Explanations in Iconography

Dedication

This book is respectfully and lovingly dedicated to
Patty Jo Watson
Professor Emerita Department of Anthropology,
Washington University, St Louis, Missouri

Explanations in Iconography

Ancient American Indian Art, Symbol, and Meaning

edited by

Carol Diaz-Granados

AMERICAN LANDSCAPES

American Landscapes is an imprint of Oxbow Books

Published in the United Kingdom in 2023 by
OXBOW BOOKS
The Old Music Hall, 106–108 Cowley Road, Oxford OX4 1JE

and in the United States by
OXBOW BOOKS
1950 Lawrence Road, Havertown, PA 19083

Paperback Edition: ISBN 979-8-88857-042-5
Digital Edition: ISBN 979-8-88857-043-2

A CIP record for this book is available from the British Library

Library of Congress Control Number: 2023942198

Printed in the United Kingdom by CMP Digital Print Solutions
Typeset in India by DiTech Publishing Services

For a complete list of titles, please contact:

UNITED KINGDOM
Oxbow Books
Telephone (0)1226 734350
Email: oxbow@oxbowbooks.com
www.oxbowbooks.com

UNITED STATES OF AMERICA
Oxbow Books
Telephone (610) 853-9131, Fax (610) 853-9146
Email: queries@casemateacademic.com
www.casemateacademic.com/oxbow

Oxbow Books is part of the Casemate Group

Front cover: Picture Cave, Glyph 43, Prehistoric Pictographs, Panel No. 3, Warren County, Missouri 2, Alan Cressler
Back cover: Face Mask Gorget, Campbell Site (23PM5, photograph by David H. Dye)

Contents

Contributors

**Alex W. Barker*, Ph.D. is an anthropological archaeologist and museum anthropologist. He is currently Director of the Arkansas Archeological Survey, and past president of the American Anthropological Association. He served as Director of the Museum of Art and Archaeology at the University of Missouri from 2006–2020. In addition to his North American work, Barker has also conducted projects in eastern Europe. In 1997 Barker coordinated a National Geographic-funded visit by leading prehistorians to Monte Verde, Chile, to assess claims that the site predated Clovis occupations.

**Steven L. Boles* earned his M.A. at Southern Illinois University, Carbondale. He is a Senior Research Archaeologist with the Illinois State Archaeological Survey, a division of the Prairie Research Institute, University of Illinois Champaign-Urbana. His research interests include Mississippian iconography, rock art, landscape archaeology, and precontact lithic studies from Paleoindian to Late Mississippian.

Robert "Ernie" Boszhardt is a Wisconsin archaeologist with nearly 50 years' experience, including three decades with the Mississippi Valley Archaeology Center at the University of Wisconsin-La Crosse. His research has focused on the unglaciated Driftless Area of the Upper Mississippi River valley. He has published on ceramics, lithics, rock art, Paleoindian, Hopewell, Effigy Mounds, Oneota, and Middle Mississippian. He is an Honorary Fellow with the University of Wisconsin-Madison.

**Carol Diaz-Granados*, Ph.D. is a Research Associate in the Department of Anthropology, Washington University in St Louis where she has taught for 39 years. Her major research focus is American Indian petroglyphs and pictographs and the interpretation of their complex imagery. Her books include *The Rock-Art of Eastern North America: Capturing Images and Insight*, which received an Outstanding Academic Title award. She is most noted for her 2005–8 Interdisciplinary Project that resulted in the co-edited volume, *Picture Cave: Unraveling the Mysteries of the Mississippian Cosmos*. In addition, she was senior editor for *Transforming the Landscape: Rock Art and the Mississippian Cosmos* (2018) in this series.

**James R. (Jim) Duncan* is a former Director of the Missouri State Museum, educator, archaeologist, author, and historian. One of his major interests is late pre-Columbian imagery on artifacts and rock art. He has co-written or co-edited books including *The Petroglyphs and Pictographs of Missouri* and *Picture Cave*, and numerous papers. Jim has lectured at Washington University, the Missouri History Museum, and throughout the state while on the Missouri Humanities Council Speakers Bureau.

Duncan has Osage and Cherokee heritage and is noted for his knowledge of Dhegiha Sioux oral traditions. He is also a known expert on frontier technology.

**David H. Dye*, Ph.D. is professor of archaeology in the Department of Earth Sciences at the University of Memphis. His archaeological research includes investigating ritual practice, social collapse, and warfare, as well as archaeological landscape and object photography. He is author of *War Paths, Peace Paths* and editor of several books including *Towns and Temples along the Mississippi*, *Cave Archaeology of the Eastern Woodlands*, and *Mississippian Culture Heroes, Ritual Regalia, and Sacred Bundles*.

Tod Frolking is Professor Emeritus in the Department of Earth and Environmental Sciences at Denison University in central Ohio. Much of his research has focused on fluvial and glacial geomorphology as well as pedology with particular emphasis on fluvial and hill slope changes in the Midcontinent late glacial period and Holocene. His collaborative geoarchaeological work has examined both natural and anthropic sediments at numerous pre-Columbian settlement and earthwork sites, mainly in central Ohio, and then utilized soil genesis within those sediment packages to better ascertain the environmental conditions during and since the period of human occupations and activity. His work on Holocene drainage evolution has helped characterize the relative stabilities of various valley bottom occupation sites.

**Adam King*, Ph.D. is a research professor at the University of South Carolina and director of the South Carolina Institute of Archaeology and Anthropology. He studies the deep past of Indigenous people of Southeast through traditional archaeological survey and excavation as well as iconography, remote sensing, and absorbed residues. His research focuses on societies of the Mississippian period (AD 1000–1600) in South Carolina and Georgia. King is author of *Etowah: A Political History of a Chiefdom Capital* and editor of *Southeastern Ceremonial Complex: Chronology, Content, Context* and *Archaeology in South Carolina: Exploring the Hidden Heritage of the Palmetto State.*

**Brad Lepper*, Ph.D. is Senior Archaeologist, World Heritage Program for the Ohio History Connection's World Heritage Program. Lepper has published numerous scholarly papers and is author of *Ohio Archaeology: an illustrated chronicle of Ohio's ancient American Indian cultures*, which received the Society for American Archaeology's Public Audience Book Award in 2007. The Ohio Archaeological Council presented Dr Lepper with its Public Awareness Award in 2008 in recognition of his efforts to promote the archaeology of the state.

**George Sabo III*, Ph.D. is a retired Professor of Anthropology at the University of Arkansas and former Director of the Arkansas Archeological Survey, a unit of the University of Arkansas System. He is author or co-author of, among other books, *Arkansas: A Narrative History* and *Paths of Our Children: Historic Indians of Arkansas*, as well as *Transforming the Landscape: Rock Art and the Mississippian Cosmos* (2018) in this series.

Grant Stauffer, Ph.D. received his MA from Texas State University and his PhD from Washington University in St. Louis. He is the Natural Resource Archaeologist at the Choctaw Nation of Oklahoma. His interests include Native American cultures of the Eastern Woodlands, their artwork and architecture, and the chronology of unwritten events in their material history. To investigate these topics, he employs material (ceramic and lithic) analysis, iconographic analysis, and geoarchaeological field methods. Stauffer is senior co-editor of *Archaeologies of Cosmoscapes in the Americas* (2023) in this series.

*Longtime participants in the spring Iconography Workshops (aka Mississippian Iconography Workshop), organized and hosted by Dr F. Kent Reilly III, Professor and Director, Center for the Study of Arts and Symbolism of Ancient America at Texas State University in San Marcos, Texas.

Preface

As many colleagues are aware – edited volumes are not for the faint of heart. This one was no exception. It has taken a few twists and turns before arriving at what my fellow authors and I believe is a substantial contribution to the field of Ancient North American Indian symbolism and interpretation – that is, iconography.

This edited volume delves into American Indian symbol and meaning and has been written to appeal to anyone interested in this topic of rapidly growing importance. Although interpretation of American Indian symbolism has been covered in several other books and volumes, it is not always offered with such clarity and ease of reading as is found in this volume.

This edited volume contains chapters that are basic to the understanding of both the field of iconography as well as to the specific topics which they address. Topics cover examples of imagery on materials including pottery, engraved gorgets and shell cups, burial architecture and grave furniture, hammered copper, mounds, rock art, and other media. Contributing authors have studied and learned the process of delving into the past by examining ancient North American symbolism coupled with style, and the ethnography and oral traditions from historic groups located in the regions where the objects they are studying likely occurred. Is it a "perfect" process? Maybe not perfect, but it is rapidly developing into a valued field, because the findings are being recognized and accepted by a selection of well-respected archaeologists, art historians, American Indian researchers, along with corroboration from various American Indian elders.

Seven of the nine contributing authors have participated in the yearly Iconography Workshop, conceived, arranged, and hosted by Dr F. Kent Reilly III in the Anthropology Department at Texas State University in San Marcos, Texas. Reilly is Director of the Center for the Study of Arts and Symbolism of Ancient America. To explain this workshop in short – during this workshop, the ten or so invitees are split into two or three divisions. Each group studies and discusses a different symbol/motif, artifact, and/or style. The last day of the workshop, each section gives its report to the whole group on their findings. The "whole group" includes all participants including the scholars, graduate student helpers, and sometimes visitors from various universities, museums, and patrons. These workshops have resulted in a significant amount of new research, discovery and enlightenment encompassing a large selection of ancient artifacts. Two major books have been published with the findings *Ancient Objects and Sacred Realms: Interpretations of Mississippian Iconography* (F.K. Reilly III and J.F. Garber (eds) 2007), and *Visualizing the Sacred: Cosmic Visions, Regionalism, and the Art of the Mississippian World* (G.E. Lankford, F.K. Reilly III, and J.F. Garber (eds) 2011). Several of the invitees have published elsewhere on the iconography of American Indian symbolism in books as well as chapters in other edited volumes. I am very honored to be a part of this workshop (since 2003). It has been a richly rewarding experience.

The field of iconography, as it relates to archaeological materials from the ancient American Indian past, is fast coming into the mainstream of Anthropological inquiry.

Carol Diaz-Granados, March 2023

Acknowledgements

First and foremost, I wish to thank our many Osage friends who have come to be like family over the past 30 years. Their friendship, conversations, information, and insights regarding ancestral oral traditions have been invaluable. On 27 June, 2007, in a beautiful ceremony, I was adopted into the Osage Tsi-zhu Wah-shta-geh (Gentle Sky Clan), and given an Osage name. It was a most meaningful ceremony and singular honor that I will forever cherish.

I would also like to sincerely thank Jim Duncan, my colleague and partner, who got me interested in American Indian oral traditions way back when. As one of Osage ancestry, Jim was able to relate to the ancient stories. Moreover, he saw the need for those stories, in understanding the Cosmos through the imagery in the petroglyphs, pictographs, and other American Indian artifacts.

My editor, Julie Gardiner, has been an absolute joy to work with during the long process of book compilation, editing, proofing, and publishing. This being my second book with Oxbow Books, I can honestly report that Julie is not only very patient and understanding – she is also very brave! Julie can not only do the impossible, but miracles are in her kitbag, too! I also thank the others at Oxbow involved in this book: Jessica Hawxwell, Declan Ingram, Eduard Cojocaru, and Mette Bundgaard.

Next, I would like to thank my contributing authors: Alex Barker, Steven Boles, Robert (Ernie) Boszhardt, David H. Dye, Tod Frolking, Adam King, Bradley Lepper, George Sabo, and Grant Stauffer. They stuck it out with me while waiting an inordinate period of time for a couple of chapters to come in.

Last, but certainly not least, I wish to thank my dear friend and colleague, F. Kent Reilly III, who approached me at a conference many years ago (in 2003) and, because of my work and research in American Indian art and iconography, invited me to join his Iconography Workshop in San Marcos, TX. For his ongoing interest in and support of my research, plus his cherished friendship, I am deeply grateful. I also want to give a shout-out to Michael Scanlon, who has been a wonderful scholar, communicator, and friend.

1

Thoughts and ideas on how iconography works: a basic primer on how "to do" iconography

Carol Diaz-Granados

It seems that the $25 word, "Iconography", has a tendency to scare away some readers, including colleagues, other professionals, students, and people in general. Case in point: I was teaching my course at Washington University titled: *American Indian Art and Iconography*. Every semester I taught this elective course, it garnered the required number or more of students. Then it dawned on me that the term, "iconography", might be scaring away some students. I changed the title of the course to: *American Indian Art, Symbol, and Meaning*. Class numbers increased markedly as expected.

So, what I want to do in this introductory chapter is, first of all, not scare away anyone! Iconography, put most succinctly, is the study of symbols and their interpretation. It is a rich and fascinating field when applied to the complex imagery on ancient American Indian artifacts and viewed through the lens of early ethnographic records and American Indian oral traditions. Second, I hope that this volume will bring to colleagues in art and archaeology, art history, American Indian studies, as well as to anyone in the general, interested public, a greater understanding of just how "iconography works" and how it can be carefully employed for a greater understanding of ancient American Indian cultural materials. The symbols representative of a culture define that culture's ideology and offer insight into their very lives, thought processes, and rituals. That is because those symbols can demonstrate what was important to the people who created them.

Granted, it can be a rather involved process and takes a substantial amount of time to come to most realizations of possible meaning behind the symbolism. However, it is not an insurmountable task in most instances and is definitely worth the effort. A major issue here is that it requires a tremendous amount of reading and synthesis – a time-consuming task in which many archaeologists choose not to participate. Oral traditions are not just entertaining stories that touch on behavior and morality, "they are the emblems of a living religion"

(Erdoes and Ortiz 1984, xv). Taking just one example, the value of the lore embedded in oral traditions was such that the knowledge of this lore was the determining factor in Mandan society of the social status of those who preserved it (Bowers 1950, 75–6). In addition, the imagery and symbols provided ways to record and recall stories. It engendered memory aids (mnemonic devices) to tell the stories that the imagery depicted.

"Art"

Before I delve into the basic details of this essay on "doing iconography", I would like to clarify two things. First and foremost is the term "Art" used in the title and throughout. Without entering into a lengthy discourse on the philosophy of art, I would just like to say a few words to clarify where I am coming from in this discussion. I am using this term very loosely and in a rather generic way to refer to all ancient cultural items that contain graphic symbolism and imagery.

Here at least, is one reason why I continue to use the term. When I was finishing up my doctoral dissertation and subsequent first book on rock art (Diaz-Granados and Duncan 2000), I decided to use "rock graphics" in the title rather than rock art, and also use the term "graphic communications" within the text. The reason is that I do not believe rock art should be viewed as "art!": I rather, and firmly, believe that rock art is primarily a means of communication, a means of transferring information. Beals and Hoijer wrote some time ago, "One of the main functions of the arts as communication is to reinforce beliefs, customs, and values (Beals and Hoijer 1955, 548). I would emphasize that the "art's" *main* function is as a means of communication. It can also serve as symbols of power, position, and identity (but that also is a form of communication!). In short, it is a way to send messages in order to pass along information to the viewer -- or to the spirits who control the Cosmos. That said, I was advised by one of the peer reviewers of my first book that if I titled it *Rock Graphics of Missouri*, it would not be available in the "rock art" literature. I compromised and instead of using "rock art" I went with "petroglyphs and pictographs", in the title (Diaz-Granados and Duncan 2000). Still, I am admittedly uncomfortable using the term "art", but will forge ahead now that you know where I stand on the matter.

The other issue is that of the "endurance of oral traditions". So many archaeologists (at least the naysayers) will deny the longevity of oral traditions, saying that people's stories change over the decades and centuries. Of course, they can change and some do. However, they can also endure, as in the Bible stories, in Greek and Roman mythology, and in the oral traditions handed down in worldwide cultures for many generations. In fact, those studying oral traditions – still referred to as mythology by some -- know that many cultures share very similar oral traditions. There are many commonalities across the spectrum of world cultures. Mythologies can sometimes be viewed simply as "stories that explain things". They can also be stories that guide the listener in their moral obligations. I have learned that many American Indian elders shy away from the term "myth" in preference to "oral traditions". In fact, I was told by an Osage elder (Jake Waller, pers. comm. 2000), that he resented the term "myth" because it implies an artificially created story, whereas oral traditions are stories recounted in their culture and believed to be true. Always keep in mind that when these extraordinary cultural materials were being created, with their detailed imagery, storytelling was one of the prime means of communication, education, influence, control, and entertainment.

In 1945, Antonio Waring and Preston Holder published a list they had composed describing and graphically showing a large number of motifs found in Mississippian symbolism (Waring and Holder 1945). In 1978, Phillips and Brown published their two-volume opus *PreColumbian Shell Engravings* which contains hundreds of designs, motifs, and symbols. In 1996, Brain and Phillips published their major work *Shell Gorgets: Styles of the Late Prehistoric and Protohistoric Southeast*. Since 1945, recognized motifs have both increased in number and broadened in perspective. For one example, the wide array of female motifs or symbols were only recognized later. This extensive list of motifs in these three resources may have been the catalyst for the field of iconography, or at least the "seeds". In the 1990s, the list expanded further using repeated symbols and motifs from Missouri's 150+ petroglyph and pictograph sites. The concepts have changed over the decades, too, and the utilization has shifted to a system similar to those employed by Mesoamerican scholars Friedel and Reilly and explained in their 2011 volume (Lankford *et al.* 2011). This system recognizes, among other things, regional differences, chronological change, cultural exchange, and the concept that cosmology and religion are tightly connected.

Viewed as an "equation"

Getting back to the discussion on "iconography" – put in the simplest of terms (which I am attempting to do here, adapting the approach of Occam's Razor), one might say that "doing iconography" follows a basic "equation". I must note that different researchers have different methods of creating their own "equations" or methods. However, one such equation that can be used is as follows:

1. First, begin with an example of American Indian symbolism found on numerous artifacts: pottery, shell, copper, or, of course, petroglyphs and pictographs (rock art). For example, this can be a single motif such as a foot (Fig. 1.1a), two co-occurring motifs such as the cross-in-circle with avian (Fig. 1.1b; and see Diaz-Granados 2004, 143), or a detailed and complex motif panel, such as the Morning Star panel at Picture Cave, Missouri (Fig. 1.1c). Take special note of the symbols that are both repeated and depicted in conjunction with other symbols, recording those motifs that co-occur most frequently. These co-occurrences provide valuable clues with regard to their importance and meaning. The most detailed and complex imagery is always the best bet for delving into possible interpretations. Although I am using mostly rock art imagery here, the same can apply to imagery on shell gorgets, shell cups, hammered copper, and the like.

2. The second part of the equation is a basic understanding of stylistic variation. Styles can vary through time and across regions. These variations can be, at least in part, the result of different graphic norms within different cultural groups and/or different artisans. In addition, one should understand how the same symbol can be depicted in various ways depending on the medium used (copper, wood, clay, shell, stone, pigments). That is, the depiction of an Underwater Spirit on a cave wall (Fig. 1.2a) as opposed to one rendered in clay (Fig. 1.2b) will look and be quite different. Still, they will retain identifying features such as horns, fangs, a long tail, etc. Another consideration is the expertise of the person/artisan creating the image. Needless to say, some are better than others! One must be aware of these variations without being thrown off track. It takes careful consideration of these issues as well as recognizing the attributes that are connected to a symbol or supernatural being.

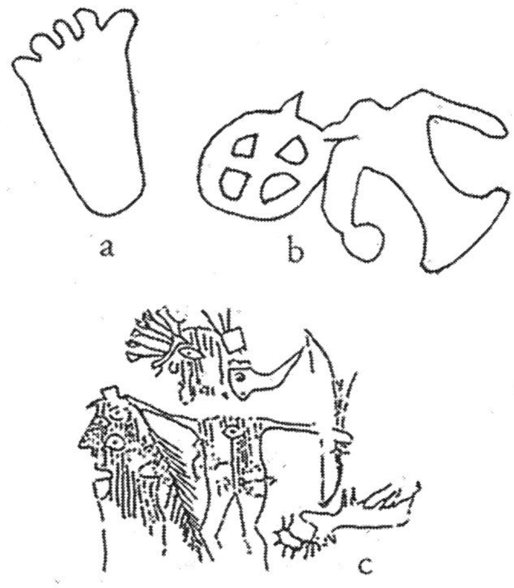

Fig. 1.1 Examples of petroglyphs found in repeated locations in Missouri: a. foot; b. cross-in-circle with Avian (bird) petroglyph, Three Hills Creek Site; c. Morning Star pictograph Panel at Picture Cave.

3. The third part of the equation is the ethnography and oral traditions that have been recorded by many historians, scholars, and American Indian informants over the ages. If one, and that one being an archaeologist, art historian, or any dedicated researcher, puts forth the effort to do the time-consuming research and reading, then I strongly believe this goal of preliminary interpretation can be accomplished.
4. As with any task, there are these "steps" that need to be taken to achieve reasonable, convincing, conceivable results. Completion of all the steps above is followed by synthesis; that is, a synthesis of the repeated, co-occurring symbol(s) coupled with the information gleaned from the ethnography and oral traditions.

Speaking with knowledgeable American Indian scholars and elders is extremely valuable, too. I do not mean to minimize the task involved, because it can be time-consuming to do the reading, and/or listen and record hours of oral traditions and recollections. As stated earlier, oral traditions are basically stories handed down from one generation to another – and they are often handed down for centuries. Again, there can be regional differences, but there are still the core stories that remain solid and enduring. Oral traditions are not just entertaining stories that touch on behavior and morality, they encode the rules of how to live, how to surmount obstacles, and how to deal in relations with others, to weather, and to creatures that roam the earth and Cosmos.

Not to confuse the matter (hopefully to "simplify it"), I should mention here that, in some cases, the process started with, or can start with, the oral

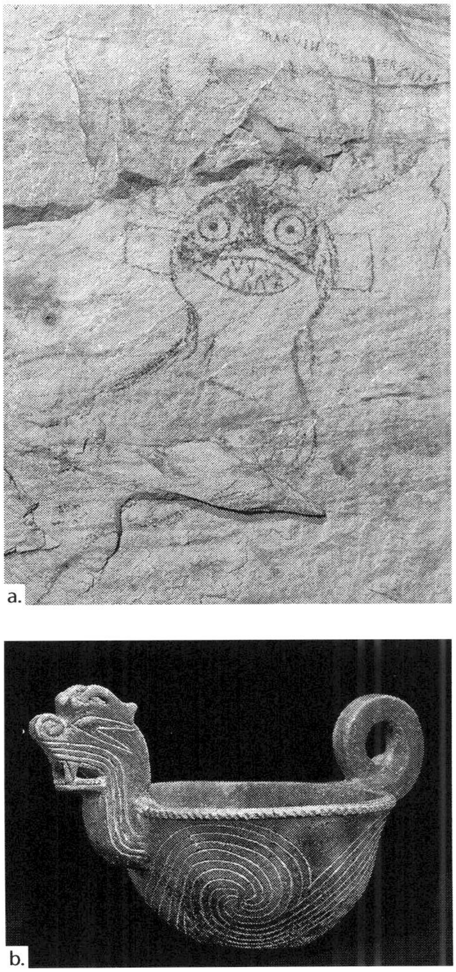

Fig. 1.2 Underwater Spirits a. Picture Cave, Missouri; b. Campbell Site Missouri (photograph courtesy of David H. Dye).

traditions. Yes, it can go either way. For example, say you are reading an oral tradition and you find a story about "The Old Woman" who can turn herself into a deer (Bowers 1992 [1965]). How curious is that? Then, on one of your travels to a rock art site, one that you have visited many times before, you run across a figure birthing her offspring (Fig. 1.3). You have seen this figure several times but then you notice something you had not noticed before – one of her hands bears the shape of a deer hoof! You begin thinking – maybe this carving is a mnemonic (memory) device for telling one of the stories about The Old Woman shape-shifting into a young doe. In other words, the reading of oral traditions and the data in those traditions, can bring about recognition of a complex symbol. That is, the oral traditions can inform the imagery if one is observant and perseverant.

Another way to view this is to consider "the artifact" as just *one* part of the equation. In anthropology, we try to understand who made the artifact, why it was made, how it was used, its context in the culture, and so on. This same approach could and should include any possible meaning derived from the style, ethnography, and any oral traditions that can be found from American Indian groups within a reasonable proximity to where the artifacts/symbols were found (or from their original location if that can be known). Realizing full well that artifacts have a way of moving around, sometimes great distances, there are often ways to resolve that issue from studying the materials used, style, or symbolism, to determine the general place of origin.

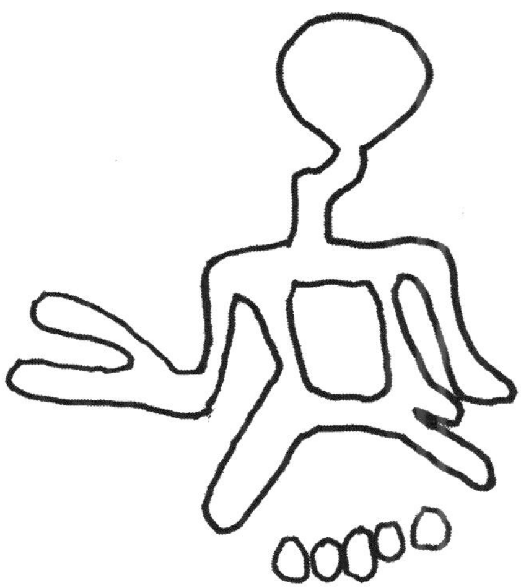

Fig. 1.3 Petroglyph of Old Woman/First Woman birthing her supernatural offspring. Her raised hand has morphed into a deer hoof. Maddin Creek, Missouri.

One of the many reasons that I became attached to, and enamored of, rock art is its *in situ* nature. As an *in situ* artifact it is in the very place where it was created. This offers a huge advantage over portable artifacts and sometimes even has the ability to anchor portable artifacts to a region.

To ignore any attempts at interpretation and understanding does the artifact and its imagery an injustice. The ethnography and oral traditions can open up avenues of insight into the basic ideology behind the cultural materials we study. Two pioneering scholars in the field of iconography, Robert L. Hall and F. Kent Reilly III, have labored to overcome the barrier of strictly descriptive discourse (and quantitative analyses) regarding archaeological materials from the Midwest and Eastern Woodlands of North America. Their quest was to delve more deeply into the cultural materials they were studying to extract meaning and ideology. They have largely succeeded (Hall 1997; Reilly and Garber 2007; and Lankford *et al.* 2011, among others). In general, Mississippian materials contain the most graphically complex designs in this region. Mississippian (last period before the Historic) symbolism is so widespread, regional styles are bound to exist, as well as variations in the inherent manner of the depictions, the canonical values used by the artisans in rendering the imagery. This expanse is a major region of detailed graphic imagery (and ideology) that was labeled the Mississippian Art and Ceremonial Complex by Reilly (2004, 125), and later the Mississippian Ideological Interaction Sphere (MIIS), (Reilly and Garber 2007, 39). The earlier designation of SECC, Southeastern Ceremonial Complex (Waring and Holder 1945) remains preferable to some, although I personally believe that the MIIS is the most "accurate" at this place in time.

Using Allison Wylie's theme of "cables and tacking" (Wylie 1989; 2002), what we do, therefore, is look at the often-repeated and co-occurring symbols within a geographic region coupled with supporting information from the ethnography, oral traditions, and conversations with American Indian elders. Of course, I am using rock art as my basis – American Indian petroglyphs and pictographs. These are the most predictable and unquestionably *in situ* category of artifacts known. We research the acknowledged American Indian groups from the area, often referring to ethnographies gleaned from the earliest established indigenous groups in the region. After reading everything we can find by the ethnographers who cared enough to record the data, and researching all the oral traditions that can be found, we begin comparing these with the symbolism found in the rock art. Quite often, many of the symbols and motifs we see depicted on the artifacts are reflected in the oral traditions. Oral traditions contain the basic ideology of a group's beliefs, this serves as the basis behind the cultural artifacts which the ancient people produced. When we find a symbol repeated frequently in the rock art and discussed frequently in the oral traditions, we can begin to determine its importance and determine any probable connections and meanings.

We do not focus on just one or two basic motifs such as squares, dots, and the like – it must be a clearly depicted symbol, frequent, and fairly widespread. Also, we have found that the most decipherable of the symbols are those that are rich in motifs and graphic complexity. That is, we do not make any attempt, nor do we believe it is possible to decipher, for example, a single dot or circle, a line, or an "X". A symbol such as the bi-lobed arrow and its co-occurring motifs, is a good example of just one on which we have focused in the past (and see Chapter 2). Another motif that can be considered complex is the cross-in-circle (Diaz-Granados 2011, figs 4.1 and 4.11), but not *just* the cross-in-circle, rather that symbol in conjunction with other recognized motifs such as an avian motif (Fig. 1.1b) or its variations (Reilly 2004, 127–30, fig. 7 a, b, c; Lankford 2007). Another is the long-nosed maskette (see Duncan and Diaz-Granados 2000).

In 1978, Binford gave a push to the idea of interpretation when he wrote,

> ... there seemed to me to be every reason to suspect that we could develop ways of extracting from the archaeological record information regarding properties of cultural systems, including social and ideological components, since they were organizationally integrated with the matter remaining in the archaeological record – the relic of an ongoing system in the past. (Binford 1978, 51)

Patty Jo Watson, Professor Emerita, Department of Anthropology, Washington University in St Louis, Missouri, understood the growing desire and need to delve into "interpretation" of archaeologically retrieved cultural materials. She wrote (with her co-authors):

> If archaeological material is recognizably primarily and deliberately symbolic – as many grave goods are, for example – then interpretations of past belief systems are possible. . . Materials that are most probably symbolic, thus provide the best data for inferring past belief systems. (Watson *et al.* 1984, 274)

It may seem to some a forbidding activity to delve into this area of "interpretation" and even to consider that we can know the ideology of long past cultures. It is not, and several well-respected archaeologists have done this successfully (Hall 1997; Reilly and Garber 2007; Lankford *et al.* 2011) as well as their students (Giles and Lambert 2021; Stauffer *et al.* 2022, and others). A number of archaeologists who once frowned upon making any attempts at interpretation of ancient cultural materials, have since "crossed over that bridge" – I will not name names, but you know who you are!

Co-occurrences are often the key

Symbols are difficult to understand when they occur singly or in a repetitive design. If, however, two or more different symbols/motifs occur together it allows for a glimpse into their past meaning. For example, a vulva in association with a serpent motif offers insight into the possible meaning of this co-occurrence. Oral traditions tell us of The Old Woman who is often associated with serpents (Bowers 1950; 1992, among others). In Siouan ethnographic stories and oral traditions this is a common theme, especially in sedentary, agrarian, Siouan societies. In addition, the vulva is the initial "portal" of entry into life for human beings. So why, you ask, are snakes connected to the vulva in ancient imagery? Check the ethnography and you will find stories of The Old Woman and her consort The Great Serpent (see Chapter 5 and Chapter 10). Another feature of this union is that The Great Serpent can impart immortality to The Old Woman and to her offspring enabling her children to be reborn – a major feature of many American Indian oral traditions.

In studying Missouri's rock art, we were seeing certain motifs repeated again and again. That is a first clue to their importance! After reading the ethnographies and oral traditions, associations began to emerge that were obviously depicted by the motifs or co-occurring motifs. Are these connections 100% accurate? There is no way to know for certain but they are extremely compelling and definitely worthy of serious consideration. This is actually how Jim Duncan and I embarked on an early focus searching out the iconography of the symbols in Missouri's petroglyphs and pictographs. As a scholar with American Indian ancestry (Osage and Cherokee), Duncan believed that there was more than mere description to be had, if he thoroughly searched the literature. He was correct.

It was not long after that we were introduced to the "gift" of Picture Cave with its hundreds of red and black drawn and detailed images laden with motifs, co-occurrences, "storyboards", and complex panels full of symbolism (Diaz-Granados *et al.* 2015). If that did not wake up the desire to "know" the past better, I cannot imagine what would. Up to that point, we had identified a group of petroglyphs in east/southeast Missouri that I termed "The Big Five". Found at The Big Five sites were similarities in both graphic style as well as themes and motifs. There are birds, serpents, feet and hands, vulvar motifs, squares, and more. The example of themes that I will discuss in the final section of this chapter include an often singular motif, the *vulva*, a "double" motif, *the "twin" figures*, and a complex motif, *the bi-lobed arrow*. I will not be discussing these in depth, but more as an introduction to "doing iconography" – that is, giving the reader a "taste" of how these three motifs figure into the ethnography, oral traditions, and interpretation.

The vulva

To begin, the vulva is depicted at multiple rock art sites in Missouri in at least seven different forms. The most typical is the simple U-shape (Fig. 1.4a). A few other versions include the U-shaped with line (Fig. 1.4b), the anatomically graphic version (Fig. 1.4c), and the symbolically graphic "Bushberg" vulva (Fig. 1.4d). Of course, there are others in Missouri as well as others at rock art sites around the world. Curiously, all versions are pretty obvious and identifiable. You might wonder what is going on with all these vulvar depictions but there is a basic and simple explanation: This motif, pecked into stone in Missouri (and around the world), is a way to honor the Earth, our Mother (known by such names as First Woman, Old Woman, Old-Woman-Who-Never-Dies, Earth Mother, Grandmother, as well as by other names). In fact, she might be the most ancient of all supernatural

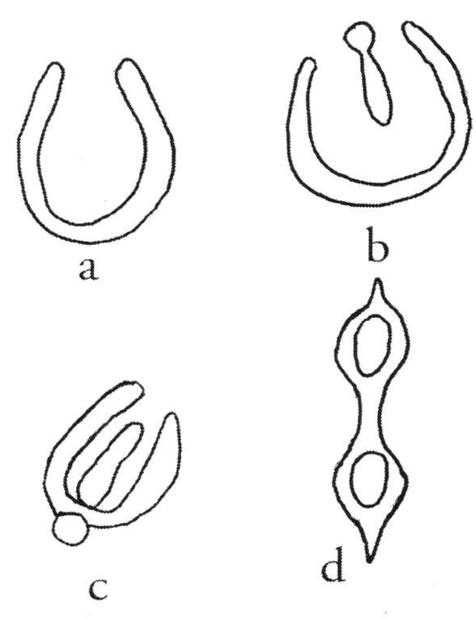

Fig. 1.4 Vulvar petroglyph motifs from sites in Missouri: a. basic vulvar motif; b. basic vulvar motif with line; c. graphic vulvar depiction, Washington State Park; d. symbolic vulvar depiction, Bushberg site.

spirit beings. Because humans are "birthed from within" she is especially associated with caves (considered to be her womb). Picture Cave has been referred to as "Womb of the Universe" by Osage elder, Charles Pratt (pers. comm. 2009).

Caves served as a sacred location for American Indian groups, places to be consecrated by cave drawings and places to be taken for ritual consecration. It is in caves such as Picture Cave that we first saw a symbol that was truly an ideograph (Diaz-Granados *et al.* 2015). This was a *Ho-e-ga*, a trident shape that denotes the Middle World, the web or trap of the fleeting "Breath of Life" (LaFlesche 1975). Because the largest panel of imagery at Picture Cave represents the Night Sky, the top layer of the four levels of the Beneath (or Lower) World; the artist carefully drew two *Ho-e-ga* symbols (Diaz-Granados *et al.* 2015, 88), reinforcing the position of the Middle World to the viewer. We had seen this symbol as depicted on the antlers of the Great Elk, a Dhegiha ideograph for the Middle World, the world in which we presently reside. First Woman/Old Woman/Earth Mother is the female deity who brings life to the earth, releases the animals into the Middle World, nurtures her supernatural offspring, enables agriculture. To peck her "symbol" into the stone is a way to honor her, to let her know that you are there, or that you are asking for a favor. If you are the recipient of a favor, you honor her by leaving an offering or pecking her symbol into the stone to thank her and acknowledge her as your most ancient "Grandmother". This ubiquitous motif is found singularly as well as in conjunction with other symbols including birds, serpents, squares, and other motifs. When positioned adjacent to a bird, it reminds us that First Woman views the birds as her messengers. When they return in the spring, it is a signal for planting to begin. The Old Woman/Grandmother, spirit of the earth, plays a prominent role in many oral traditions. So it was not unusual to find a large number of vulvar motifs carved or pecked at many of Missouri's rock art sites.

"The Celestial Twins"

These occur at a minimum of four rock art sites, mostly within The Big Five grouping, but there are also two examples in Picture Cave. These "twins" appear in petroglyph form at Three Hills Creek (Fig. 1.5a), at Washington State Park (Fig. 1.5b), at Maddin Creek (Fig. 1.5c), and in pictograph form at Picture Cave (Fig. 1.5d, one of two examples. For the other example at Picture Cave, see Chapter 2, Fig. 2.6a). The Celestial Twins, Hero Twins, or Children of the Sun (depending on the group/ethnographer), are the principal "good guys" found in the oral traditions of the Prairie/Plains dwellers, especially the Siouan speakers and their neighbors. When we began working on interpreting a selection of the images at The Big Five petroglyphs, and the Picture Cave iconography, we began to recognize the telling of the Great Medicine Rite: "The making of the Earth". Much later, this rite was thought by many ethnographers to be an adaptation by later native groups of the Christian doctrine brought by early European missionaries, especially the Jesuits. This genesis epic acknowledges an "Earth Maker", Old Man immortal, a supreme creative spirit. In reading the early Jesuit relations, they often pointed out the congruency between the Great Medicine Rite and Christian teachings, revealing the reason that the latter was easily adopted by indigenous groups. This congruency indicated that the Great Medicine Rite was indeed quite ancient. A recent review of these oral traditions anchors their origins in antiquity (Hall 1997; Duncan 2015).

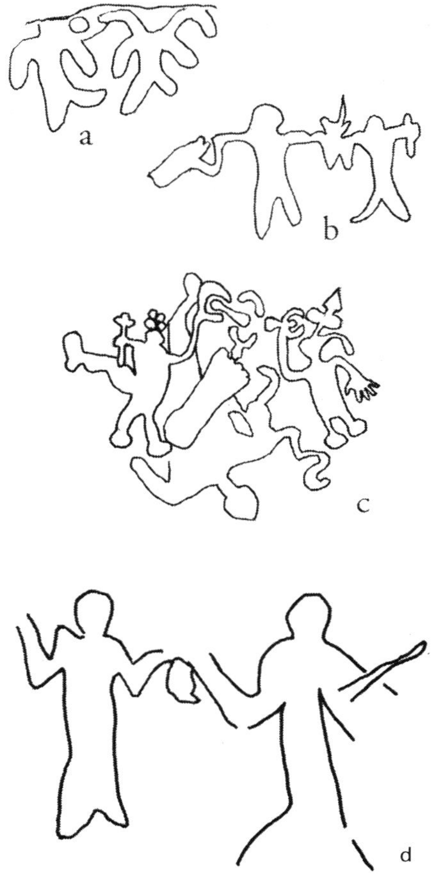

Fig. 1.5 The Twins motifs from sites in Missouri: a. Three Hills Creek, petroglyph; b. Washington State Park, petroglyph; c. Maddin Creek, petroglyph; d. Picture Cave, pictograph.

The bi-lobed arrow

The third motif to consider is the bi-lobed arrow (Fig. 1.6). It has been found archaeologically in hammered copper, painted onto pottery, engraved onto shell, and is plentiful in the rock art and artifacts of Missouri and some surrounding states, stretching down into Alabama (see Knight and Steponaitis 2011, fig. 9.9; Diaz-Granados and Duncan 2000, 192, fig. 6.2c and d). This singular, yet complex, motif puzzled archaeologists for many years until the ethnographic literature was consulted (Hall 1997). It is believed that this bi-lobed arrow design portrays a pipe (or arrow) with downy feathers on either side representing the lungs of a deer. As one reads the ethnographer, Paul Radin (1948), one learns about a supernatural being who is adopted and ceremoniously "hit with deer lungs". What is described in the adoption ritual is a key part of the Great Medicine Rite where the Celestial Twins are re-united by the adoption ritual conducted by their maternal uncle or father. This ritual uses two special pipes, each with two feather "tassels" made of red painted, downy, owl feathers. While the oral tradition is found among the Caddo, Chiwere and Dhegiha speakers, it is only the Dhegiha who have a "Deer Lung Clan" that makes the adoption pipe tassels (Hall 1997; Duncan 2015).

You will find that the hero figure, Morning Star, goes by various names including Red Horn, Morning Star, Hawk, and "he-who-is-hit-with-deer-lungs" (see Radin 1948). It is the oral traditions that connect this hero figure to the bi-lobed arrow. Most everyone has read "hero stories" from other cultures and countries. For the Plains and eastern tribes, this supernatural being was a major player in the oral traditions. He is found battling the Giants, in sports competitions, getting killed and resurrected, and so on. Radin (1948) refers to these stories as "Hero cycles". These oral traditions were an exceedingly important part of one's daily life and often shared around a fire on cold winter nights. Along with Radin, another important

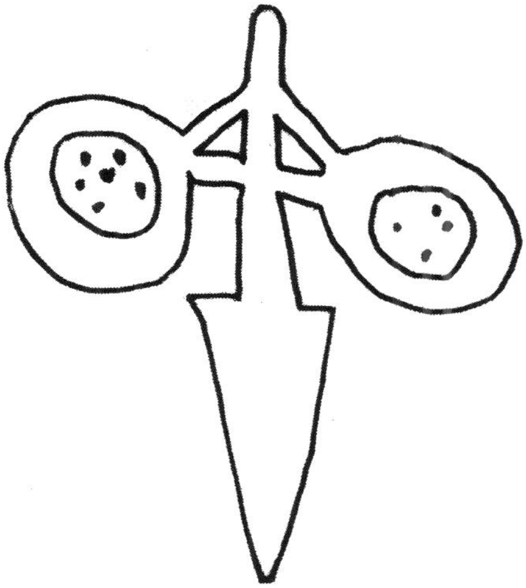

Fig. 1.6 Bi-lobed arrow in red pigment at Lost Creek pictograph site, Missouri.

ethnographer who discusses this hero figure is Skinner (1923). In Missouri's petroglyphs, the bi-lobed arrow is often seen paired with a sun symbol (see Chapter 2) thus depicting in symbols – The Son of the Sun!

Conclusion

I have been intentionally brief in this explanation and have made every attempt to use basic, clear terminology. For that reason, it is my hope that readers wishing to delve into the field of interpretation of graphic imagery on artifacts – i.e., iconography, will look to this chapter for initial guidance. As Binford (1983); Watson (*et al.* 1984); (Hall 1997); Reilly, Lankford, and quite a few other scholars believe – ideological information can indeed be extracted from ancient imagery. If one is looking for a much more in-depth, theoretical, and philosophical approach one might refer to Knight (2012). Those interested in pursuing a study of ancient American Indian iconography are also encouraged to read the remaining chapters in this volume and to do the reading included in the references at the end of this chapter, particularly Hall (1997), Reilly and Garber (2007), and Lankford *et al.* (2011). I hope that readers will see it is not an insurmountable task just one that requires time, thought, reading, and study, as any worthwhile academic endeavor does.

Bibliography

Beals, R.L. and Hoijer, H. (1953) *An Introduction to Anthropology*. Macmillan, NY.

Binford, L.R. (1978) On covering law and theories in archaeology. *Current Anthropology*. 19(3), 631–2.

Bowers, A.W. (1950) *Mandan Social and Ceremonial Organization*. University of Chicago Press, Chicago IL.

Bowers, A.W. 1992 [1965] *Hidatsa Social and Ceremonial Organization*. University of Nebraska Press, Lincoln NE.

Brain, L.P. and Phillips, P. (1996) *Shell Gorgets: Styles of the Late Prehistoric and Protohistoric Southeast*. Peabody Museum of Archaeology and Ethnology, Harvard University, Cambridge MA.

Diaz-Granados, C. (2004) Marking stone, land, body, and spirit. In *Hero, Hawk, and Open Hand: American Indian Art of the Ancient Midwest and South*. R.F. Townsend and R.V. Sharp (eds) 139–49, Yale University Press and Art Institute of Chicago, New Haven CO and London.

Diaz-Granados, C. and Duncan, J.R. (2000) *The Petroglyphs and Pictographs of Missouri*. University of Alabama Press, Tuscaloosa AL.

Diaz-Granados, C., Duncan, J.R. and Reilly, F.K. III 2015. *Picture Cave: Unraveling the Mysteries of the Mississippian Cosmos*. University of Texas Press, Austin TX.

Duncan, J.R. (2015) Identifying the characters on the walls of Picture Cave. In Diaz-Granados *et al.* (eds) 2015, 209–40.

Duncan, J.R. and Diaz-Granados, C. (2000) Of masks and myths. *Midcontinental Journal of Archaeology* 25, 1–26.

Erdoes, R. and Ortiz, A. (eds) (1984) *American Indian Myths & Legends.* Pantheon Books, New York.

Giles, B.T. and Lambert, S.P. (2021) *New Methods and theories for Analyzing Mississippian Imagery.* Florida Museum of Natural History, Ripley PP. Bullen Series, Gainsville FL.

Hall, R.L. (1997) *An Archaeology of the Soul: North American Indian Belief and Ritual.* University of Illinois Press, Urbana IL.

Knight, V.J., Jr (2012) *Iconographic Method in New World Prehistory.* Cambridge University Press, Cambridge.

Knight, V.J. Jr and Steponaitis, V.P. (2011) A redefinition of the Hemphill style in Mississippian art. In Lankford *et al.* (eds) 2011, 203–39.

La Flesche, F. (1975) *Dictionary of the Osage Language.* Smithsonian Institution Bulletin 109, Washington DC.

Lankford, G.E. (2007) Some cosmological motifs in the Southeastern ceremonial complex. In Reilly and Garber (eds) 2007, 8–38.

Lankford, G., Reilly III, F.K. and Garber, J.F. (2011) *Visualizing the Sacred: Cosmic Visions, Regionalism, and the Art of the Mississippian World,* University of Texas Press, Austin TX.

Phillips, P. and Brown, J.A. (1978) *PreColumbian Shell Engravings from the Craig Mound at Spiro, Oklahoma, Part 1.* Peabody Museum of Archaeology and Ethnology, Harvard University, Cambridge MA.

Radin, P. (1948) Winnebago Hero cycles: a study in Aboriginal literature. *International Journal of American Linguistics* 14(3).

Reilly, F.K. III (2004) People of Earth, People of Sky. In *Hero, Hawk, and Open Hand: American Indian Art of the Ancient Midwest and South.* R.F. Townsend and R.V. Sharp (eds), 125–37. Yale University Press and Art Institute of Chicago, New Haven CT and London.

Reilly, F.K. III (2007) The petaloid motif: a celestial symbolic locative in the Sheel art of Spiro. In Reilly and Garber (eds) 2007, 39–55.

Reilly, F.K. III and Garber J.F. (eds) (2007) *Ancient Objects and Sacred Realms.* University of Texas Press, Austin TX.

Skinner, A.B. (1923) Traditions of the Iowa Indians. *Journal of American Folklore* 38. 425–506.

Stauffer, J.G., Giles, B.T. and Lambert S.P. (2022) *Archaeologies of Cosmoscapes in the Americas.* American Landscapes 5, Oxford.

Waring, A. and Holder, P. (1945) A prehistoric ceremonial complex in the Southeastern United States. *American Anthropologist* 47(1), 1–34.

Watson, P.J., LeBlanc, S.A. and Redman, C.L. (1984) *Archaeological Explanation: The Scientific Method in Archaeology.* Columbia University Press, NY.

Wylie, A. (1989) Archaeological cables and tacking: the implications of practice for Bernstein's "Options Beyond Objectivism and Relativism". *Philosophy of Social Sciences* 19, 1–18.

Wylie, A. (2002) *Thinking from Things: Essays in the Philosophy of Archaeology.* University of California Press, Berkeley CA.

2

Son of the sun: iconography in rock art and artifacts that reveals important associations between symbolism associated with Dhegiha religion, celestial bodies, and Western Mississippian ideology

James R. Duncan and Carol Diaz-Granados

For many years, archaeologists have marveled at the large inventory of pre-Columbian artifacts displayed in various museums, originating in the central Mississippi Valley. This region, beginning at the confluence of the Missouri and Mississippi and continuing south to the confluence of the Ohio and Mississippi rivers, contains five of the eight largest mound groups in North America. The largest concentration of rock art sites in the Eastern United States is just to the west. Sadly, because of urbanization and advances in farming technology, most of these archaeological sites have been adversely impacted. In the relatively short time span of 100 years, many of the archaeological sites within this corridor have been damaged, some totally destroyed. The southeastern quadrant of Missouri, especially the broad Mississippi River floodplain, south of Commerce, has been cleared, land leveled, channeled, and leveed; few archaeological sites have survived untouched (Fig. 2.1).

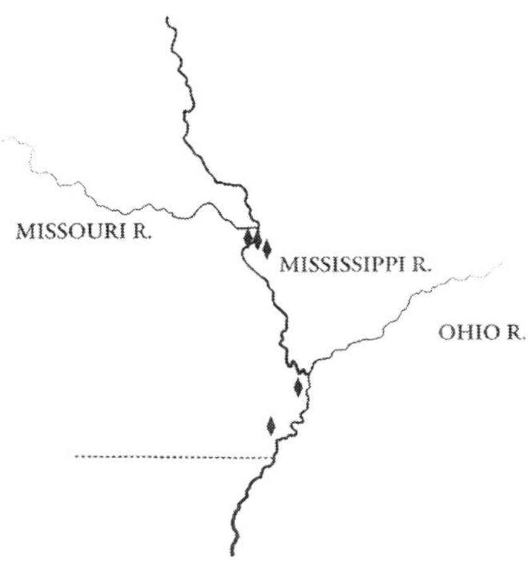

Fig. 2.1 Map of the Central Mississippi River Valley showing the locations of the five large mound groups between the confluences of the Missouri and the Ohio Rivers with the Mississippi River. The northeastern-most site is Cahokia, the largest mound group in North America. Not to scale.

In our discussion, we will use material from Missouri rock art sites, as well as artifacts from the same quadrant and adjoining regions in Arkansas, Kentucky and Tennessee. The rock art records, especially photographs and maps by Frank Peter Magre, Benedict Ellis and Robert Elgin, are crucial in linking traditions and practices to the artifacts. We will also build on previous Boasian patterned research that links the oral traditions of the Dhegiha, their Siouan kin and their neighbors to this imagery, while constructing a more complete perspective of a small segment of Western Mississippian culture. A key to our study is the interviews with important Osage priests by Francis La Flesche that give us a window into the past of a pre-Columbian North America now gone (Emerson 2022, 273–5). These priests have provided us with a glimpse inside the minds of the ancient Osage and thus the minds of their Mississippian forebears (Bailey 1995, 285).

The rock art

During the Summer of 1961 one of us (JD) began working for the Missouri State Parks Department at Washington State Park. The two principal rock art sites in the park and several other closely related sites contained a large number of well-defined petroglyphs. The inventory of individual symbols was impressive for this Midwestern rock art (Fig. 2.2). It contained many clear representations of motifs initially linking it to a southeastern centered taxonomic catalog of Mississippian symbols compiled by Antonio J. Waring and Preston Holder (Waring and Holder 1945, 1–34).

Their catalog had quickly morphed into a catch-all depository for any and all elaborate Mississippian art forms and symbols found throughout the Eastern United States and labeled as belonging to the "Southern Cult" (Muller 1989, 12–13). When the second author of this paper (CD-G) began work on a state-wide survey of Missouri rock art in the mid-1980s, we were drawn into the rapidly evolving offshoot of Waring and Holder's system, then called the Southeastern Ceremonial Complex or SECC (Galloway 1989, 1–7). As this system evolved, it began to take on multiple regional irregularities (Howard 1968, 25–36; Williams 1968, 30–69). That is, motifs appeared in some regions and not in others.

The northwestern regional rock art, especially that found along the eastern Ozark uplift between the Missouri and Ohio confluences, best modeled Dhegiha patterns (Diaz-Granados 1993, 382; Griffin 1952, 106; Duncan and Diaz-Granados 2000, 2; 2004, 215; 2018, 30; 2022, 175; Brown 2007, 56; 2011, 36–41; Kehoe 2007, 246–61; Diaz-Granados *et al.* 2015). This region we labeled "Western Mississippian" which includes the central Mississippi River Valley, the Cahokia area surrounding the confluence of the Missouri and Mississippi Rivers, and its southern extension, the Ohio-Mississippi confluence. This Western Mississippian symbolism displayed a distinct anomaly, a plethora of female symbolism in contrast to the then, largely masculine SECC (Duncan and Diaz-Granados 2000, 2; 2004, 190–1). We have since gathered more information from various sources, especially from Osage Native American Church members, as well as artifact collections, both institutional and private. It is our intent in this chapter to further utilize the American Indian ethnography and oral tradition, especially Dhegiha, to define the cosmology of the

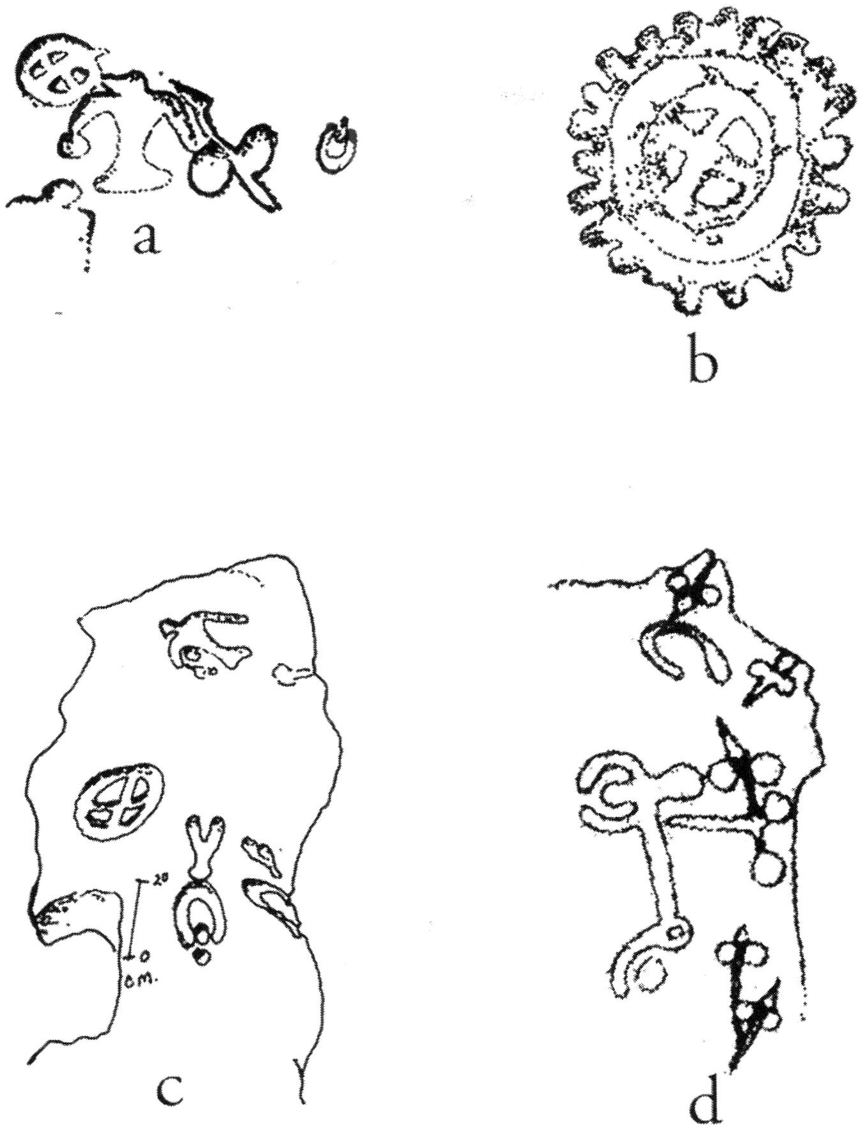

Fig. 2.2 Petroglyphs found on sites in the northeastern Ozark escarpment, south of the Missouri River in Washington County, Missouri. These sites have symbols comparable to Waring and Holder's list of Mississippian icons belonging to the Mississippian interaction sphere, with regional differences: a. cross-in-circle and vulvar symbol from the Three Hills Creek Site; b. petaloid cross-in-circle from the Maddin Creek site; c. cross-in-circle, Raptor and Vulvar symbol, Three Hills Creek Site; d. hafted spatulate celt or spud and bi-lobed arrows from the Maddin Creek Site.

Western Mississippian societies who so prominently depicted cosmic symbolism in their sacra, both their rock art and portable artifacts. One of these sacred places was a cave in the Lower Missouri River Valley, Picture Cave. Widespread familiarity with specific rituals aided in the peaceful interaction by multiple groups at such sacred places. Using the radiometric dates from this cave, we believe the beginning of this interaction might have taken place as early as AD 950. The signature of this Emergent Mississippian cultural expression at Picture Cave was the beautifully rendered early artistic expression, a formative Braden style imagery (Fig. 2.3) (Phillips and Brown 1978, 36–7; Brown 2011, 38; Duncan and Diaz-Granados 2022, 175–92).

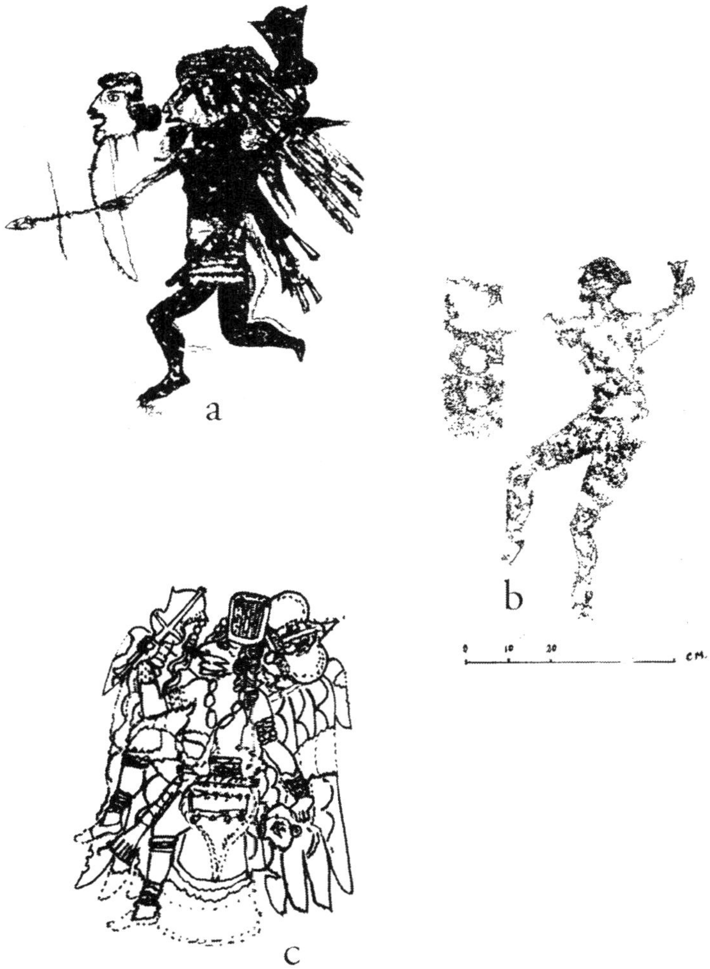

Fig. 2.3 A comparison of anthropomorphic figures from rock art sites and a repoussé copper plate image found at the Etowah Site in Georgia: a. a warrior armed with a large war club and a bow, drawn in black pigment, from Picture Cave in Warren County, Missouri AD 950–1025; b. a warrior armed with a war club, carrying a large rectangular shield from the Rattlesnake Bluff Site, in Franklin County, Missouri. This 1 m tall figure was painted in red ochre *c.* AD 1050–1200; c. the Rogan Copper Plate found at Etowah. This Classic Braden style repoussé plate, while found in Mound C at Etowah, Georgia this plate is attributed to Cahokia, Illinois *c.* AD 1100–1200.

Rock art sites displaying thematic subject matter

Graphic support for the father/son dynamics present in the ethnography and oral traditions could be observed using the petaloid cross motif interpreted as the Above Worlds, the Sun/First Man-All Father (Fig. 2.4a; Diaz-Granados and Duncan 2000, 21; Duncan and Diaz-Granados 2004, 201–3; Reilly 2004, 132, 136; 2007, 48, 52), and seeing it often paired in the rock art with the bilobed arrow (Fig. 4.2c), a symbol which we interpret as denoting Morning Star/Hawk – the son (Ponziglione 1897, 11–14; Bowers 1950, 155; Duncan and Diaz-Granados 2004, 200–3). This pairing is evidence that these two characters in the cosmic family indeed interact. This pairing is seen at Maddin Creek (Fig. 2.4b), at Lost Creek (Fig 2.4c) in a unique pictograph version, and another version can be seen at the Three Hills Creek petroglyph site (Fig. 2.4a) in which the sun motif is actually paired with a raptor.[1]

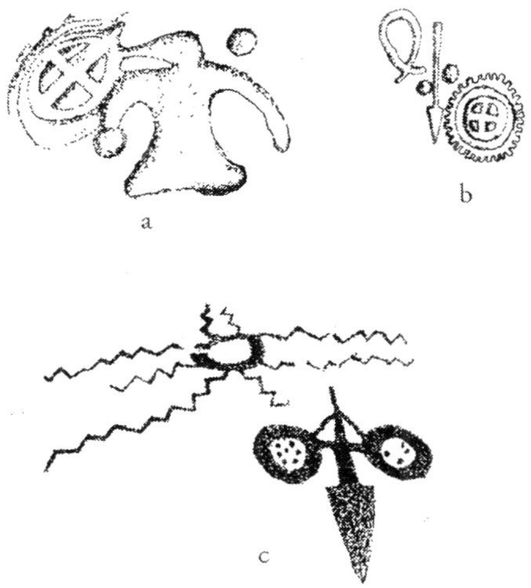

Fig. 2.4 Petroglyphs and pictographs of powerful symbols: a. an avian figure holding a discoidal (small circle) also holding a quartered circle in his beak at the Three Hills Creek petroglyph site; b. the petaloid cross-in-circle, bi-lobed arrow and the mobius eye surround found on Braden Water Spirit images linked to Cahokia at the Maddin Creek petroglyph site; c. the power radiating sun and bi-lobed arrow pictographs are painted in red on a Lost Creek bluff.

In American Indian art we often see the use of metaphors; that is, an icon or motif used as a type of "shorthand" to symbolize a supernatural being or concept. That icon, when paired with another, can confer special meaning. So, rather than taking the motifs as having a singular meaning, we believe what we are seeing – what was carved and painted several hundred years ago, are mnemonics for a story conveying data from oral traditions and these motifs relating to the interactions of two related supernatural beings – the Sun(father) and the Morning Star(son). This in turn may be an allusion to the importance of the father/son relationship so often expressed in the Dhegiha oral tradition and important inherited roles.

If one believes, as we and many of our colleagues do, that the imagery carved, drawn, and painted by the ancient American Indians on boulders, bluff facades, and on shelter and cave walls, is not mere graffiti, but had meaning for the people creating it, then we can be confident that repeated pairings in the imagery bear notice and can and should be interpreted using the widespread Siouan oral traditions. Many of the major sites in Missouri's southeastern quadrant contain symbolism associated with the Mississippian Idealogical Interaction Sphere (MIIS) (Reilly and Garber 2007, 3).

When we first began to link the rock art symbolism with Dhegiha oral traditions we had to synthesize a great deal of information. We came to understand that much of the surviving Siouan oral traditions present in translated collections, Mandan, Hidatsa, Lakota, and especially Chiwere and Dhegiha material, all shared a common core ideology (Diaz-Granados 2004, 142–4; Duncan and Diaz-Granados 2004, 190–1). We were most interested in the prominent recurring theme of these traditions in the Dhegiha version as noted by Francis La Flesche (Fletcher and La Flesche 1992, 171). We believed this to be the Dhegiha genesis story, and this story involved an important concept, that the father, First Man, and his eldest son (Hawk/Morning Star, etc) chartered a father-son affinity, even a dependency. We have long believed at least some of this oral tradition to be quite ancient and, today, we are even more convinced of its antiquity. We, along with many of our colleagues, agree that some of the Middle Woodland cosmology, with its attendant spirit beings, demonstrates ontological roots that resonate metaphorically within the Western Mississippian religion, roughly 700 years later (Reilly *et al.* 2011, xiii; Giles *et al.* 2022, 213–16). We think that the antiquity of this layered cosmos may be even greater: not only is the basic cosmology ancient, it is widespread (Reilly *et al.* 2011, xiv). Being widespread and ancient, some of the lore has survived in isolated pockets into modern times. One such survival is among the Osage of Eastern Oklahoma.

The Osage, largely because of their wealth, have achieved a remarkable degree of cultural stability. They have been able to preserve their ancient traditions in their Native American Church rites (Duncan and Diaz-Granados 2004, 191–2; 2018, 65–7; 1; Swan 2004, 122–3; Duncan 2015, 210–11). However, and most significantly, the Dhegiha, particularly the Osage, have valued literate tribal members for more than 200 years because of two important factors, they encouraged intermarriage with the French and they began interacting with the Jesuits as educators early, perhaps before 1760 (Edward Red Eagle Jr; John Mathews; Louis Burns; Francis La Flesche).

The Osage and their cognate kinsmen, the Omaha, Ponca, Quapaw, and Kansa have shared a long-established ideology (Mathews 1961, 744–56). Much of this ideology, especially the core themes, we believe to be common to sedentary Siouan speakers and their neighbors (Duncan 2021, 29).

Several important themes are depicted in the rock art of Missouri's southeastern quadrant and lower Missouri River, especially in Picture Cave. Two of these themes are of such importance that they are present at multiple sites, the *Mon-thin-ka ga-xe* or "The Making of the Earth" and *Wa-ko pa-hon* or *Wa-kon-da hon-non-pa-ce*, "First Woman" (La Flesche 1975, 194; Fletcher and La Flesche 1992, 171). It is no surprise why we selected these two themes and the supporting themes that connect the ritual practices of the Mississippian period with the ethnographic record of the post-contact period. There is strong supporting thematic information in the imagery. Most importantly, rock art is *in situ*. It ties the iconography to a specific location. Furthermore, its motifs often link with similar symbols found in portable artifacts. A recurrent issue is whether or not the cultural values or definitions change over time. We have discussed this in the past and we will again reiterate our findings: we find that Dhegiha core religious concepts have not been subjected to radical change. The principal religious rites and oral traditions are remarkably complete and intact (Parks 1991; Mooney 1996). We have learned that the modern Dhegiha, especially the Osage, have greatly simplified these oral traditions while still retaining the key chartering points that govern and instruct the listener about important cultural values.

Theme I: the making of the earth, a remarkable relation

This theme lies at the core of the Dhegiha religious beliefs and is included here to help the reader better understand the father/son continuum. In 1851 a well-educated Jesuit, Father Paul M. Ponziglione came to the Osage Mission on the Neosho River in Kansas (Fitzgerald 1939, 89). Ponziglione learned the Osage language and kept a journal enabling him to write a "history" – incorporating a great deal of theological material concerning the Osage, in 1897. It is from this history we learn that the Osage were monotheists, giving the role of creator and "Master of life" to some "Great One" (Ponziglione 1897, 12). This great, mysterious power was called *Whaconta* or *Wa-kon'-da* (Fitzgerald 1939, 25; La Flesche 1975, 194). What follows is a brief version of the Osage cosmology. Ponziglione, bemoaning the lack of a written history of the Osage People, began to write one, and he began his efforts: "The only reliable document one can have about their history is that of oral tradition" (1897). He recognized that Osage oral traditions chartered important cultural values and behaviors. We will annotate select parts of Ponziglione's history; the annotations are preceded by an asterisk (*).

Ponziglione begins this "remarkable legend" by relating what was told to him by "one of the more intelligent priests": "First Osage Man who walked down from the Sun and the First Osage Woman from the Moon" (1897, 11). First Man and First Woman cohabit and have six children, three boys and three girls. After watching the motions of the stars and the changing seasons, being well furnished with everything they need including fresh water, the genesis family begin to feel that there had to be some Great One, a Master of all things by whom the entire universe was governed. They could not see this Great Spirit but they incessantly call for assistance. Beginning with the eldest son, who decides to offer some act of self-punishment to the Great Spirit that they might gain his favor and obtain the knowledge they so much coveted. He undertakes a journey to the west, strictly fasting and mourning for seven days but to no avail. Finally, after all five of the eldest children undergo the journey, fasting and mourning to no avail, the youngest daughter begins her seven-day journey, fasting and mourning. On the seventh day she finds a wondrous cave and entering it she experiences a beautiful and moving experience where she gains the knowledge of how the cosmos moves in a balanced manner and how all life begins. It seems to her that a heavy veil is removed from her mind! Enlightened and with a calm soul, she returns to her family who rejoice in her successful return. She then gives to all of her family, the information she has gained from her successful vision quest (Ponziglione 1897, 13–16). *This introductory genesis tradition emphasizes the importance of *Wa-kon'-da* as the creator and governor of the universe. It also explains the roles of the Sun and the Moon as housing powerful ancestral spirit beings and finally, it emphasizes the important role of women in the dichotomous Dhegiha society, for women create life both as mothers and as farmers, as well as practicing fasting and vision quests as the means by which all Dhegiha can gain help from *Wa-kon'-da*. A part of the cosmology was tattooed on the throats and chests of the Osage priests belonging to the Men of Mystery clan. Birthing scenes in rock art, where a female figure (First Woman) is shown giving birth to multiple offspring, usually six, are found at the Maddin Creek site and the Three Hills Creek site (Fig. 2.5), as well as in other locations in North America.

Stories surrounding the eldest daughter abound in the oral traditions. One in particular describes the eldest daughter getting impregnated by ingesting a downy eagle feather, being struck by a ray of sunlight, or other scenarios, depending on the cultural group's version. After conception, Evening Star hears singing coming from her belly. She is ashamed and asks her brother, Morning Star to move away with her and hunt for her. While pregnant she is confronted by a monstrous, smelly character, "Sharp Elbow". She feeds him, but upon leaving her lodge, he hears her insult him. He rushes back and rips open her belly and he throws one of her two male fetuses into the corner and the other into a spring. The eldest brother returns to find his slain sister and her son crying in the corner of the house.

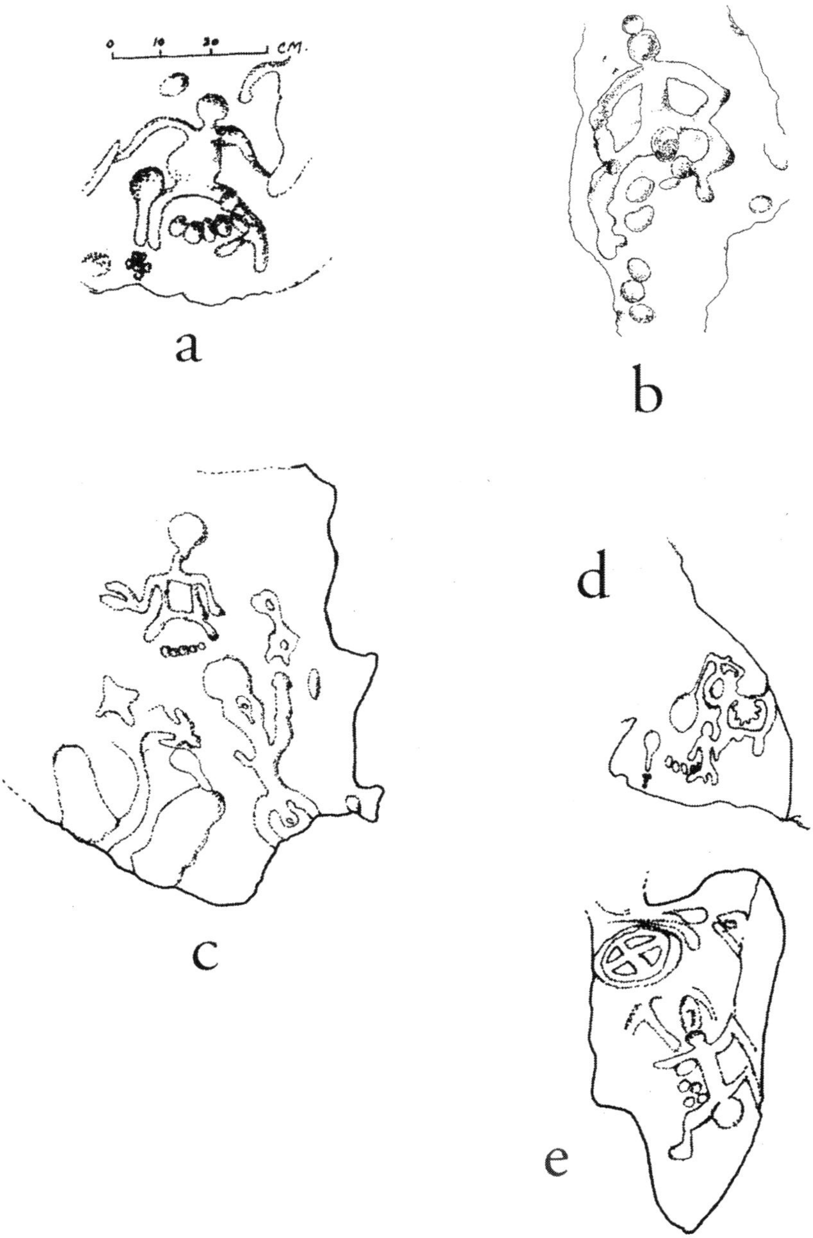

Fig. 2.5 Petroglyphs of First Woman birthing her six children: a. a wavy armed example with a conventional vulvar symbol by her right leg; b. a shape-shifting *Iko* (Grandmother) with deer hoofs for feet; c. Iko with a deer hoof for her right hand; d. an interesting composition, Iko birthing with a conventional vulvar symbol and a house (square motif) containing a petaloid sun symbol (a.–d. from the Maddin Creek site); e. Iko birthing with a quartered circle at the Three Hills Creek Site.

The brother raises the little boy who is called "Stone" (*I'n tha-thgin*). Since there is no trace of the other fetus, who was thrown into a spring, the maternal brother knows nothing of him. This fetus is raised by a powerful Water Spirit who (we believe) names him "Dark Wolf" (*Shon'-ge ca-be*). These two boys grow up independent of each other, one with his maternal uncle "Elder Brother" who is Morning Star or Hawk and the other is the foster son of the Great Water Spirit

(La Flesche 1975, 175, 336; Fletcher and La Flesche 1992, 171). *This section contains very important chartering information: the boy "Stone" who is raised by his maternal uncle, Morning Star, represents the closest bond between a young man and a mentor, that of his mother's brother, who will be his principal teacher. The raising of the eldest child by his uncle Morning Star while his younger brother "Dark Wolf" by the Great Water Spirit establishes the two great divisions of the Osage, that of the Sky Above division, the *Tsi'-zhu* and the Earth/Water division, the *Hon'-ga*.

The younger brother leaves the spring and the two boys play together during the day, when the maternal uncle, Morning Star, is away hunting. They often play roughly, as young boys will do, and Morning Star finds strange bite marks on his nephew's toys and clothing. Morning Star's nephew, Stone, asks his uncle to make two bows and arrows for him and his playmate to use the next day. Thus, Morning Star finds out that his nephew has a companion. For several days he tries to catch the little boy who is not only very shy, but also wild, cunning and powerful. Using several magical guises Morning Star finally catches the wild boy. This little boy is strange looking, he has a long nose, strange owl-like eyes and the fangs of a water spirit. Morning Star trims his nose, washes him and cleans and dresses his hair, a feat that takes six days (Fletcher and La Flesche 1992, 122–3; Duncan and Diaz-Granados 2000, 8). He then performs the adoption rite and the two brothers, Stone and Dark Wolf, officially become brothers (Bowers 1950, 329–31; Hall 1997, 44–7; Duncan 2015, 226–7). *This section contains the adoption rite. This rite was so important in establishing peaceful relations between leaders of non-aligned bands. It allowed principal men and women to adopt alien people as children or siblings to further economic and social relations. The allusion to the trimming of the wild boy's nose is an indelible link to the "Long-Nosed Maskettes", often called "Long-Nosed God" ear ornaments by some authors; however, they do not represent "Gods", they are ancestral spirits (Williams and Goggin 1956, 7; Diaz-Granados 1993, 205; Duncan and Diaz-Granados 2000, 1–26, King and Reilly 2011, 316–17). These two brothers, often called the "Hero or Celestial Twins", Stone and Dark Wolf, are the champions of humanity in their epic struggle with monsters and their other foes. They are depicted at Picture Cave shooting the Giant Water Spirit with their magic arrows (Fig. 2.6). This tradition is widespread throughout North and Middle America. The Celestial Twins aid their father/uncle in his role as the guardian of Humanity (Bowers 1992, 64, 290–3). Morning Star, wearing the Long-Nosed maskette, is beautifully depicted in a very early pictograph at Picture Cave (Diaz-Granados *et al.* 2015, 71; Fig. 2.7). The twin boys also represent the role of dual chiefs, so important to Dhegiha (Osage) government (Bailey 2010, 43–4).

The two brothers Stone and the Dark Wolf travel throughout the cosmos and have many adventures. They travel on the back of the Great Serpent, the Milky Way to visit their grandmother, First Woman. *The boys, Stone and Dark Wolf travel the Great Serpent, the Milky Way or Path of Souls to visit their grandmother, First Woman. This is an important statement about how spirits of the dead travel to First Woman's house (Lankford 2004, 207–17). First Woman is the creator of the "fleeting snare of the breath of life" engraved on thin ware Bell Plain ceramics from Southeast Missouri and Northeast Arkansas (Fig. 2.7).

The Celestial Twins travel from their home in the Upper Worlds (north) to the Lower Worlds (south), to the house of their grandmother to be given greater powers. It is especially important to remember that the weather is only one of First Woman' domains in Dhegihan cosmology. With her dried sunflower stalk whistle she can summon the Great Serpent and her two grandsons the Celestial Twins who bring terrible storms with wind and hail. The Great Serpent and the two brothers with sacred bundles are the subjects of a vignette at Washington State Park A (Fig. 2.6b).

Returning to the Father/Son relationship, we argue that the iconography of the Western Mississippians contains encoded information that, when linked to Dhegihan ethnography, fleshes out a more balanced look at societal beliefs in the Mississippi River Corridor. These are two symbols that we wish to describe and interpret. They are depicted either alone or attached to a figure. Again, they are the bi-lobed arrow (the Son/Hawk/Morning Star) and a Sun or Solar symbol (the Father) (Fig. 2.4b). Both seem to relate to the same spirit beings, First Man and his son,

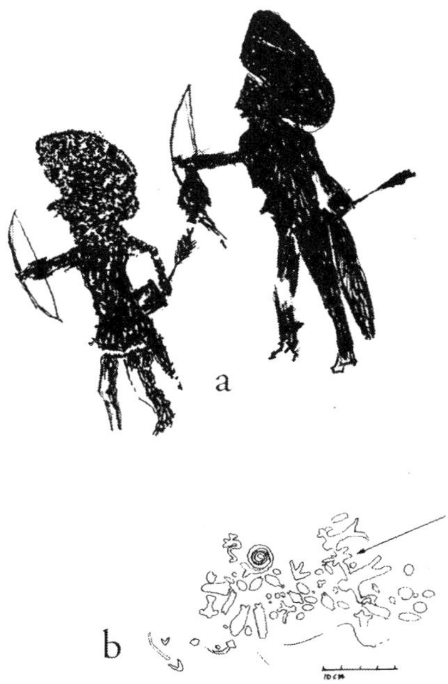

Fig. 2.6 The Celestial Twins: a. the Twins with towering "True Dog" headdresses and carrying bows with quivers of arrows, drawn in black pigment at Picture Cave, Warren County, Missouri; b. the conjoined Celestial Twins at Washington State Park, site A. The Great Serpent and numerous medicine bundles are included in this vignette.

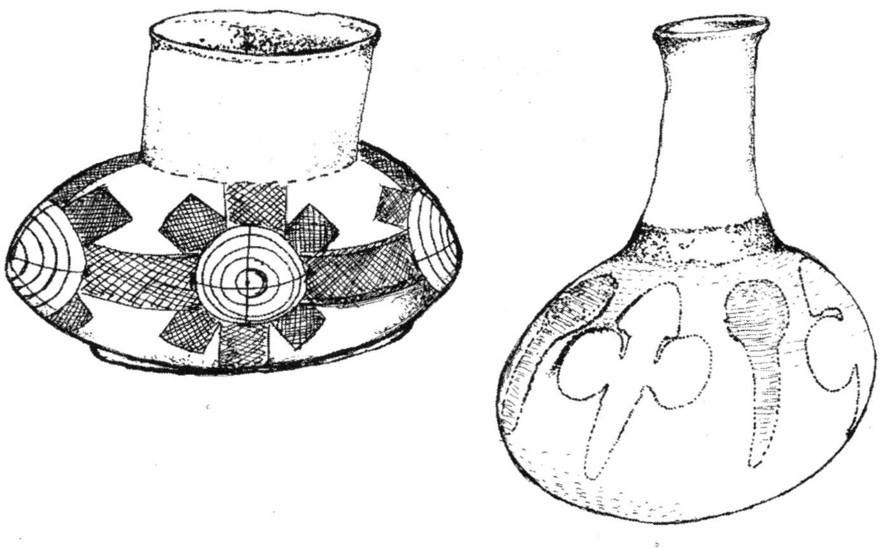

Fig. 2.7 Late Mississippian ceramics displaying cosmic symbols: left. a fine ware (Bell Plain) bottle from the Murphy Mound, Pemiscot County, Missouri engraved with a *Ho'-e-ga*, the "snare or trap of the breath of life", a definition for the Middle World where human beings live; right. the bi-lobed arrow and a conventional vulvar design painted on a Late Mississippian (Quapaw) polychrome bottle from the Soudan site, Lee County, Arkansas. These two important icons represent the Great Portal, First Woman's vulva, and the spirit of Symbolic Man who will precede in birth, the Rising Sun at dawn.

Morning Star. These occur along the eastern Ozark uplift, usually carved on sandy dolomite outcrops on or near glades and as pictographs on vertical dolomite bluffs. We are convinced that the bi-lobed arrow and its frequently used icon relates to Morning Star, the eldest son and successor of First Man. The Sun represents First Man in his "Sky Lodge" (Ponziglione 1897, 11). Ponziglione said that the Osage had many origin stories but that the one about First Man and First Woman was the one that he obtained from the "most intelligent priest" (Ponziglione 1897, 10–11). While it is true that all clans and sub-clans had their own genesis traditions, the Tsi-zhu version contained a part of these, in a unified and lengthy narration. All the clans had knowledge of the Tsi-zhu genesis account, but each also had a unique genesis story, while sharing the power of narration.

The central spirit helper, Morning Star, and his nephews the Celestial Twins are also the ancestors of the Dhegiha (Ponziglione 1897, 12). With the advent of horses, the Pawnee of the Platte, the Hidatsa, Mandan, Oto, Osage, and Iowa of the lower Missouri River enhanced their agricultural ways with the new equestrian culture. In the 19th century General Kearney noted in his journal that the Osage treated "images they carried" as the Hebrews of old treated the arc of the covenant (Penney and Longfish 1994, 82). These images are probably the two great swanskin covered staffs representing the great white plumes of the rising Sun and Morning Star carried at the head of Great Bands as they moved as a nation during migrations and buffalo hunts. These staffs have the same anatomical parts as holy arrows and the great pipe stems, they encompass the breath of life. Once they were confined to a reservation, Road men's striped staffs (see below) probably replaced the ancient sun staffs, the heralds of war and conquests, in authority.

These staffs have ancient counterparts that are found throughout sedentary Siouan speaking societies as well as their neighbors, the Cadddoan speakers, Algonkin speaking Cheyenne, and even the Kiowa, they are the sacred arrows. These sacred arrows represent powerful spirit beings who travel from the Upper Worlds to the Earth and the Beneath Worlds as lightning. The bodies of these sacred arrow beings have the same anatomical names and structures as do the pipe stems for the great pipes present in sedentary Plains Siouan societies. These symbols were used to repel evil spirits as well as quelling disputes among members of those societies (Bowers 1992, 290–30; Hall 1997, 41). With the appearance of single poles with oriented offering pits in the American Bottom during the Late Woodland Patrick Phase, the locus for the antecedent of the First Man ancestor and the accompanying son, Morning Star is established (Kelly *et al.* 1984; Brown 2007, 57–9). This sacred arrow/pole symbolism becomes expressed as the bi-lobed arrow by AD 1200 in the Cahokia area, remembering the definitive Rogan plates found at Etowah, were manufactured at Cahokia (Brown 1989, 201; Hall 1989, 250–2; Muller 1989, 15). Cahokia's Braden style has the greatest number of variations of bi-lobed arrow adornment which seem to be the label of Morning Star, the son of the First Man. First Man (Sun) and his eldest Son, Morning Star whose principal symbol is the bi-lobed arrow, along with Sun's grandsons the Celestial Twins who are Morning Star's nephews, make a foursome of powerful ancestral spirits, all with thunder and lightning powers who come to the aid of humanity in quelling evil spirits and monsters. This basic tradition is found throughout the prairie/plains, the mid-continental Mississippi corridor and the southeast.

Historic descriptions of the plaza-like areas occupying the centers of fortified towns on the lower Missouri River state these spaces were considered to be sacred and were used for ritual religious gatherings and dances. Cleared areas adjacent to the towns were used for games, in particular stick ball games. Stick ball is universal and was played by men and women. Among the Dhegiha the stick ball game was played between boys of the two great divisions, usually at the beginning of the new year in the spring. The outcome of this sacred game alluded to the winds, the bringers of life (Fletcher and La Flesche 1992, 96–8).

The game of chunkey, the rolling of the round disc-shaped chunkey stones, emulates the sun's path and is well documented for the Dhegiha and their Mandan relations. This essential ritual of rolling the chunk stone is also connected to bringing rains favorable to agriculture and is used to foretell the future of the buffalo herds (Fletcher and La Flesche 1992, 148–9, 171–2). Both the great stick ball game between the two great tribal divisions and the chunkey game were of ritual nature. There was no betting allowed during the ritual ball game and the tribal officers and clan priests carefully watched the young participants for bravery and leadership skills (Fletcher and La Flesche 1992, 196–8). These rites were part of the annual celebration of the creation of the earth and is found repeated in the oral tradition.

Warfare is a dominant theme at a number of the rock art sites. The rock art, the *xthe-xthe'* or symbolic tattooing on the sacred body of First Woman, the Earth, the mother of all things, is testimony to the warlike nature of the Western Mississippians (La Flesche 1975, 220; Diaz-Granados 2004, 142–6; Duncan 2015, 236). There is little doubt that Morning Star (The Symbolic Man) and his two nephews/sons, Stone and the Gray Wolf are the paramount role models for all young Dhegiha males with regard to military behavior. Warfare was carefully regulated by the *Non'-hon-zhin-ga*, the assembled clan priests/leaders (La Flesche in Bailey 2010, 31). Only warfare sanctioned by this governing body, warfare that would benefit the nation was allowed to proceed.

Two major risks confronted Western Mississippian society when engaging in warfare: the loss of warriors killed in combat had to be compensated for, and the taking of the life of enemies had to be atoned for because only *Wa-kon'-da*, the great creator, was the source of life. Destroying any "gift" from *Wa-kon'-da* was considered to be a sacrilegious act.

Since we began working with Osage informants in the early 1990s, we have interviewed several important Osage elders and religious leaders. Two of the men we interviewed, referred to as "doctors" by members of their Osage Indian churches, were Preston Morrell and Edward Red Eagle Sr. Both of these men were important second-generation leaders in the Osage Indian church, after Chief Fred LookOut and the few remaining clan priests reinstated the essential ancient Dhegihan religious narratives into the Osage church rites. The ancient name for these men would have been *Wa-kon'-da-gi*, "those who communicated with the holy and sacred" (La Flesche 1975, 194). They gladly imparted their sacred knowledge with their associates, counseled church members and friends, and performed naming ceremonies, as well as helped to heal church members of their afflictions. This seems to be just a part of the general role of these religious leaders. Preston Morrell (Good Eagle) traveled extensively and attended many Native American peyote church prayer meetings. He was a very interesting and well informed person. Francis Holding requested that "Uncle" Preston spend an afternoon during the Hominy Il-lon'-ska dances with the senior author. He was especially knowledgeable about Morning Star and his descriptive narratives have been the foundation for much of our research on the Morning Star subject. The genesis narrative at the beginning of this chapter should probably be called by its proper name, the *Wi'-gi-e ton-ga*, "the great prayer" (La Flesche 1975, 216). Equally important in the synthesis was the help from Charles A. Pratt, the Hominy West Moon Osage Native American Church leader, who was instrumental in corroborating our synthesis. Charles also furnished a large corpus of data relating to the stars, church rites, and Osage terms for the principal spirit beings. Charles Pratt was a champion of Osage religious thought and practice! It was Charles who worked with the Picture Cave interpretive narrative so that this "ancient genesis story" would be preserved. Finally, Johnny Williams, Eddy Red Eagle Jr and Mark Sims have been essential in corroborating symbolism connected to the ancient religion as well as the current Osage peyote church.[2]

All the Dhegiha groups have an oral tradition in which they were one great nation. It is believed that they split apart into the five cognate tribes (Fletcher and La Flesche 1992, 37). This split occurred around AD 1200–1250. However, the Kansas remained closely associated with the Osage until the late 18th–early 19th century as did the Omaha and Ponca. For many years the archaeological community has known of the fragmentation and dispersal of the Cahokian population. This would then serve as a partial explanation with respect to what happened at the Western Mississippian religious centers during and following the Cahokian florescence. A part of this group, today called the Osage, remained closest to the Missouri and Mississippi confluence, the closest to ancient Cahokia. They were encountered there by the French during the late 17th century. While the Dhegiha focus was the lower Missouri River valley, especially its northern prairie and the eastern prairies adjacent to the Mississippi River, one large division, the *Hon'-ga U-ta-non-dsi* traveled south to find suitable supplies of wild fruit, paw-paws and plums (La Flesche in Bailey 2010, 76). This division inhabited both sides of the Mississippi River floodplain below the Ohio River confluence, east of the Little River, along the Pemiscot Bayou until the late 17th and early 18th centuries (Duncan 2013, 207–9; 2015, 106–109).

In refocusing on the relationship between the First Man (Sun) and his eldest son, Morning Star, we see these two figures, universally tied to the paramount, great, or grand chief concept of the Mississippian world. This symbolism is present throughout the Western Mississippian corridor, the earliest being on the lower Missouri River, Picture Cave (Diaz-Granados *et al.* 2015), on classic Braden shell cups from Cahokia, and finally on superlative repoussé copper plates. The images of the spirit beings, Sun and his son, Morning Star, are charged with unmistakable symbolism – the Sun is preceded in its birth, at dawn, by Morning Star (Fig. 2.8). In order to accomplish this reversal in time, the son before the father, the body of the First Woman, the Earth, acts as a birth canal or portal for both and for the son preceding his father. This is a difficult concept for a western European mind but it works in the minds of Western Mississippians attuned to the asynchronous gestation period in the house of the First Woman. This miracle is still accomplished during the 15 hour rite of vigil during the Osage Native American Church service.

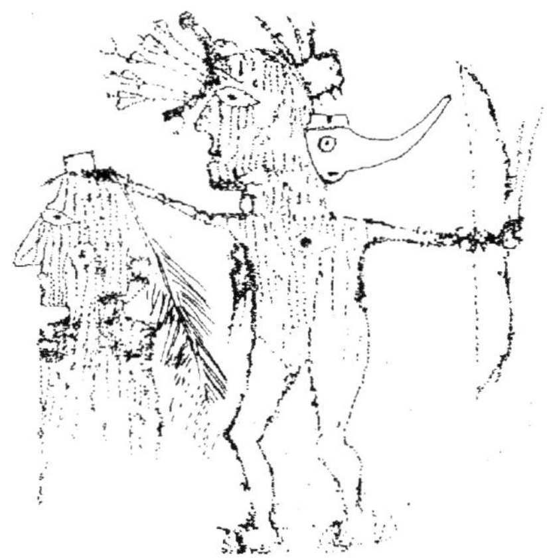

Fig. 2.8 Morning Star raising his father, the Sun, at dawn on the first day of the creation of the Middle World. This important image possibly dates to the Terminal Late Woodland as its distinctive style of execution is unique. Its polychrome appearance is due to engraving and scraping of the sandstone cortex to remove iron pigments and adding fine detail with a brush and black pigment. The great importance alludes to the antiquity of the striking iconography, especially the forehead plaque which depicts First Woman's vulva with the five arrows embedded in it, the arrows representing the number of portals in the Beneath Worlds he must pass through in order to be reborn.

After his birth, First Man assumes the metaphorical form of the axis of the Universe, the Great Red Oak Tree, the Sacred Pole. This too is symbolically and reverently achieved by the Osage Native American Church. This is the work of the two principal church officers, the "Road Man" and the "Fire Man" (Mathews 1961, 740–56). These officers likely represent the Celestial Twins, the Thunderers, Stone and Dark Wolf, the sons of Evening Star. The most important depiction of this rite is the Potter Gorget from the Lilbourn site 23NM38 (Fig. 2.9).[3]

The Lilbourn site is one of the largest mound sites in the US, measured in the mid-19th century as *c.* 22 acres. It lies on the west side of the Mississippi River, near the mouth of the Ohio River. Lilbourn has a large plaza area and nine mounds with the largest, on the south side of the plaza having a base covering 2.41 acres (*c.* 1 ha). The great mound at Lilbourn, 23NM38, is probably the largest remaining mound in Missouri. On the Potter Gorget we see Stone holding an animated First Man staff. The animated First Man staff seems to be wearing a distinctive decorated leather cap similar to the caps worn by Siouan priests described in the journals of Tabeau (Fig. 2.10; Tabeau 1939, 210–11). The striped pole is identified as a distinct thunder spirit being, and since it has a companion, the ancient cedar pole, we know that there are two Thunder Beings or Celestial Twins and the poles are their metaphors (Fletcher and La Flesche 1992, 171, 229).

The Osage also celebrate their Big Moon rites in two distinct round houses, the West Moon and the East Moon Church houses, each with its attendant staff, so there are again two Thunder Beings. This makes for a complicated situation as the staff or pole is usually referred to as First Man. So how do we account for the two Thunder Beings (Fletcher and La Flesche 1992; 229, La Flesche in Bailey 2010, 101)? To answer this question, we will have to refer to a very old formative Braden image at Picture Cave, the "womb of the universe". In Picture Cave the images of First Man and his son Morning Star have the same facial markings, vertical lines, 13 of them as best as we can tell (Fig. 2.8). La Flesche answers this conundrum in his amusing story of when he was a youngster and Omaha boys

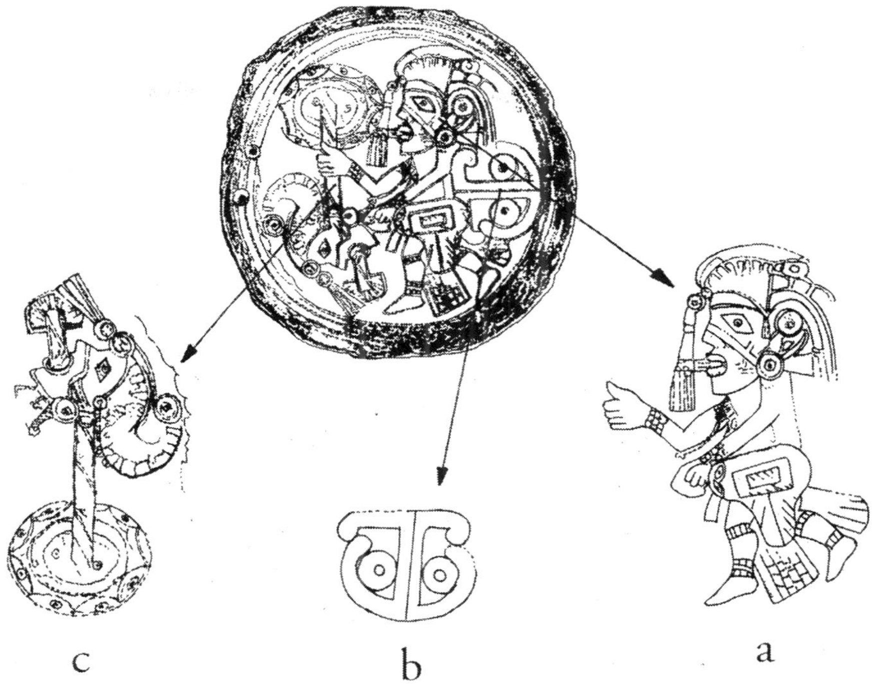

Fig. 2.9 The Potter Gorget, excavated from Mound 3 at the Lilbourn site in New Madrid County, Missouri. The attachment holes indicate that the (a) figure of a priest floats horizontally above (b) a ceramic vessel that represents First Woman's body (Earth) depicted with two vulvar shaped altars flanking a central cosmic tree or ***axis mundi***. The priest is holding (c) an animated Striped Pole or Staff representing the Symbolic Man or Morning Star who is wearing an unusual decorated leather(?) cap. Opposite the head of Symbolic Man, the Striped Staff is emerging from a celestial symbol. Both the priest and Symbolic Man are smoking tubular "cigarros" made of tobacco wrapped in a maize husk. All this symbolism is still found in today's Osage Native American Church.

had a festival in the Spring, after the thunder had sounded. The boys took dried buffalo bladders and made masks, cutting eye and mouth holes and painting the masks with vertical stripes symbolizing, in this case, lightning, according to La Flesche. Going to the lodge of Mother's brother, the masked boy would beat on the door pole with a war club while making a growling sound like distant thunder. When asked "what does Thunder want?" the boy would ask for leggings or moccasins. If the uncle did not give the masked boy a gift, the boy could punch a hole in the lodge cover (Fletcher and La Flesche 1992, 370). Thus, we see that vertical facial stripes that symbolize the Sun can also symbolize thunder power. It seems that First Man, his eldest son Morning Star, and his two Grandsons, all have thunder power and are therefore "Thunderers". And, by the way, they are all four depicted as bird men.

Theme 2: First Woman as the giver of life

Since the excavations of the FAI-270 archaeological mitigation project (undertaken by IDOT – Illinois Department of Transportation) of 1978–81, a great deal has been written about the female figures carved from Missouri flint clay that appeared to be made during the Sterling period at Cahokia. These have been identified and given names using ethnographic sources ranging from Shawnee to Muskogean (Prentice 1986, 239–66). Since Emerson and his team have determined that all

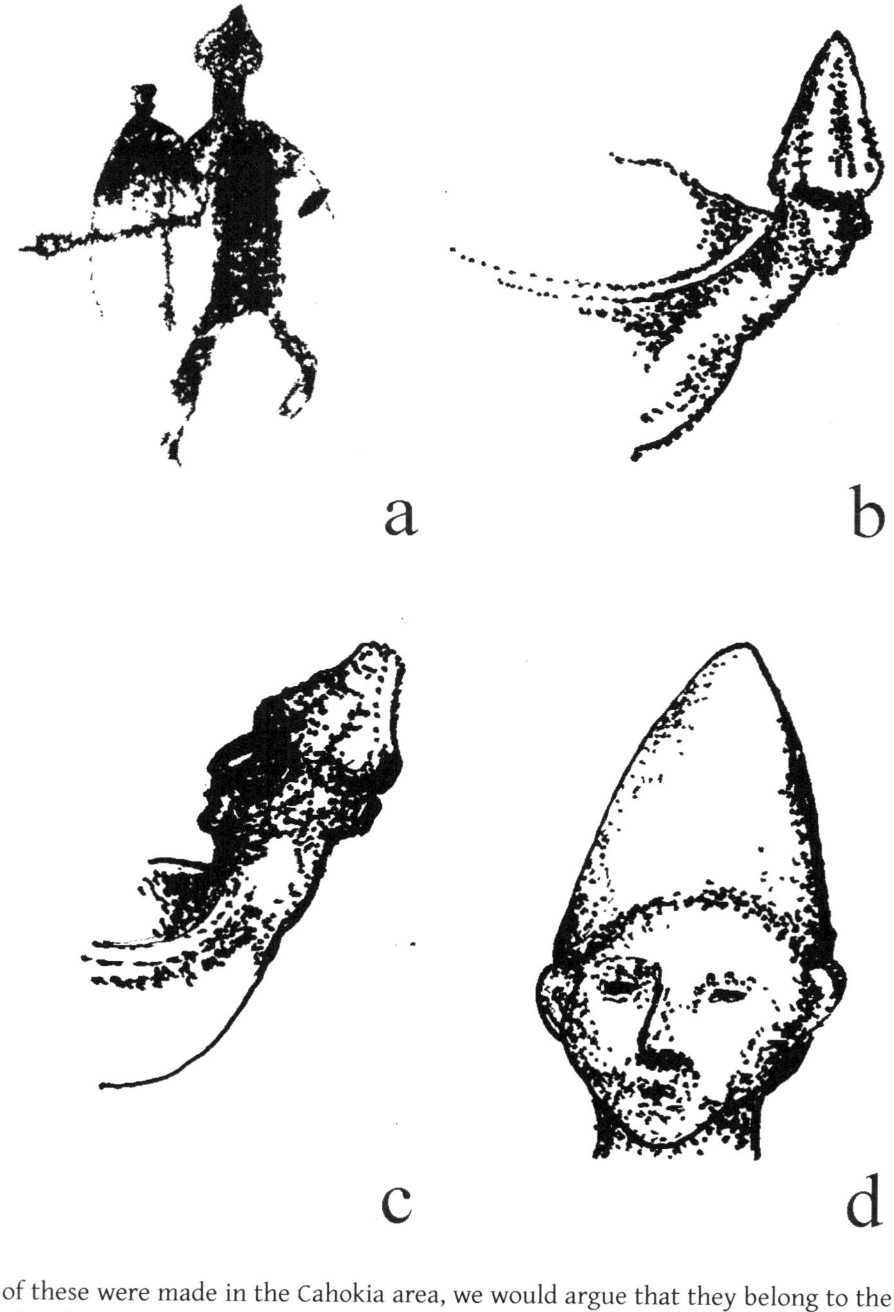

Fig. 2.10 Examples of the conical headdress found on ceramic bowls and drawn on a figure from Picture Cave. These important Western Mississippian icons span the entire period: a. Picture Cave, Early or formative Mississippian period; b. Bell Place, Mississippi County, Arkansas; c. Lilbourn, New Madrid County, Missouri; d. Nashville area, Tennessee.

of these were made in the Cahokia area, we would argue that they belong to the Dhegiha's ancient oral traditions, namely, First Woman (Old-Woman-Who-Never-Dies) and some may even be images of her daughters (Emerson *et al.* 2002, 328; 2003, 290). The First Woman is a powerful spirit being, the foundation of Dhegiha religious concepts. She is the mother of all things, she is the ruler of the night sky with the Moon as her sky lodge, and she is the sacred vessel or receptacle of life having been given this spiritual power by the Great Serpent (La Flesche 1975, 30–71, Diaz-Granados and Duncan 2000, 219, Duncan and Diaz-Granados 2004, 202–3).

The vulvar or earth altars of the First Woman is the focus of the ritual in the Osage Native American Church; it is in this great portal that a fire representing the life-giving powers of the Sun is manipulated by the Fire man. This fire is divided and rekindled arrow fashion to allow the Symbolic Man or Morning Star to pass through the four layers of the Beneath World and emerge reborn at Dawn (Mathews 1961, 746). To this day, Morning Star's footprints are present at the entrance to the western portal, First Woman's vulva (Fig. 2.11b). To preserve the balance of the universe, there is also an east facing church alter. In the Osage Native American church the two separate alters, one east facing and one west facing complete the unending cycle of sunrise and sunset (Fig. 2.11).

Around the year AD 1160, the summit of Monks Mound at Cahokia had its buildings dismantled and the sacred precinct at the top was carefully buried (Reed 2009, 62). Similar scenarios occurred at other Western Mississippian mound groups, especially with the larger mounds. The center of the Western Mississippian populations shifted southward from the Missouri-Mississippi confluence, the Cahokia area, to the Cairo Lowlands opposite the mouth of the Ohio River after AD 1200 (Morse and Morse 1983, 238). The radiometric dates from Carl H. Chapman's excavations at the Lilbourn site in New Madrid County, Missouri average AD 1240, and neatly coincide with this exodus (Chapman 1977, 312–14). At about this same time a general southeastern spread of Classic Braden style art objects occurred. This "Braden Corridor" allowed the flow of ritual objects and most importantly, people (Sawyer 2011, xii). King notes that ideas, as well as objects, traveled this corridor (2011, 293). One such person seems to have been interred at Cemochechobee on the Chattahoochee River (Schnell *et al.* 1981, 75–9). This burial, number 4, consisted of the poorly preserved skull of an aged woman. This woman

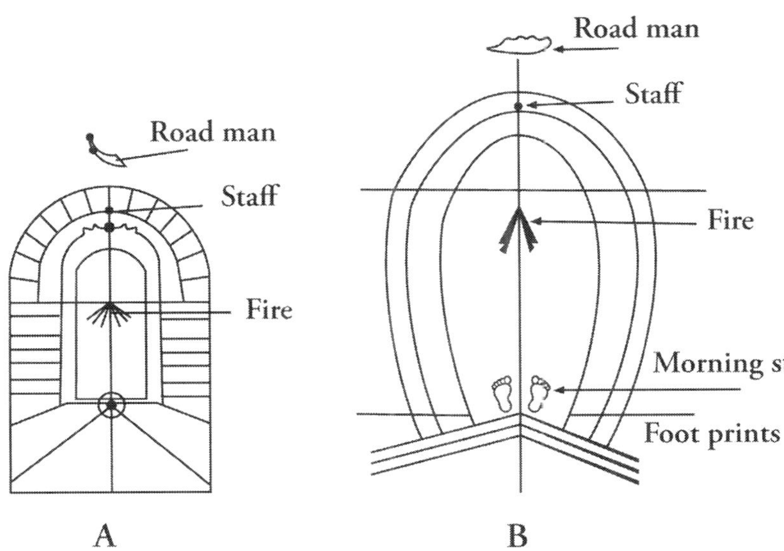

Fig. 2.11 The two altars used by the Osage Big Moon Church: a. East Moon Church Altar; b. West Moon altar. Fifteen hour meetings take place around the altar, called a "Grave", 19th century photographs show early round structures called *Tsi Wakan* or Houses of Mystery.

was accompanied by two Sikeston Ridge style, negative painted pottery vessels, a water spirit, and a female figure, both made in the Cairo Lowlands area. Knight's date for the burial places it before AD 1350, not unreasonable and possibly a little on the late side (Knight and Schnell 1981, 250–1). King places the burial of the famous Rogan copper plates, the chartering symbols of the Braden style in Early Wilbanks at Etowah, around AD 1250–1325 (2003, 70, 146). Brown agrees with King's placement (Brown 2007, 237–9). Allowing a generation or two for the use of the ritual Braden objects, they were probably manufactured closer to AD 1250 or earlier. These items traveled south and east accompanied by persons adept in interpreting their meaning and ritual purposes. It is probable that the symbolism and use was known to the recipients of these highly desirable sacra. Much like the present day Dhegiha (Osage) Native American churches, ancient travelers from far away were welcomed to participate in the *wi-gi-e*, prayer meetings accompanying the rites of vigil in the Western Mississippian (Dhegiha) houses of mystery.

Many of the large Mississippian centers in southeastern Missouri were abandoned, beginning about AD 1350. The populations began to cluster in densely occupied towns along the Pemiscot Bayou, east of the Little River (Morse 1990, 95; O'Brien 1994, 17–20). One of the last mound centers to be used by the Dhegiha was the Murphy Mound site in Pemiscot County, Missouri.

Summary and closing remarks

The most important ancestral spirit is First Man, who is associated with the Sun and rebirth. One of his many manifestations is a pole, the First Man Pole, still in use by the Osage Native American Church. In a recent comparison between the Mandan and the Dhegiha rites involving the First Man Poles, the anatomical nomenclature is similar; the pole has the same name as a sacred arrow or the stem of a great pipe, it is called a *Mon'-ka*, the pathway of the breath of life. The spirit of the pole travels like a sacred arrow, as lightning. In both cases the poles have their own lodge, along with sacred bundles containing paints, pipes, and myriad accessories including clothing. They are addressed and treated as if they were sensitive, living beings (Fletcher and La Flesche 1992, 217–60).

While there are many oral traditions that relate how the cosmos came to be, the *Tsi'-zhu Wa-non* version seems to dominate. This is certainly true at Picture Cave. Its early dates compare nicely with the early growth of the mound centers in the Cahokia area. As Cahokia grew in size and importance, as well as its two large attendant mound sites in East St Louis and St Louis, so did the sanctity of these sites. Oral traditions reflect ideo-political agendas and as the basic doctrine spread, it also was modified to best be adopted by other groups. Versions of the basic genesis story, traveled north and west of the Missouri/Mississippi River confluence very early, much like the old-fashioned revivals and it is the localized versions that were collected by Radin and Skinner on the northern and western peripheries (Skinner 1926, 252–4; Duncan 2000, 15–16). Francis La Flesche was unable to collect the Dhegiha genesis traditions, except in small segments as it seemed to be long and complex. However, matching imagery from Picture Cave with extant descriptions in La Flesche's collections, we find that bison or buffalo imagery occupy a prominent place in these traditions. Several images of bison, including an important ritual bison image connected with "Sharp Elbow" or Long Arm can be seen at Picture Cave. These images have a weighted mean (N=4) of 994±42 BP; AD 985–1165 at 2 sigma; Diaz-Granados *et al.* 2001, table 1). Focusing again on the First Man, the Dhegiha (Osage) Grand Chief's name, the direct descendent of First Man, is always *Pa-hiu'-cka*. This name relates him to the sacred white buffalo, another solar symbol. The combining of a solar symbol and the bison, along with the presence of two clans, the Buffalo-Face and Buffalo Bull clans, attests to the ancient origins of these titular elite names (La Flesche 1975, 125; La Flesche in Bailey 2010, 41).

During the Late Mississippian period, the Pemiscot Bayou towns seem to have shifted their attention, at least in part, to Moundville, Alabama. Two of the sites represented in Leo O. Anderson's collections, formerly in his museum at Van Buren, Missouri, produced fragments of Moundville style palettes. One fragment was a surface find at the Campbell site (23PM5). Three engraved fragments with serpentine motifs were surface collected from the McCoy site (23PM21) (Price and Price 1980, 44, 54). Additional intact palettes were found: one in the shaft grave excavated by the Main brothers in the mound at the Campbell Site (23PM5), and another oval, scalloped palette just north of Steele, Pemiscot County, Missouri (Aid 2016, 114, 116). These towns were likely inhabited by the Isolated or Sacred Earth division, a division of the Osage tribal organization that, after reunification, stood alone in many rites and possessed some interesting life symbols including the spider, rattlesnake, and the red boulder. Both Francis La Flesche and Charles Pratt called these people "the teachers of the rites" and ascribed to them great spiritual knowledge and power, especially related to rebirth and horticulture lore (Fletcher and Le Flesche 1992, 59; C. Pratt, pers. comm. 2010). This is borne out by several oral traditions collected from these people (La Flesche in Bailey 2010). The iconography of the Walls Engraved ware from Pemiscot Bayou is closely related to Moundville. This unusual symbolism also involves the "full face" representations of the Great Serpent in the "Bellaire style", a post AD 1400 style (Brain and Phillips 1996, 191–2; Brown and Muller 2015, 121). The Son of the Sun symbolism is well represented, especially in the Hawk motifs engraved on bottle forms and the famous "head pots" (Cherry 2009; 193–6; Giles 2021, 165–92).

At an iconography workshop held in the Chickasaw Culture Center near Sulfur, Oklahoma in 2013, the definition of the "Striped Pole" was discussed. The Chickasaw and the Dhegihan cosmic definitions were congruent; their cosmogony was remarkably similar. This symbol, the Striped Pole, was referred to as "The Eldest Son of God", a metaphor for First Man by both Chickasaw and Dhegiha. We may never know how widespread the meaning was of this important symbol. However, by inference and archaeological evidence, we believe it to have been understood and accepted by Mississippian and Oneota groups of the Midwest and southeastern United States. While the rock art involving this symbolism occurs only in the Western Mississippian corridor, on convenient outcrops of arenaceous dolomite, it occurs on scattered ceramic vessels distributed throughout the southeast. These vessels were probably manufactured in select workshops associated with the principal mound centers in the Western Mississippi corridor. First Man was well described among the Dhegiha Tsi-Zhu elite in Ponziglione's writings, dating from the 1850s. The last "White Hair" Grand Chief, George White Hair, also known as Iron Necklace, died in 1854 and was buried in Kansas Indian Territory (Ponziglione 1897, 243–6). Iron Necklace had no sons, only daughters and his adopted son died of tuberculosis before any of his three wives could bear him a son.

The Dhegiha Grand Chief, the direct descendant of First Man was recognized during the early 19th century as a unifier, a Father figure, and his followers acted as an extended family. His sanctity was supported by a body made up of the clan priests, middle aged men with outstanding military records and possibly several women with recognized healing abilities, who met daily, discussing the means to improve unity, living conditions, and community safety. Images of a principal being, a First Man, are rare in the region around Cahokia and the Confluence, and in the central Mississippi Valley. They are found in the Braden Corridor to the east (Sawyer 2011, xii). The best candidate for this character in the Cahokia region is a badly damaged, large Missouri flint clay figure of a nude male, seated cross-legged, curated by the Missouri History Museum. This figure was accidently found by railway workers who broke it into pieces so that each worker might have a souvenir. This sculpture, the Mangum Plate and an enigmatic engraved figure on a shell cup are probable Classic Braden style images of members of the very powerful First Man lineage (Fig. 2.12). There are several possible reasons for this scarcity, one that separates this image from the other representations, might simply be that this image was the ritual property of only the elite, Sky division (Tsi-Zhu) while the more plentiful spirit images were parts of clan ritual equipment.

Another reason could be that the Dhegiha elite priesthood did not believe in separate gods and goddesses but rather that a central creative or animistic force could reside in a specific living individual (Bailey 1995, 31–2, 288). The First Man Pole used in the Osage peyote church meetings, today, is a metaphor for the ancient First Man. Not only does it represent the continuity of the lineage, it also represents the cosmic axis, the center of this universe insuring a stable and balanced structure by binding all of the creative and animating powers to the web of life (*Ho'-e-ga*) the Middle World or Earth. Another reason just might be that the specially treated remains of First Men were curated in special structures and eventually were reburied or they were perhaps

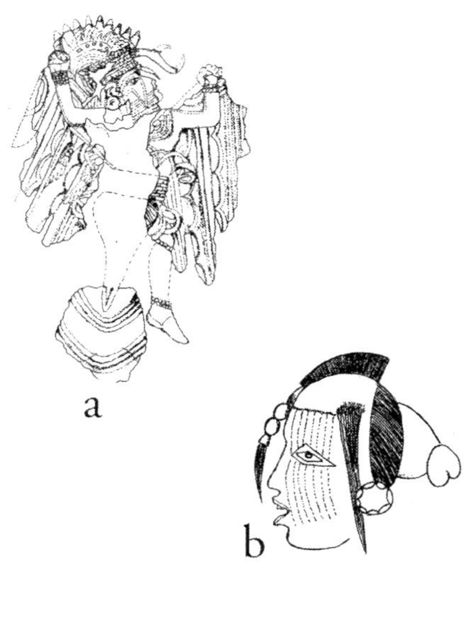

Fig. 2.12 Two images of First Man, "He Who Dwells in the Sun"; a. The Mangum Plate, a classic Braden style repoussé copper plate image of the resurrected First Man. This image has fragments of basketry parts of his burst burial shrine; b. a classic Braden style image from an engraved marine shell cup found in the Craig Mound, Spiro, Oklahoma.

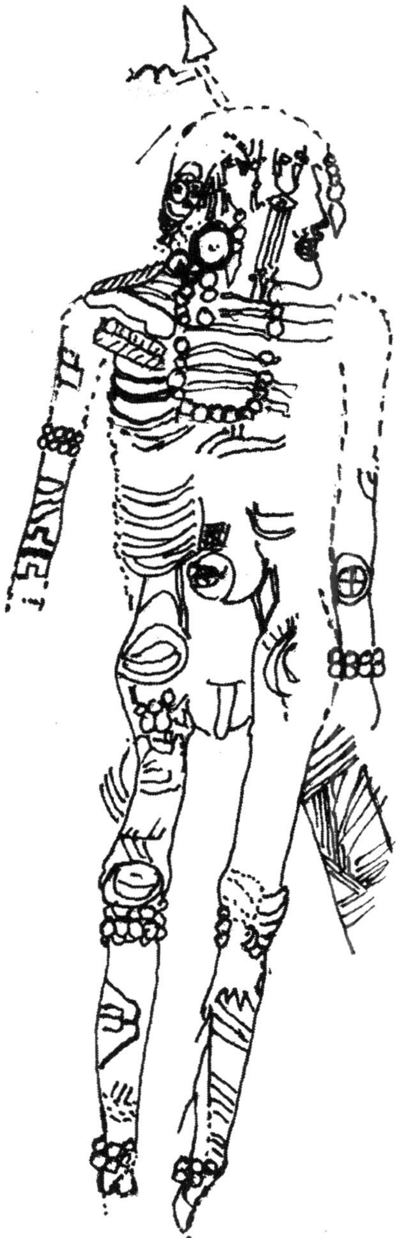

Fig. 2.13 A reconstruction of the several engraved figure fragments on shell cup No. 21 found in the Craig Mound, Spiro, Oklahoma. We do not believe it has anything to do with sacrifice. It would better fit the mummified ancestor role. The figures appear to have all the characteristics of mummified human bodies including tattoos; it is a well engraved record. The mummies have pupils in their eye(s) indicating that the artist considered them to still be alive, but probably on another spiritual plane. These mummified ancestors were probably housed in a large shrine, like Nelson Reed's reconstruction of the building on the top of Monk's Mound at Cahokia prior to AD 1160. These revered ancestors were also pictured by John White showing mummified "chiefs'" bodies on a raised platform and also basketry bone chests in the 1580s. Major Western Mississippian towns described by the de Soto journals depict these mortuary houses as well as the treasures, especially freshwater pearl beads bedecking the mummified remains. The disarray of the bodies on the shell cup is a bit disturbing for the subject matter. Is this a record of a major town's defeat where the hallowed ancestors, the bodies of the Grand Chiefs and their relations are thrown about, trampled, and scattered as described in which the Tunican Cascui enter the abandoned Quapaw (Dhegiha) town of Pacaha and gleefully desecrate the mortuary temple?

bundled (Penney and Longfish 1994, 18; Fig. 2.13)

In Dhegiha and other sedentary Siouan speaking groups, with patrilineal descent the eldest son receives his father's bundle responsibilities and clan determined titles (Bailey 2010, 16–17; Bowers 2004, 30–6). Both the pictographs of a sun disc emanating jagged linear energy (lightning) motifs and an associated bi-lobed arrow are depicted together on the bluff at Lost Creek (Fig. 2.4b). We believe, because of its location near Cahokia, that these images are metaphors for First Man and his eldest son, Morning Star or Hawk who are identified as one single spiritual entity in the Rites of Chiefs (Bailey 1995, 255–7; Duncan 2015, 230–1). The clan Hawk/Morning Star bundles are said to represent the valor and death-dealing abilities of the young warriors and are the center of clan rites. Their power is closely regulated by the body of acclaimed warriors with priestly duties called The Little Old Men (*Non'-hon-zhin-ga*). Likewise, the First Man Grand Chief, while much revered, has strict perimeters regarding judgmental powers; this is also delegated by the Little Old Men. This model is widespread among plains/prairie tribes and well recognized among ethnologists (Provinse 1970, 344–60).

There are several additional safeguards among the Dhegiha to promote stability and avoid differential treatment, especially sacrifice within the society and outside of it upon the death of a First Man. There was a time in the past when ritual killing by garroting, poisoning, or the clubbing of large numbers of retainers, was practiced in a southeastern manner (Emerson 1997, 187). The presence of Coles Creek ceramics in early Western Mississippian contexts at Cahokia and the presence of many ritually slain retainers in Mound 72 both resonate with descriptive narratives from the early European accounts among several southeastern Late Mississippian groups, especially the Natchez (Morse and Morse 1983, 201–2). We suspect that the ideology has evolved to no longer require that behavior to accomplish rebirth or acquiesce the notice of supernatural beings. However, the mourning rite persisted until 1911 among the elite Dhegiha, the Osage, which involved the taking of the scalp of a foreign or enemy person. The rite usually involved sending a party of warriors to kill a person, preferably an enemy outside of the Osage society, and bring the head or scalp of the slain so that its spirit would accompany the elite spirit. A likely candidate for the preference of delegating this power from a single elite lineage would be all the clans participating in the ritual of slaying an outsider as a retainer. While central figures do occupy places of authority and power, there seems to be adequate authority within the clans to avoid differential treatment within the group, the clans being the principal corporate groups. Arrangements having been made, a prostitute awaited the mourning warriors that day in 1911. She cut off her long hair for the mourning warriors after being paid handsomely for it.

On a lighter note, on the celebration of the New Year, which occurred in the Spring at the equinox, a great gathering of all the Osage people occurred, with the Grand Chief officiating with the help of the Black Leggings Warrior Society members at a distribution of provisions, goods, and monies from Government annuity payments and income from the rental of reservation lands for Texas drovers to graze their livestock. Widows and orphans of gallant warriors slain in battle were also given ample quantities of dressed deer skins, buffalo robes, cloth, blankets, and dried meat to compensate them for their loss (Ponziglione 1897). This echoes the oral tradition that the Omaha left the Missouri/Mississippi confluence region because they were slighted in the distribution of sinew and deer skins. Because of this biased distribution, the Omaha (Dhegiha) always appointed twice as many chiefs for the Honga or Earth division to counter the decisions of the Tsi-Zhu or sky division chiefs (Fletcher and La Flesche 1992, 197).

First Man and his eldest or son, Morning Star, form a complex duality, an ontological bridge that rationally connected the pietistical government with the Dhegiha populace. Also, the appearance of single posts, in a sanctified plaza setting, representing the First Man as a common ancestor, was a unifying trait. Additionally, we believe that this exercise of authority over rapidly growing populations during the Late Woodland period was linked not only to sanctioned unification rites but also to more efficient agricultural technology. Both sanctioned unification and a more stable economy anchored by a stable, plentiful food supply were an antecedent of the building of the large mound groups in the Central Mississippi valley. Ritual was still practiced in glades, shelters, caves, and at spring sites, as it had no doubt been prior to the construction of the major mound centers. The associated symbolism in the rock art, precisely the "Son of the Son", reveals an acute awareness of the celestial realm. It reflects both the Late Woodland period before such construction, and the diaspora that followed, when the populations dispersed away from the major mound centers, particularly those around the confluence of the Missouri and Mississippi rivers.

Notes

1. When we first started studying Osage oral traditions, a great friend with a keen sense of humor, Charles Red Corn, told us without reservation that the Osage did not believe in Thunder Birds. A lot of questioning along with a lot of reading led us to believe that certain clan members, along with ancestral spirits, were in possession of these thunder and lightning powers. This was of course an ancient concept, but many Osages would talk about these abilities and the various degrees of the thunder and lightning powers. Just like the Little People, these powers had their place in modern Osage society. Likewise, a person with knowledge of this power could make contact with the thunder spirits and ask them to not use their power to destroy barns full of hay and livestock. These same members of Osage society could also stop powerful storms from damaging property.
2. Charles Red Corn gave us a wonderful account of his paternal great-uncle Wakan Iron and the quest to make some of the good, old time Osage tobacco mix that was used in their great pipes. Uncle Wakan and one of his friends, who could still drive an automobile, spent several days driving about, looking and gathering several special aromatic plants, bark from the red willow tree, and several other secret ingredients. Charles told us that he helped the old men strip, scrape, cut, mince, and oven dry the very carefully mixed herbs and a strong home raised tobacco. Charles noted that before the Osage left Kansas, they also remembered how to make several herbal brews that they drank before meeting in their Mystery Houses or when they needed a "healing" session. He also said "That the old-time priests knew how to make some potions that if they were not mixed correctly, could kill a person". He was, of course, referring to a brew that contained *Datura* (jimsonweed, a poisonous member of the nightshade family) and possibly other extremely dangerous plant parts and extracts.
3. The Potter Gorget was found in mound 3, MAS file map (#9 on Carl Henrich's map of 1878) of the Lilbourn Site 23NM38 on the southern end of Sikeston Ridge next to the town of New Madrid. This large mound group was first extensively excavated in 1858 by enslaved African Americans using mule pulled slips or scoops, supervised by members of the St Louis Academy of Science. The extensive collection of the excavated materials was divided between several St Louis Institutions. Prof. W.B. Potter retained a portion of the collection, pottery and other artifacts, including the gorget, kept in his summer home in the Arcadia Valley, south of St Louis. A fire destroyed this summer home in the early 20th century and all that remains of the collection are a few small pottery vessels. The only record of the Potter Gorget is an engraving from a photographic plate published by Holmes and a drawing of the photo engraving in Thruston's *Antiquities of Tennessee* (1890). Thruston describes the gorget as "rather small", about 4½ inches c. 11.4 cm) in diameter. The principal figure holding the animated staff floats horizontally (above the "Earth" or "Owl pot") in the same manner as the Castalian Springs "Morning Star" figure.

Bibliography

Aid, C.T. (2016) *The Roy Hathcock Collection*. Privately published.

Bailey, G. (ed.) (1995) *The Osage and the Invisible World: From the Works of Francis La Flesche*. University of Oklahoma Press, Norman OK.

Bailey, G. (2010) *Traditions of the Osage*. University of New Mexico Press, Albuquerque NM.

Bowers, A. (1950) *Social and Ceremonial Organization*. University of Nebraska Press, Lincoln NE.

Bowers, A.W. (1992) [1965] *Hidatsa Social and Ceremonial Organization.* University of Nebraska Press, Lincoln NE.

Bowers, A. (2004) *Mandan Social and Ceremonial Organization.* University of Nebraska Press, Lincoln NE.

Brain, J. and Phillips, P. (1996) *Shell Gorgets: Styles of the Late Prehistoric and Protohistoric Southeast.* Peabody Museum Press, Cambridge MA.

Brown, J.A. (1989) On style division complex – a revisionist perspective. In *The Southeastern Ceremonial Complex: Artefacts and Analysis. The Cottonlands Conference*, P. Galloway (ed.), 183–204. University of Nebraska Press, Lincoln NE.

Brown, J.A. (2007) Sequencing the Braden Style within Mississippian Period art and iconography. In Reilly and Garber (eds) 2007, 213–45.

Brown, J.A. (2011) The Regional culture signature of the Braden Art Style. In Lankford *et al.* (eds) 2011, 37–63.

Brown, J.A. and Muller, J. (2015) Tradition and horizons in Southeastern representation: lessons from Picture Cav. In Diaz-Granados *et al.* (eds) 2015, 113–24.

Chapman, C.H. (1977) *Investigation and Comparison of Two Fortified Mississippi Tradition Archaeological Sites in Southeastern Missouri. The Missouri Archaeologist* 38

Cherry, J.F. (2009) *The Headpots of Northeast Arkansas and Southern Permiscott County, MO.* University of Arkansas Press, Fayetteville AR.

Diaz-Granados, C. (1993) The Petroglyphs and Pictographs of Missouri – A Distributional, Stylistic, Contextual, Temporal, and Functional Analysis of the State's Rock Graphics. Unpublished Ph.D. Dissertation, Washington University, St Louis MO.

Diaz-Granados, C. (2004) Marking stone, land, body, and spirit. In *Hero, Hawk, and Open Hand: American Indian Art of the Ancient Midwest and South.* R.F. Townsend and R.V. Sharp (eds) 139–49, Yale University Press and Art Institute of Chicago, New Haven CT and London.

Diaz-Granados, C. and Duncan, J.R. (2000) *The Petroglyphs and Pictographs of Missouri.* University of Alabama Press, Tuscaloosa AL.

Diaz-Granados, C., Duncan, J.R. and Reilly, F.K. III (eds) (2015) *Picture Cave: Unraveling the Mysteries of the Mississippian Cosmos.* University of Texas Press, Austin TX.

Duncan, J.R. (2013) Dhegihan tattoos. In *Drawing With Great Needles: Ancient Tattoo Traditions of North America*, A. Deter-Wolf and C. Diaz-Granados (eds), 195–213. University of Texas Press, Austin TX.

Duncan, J.R. (2015) Identifying the characters on the walls of Picture Cave. In Diaz-Granados *et al.* (eds) 2015, 209–40.

Duncan, J.R. (2021) Dressing and caring for the spirits: the role of sacred bundles in Siouan society. In *Mississippian Culture Heroes, Ritual Regalia, and Sacred Bundles*, D.H. Dye (ed.), 29–56. Lexington Books, New York and London.

Duncan, J.R. and Diaz-Granados, C. (2000) Of masks and myths. *Midcontinental Journal of Archaeology* 25, 1–26.

Duncan, J.R. and Diaz-Granados, C. (2004) Empowering the SECC: The "Old Woman" and Oral Tradition. In *The Rock Art of Eastern North America: Capturing Images and Insight*, C. Diaz-Granados and J.R. Duncan (eds), 190–215. University of Alabama Press, Tuscaloosa AL.

Duncan, J.R. and Diaz-Granados, C. (2018) The Big Five petroglyph sites: their place on the landscape and relation to their creators. In: Diaz-Granados, C., Simek, J., Sab, G. III and Wagner, M. (eds), *Transforming the Landscape: Rock Art and the Mississippian Cosmos*, 30–56. American Landscapes 4, Oxford.

Duncan, J.R. and Diaz-Granados, C. (2022) Picture Cave and the birth of the Braden art style. In *Archaeologies of Cosmoscapes in the Americas.* J. G. Stauffer, G.T. Giles and S.P. Lambert (eds), 175–92. American Landscapes 5, Oxford.

Emerson, T.E. (1997) Cahokian Elite Ideology and the Mississippian Cosmos. In *Cahokia: Domination and Ideology in the Mississippian World*, T.R. Pauketat and T.E. Emerson (eds), 190–228. University of Nebraska, Lincoln.

Emerson, T.E. (2022) Book review of *Mississippian Culture Heroes, Ritual, Regalia, and Sacred Bundles*, Dye, D.H., ed. *Southeastern Archaeology* 41(4), 273–5.

Emerson, T.E., Hughes, R.E., Haynes M.R. and Wisserman, S. (2002) Implications of sourcing Cahokia-style flint clay figurines in the American Bottom and the upper Mississippi river valley. *Midcontinental Journal of Archaeology* 27(2), 309–38.

Emerson, T.E., Hughes, R.E., Hynes, M.R. and Wisseman, S.U. (2003) The sourcing and interpretation of Cahokia-style figures in Transmississippi south and southeast. *American Antiquity* 68, 287–314.

Fitzgerald, M.P. (1939) Beacon on the Plains. Unpublished Ph.D. Dissertation, St Mary College, Leavenworth KS.

Fletcher, A. and La Flesche, F. (1992) *The Omaha Tribe*. University of Nebraska Press, Lincoln (originally published 1911).

Galloway, P. (1989) Introduction. In *The Southeastern Ceremonial Complex: Artefacts and Analysis. The Cottonlands Conference*, P. Gallow (ed.), 1–7. University of Nebraska Press, Lincoln.

Giles, B.T. (2021) Mnemonic parallelism and the cosmologies materialized in the Late Mississippian Pecan Point Head pots. In *New Methods and theories for Analyzing Mississippian Imagery* B.T. Giles and S.P. Lambert (eds), 165–95. Florida Museum of Natural History, Ripley PP. Bullen Series, Gainsville FL.

Griffin, J.B. (1952) An interpretation of the place of Spiro in Southeastern Archaeology. In *The Spiro Mound*, H. Hamilton (ed.), 89–106. *Missouri Archaeologist* 14.

Hall, R. (1989) Cultural background of Mississippian symbolism. In Galloway (ed.) 1989, 239–78.

Hall, R. (1997) *An Archaeology of the Soul*. University of Illinois Press, Urbana IL.

Howard. J.H. (1968) *The Southeastern Ceremonial Complex and Its Interpretation*. Missouri Archaeological Society Memoir 6, Columbia MI.

Kehoe, A.B. (2007) Osage texts and Cahokia data. In Reilly and Garber (eds) 2007, 246–61.

Kelly, J.E., Ozuk, S.J., Jackson, D.K., McElrath, D.L., Finney, F.A. and Esarey, D. (1984) Emergent Mississippian Period. In *American Bottom Archaeology*, C.J. Bareis and J.W. Porter (eds), 128–57. IDOT, University of Illinois, Urbana IL.

King, A. (2003) *Etowah, the Political History of a Chiefdom Capitol*. University of Alabama Press, Tuscaloosa AL.

King, A. (2011) Iconography of the Hightower Region of eastern Tennessee and northern Georgia, In Lankford *et al.* (eds) 2011, 279–93.

King, A. and Reilly, F.K. III (2011) Raptor imagery at Etowah. In Lankford *et al.* (eds) 2011, 313–20.

Knight, J. and Schnell, F.T. (1981) *Cemochechobee*. University of Florida Press, Gainesville FL.

La Flesche, F. (1975) *A Dictionary of the Osage Language*. Smithsonian Institution Bulletin 109, Washington DC.

Lankford, G.E. (2004) World on a string: some cosmological components of the Southeastern Ceremonial Complex. In *Hero, Hawk, and Open Hand*, R.F. Townsend and R.V. Sharp (eds), 207–18. Yale University Press and Art Institute of Chicago, New Haven CT and London.

Lankford, G., Reilly III, F.K. and Garber, J.F. (2011) *Visualizing the Sacred: Cosmic Visions, Regionalism, and the Art of the Mississippian World*, University of Texas Press, Austin TX.

Mathews, J.J. (1961) *The Osages: Children of the Middle Waters*. University of Oklahoma Press, Norman OK.

Mooney, J. (1996) *The Ghost Dance*. J.G. Press, North Dighton MA.

Morse, D.F. (1990) The Nodena Phase. In *Towns and Temples along the Mississippi*, D.H. Dye and C.A. Cox (eds), 69–97. University of Alabama Press, Tuscaloosa AL.

Morse, D.F. and Morse, P.A. (1983) *The Archaeology of the Central Mississippi Valley*. Academic Press, New York.

Muller, J. (1989) The Southern Cult. In Galloway (ed.) 1989, 11–26.

O'Brien, M.J. (1994) *Cat Monsters and Head Pots*. University of Missouri Press, Columbia MO.

Parks, D.R. (1991) *Traditional Narratives of the Arikara Indians*, University of Nebraska Press, Lincoln NE.

Phillips, P. and Brown, J.A. (1978) *Pre-Columbian Shell Engravings from Craig Mound at Spiro, Oklahoma*. Peabody Museum of Archaeology and Ethnology, Harvard University, Cambridge MA.

Ponziglione, P. (1897) *The Osages and Father John Schoenmakers, S.J. Interesting Memoirs Collected from Legends, Traditions and Historical Documents*. Handwritten Manuscript on File at Midwest Jesuit Archives, St Louis MO.

Penney, D.W. and Longfish, G.C. (1994) *Native American Art*. Hugh Lauter Levin Associates/ Rizolli, Fairfield CT.

Prentice, G. (1986) An analysis of the symbolism expressed by the Birger figurine. *American Antiquity* 51, 239–66.

Price, J. and Price, C. (1980) *An Inventory and Assessment of the Leo Anderson Collection of Archaeological and Historical Specimens*. Southwest Missouri State University, Springfield MO.

Provinse, J.H. (1970) The underlying sanctions of Plains Indian Culture. In *Social Anthropology of North American Tribes*, F. Eggan (ed.), 341–76. University of Chicago Press, Chicago IL.

Reed, Nelson A. (2009) Excavations on the Third Terrace and Front Ramp of Monks Mound, Cahokia, a personal narrative. *Illinois Archaeology* 21, 1–89.

Reilly, F. K. III (2004) People of the Earth, people of the sky: visualizing the sacred in Native American art of the Mississippian Period. In *Hero, Hawk, and the Open Hand*, R.F. Townsend and R.V. Sharp (eds), 124–37. Yale University Press and Art Institute of Chicago, New Haven CT and London.

Reilly, F.K. III (2007) The petaloid motif: a celestial symbolic locative in the Sheel art of Spiro. In Reilly and Garber (eds) 2007, 39–55.

Reilly, F.K. III and Garber, J. (eds) (2007) *Ancient Objects and Sacred Realms*. University of Texas Press, Austin TX.

Reilly, F.K. III and Garber, J. (2011) Introduction. In Lankford *et al.* (eds) 2011, xi–xviii.

Sawyer, J. (2011) Braden Style Corridor, Map 1. In Lankford *et al.* (eds), 2011.

Schnell, F.T., Knight, V.J. Jr and Schnell, G.S. (1981) *Cemochechebee*. University of Florida Press, Gainsville FL.

Skinner, A. (1926) Ethnology of the Ioway Indians. In *Ethnology of the Ioway and Sauk Indians*, 181–352. Milwaukee Public Museum Bulletin 5(4), Milwaukee WI.

Swan, D.C. (2004) The Osage Peyote religion. In *Art of the Osage*, G. Bailey and D.C. Swan (eds), 108–35. St Louis Art Museum with University of Washington Press, Seattle WA.

Tabeau, P.A. (1939) *Tabeau's Narrative of Loisel's Expedition to the Upper Missouri* A.H. Abel (ed.), University of Oklahoma Press, Norman OK.

Thruston, G.P. (1890) *Antiquities of Tennessee*. Cincinatti MO.

Waring, A.J. Jr and Holder, P. (1945) A Prehistoric Ceremonial Complex in the Southeastern United States. *American Anthropologist* 47(1), 1–34.

Williams, S. (1968) *The Waring Papers*. Papers of the Peabody Museum of Archaeology and Ethnology 58, Harvard University Press, Cambridge MA.

Williams, S. and Goggin, J.M. (1956) The Long-Nosed God Mask in Eastern United States. *Missouri Archaeologist* 18(3), 3–72.

3

Vestiges of the Birdman at Etowah

Adam King

For decades archaeologists, folklorists, and art historians have been exploring the ideas represented in the images made by Native Americans during the Mississippian Period (Reilly and Garber 2007). Those studies have made it clear that much of that imagery depicts otherworldly realms and the activities of supernatural beings (Knight *et al.* 2001). In the 12th–14th centuries, one of the most prominent themes in Mississippian imagery depicts a figure known most frequently as the Birdman (Brown 2007). This figure seems to first appear as part of the Braden style school tradition in the cultural milieu of the great site of Cahokia (Brown and Kelly 2000; Duncan 2015). The Birdman and his regalia appear in caves and on, or as, objects made of embossed copper, engraved shell, ground and flaked stone, and ceramics and are most frequently found in graves placed in special contexts. Using ethnographic texts and modern-day Native American practice, several different scholars have connected the pre-Columbian Birdman to a key figure or figures who feature prominently in an epic narrative still told by native inhabitants of the Upper Midwest and Prairie Plains (Hall 1997; Diaz-Granados and Duncan 2000; Duncan and Diaz-Granados 2000; 2004; Brown 2007). In this paper, I explore evidence for the presence of the Birdman at the Etowah site in northwestern Georgia.

The Birdman in narrative

Starting with Hall (1997) and continuing with Diaz-Granados and Duncan (2000; Duncan and Diaz-Granados 2000; 2004) and Brown (2007), the identity of the Birdman has been explored extensively, and these scholars agree that the figure is a culture hero known to many different groups. The names of the protagonist in this saga vary from group to group – Hawk, Morning Star, Red Horn, First Man – and, in some cases, the plot lines vary. Still there are enough connections and similarities among the various versions to show convincingly that they all reference the same basic set of themes and figures.

The work of Duncan and Diaz-Granados (2004; Duncan 2015) on these narratives has drawn out those themes and figures in their broadest sense. Here is the outline of the saga:

Before the Middle World of the Native American cosmos was created, there was only water and sky. A male creator figure, sometimes referred to as First Man, was the sun and therefore an important figure in the Above Realm. He, as the epitome of order and life, often did battle with beings of the Beneath World – a place of chaos and death. During one of these battles, First Man was defeated and his head was cut off. This represented the defeat of life and day, by removing the sun from the sky. Male relatives of First Man (sometimes two sons and sometimes a son and nephew) set out to avenge his death. They accomplished this, retrieved First Man's head, and brought it to the house of their mother. She was the wife of First Man – an Earth Mother figure sometimes called Old-Woman-Who-Never-Dies. In her house, which was conceived of as a wooden house, a woven basket, and also a mound of earth, First Man was brought back to life. Upon being requickened, First Man burst out of his wife's house and pushed the water and sky apart, creating room for the Middle World. In doing so, he established himself as the center of the cosmos and an *axis mundi* that connected all three realms. Thus, creation of the cosmos and the natural world began.

From this we can draw some generalizations. First Man was the sun and the one who put creation into motion. He started a line that shared many of his same qualities and associations. Among those was the status of great warrior of the Sky Realm, which was symbolized by raptor characteristics. Another was the ability to rescue day from night, life from death, and even renew life (Hall 1997). These abilities were retrieved by First Man from the Beneath World beings and symbolized each day by the rising sun (Duncan 2015).

The Classic Braden Birdman

Systematic iconographic studies by scholars including Hall, Duncan, Diaz-Granados, and Brown show that many aspects of the Classic Braden Birdman's regalia seem to connect to the themes and associations of First Man and his line. It is important to emphasize that none of these scholars thinks that the intended meanings of the Mississippian Period imagery correspond one-to-one with what is described in narratives collected as many as 800 years later. As Knight (2012) has argued, it is wise to think of the themes in the imagery and those in the narratives as cognates. They are part of the same historical stream and are therefore related, but they do not necessarily mean exactly the same thing nor were those ideas put to the same uses in the Mississippian Period and 19th century. However, as Keyes (1994) has pointed out in his study of Apalachee Ball Game narratives, certain themes and ideas are so fundamental within a cultural group's history that they persist through changes resulting from the passage of time.

One of the clear connections between the Birdman and the First Man line is the association with the raptor. Sacred narratives reveal that First Man and his male

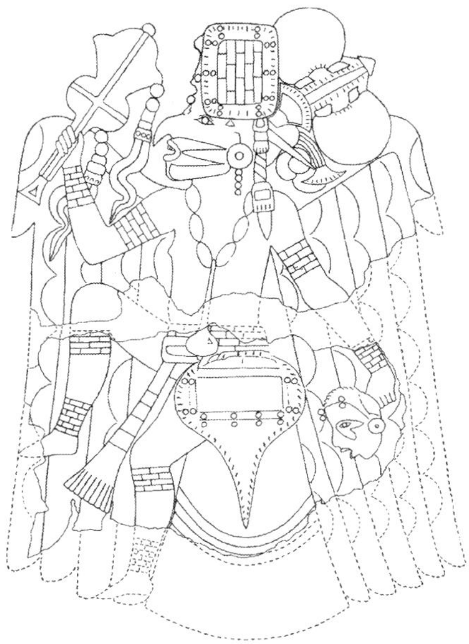

Fig. 3.1 Rogan Plate A (Moorehead 1932, fig. 14).

children are great warriors, beings of the Sky Realm, and associated with raptors (Hall 1997). As Brown (2007) summarizes, Classic Braden Birdman imagery makes this explicit. For example, the figure depicted on the Rogan plates (Fig. 3.1), as well as others, possess raptor elements including wings, a tail, and a beak-like nose. Other images, like the Maldin Plate, depict a figure with the same regalia possessing the head of a human and the body of a raptor (Brose *et al.* 1985).

Hall (1997) outlined a more complex connection between the Classic Braden Birdman and the line of First Man – the shared ability to bring souls back from the land of the dead. The Classic Braden Birdman very often wears a headdress containing a motif called the bi-lobed arrow. Hall argued that this motif is connected to the historically-described Captain of the Calumet ceremony and the ability to bring souls of deceased relatives back into bodies of the living. The narratives indicate that this is an ability First Man captured from the beings of the Beneath World and brought back with his requickening (Duncan 2015). This ability is referenced in the Ho-Chunk version of the saga, which features Red Horn (likely one of First Man's male descendants). One of Red Horn's names is He-Who-is-Hit-with-Deer-Lungs. As Hall (1997) summarized, being hit with deer lungs is a metaphor for being requickened.

The Classic Braden version of the Birdman is often depicted with other features connecting it to heroes of later narratives. One of those features is human-headed earrings, present on the Resting Warrior pipe (see Townsend and Sharp 2004, 132; Brown 2007) and visible in multiple images found on engraved shell cups (Brown 2007). The Ho-Chunk's Red Horn is also known as He-Who-Wears-Human-Heads-on-His-Ears. Another feature connecting the Classic Braden Birdman to more recent narratives is the long braid of hair that gave Red Horn his name. To the Ho-Chunk, Red Horn is a metaphor referring to a long braid of red hair that is a symbol of manliness and male virility (Hall 1997). That braid is visible both on the Resting Warrior pipe and on the Rogan Plates.

As Brown (2007) has noted, at least some of the Classic Braden imagery appears to depict pieces or snapshots of the epic narrative featuring First Man and his descendants. Duncan and Diaz-Granados (2001) have argued that the Mangum Plate represents a First Man figure at the moment of creation – bursting through the basket that is his wife's house (Fig. 3.2). The images on a Craig A style gorget and the Lightner Cup published in Phillips and Brown (1984, pls 132 and 157) show a

Birdman figure as the center of the cosmos. Additionally, Brown (2007) has argued that the Rogan plates and the Castilian Springs and Douglass gorgets (Fig. 3.3a and b, respectively) all depict the recapture of First Man's head by one of the sons.

While the names of the protagonists may change and their motives may be explained differently depending on the group telling the saga, it seems that the underlying theme of this saga is the same. It is about the lineage that puts creation into motion, rescues day from night, and makes it possible for kin groups to perpetuate by recycling souls. It is about the continuation of life. I think those fundamental thematic associations carried from the 12th century to the 19th among Siouan speakers of the Upper Midwest and Prairie Plains.

The Etowah Birdman

Sometime late in the 13th century a figure similar to the Classic Braden Birdman appeared on shell gorgets made in the Hightower style of northern Georgia and eastern Tennessee (King 2011). This anthropomorphic themed gorget is most abundant at Etowah, suggesting the site was the locus of its production. Because this new theme appeared at the same time that Classic Braden imagery was buried in Etowah's Mound C, I have argued that its creation was inspired by the arrival of Classic Braden imagery (King 2010). More than just superficial similarities, the Hightower figure has clear motif and

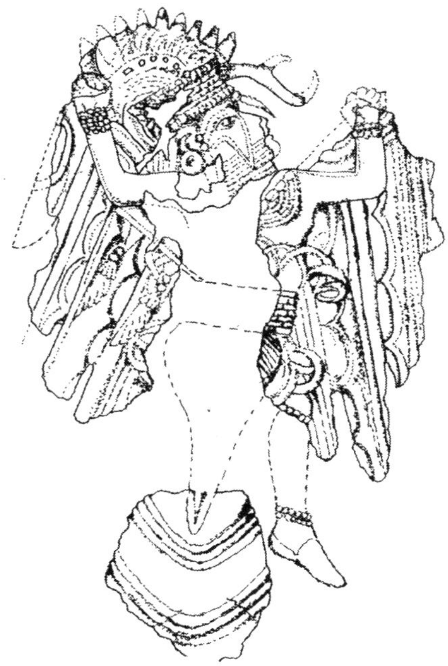

Fig. 3.2 Mangum Plate (drawing by James Duncan).

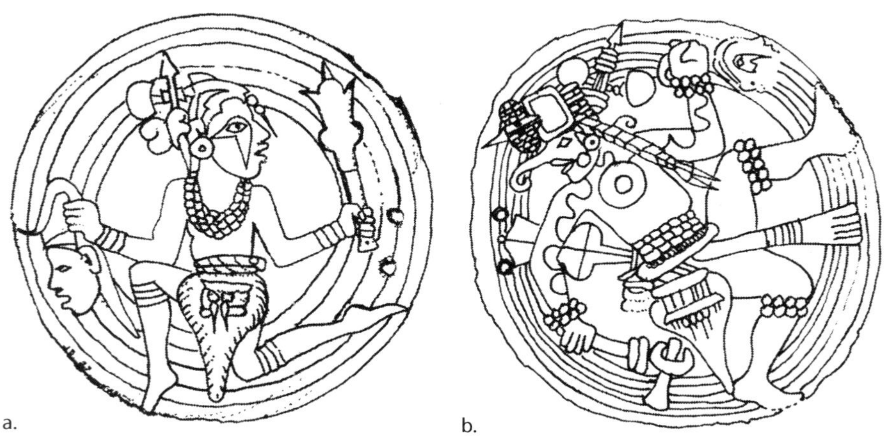

a.

b.

Fig. 3.3 a: Castalian Springs Gorget and b: Douglass Gorget (drawings by James Duncan).

thematic connections to the line of First Man and the Classic Braden Birdman. In addition, as will be discussed, the mortuary treatment of many individuals buried in Etowah's Mound C includes the regalia of the Birdman, suggesting that people were connected to the Birdman in death.

The raptor

The Siouan narratives make it clear that First Man and his children are beings of the Above World and the male relatives all have characteristics of birds of prey or raptors. This raptor connection is apparent in Classic Braden images like the Rogan plates (Fig. 3.1), as the figure possesses wings, a tail, and a "drooped" nose that presumably is meant to refer to a beak. The figure depicted in the Hightower imagery has the same wings, tail, and beak-like nose. In addition, that figure has feet, and sometimes hands, that are replaced by the talons of a raptor, reinforcing the connection (Fig. 3.4).

Another potential indication of the presence of the Birdman at Etowah is illustrated by Burial 57 excavated by Lewis H. Larson on the north side of Etowah's burial mound, Mound C (Larson 1971). This grave contained the body of an adult male laid out on a surface and enclosed within a small single-set post building. Upon completion of the building, it was covered by a small earthen mound that was appended to the northern margin of Mound C. The individual buried in the grave was placed on a cape of feathers and wore a massive bead necklace and a headdress containing a Classic Braden Birdman-themed copper plate. He had copper celts on either side, another Classic Braden Birdman plate at his waist, and was surrounded by a ring of marine shell cups. The assemblage of grave goods suggests an individual buried wearing the regalia of a Birdman figure (King 2010). As I have suggested elsewhere (King and Sawyer 2017; King 2020), the placement of this grave marks the start of an important set of ritual events in Mound C, and symbolically sets the stage for the requickening of the Birdman and the creation of the Middle Realm of the cosmos.

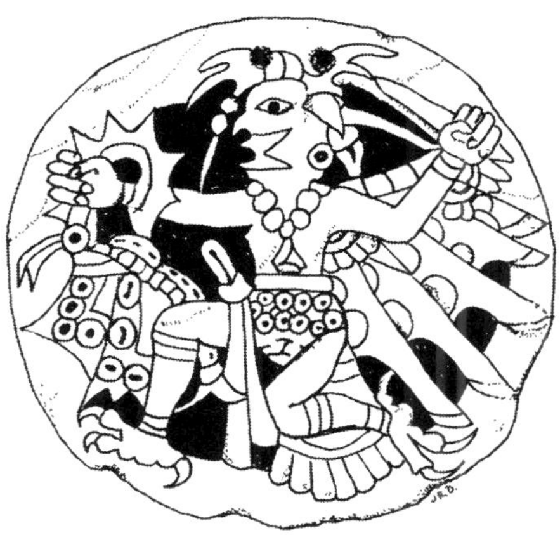

Fig. 3.4 Hightower style anthropomorphic themed gorget (Reilly and Garber 2011, drawing by James Duncan).

The triumph of life over death

One theme that is emphasized in the Siouan creation saga is the triumph of life over death. As Hall (1997) has argued, this is referred to symbolically in the Ho-Chunk version of the narrative through Red Horn's alternative name, He-Who-Is-Hit-With-Deer-Lungs. To the Ho-Chunk, being hit with deer lungs is the same as being brought back to life.

Hall (1997) has further shown that the Captain of the Calumet ceremony, known primarily as an adoption ceremony, actually was a ritual intended to bring the soul of a deceased relative back into the body of a newly adopted member of the community. According to Hall (1997), the bi-lobed arrow motif (Fig. 3.5), closely associated with the Classic Braden Birdman, is a cognate of the paired calumets which function as a conduit through which souls are recycled. The bi-lobed arrow, then, is a motif representing the power to bring souls back from the realm of the dead. That same motif is associated with the human figure in the Hightower shell gorgets. In addition, four people buried in Etowah's Mound C were buried with a copper or mica version of the bi-lobed arrow as an element of regalia (Brain and Phillips 1996).

The triumph of life over death is most vividly symbolized in the Siouan creation saga by the return of First Man's head from the Beneath World and his eventual requickening. This act returned the sun to the sky and literally rescued day and life from night and death. As noted above, Brown (2007) has convincingly argued that the Classic Braden Rogan plates depict that return of First Man's head and essentially symbolize this key theme. Larson's Burial 67 contained an adult male with a variety of grave goods, including a wooden rattle covered with copper that is a precise copy of the severed head motif found in Classic and Late Braden imagery (Brain and Phillips 1996, 159). A reasonable case can be made that this rattle is meant to represent the head of First Man as depicted in the Braden School imagery.

Brown and Dye (2007) have argued that the missing lower jaw, found on the Etowah rattle and its analogs, embossed in copper and engraved in shell, is intended to indicate that the head was taken in battle or as a trophy. This fits well with its identification as the head of First Man, which was severed by beings of the Beneath World after his defeat by them. That same missing lower jaw is evident on a wooden mask Larson recovered from Burial 79 in Mound C (Fig. 3.6). The mask was carved of wood and had eyes and teeth of inlaid shell. Like the Birdman imagery found on the Hightower gorgets (Fig. 3.4) and the Mangum Plate (Fig. 3.2), the mask also had antlers, in this case, made of wood and covered with copper. While the rattle may have been part of ritual regalia representing the head of First

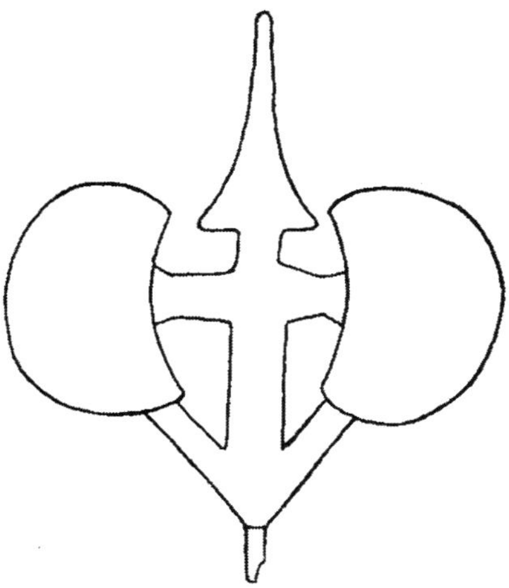

Fig. 3.5 Bilobed arrow (Moorehead 1932, fig. 21 c).

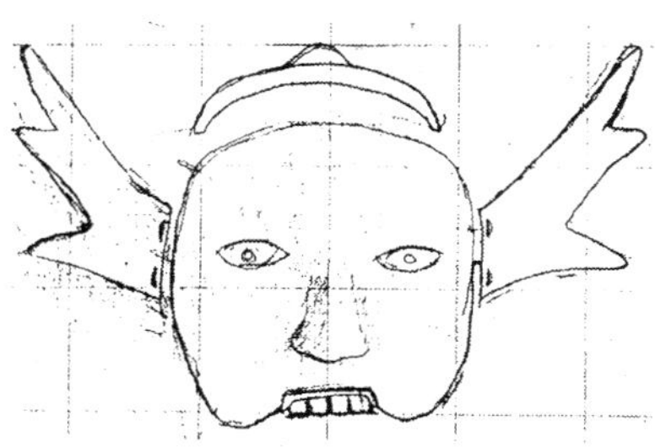

Fig. 3.6 Sketch of wooden mask from Burial 79, Mound C, Etowah (Lewis H. Larson unpublished field notes).

Man as it was returned from the Beneath World, the mask from Burial 79 may have represented First Man in a different way. While the mask itself lacks a lower jaw, when it is worn, that lower jaw is replaced by the jaw of the wearer. In that way, the wearer of the mask may have become the requickened First Man.

At least one sub-theme in the Hightower style may depict the same theme (rescue of life from death), but in a uniquely Etowah way. That sub-theme, called *Dances with Moths* by Reilly and Garber (2011), depicts the Etowah Birdman brandishing a blade in the left hand while holding an insect-like creature in the right (Fig. 3.4). If we accept that the Etowah Birdman is intended to reference a male in the line of First Man, then he too is associated with the Sky Realm. Knight and Franke (2007) identify the insect as a cognate of a Hawk or Sphinx moth, which is most active at dusk and pollinates important medicine plants like tobacco and *Datura*. This moth was likely considered a being of the night sky along with its counterpart, the Beneath World. In the Hightower Dances with Moths theme, the Night Sky Being appears to be getting the worst of the encounter with the inhabitant of the day sky, suggesting it too depicts the triumph of day over night and life over death.

Weapons of rebirth

When First Man's male descendants defeated the powers of the Beneath World, as a prize they took the power to bring souls back (Duncan 2015). This became an important ability possessed by the line of First Man and a power passed on to human men. Using historical information Dye (2013) has shown that Native American men, from the Great Lakes to the Plains, understood that they could control the life force of those they killed in battle. That ability was won for them by First Man and his male descendants. In the proto-Braden imagery of Picture Cave and the Classic Braden imagery of the Rogan plates the weapon that defeated the Beneath World beings was a crown-form mace (Diaz-Granados and Duncan 2015). In later Braden images, like the Douglass Gorget (Fig. 3.3b), that weapon takes the form of a hafted celt which likely corresponds to the monolithic axeheads and copper celts found as grave goods in Etowah's Mound C, as well as other special contexts and sites such as Moundville in Alabama and Hixon in Tennessee (see Brain and Phillips 1996). In the Hightower imagery, that weapon takes the form of a long blade. Beautifully flaked versions of this blade also appear as grave offerings in Mound C (King 2007; Marceaux and Dye 2007).

The cosmological center

The Siouan narratives make it clear that First Man became the central axis of the cosmos when he pushed sea and sky apart, making room for the creation of the Middle Realm. This aspect of the First Man narratives is illustrated in Braden-related imagery in various ways. For example, an anthropomorphized Striped Pole (considered the axis of the cosmos in Mississippian imagery; see Lankford 2004; 2007)

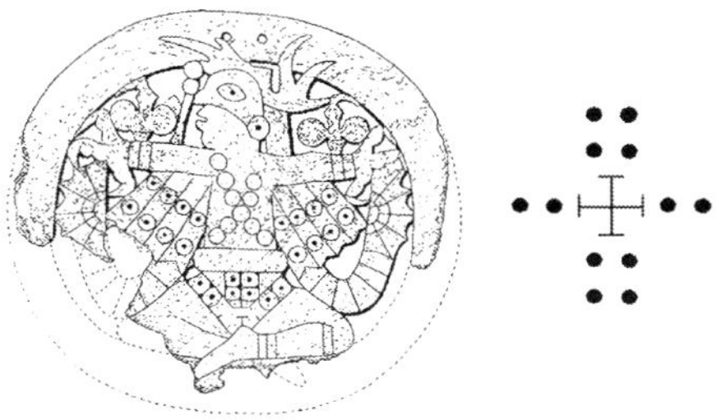

Fig. 3.7 Hightower style anthropomoprhic themed gorget (Moorehead 1932, fig. 29) and breechcloth reconstruction.

appears on an engraved shell cup recovered from the Spiro site (Lightner Cup; Phillips and Brown 1984, pl. 157). In a gorget also recovered from Spiro (Phillips and Brown 1984, pl. 132), the axis of the cosmos emerges from an individual who is in turn emerging from a ceramic vessel which Sawyer (King and Sawyer 2012) has identified as the Earth Vessel. This same idea is represented by at least one key element of the Classic Braden Birdman's regalia: that is, the columella pendant that is often worn by Birdman figures in Braden imagery. The columella is the central spire of a whelk shell that remains after the outer whorls have been removed. It is a spiraling column of shell that echoes the form of the Striped Pole found widely in Mississippian imagery (F. Kent Reilly pers. comm. 2014). As Brown (2007) notes, this element of regalia is consistently associated with the Birdman in Classic and Late Braden imagery. Like the bi-lobed arrow, the Hightower Birdman also wears a columella pendant. Additionally, actual columella pendants were found as regalia buried with some individuals in Etowah's Mound C (Larson 1971; Brain and Phillips 1996). Among those was the individual placed with a variety of other Birdman regalia in Larson's Burial 57.

There is another element of regalia, found only on the Hightower Birdman, that also could be interpreted to reference his place at the center of the cosmos. It has long been argued that various renditions of the cross-in-circle motif represent the center of the cosmos. Howard (1968), and Waring (1968) before him, argued that the cross-in-circle represented a version of the sacred fire kindled at ceremonial grounds. That sacred fire was, and still is, understood to be part of an axis that connects the Middle Realm of the cosmos to the sun at the center of the Above World. Lankford (2007) has argued that the spinning cross represents the same idea, but the center of the cosmos in the Underwater Realm or Beneath World. Reilly (2004) suggests that the cross-in-circle surrounded by the petaloid motif is that same center, but in the Sky Realm or Above World.

The Hightower Birdman wears another version of this same motif on his breechcloth. While the nature of his wings and the content of his hands may change with sub-themes (Reilly and Garber 2011), the breechcloth he wears always bears the same image. In all cases, only the front side of the decoration is visible. Still enough can be seen to suspect that the other side of the garment likely is a mirror image. Following this assumption, a reconstruction of that image is presented in Figure 3.7. It is worth suggesting that this decoration is no accident, but instead refers back to an important aspect of this person and associated line – they are the center of the cosmos.

Regalia referencing the Birdman

The final set of graves interred at Mound C contain a series of unique headdresses known as the Larson-type headdress (Larson 1959). This headdress type was made of a bone framework and leather cap and was decorated with feathers and copper ornaments. Headdresses with copper ornamentation appear in earlier graves in Mound C, but the copper elements consist of embossed copper plates depicting the Birdman or his raptor avatar or bi-lobed arrow hair pins. The copper ornamentation found in the Larson-type headdress consists of small pieces cut in three distinct shapes: the arrow point, the feather, and the mace. Each of these three motifs can be connected directly to the original Classic Braden Birdman imagery. The mace references the raised mace held by the Birdman in the Rogan plates. As noted above, it is the weapon used to return order to the cosmos and capture the ability to recycle souls. The feathers represent the wings that mark the Birdman as a raptor and a being of the Sky Realm. The arrow point is found as a key element of the bi-lobed arrow motif, which represents the Birdman's ability to bring souls back from the realm of the dead (Hall 1997; Brown 2007).

The Birdman at Etowah

It appears that the imagery and ideas associated with the Birdman arrived at Etowah, and probably the Hightower region generally, sometime after AD 1200. Analyses of decorative style make it apparent that the Birdman was an integral part of the imagery associated with the Braden style school and especially the Classic and Late Braden styles that emerged from it. That style school had its origins in the American Bottom and surrounding areas of Missouri and Illinois (Diaz-Granados and Duncan 2000) and is intimately tied to the version of Mississippian religious and political traditions of the great site of Cahokia (Brown 2004). It is certainly no accident that canonical imagery of Cahokian Mississippian began to appear in the Eastern Woodlands as the social and political import of Cahokia transformed in the 13th century. In the same way that people from surrounding regions were drawn to Cahokia as it ascended in the 11th century, people and their regalia left Cahokia in the 13th. Some of the objects, ideas, and likely people from that Cahokian dispersal made their way to sites like Etowah, as well as others in the Deep South (King 2010; 2020; King and Sawyer 2017).

The Birdman imagery and associated belief practices arrived at Etowah along with a broader set of objects, including shell gorgets and elaborate ceramic vessels, whose place of origin was the central Mississippi valley (King 2005; 2020). This occurred at a point in the history of Etowah immediately after a period of abandonment or at least a period of dramatic material change, suggesting that people and objects from the central Mississippi valley were part of the reimaging of Etowah after AD 1250 (King 2010; 2020). Changes in the nature and distribution of imagery in Mound C, especially those connected to the Birdman, show that this supernatural became an integral part of the belief traditions of this new Etowah.

In fact, it is possible to see the creation of a new social order at Etowah that blended new and local traditions through the mortuary ceremonialism in Mound C. In the Early Wilbanks stages (AD 1250–1325) of Mound C, Classic Braden Birdman imagery was buried with a different set of people than the local Birdman Hightower gorgets. These may represent both foreign and local members of a social segment attached to the Birdman. I suspect they represent people who were believed to be descended from the founder of the Birdman line – possibly some cognate of the Siouan First Man.

In Burial 57, discussed above, both the local and non-local Birdman imagery is united in one figure's regalia, which matches closely the regalia of the Classic Braden Birdman (King and Sawyer 2017). According to Larson (1971), the excavator of Burial 57 and later graves in Mound C, the placement of Burial 57 set in motion a series of mortuary events that occurred in a short span of time. In the graves that followed Burial 57, a new form of regalia appeared and both the Classic Braden imagery and Hightower Birdman gorgets all but disappeared. That new form of regalia was the Larson-type headdress discussed above, with its shorthand allusions to key thematic associations of the Birdman. In essence, through Burial 57 the local and non-local branches of the Birdman line were united and what emerged was a single Birdman line at Etowah whose membership was symbolized by a new kind of regalia.

I have also argued that the sequence of mortuary activities in Mound C did more than blend local and non-local traditions (King 2010). The completion of Burial 57 was followed in rapid succession by a series of mortuary events that used people and objects to re-live the creation of the This Middle World. Following some cognate of the Siouan First Man epic, the Birdman figure played a key role in that creation. The end result of re-living creation was that the people of Etowah recreated their community and their society with a Birdman-descended social segment at its head.

Concluding comments

The Birdman was a prominent theme in 13th and 14th century imagery of the Southeast and Midwest. The beginnings of those images lie in the formation of the Braden style school in the Upper Midwest, and the ideas behind them became an integral part of the Cahokian version of Mississippian political culture. Birdman imagery and ideas were dispersed far beyond the confines of the American Bottom, especially after the decline of the Cahokian polity in the 13th century. Sometime after AD 1250 those images and ideas arrived at Etowah and had a rapid and profound impact on belief traditions, crafting, and the ideology underlying a ranked social structure. The influences of the Birdman are apparent in Etowah's Mound C through the burial of specific imagery and regalia with a special set of people. Those people used Birdman imagery and regalia to link themselves to a powerful supernatural and ultimately rewrite the social structure of Etowah.

Bibliography

Brain, J.P. and Phillips, P. (1996) *Shell Gorgets: Styles of the Late Prehistoric and Protohistoric Southeast*. Peabody Museum Press, Cambridge MA.

Brose, D.S., Brown, J.A. and Penney, D.W. (1985) *Ancient Art of the American Woodlands Indians*. Harry N. Abrams, New York.

Brown, J.A. (2004) The Cahokian expression: creating court and cult. In *Hero, Hawk, and Open Hand: American Indian Art of the Ancient Midwest and South*, R.F. Townsend and R.V. Sharp (eds), 105–23. Yale University Press and Art Institute of Chicago, New Haven CT and London.

Brown, J.A. (2007) On the identity of the Birdman within Mississippian Period art and iconography. In Reilly and Garber (eds) 2007, 56–106.

Brown, J.A. and Dye, D.H. (2007) Severed heads and sacred scalplocks: Mississippian iconographic trophies. In *The Taking and Displaying of Human Body Parts as Trophies by Amerindians*, R.J. Chacon and D.H. Dye (eds), 278–98. Springer, New York.

Brown, J.A. and Kelly, J.E. (2000) Cahokia and the Southeastern Ceremonial Complex. In *Mounds, Modoc, and Mesoamerica: Papers in Honor of Melvin L. Fowler*, S.R. Ahler (ed.), 469–510. Illinois State Museum Scientific Papers 55, Springfield IL.

Diaz-Granados, C. and Duncan, J.R. (2000) *The Petroglyphs and Pictographs of Missouri.* University of Alabama Press, Tuscaloosa A.L.

Diaz-Granados, C. and Duncan, J.R. (2015) Transmogrification, healing, and resurrection: extraordinary themes in Picture Cave. In Diaz-Granados *et al.* (eds) 2015, 209–40.

Diaz-Granados, C., Duncan, J.R. and Reilly, F.K. III (eds) (2015) *Picture Cave: Unraveling the Mysteries of the Mississippian Cosmos.* University of Texas Press, Austin.

Dye, D.H. (2013) Snaring life from the stars and the sun: Mississippian tattooing and the enduring cycle of life and death. In *Drawing with Great Needles: Ancient Tattoo Traditions of North America*, A. Deter-Wolf and C. Diaz-Granados (eds), 215–51. University of Texas Press, Austin TX.

Duncan, J.R. (2015) Identifying the characters on the walls of Picture Cave. In *Picture Cave: Unraveling the Mysteries of the Mississippian Cosmos*, C. Diaz-Granados, J.R. Duncan, and F.K. Reilly III (eds), 209–40. University of Texas Press, Austin TX.

Duncan, J.R. and Diaz-Granados, C. (2000) Of Masks and myths. *Midcontinental Journal of Archaeology* 25, 1–26.

Duncan, J.R. and Diaz-Granados, C. (2004) Empowering the SECC: The "Old Woman" and oral tradition. In *The Rock Art of Eastern North America*, C. Diaz-Granados and J.R. Duncan (eds), 190–218. University of Alabama Press, Tuscaloosa AL.

Hall, R. (1997) *An Archaeology of the Soul: North American Indian Belief and Ritual.* University of Illinois Press, Urbana IL.

Howard, J.H. (1968) *The Southeastern Ceremonial Complex and its Interpretation.* Memoir of the Missouri Archaeological Society 6, Columbia MO.

Keyes, J.G. (1994) Myth and social history in the early Southeast. In *Perspectives on the Southeast: Linguistics, Archaeology, and Ethnohistory*, P.B. Kwachka (ed.), 106–15. University of Georgia Press, Athens GA.

King, A. (2005) Deciphering Etowah's Mound C: the construction history and mortuary record of a Mississippian Burial Mound. *Southeastern Archaeology* 23(2), 153–65.

King, A. (2007) Mound C and the Southeastern Ceremonial Complex in the history of the Etowah Site. In *Southeastern Ceremonial Complex: Chronology, Content, Context*, A. King (ed.), 107–33. University of Alabama Press, Tuscaloosa AL.

King, A. (2010) Multiple groups, overlapping symbols and the creation of a sacred space at Etowah's Mound C. In *Mississippian Mortuary Studies: Beyond Hierarchy and the Representationist Perspective*, L.P. Sullivan and R.C. Mainfort, Jr (eds), 54–73. University Press of Florida, Gainsville FL.

King, A. (2011) Iconography of the Hightower region of eastern Tennessee and northern Georgia. In *Visualizing the Sacred: Cosmic Visions, Regionalism, and the Art of the Mississippian World*, G.E. Lankford, F.K. Reilly III and J.F. Garber (eds), 279–93. University of Texas Press, Austin TX.

King, A. (2020) The Cahokian diaspora, Etowah, and south Appalachian Mississippian. In *Cahokia In Context: Hegemony and Diaspora*, C.H. McNutt and R.M. Parish (eds), 352–68. University of Florida Press, Gainesville FL.

King, A. and Sawyer, J.A. (2012) The Sacred Geography of the Pot. Unpublished paper presented at the 69th Annual Meeting of the Southeastern Archaeological Conference, Baton Rouge FL.

King, A. and Sawyer, J.A. (2017) Shell gorgets, hybridity, and identity formation in the Hightower region. In *Forging Southeastern Identities: Social Archaeology, Ethnohistory, and Folklore of the Mississippian to Early Historic South*, G.A. Waselkov and M.T. Smith (eds), 1–15. University of Alabama Press, Tuscaloosa AL.

Knight, V.J. (2012) *Iconographic Method in New World Prehistory*. University of Alabama Press, Tuscaloosa AL.

Knight, V.J. and Franke, J.A (2007) Identification of a moth/butterfly supernatural in Mississippian Art. In Reilly and Garber (eds) 2007, 136-51.

Knight, V.J., Jr, Brown, J.A. and Lankford, G.E. (2001) On the subject matter of Southeastern Ceremonial Complex art. *Southeastern Archaeology* 20, 129–53.

Lankford, G.E. (2004) World on a string: some cosmological components of the Southeastern Ceremonial Complex. In *Hero, Hawk, and the Open Hand: American Indian Art of the Ancient Midwest and South*, R.F. Townsend and R.V. Sharp (eds), 207–18. Yale University Press and Art Institute of Chicago, New Haven CT and London.

Lankford, G.E. (2007) Some Cosmological motifs in the Southeastern Ceremonial Complex. In Reilly and Garber (eds) 2007, 8–38.

Larson, L.H. (1959) A Mississippian headdress from Etowah, Georgia. *American Antiquity* 25, 109–12.

Larson, L.H. (1971) Archaeological implications of social stratification at the Etowah Site, Georgia. In *Approaches to the Social Dimensions of Mortuary Practices*, J.A. Brown (ed.), 58–67. Society for American Archaeology Memoir 25, Washington DC.

Marceaux, S. and Dye, D.H. (2007) Hightower anthropomorphic marine shell gorgets and Duck River sword-form flint bifaces: Middle Mississippian ritual regalia in the southern Appalachians. In *Southeastern Ceremonial Complex: Chronology, Content, and Context*, A. King (ed.), 165–84. University of Alabama Press, Tuscaloosa AL.

Moorehead, W.K. (1932) *Etowah Papers*. Yale University Press, New Haven CO, for the Phillips Academy, Andover.

Phillips, P. and Brown, J.A. (1984) *Pre-Columbian Shell Engravings from the Craig Mound at Spiro, Oklahoma* Vol. 2. Peabody Museum Press, Cambridge MA.

Reilly, F.K. III (2004) People of earth, people of sky: visualizing the sacred in Native American art of the Mississippian Period. In *Hero, Hawk, and Open Hand: American Indian Art of the Ancient Midwest and South*, R.F. Townsend and R.V. Sharp (eds), 125–37. Yale University Press and Art Institute of Chicago, New Haven CO and London.

Reilly, F.K. and Garber, J.F. (eds) (2007) *Ancient Objects and Sacred Realms: Interpretations of Mississippian Iconography*. University of Texas Press, Austin TX.

Reilly, F.K. III, and Garber, J.F. (2011) Dancing in the Otherworld: the human figural art of the Hightower style revisited. In *Visualizing the Sacred: Cosmic Visions, Regionalism, and the Art of the Mississippian World*, G.E. Lankford, F.K. Reilly III and J.F. Garber (eds), 294–312. University of Texas Press, Austin TX.

Waring, A.J. (1968) The Southern Cult and Muskhogean ceremonial. In *The Waring Papers: The Collected Works of Antonio J. Waring, Jr*, S. Williams (ed.), 30–69. Peabody Museum, Harvard University, Cambridge MA.

4

The house between life and death: interpretations about the organization of Mound 3 at the Lake Jackson Site

J. Grant Stauffer

The fact that mound architecture is both a symbolic expression and physical manifestation of politically charged cultural behavior has become widely acknowledged in the archaeological literature (Brown 1986; 2004; Knight 1986; 2001; 2006; Blakely 1995; Lindauer and Blitz 1997; Blitz and Livingood 2004; Blitz and Lorenz 2006). Across various sites and regions that comprise what has been described as the Southeastern Ceremonial Complex (SECC hereafter) – a derivation of Caldwell's (1964) "interaction sphere" concept first articulated as a "Southern Cult" for Mississippian cases by Waring and Holder (1945) – common forms of symbolism exist that once constituted shared forms of ceremonialism, including those that were adapted from pre-existing Woodland period practices (Waring 1968a; 1968b; Prentice 1986; Alt 2002; Knight 2006; King 2007a). Moreover, I use "cult" as a non-derogatory reference to "the religious acts of a culture at a sacred place" in religious studies (Christenson 2009, 17). Although researchers are divided on the use of the SECC label (*sensu* King 2007a; see also Knight 2006), I use the term to simply capture the idea that several Native American cults operated in widespread social networks across the Midwest and Southeast. In this paper, Lake Jackson's Mound 3 is examined for the purpose of identifying the possible symbolic expressions of ancestral cults, portrayed through architecture, artfully crafted grave furniture, and pre-determined arrangement of the mound's 25 known graves.

Though located at what has been called the periphery of cultural and iconographic style zones, the Lake Jackson site exists as a unique manifestation of Mississippian period (AD 1000–1500) activity in the region (Willey and Woodbury 1942, 234; Tesar 2012). Consisting of seven known mound structures clustered in a central precinct that may have included a plaza, several of Lake Jackson's known characteristics were referenced to interpret the site as a Fort Walton "capital" (Payne 1994; 2002; 2006; Payne and Scarry 1998). Moreover, complex mortuary contexts revealed from B. Calvin Jones's (1982; 1992; 1994) excavations in 1975 and 1976 included the remains of elderly women interred in timber box tombs with embossed copper plates that have been attributed to the SECC (Storey 1993).

While more recent radiocarbon dates and chronological refinements have demonstrated its Mississippian period occupation, important questions about Woodland vs Mississippian archaeological distinctions were voiced early on during investigations at Lake Jackson, based on the characteristics of materials it contained (Willey and Woodbury 1942, 234; Willey 1949; Brose 1984; Shapiro 1987, 1–2; Marrinan and White 2007). Although such questions largely concern the site's chronology, my focus is primarily centered on assemblages that appear to be tied to ancestral cults whose practices often defied these imposed time period distinctions. More specifically, a great deal of evidence suggests that late prehistoric cults focused on associations between vegetative fertility and the female gender (Swanton 1928; Prentice 1986; Colvin 2012). With reference to sites in surrounding regions and widely acknowledged Mississippian ceremonial centers (Etowah, Moundville, and Spiro), I propose that a portion of Lake Jackson's Mound 3 assemblage was created by a fertility-oriented, ancestral cult in the southeastern-most reaches of the SECC (see Steadman *et al.* 1996; Brown 1997).

Existing in the Panhandle of Northwest Florida (Fig. 4.1), the Lake Jackson site's builders and inhabitants have been contextualized within the Fort Walton archaeological culture region (Marrinan and White 2007; Shahramfar 2008). Primarily distinguished by their connection with a ceramic complex initially defined by Gordon Willey (1949), Fort Walton sites exhibit highly variable burial assemblages that frequently defy categorization (Scarry 1985; Marrinan and White 2007; Shahramfar 2008, viii). One might say that the influences of several pre-Columbian tribes washed down the Apalachicola, Chattahoochee, and Tombigbee rivers to

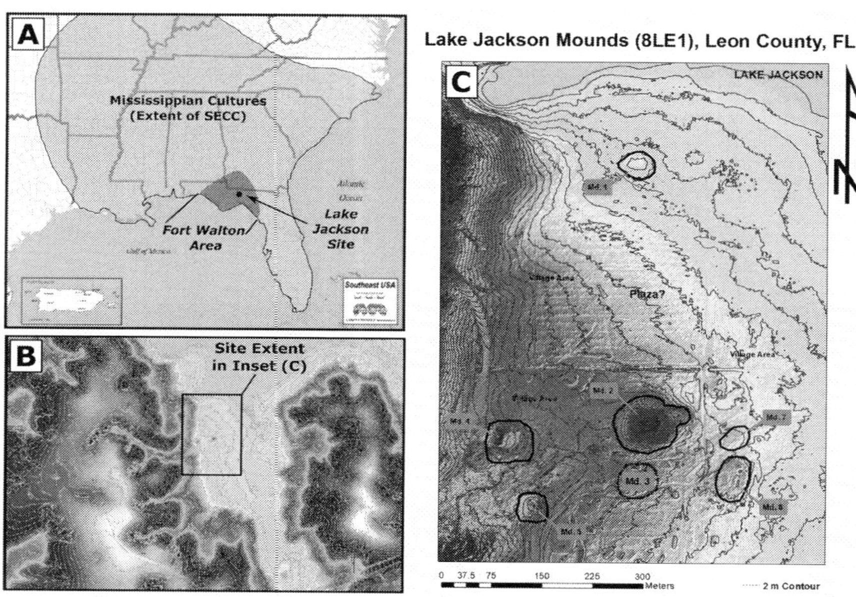

Fig. 4.1 Placement of the Fort Walton Archaeological Culture within the geographic distribution of Mississippian period sites in the Greater Southeast: A. extent of Mississippian archaeological cultures with the Fort Walton area indicated in darker gray (greyscale base map of the Southeastern United States made publicly available online by Maps & Graphics ©); B Contoured digital elevation model (DEM) of the McGinnis Arm of Lake Jackson with the site extent indicated; C. DEM of the Lake Jackson site with mound skirts indicated.

participate in Fort Walton's manifestation, but the Lake Jackson site has been specifically related to ancestral Apalachee and Muscogee Creek traditions (Hann 1988; Tesar 2012). It is for this reason that I attempt to navigate the diverse characteristics of Lake Jackson's Mound 3 in order to distinguish burials 7, 10, and 16 as "Earth Mother" representations. Drawing from Guy Prentice (1986, 239), this is accomplished by relating them to "defining characteristics of deities in the early historic Indian myths of eastern North America" in our conclusions.

The archaeology of Mound 3

Located on a sandy terrace flanked immediately to the west by upland formations, the Lake Jackson site lies on the southwestern shore of the lake from which its name is derived. Characteristic of landforms in Florida's Woodville Karst Plain, Lake Jackson is large, shallow and sinkhole rich. Sinkholes cause the lake's water levels to fluctuate often and completely dry down in sporadic occurrences (Payne and Scarry 1998, 28; McGlynn 2006). More specifically, Mound 3 is located within a six-mound group intersected by Butler Mill Creek, a spring-fed drainage that feeds into the McGinnis Arm of Lake Jackson. Situated in the center of the southern row of mounds, Mound 3 was in closest proximity to Mound 2, the largest earthen structure of the site (Willey 1949, 113; Jones 1982, 4).

Described during the first professional survey of Lake Jackson in 1940, Gordon Willey and Richard Woodbury noted Mound 3 as being truncated relatively undisturbed (1942, 232–5). B. Calvin Jones would later measure the dimensions at 44 m east–west and 48 m north–south, with a height of 4.9 m (1982, 7). Mound 3 remained relatively unchanged until 1975, when the landowner removed roughly 40% and a limited number of archaeologists conducted expedited excavations (Jones 1982, 7). Under these constrained circumstances, 15 previously undisturbed burials were recorded (Jones 1982, 7; Ledoux 2009, 50, 51). In February of 1976 the mound was cleared to ground level. Portions of the pre-mound occupation and construction stages remain intact in the sub-surface (Jones 1982, 9; 1994, 123).

In total, salvage excavators of Mound 3 recorded it as a platform burial mound whose stratigraphy revealed several construction stages (Fig. 4.2). Twelve floors were demarcated by sandy soils capped with clay mantles. A sum of 25 burials was recorded within the mound's construction layers, some of which contained up to nine internments. Over 7000 artifacts were recovered, including ornate funerary objects made from shell, stone, ceramic, and copper (Jones 1982; 1994). The most elaborate of these include exotic copper plates bearing Braden style iconography, the largest of their kind known from North America (Jones 1982, 37–9; 1994).

Cultural features encountered include structures shown by the presence of linear-oriented postholes on top of clay floors. The largest angular structure was observed on floor 11, the first level characterized as being affiliated with mound construction. Jones noted that the mound was palisaded in reference to this angular structure, which may have denoted a partitioned area of ritual

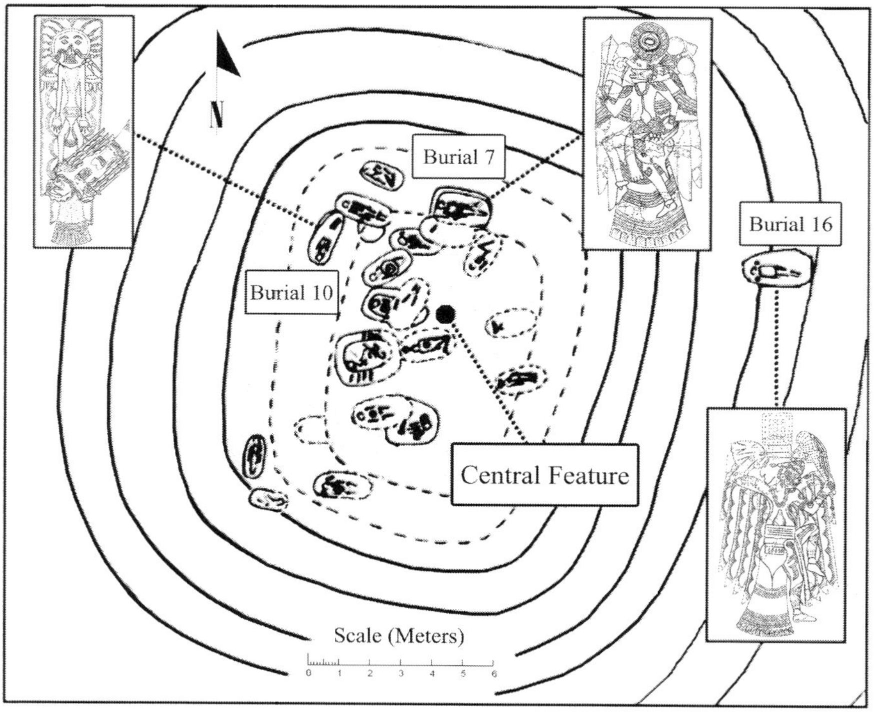

Fig. 4.2 Planview map of burials in Mound 3 at Lake Jackson (image adapted from Jones 1982, 27, fig. 4).

activity closed off from the general public (1982, 9, 10). Other postholes were located on upper mound levels 1, 2, and 7 (Jones 1982, 9; 1994, 122–5). A central midden that Jones stated was clearly not a hearth feature, was interpreted as a large center post. This post occurs in levels 2 through 7 and appears in at least three floors (Jones 1994, 126). No burials were noted to intrude into this prominent feature. Instead, it appears all burials *revolve* around this central feature of the mortuary mound.

Three radiocarbon dates from Mound 3 provide a range of construction beginning with the pre-mound midden dating to AD 1162–1410 with mound construction initiating near the initiation of the SECC manifestation at *c.* AD 1250. Mound construction appears to conclude around AD 1500 with a terminal date being AD 1416–1666 (Merrinan 2012, 194).

Adhering to known characteristics of Mississippian architecture (Lewis *et al.* 1998, 16–18; Seinfeld *et al.* 2015), Mound 3 was built on top of an existing activity area. This sequence contained a 22 cm subsurface dark midden with ceramics, burned organics, and a cache of 35 lithic projectile points. All ceramics were attributed to the Fort Walton period. The midden area was capped with a yellowish-red clay layer which, located beneath ground level, was labeled floor 12 (Ledoux 2009, 50). Floor 12, the first level of mound construction, contained an offering of charred corn and a copper badge, the first of their kind recovered from the site (Jones 1982, 9).

Mound 3 mortuary patterns

Researchers have noted changes in Mound 3's mortuary patterns through time and their associated cultural significance (Jones 1982; 1991; 1994; Scarry 1992; Ledoux 2009; Payne 2010). At the same time, however, all burials were interred in association with superimposed mound summit floors, providing a continuous mortuary sequence for the approximately 250 year span of activity at Mound 3. All burials included positioned individuals but a single cremation is associated with the uppermost mound floor and an exception to the overall pattern. The cremated individual aside, all other individuals were placed in intrusive pits, wrapped in textiles, and laid out in one of three positions: extended on their back, flexed on their side, or semi-flexed on their back or side (Jones 1994, 128; Merrinan and White 2007, 308–9). Overall, the mound's burial sequence remains relatively consistent. The first burials occur in levels 8, 9, and 10 near the mound's center. Jones (1982) notes that grave placement alternated on the ends of the structure floor in relation to previous burials from older layers. Beyond practical reasons of not disturbing earleir graves, this practice suggests a multi-generational memory concerning burial arrangement around the geometric center of the mound. This same alternating practice is encountered in the final construction sequences within floors 2, 3, and 4. Jones specifically remarks that the levels follow a *counterclockwise* order of inter-floor burial (Jones 1994, 127). The rotating swirl of earliest to latest internments reveals a consistency in mortuary practice within Mound 3.

The three burials containing the exotic and iconographically rich copper plates with falconoid characteristics also demand further discussion. All three individuals were extended on their backs with the copper plates placed over their torso on top of cloth wrapping. The bodies were then wrapped in leather, followed by cane or reed matting. Finally, they were placed into pits dug into the floor of the mound. The pits were topped with split logs, most of which had evidence of a fire burned on top of them (Jones 1982, 9–10; 1994, 126). Burial 6 from floor 11 provides circumstantial evidence that these charred deposits may have been a maize offering. The split logs covering this burial were, themselves, topped with a large mass of charred corn (Ledoux 2009, 51, 52).

Placed in association with floor 9, Burial 7 contained an extended individual within a split log tomb. Associated remains included graphite pigment, as well as large amounts of shell and pearl beads with the person. Aside from a copper badge interred during the mound's initial construction phase, Burial 7 holds the oldest copper plate to appear in Mound 3 (Jones 1982, 37–9). The estimated date Jones provides for this burial is *AD 1319* (1994, 124)[1] but Marrinan and White (2007, table 4) provide a calibrated radiocarbon date (cal AD 1372±59; 550±90 BP; Beta-64835) associated with floor 9 also. Rebecca Storey (1993), a biological anthropologist, examined the remains from Mound 3 to determine age, sex, and markers of pathology. Possessing a wide and scalloped sciatic notch that bore evidence of parturition (birthing) scars, the woman in Burial 7 lived well over 50 years of age and was one of the oldest known individuals in the mound (Storey 1993, 7).

Burial 10 contained the "Elder Hawkman" plate, shell and pearl beads, and other copper artifacts (Jones 1982, 37–9). Storey (1993, 10) described this 45–49 year-old individual as a "gracile male" but later (2001) agreed with Larson and Hutchison that it was female. Due to the burial patterns and ethnographic sources indicating females kept and maintained sacred copper, I suspect the person to have been an elderly female or, perhaps, an elderly phenotypic male that adopted a female gender identity (Bloch 2014, 80). The individual was also interred within a series of split log boards that comprised the tomb. The radiocarbon date associated with a structural log in Floor 2 is reported as cal AD 992±91 (1045±75 BP; I-9921) (Marrinan and White 2007, table 4), but Jones (1994, table 1) reports an estimated date of *AD 1457* using his phase-based schema.

Burial 16 was a 50+ year-old individual interred with cloth and cane matting, litter poles, leather, pearl beads, and an ornately decorated "hawkman style" copper plate (Jones 1982, 37–9). Chunkey stones that evoke images from Apalachee folklore were also recovered from the burial (Hann 1988). She appears to have been placed with split logs that resemble those that comprised other tombs. This burial penetrated Floors 4 through 7 and Jones estimates its age to be *AD 1398* (Jones 1994, 124). Floor 9 provides the closest underlying context that was sampled for a radiocarbon date, reported as cal AD 1293±67; 720±70 BP; Beta-64835) by Marrinan and White (2007, table 4).

Discussion: continuity and innovation in Mound 3 mortuary ceremonialism

Especially during the Mississippian Period and into historic times, mound-building practices appear to be inextricably tied to world renewal ceremonies, such as green corn or busks recorded in historical accounts of Muskogean communities (Swanton 1928; Knight 1986a; 1986b). However, it is important not to lose sight of an important distinction that has been made between platform and mortuary mounds (Lindauer and Blitz 1997; Blitz and Lorenz 2006). While the former has been linked with community-centered accession ceremonies among the Natchez and various Muskogean speaking tribes, the behaviors that produced the latter remain elusive (Lindauer and Blitz 1997; Blitz and Lorenz 2006; Knight 1986a; 1986b). Nevertheless, both categories of mound building seem to be the result of communal efforts during the Mississippian Period (Fowler 1991; Kelly 1991; 1996; 2003; Kimball *et al.* 2010), but the orientation of graves around central poles appears to be a practice that existed even earlier (Keel 1972, tables 82 and 86; Jeffries 1994, 78–81; Coe 1995; Lindauer and Blitz 1997; Knight 2001, 316–17; Kimball *et al.* 2010, 48–9). Additionally, tomb structures containing SECC materials from Mississippian Period sites also bear similarities to those from surrounding Woodland Period sites.

In the case of Woodland Period sites, log tombs are a consistent feature of Hopewell and Adena mortuary ceremonialism, particularly on the Illinois and Mississippi rivers (Milner 2004, 58–9, 67). Along the Forked Deer River in Tennessee, however, the Twin Mounds at the Pinson Mounds site host several log-lined pits, one of which includes an elderly female designated as Burial 18 (Mainfort *et al.* 1985, 58). Interestingly enough, rattles were recovered from Burial 5 at the Twin Mounds that bear iconography reminiscent of Weeden Island Incised ceramics

(Mainfort *et al.* 1985, 57). Additionally, Swift Creek paddle stamp designs have been found at the site that resemble those from southern Georgia (Mainfort *et al.* 1997; Stephenson *et al.* 2002, 349; Wallis 2007, 214). In northwest Florida, it is generally accepted that Fort Walton materials were produced by behaviors influenced from pre-existing Weeden Island and Swift Creek traditions, as well as newly developing Mississippian traditions (Milanich *et al.* 1997, 14; Tesar 1980, 123, 131; Marrinan and White 2007, 296). Although several sites in northwest Florida have components from all three archaeological cultures, the manner in which Fort Walton culture emerged around AD 1000 has been a long-lived subject of debate (Brose and Percy 1984; Tesar 1980, 131–7; Marrinan and White 2007; Shahramfar 2008).

Unlike the more recent timber box tombs identified during Jones's (1982; 1992; 1994) excavations, all the Twin Mounds' interments contained at least two individuals, deposited in a single mortuary construction effort consisting of multiple stages and residing near known charnel house and crematory facility sites (Ford 1965; Brown 1979; Mainfort *et al.* 1985, 50). The nearby crematory facilities, charnel house, and mortuary crypt structures located at the Bynum and Pharr Mounds sites serve as interesting compliments to these monumental creations (Cotter and Corbett 1951; Bohannon 1972; Mainfort *et al.* 1985). Multiple mound sites often consist of tomb burials arranged around a cremation pit at their bases, like the Robbins Mound site (Milner 2004, 59–60). Fort Walton sites that contain cremation features include Marsh Island and Rood's Landing (Shahramfar 2008, 56, 73–4). While cremated remains from Mound 3 at Lake Jackson were present, pits and other structures that would facilitate cremation have yet to be identified (Jones 1994, 125–6).

The curious circular pit (70–90 cm in diameter) located near the center of Mound 3 at Lake Jackson indicates that a central pole supported multiple structures and served as a central feature for orienting the graves interred between floors 2 and 7 (Jones 1982, 10). It is possible that the act of orienting tomb and charnel house burials around central features before burning them may be an aspect of Woodland Period practices that survived into the Mississippian Period (Brown 1979; Jones 1994, 122, 125). Perhaps these poles and cremation pits served as orienting structures for both Mississippian and Woodland Period peoples. In any case, the counterclockwise arrangements of burials in Mound 3 at Lake Jackson did catch B. Calvin Jones's (1994, 127) attention and such rotations in burial orientation remained consistent through floors 2, 3, and 4. Another site that exhibited varying grave orientations is Snow Beach, wherein burials were arranged toward the "north, west, northwest, northeast, southeast, and southwest" (Klingle 2006, 260; Shahramfar 2008, 44, 60).

Not only do the arrangement and construction of burial structures at Lake Jackson exhibit similarities with both Mississippian and Woodland Period contexts, but certain objects emphasizing the female gender and fertility also exist that were unearthed from mortuary settings in regions where SECC materials were deposited after AD 1250. More specifically, objects crafted in the forms of seated or kneeling women with bundle baskets bear strong resemblances to burials 7, 10, and 16 from Mound 3 at the site, and arguably embody female-oriented fertility symbols examined by Prentice (1986). While several examples of these figurines exist from Mississippian and Woodland Period contexts, none were found in Mound 3 at Lake Jackson. However, elderly female burials from the site were interred with copper plates in wrapped accouterments that resemble sacred bundles attributed to SECC craftsmanship (Jones 1982, 16). These mortuary objects are not unlike the bundles depicted on the small female figurine from Block-Sterns and a marble statue recovered from Mound C at Etowah (Larson 1971, 65; King 1974, 640; Jones 1982). Alternatively, log lined Weeden Island burials from Mounds D and E at Kolomoki contained both human occupants and crafted effigies depicting various animals and anthropomorphic beings (Sears 1953; Milanich *et al.* 1997; Pluckhahn 2003). Woodland and Mississippian Period objects of this sort have been examined by James Brown (1985, 104, 123–9), who identifies them as shrine house furnishings associated with ancestral cults that placed a specific focus on fertility symbolism.

Before a discussion of other Mississippian burials can take place to compare with those at Lake Jackson, it is important to discuss nearby sites that were occupied toward the end of the Woodland Period. In particular, the McKeithen mound site contained another feature that is relevant to fertility symbolism in mortuary contexts. Primarily hosting Weeden Island remains, Mounds A, B, and C at the site served as a multi-mound charnel facility that contained numerous bundle burials and a tomb for an older female (Milanich 1997, 94–117; Turner *et al.* 2005). Experiencing its greatest apogee of sociocultural complexity between AD 300 and 350, Mound B contained burial S426, its sole occupant (Milanich *et al.* 1997; Turner *et al.* 2005, 128). Being the only burial in the mound, S426 was not placed in an arrangement organized around a centering feature but was located near the geometric center of the mound and aligned with the summer solstice (Milanich *et al.* 1997, 92; Turner *et al.* 2005, 126, fig. 4.4). Like the women from Mound 3 at Lake Jackson, she was interred in a timber tomb at the base of the mound and linked to maize through her diet (Turner *et al.* 2005, 128). Isotope analysis results strongly indicate that this individual was of non-local origin and consumed maize while her dental signatures were forming during childhood (Turner *et al.* 2005, 133).

Mound C at Etowah also presents an opportunity for comparison with Mound 3 at Lake Jackson. Mound C was built during the Early Wilbanks phase (AD 1250–1325) as an enormous mortuary structure that contained roughly 350 burials (Larson 1971, 58; Cobb and King 2005, 181; King 2007b; Scarry 2007; King *et al.* 2011). Unlike the older Woodland burials at Pinson Mounds, Etowah's Mound C included log and stone tomb burials that encased single individuals who were accorded special treatment (Larson 1971, 64; King 2007b). Like Mound B at the McKeithen site, the dead were also interred in association with screens or palisades that delineated mortuary spaces and tomb structures (Larson 1971, 59–61; King 2004, 154–5; 2007b, 109; Turner *et al.* 2005, 126, fig. 4.4).

The tomb burials in Mound C did not exclusively contain females. Decorated with elaborate burial furniture made from exotic and local materials, both male and female subjects were often segregated individually by the tombs themselves, lobed mantles of earth, and palisade screens (Larson 1971, 61–5; King 2007b, 114–15).

Moreover, some tombs in Etowah's Mound C did not contain subjects that were exclusively human. In the case of Burial 15, four individuals were interred in a tomb that also contained two marble statues, each bearing male and female identifiers (Larson 1971, 65; King 2007b, 115). Additionally, the female statue bears many similarities with the Birger, West, and Westbrook figurines that Prentice (1986) has identified as referents to the "Earth Mother" character immortalized in Native American folklore (Larson 1971, 65; King 2007b, 115). It is in this instance that Burial 15 is similar to earlier Woodland Period burials that also contain several occupants alongside human effigies.

Most intriguingly, the "dancing hawkman copper breastplate" from Burial 7 at Lake Jackson Mound 3 is strikingly similar to Burial 25 from Etowah's Mound C (Larson 1971, 62, fig. 4; Jones 1994, 129, fig. 6). The former burial contained an elderly female interred with numerous shell beads and the famous Lake Jackson plate (Fig. 4.3), rendered in the same style as the Rogan plates from Mound C at Etowah (Scarry 2007, 138–9, fig. 7.4). The plate itself prominently displays an anthropomorphic subject with an enormous copper headdress ornament bearing an ogee motif, recognized by Reilly (2004, 130) as a portal symbol associated with serpents in representations of cosmic models. He has also proposed that it represents another portal that people still travel through today: the birth canal (Reilly, pers. comm. 2015). This same motif is bill-boarded on the copper plate found covering the head of Burial 25 in Mound C at Etowah (Larson 1971, 62, fig. 4). Additionally, the being depicted in the Lake Jackson plate holds a mace aloft in the right hand, a posture that is well documented in Muskogean folklore and celebrated in ideologically based rituals from recent history (Swanton 1995; Scarry 2007). I suspect that the figure is purposefully "frozen" in a dance posture.

Copper objects aside, common artifacts from mortuary contexts at both Etowah and Lake Jackson include shell beads, greenstone celts, shark teeth, and shell gorgets (Scarry 2007). Also of note is the charred corn offering found in association with Burial 6 at Lake Jackson (Jones 1994, 125). While corn offerings were not definitively uncovered from Mound C at Etowah, David Hally (2004, 166–7, fig. 1) noted multiple female burials with rattlesnake gorgets that were placed near

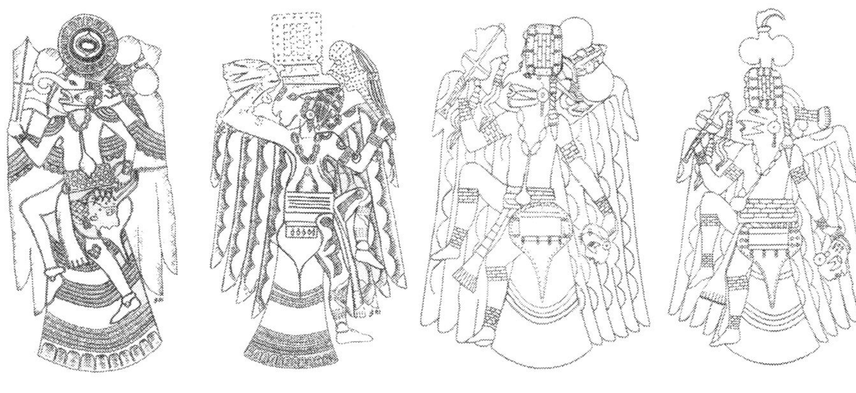

Fig. 4.3 Lake Jackson Mound 3 (left pair) and Etowah Mound C (Rogan) plate illustrations (right pair).

a corncrib at the King site. Burials BK 2, 4, and 5 at Lake Jackson were interred with Williams Island style gorgets, but their remains were mixed when delivered for forensic analysis. Nevertheless, BK 2 and 4 were labeled as biological males (Storey 1993, 24).

Like other known Mississippian mortuary structures, Lake Jackson's Mound 3 burials were situated near the structure's geometric center, where a centering feature likely existed (Duffield 1973, 7, 10; Jones 1982; 1992; 1994; Marrinan and White 2007). Moreover, remains examined by Jones (1982, 9; 1994, 122–5) indicated the presence of square house structures and a potential mortuary temple in layers 1, 2, and 7 of the mound, as well as a long narrow structure constructed with upright posts. These are not unlike other sites with central pole structures, central burial fires, and mortuary facilities across the Mississippian Period Southeast. Like Mound C at Etowah, Hollywood's Mound B was largely constructed after AD 1250 and contained elaborate objects that suggest SECC associations, but only hosted two burial phases (King 2007a; Reilly and Garber 2007; Thornock *et al.* 2015). Although the layout of these burial events differed significantly, both involved the arrangement of the deceased around a central fire (Thornock *et al.* 2015, 11). Thornock *et al.* argue that both were constructed in a cosmologically complimentary manner during a single building effort. No central pole was identified, but it is clear that the fire fulfilled a similar purpose as a centering feature nonetheless.

In addition to the meaningful arrangement of graves around a central feature at Lake Jackson's Mound 3, burials were constructed in the form of tombs, litter internments, and even a single cremation in its uppermost stratigraphy (Jones 1994, 126). However, a particular focus was placed on the "repeated burial of single individuals in graves" (Jones 1994, 126). The patterning of these burials "suggests that some record was maintained concerning grave placement" over multiple generations (Jones 1994, 127). The three elderly female tombs that are the focus of this investigation were documented in the lower half of the mound, a location that potentially bears symbolic significance.

Summary and conclusion

For the purposes of this paper, the following characteristics have been tied to Lake Jackson Mound 3 and identified as tableaux components arranged to portray specific aspects of Muskogean cosmology:

- Organization of graves around centralizing features, such as a pole, cremation crypt, or single tomb. For Lake Jackson, this is manifested as burials arranged in a steadily rotating or "swirling" orientation around a central pole.
- Interment of elderly female individuals in timber or split cane tombs that were often burned during the burial process.
- Provision of specific graves goods that may have been tied to fertility ceremonialism, such as cloth wrapped bundles with copper objects inside, corn offerings, figures, and shell gorgets.

- Association with objects bearing bird symbolism, as well as actual bird remains (Jones 1982, 38–9, table 2; Joby Kidd, pers. comm. 2015[2]).
- Whether they are manifested as center poles in Mississippian mound sites like Cahokia, central fires in the middle of Mound B at the Hollywood site, or cremation crypts at the Robbins and Pinson Mound sites from Woodland Period times, centralizing features representing a cosmic *axis mundi* that link the deposited dead to the mobile living were incorporated into burial mound architecture throughout American prehistory (Duffield 1973; Fowler 1991; Milanich *et al.* 1997; Milner 2004; Turner *et al.* 2005; Thornock *et al.* 2015).

Across cultural and temporal regions in North America during prehistoric times, mound features conform to a shared tripartite model of the cosmos represented by symbols chained together in grammatical coherency (Knight 1986b; 2006; 2010; Prentice 1986; Watson 1990, 44; Sundstrom 1996; Lindauer and Blitz 1997; Reilly and Garber 2007; 2011; Blitz and Lorenz 2006; Scarry and Payne 2006). Considering the rotating arrangement of burials interred between floors 2 and 7 in Mound 3 at Lake Jackson, it is our belief that a three-dimensional representation of the swirl cross motif in Mississippian iconography was attempted by the feature's architects (Fig. 4.4). George Lankford (2011a; 2011b) has identified this motif alongside others in cryptic representations of the "Path of Souls", a realm through which one's soul travels after death in the theologies of Muskogean speaking tribes and others. As an independent motif, it symbolizes swirling waters that become a "two-dimensional version of what was understood as a three-dimensional reality" (2011a, 255). Perhaps not unlike the relationship between the Minnetaree (whose translated name is "to cross waters") and the Missouri River, occupants of Lake Jackson's sinkhole rich environment created a representation of *Okeeheepkee*'s dry-down vortices in order to deposit their dead into "disappearing waters" (Colvin 2012, 55). With further investigation, the common relationship that these different centralizing features may have with cosmic *axis mundi* symbolism could further demonstrate their continuity from the Woodland Period into Mississippian times.

In addition to being a materialized representation of prehistoric cosmology, Lake Jackson's Mound 3 also hosted prominent individuals who carried equally symbolic objects to their graves. Especially in the case of exotic copper plates that bear pan-regional motifs observed in other Mississippian mortuary contexts, the association of such symbols with elderly female burials suggests that later recorded folklore recounted themes invoked by Lake Jackson's architects. It is my belief that these invocations established an association between these individuals and a preternatural "Earth Mother" character from Native American folklore, much like the fire-clay statues that were crafted in the Midwest and examined by Prentice (1986). However ironic it may seem, this ostensibly grim monument contained burials that housed prominent fertility symbols,

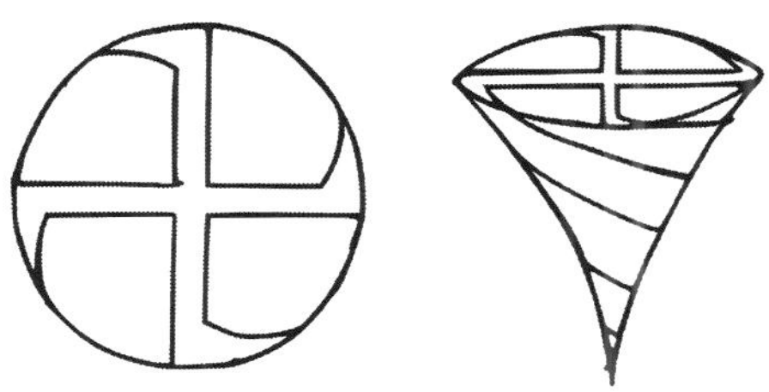

Fig. 4.4 Swirl cross motif in two-dimensional and three-dimensional perspectives.

constructed in accordance with beliefs in nature's dualistic oppositions (Hultkrantz 1967, 39–43, 132; Lévi-Strauss 1981, 353; Lankford 2008, 73–97).

The Muskogee tell of a woman from the Talmalgi clan who instructed the people to build a corncrib for her to occupy over four days. During this time, she stocked it to the brim with corn that could be ground into the soup/porridge sofki (Swanton 1995, 9–10; Lankford 2011a, 147). In several versions of this story, this "Earth Mother" character is described as the embodiment of maize. While they do admit that some Indians came from the Sky World, the Creek also expressed to Swanton (1928, 480) that others "sprang from the earth, their mother, much like corn does". Among the Koasati, another tale exists that describes an elderly woman who fills a similar corncrib with maize while taking care of orphan children (Swanton 1995, 168). Finally, the Natchez have a story much akin to those of the Creek and Koasati that describe how two children kill Corn-woman, burn her body in a lodge that is subsequently buried, and harvest corn from her grave mound every summer (Swanton 1995, 230). It is our belief that the individuals interred in Burials 7, 10, and 16 embody this "Earth Mother" character, interred with accoutrements that also reference the twins she fosters in Native American folklore.

Although only indirectly referenced in the mortuary assemblages of Mound 3, it is worthwhile to describe the significance of Hero Twin symbolism because they articulate with Earth Mother personages. In several folkloric traditions in the Southeast, Hero Twins frequently appear as orphans that interact with other-than-human-persons, in both cooperation and conflict (Swanton 1995; Lankford 2011a). While "Earth Mother" is a life symbol to balance out frequently male-supplied death symbols, Hero Twin stories similarly symbolize dualisms of proper conduct (polite:rude, war:peace, dirty:clean) among other opposing themes (Lankford 2008). Moreover, they consistently bear falconoid and, occasionally, moth-related symbols (Lankford 2007; 2011a; Reilly and Garber 2007; Bloch 2014). Thus, characters such as these portray harbingers of the following paired oppositions: day:night, conflict:cooperation, fire:water, above:below, and life:death. While Hero Twin referents communicate complete dualisms, the emphasis on fertility themes in female burials would surely compliment (and be complimented by) surrounding male burials.

While it will never be possible to understand what justified the treatment of these women in Lake Jackson's Mound 3 (Burials 7, 10, and 16), it is clear that they fulfilled communicative goals by transmitting messages in loaded symbols to a contemporary audience, even after death. Perhaps, the mound's construction provided a materialized record for future generations to reference or, as Payne (2010, 2) has suggested, capitulated an act of forgetting that marked the end of an era. Whatever the case may be, the Mound 3 tableau does demonstrate that the religious meanings were enacted and materialized in purposeful ways. Moreover, these contexts illustrate how deceased ancestors are often as vivacious and socially dependent as the people who gave them existence. By transforming the dead into mythical "Earth Mother" protagonists and ceremoniously "killing" sacred objects, these native Floridians preserved their memory just before the arrival of the Spanish triggered a widespread and drastic shift in their history.

Acknowledgements

Special thanks to Adam King and F. Kent Reilly for their ongoing efforts in, and dedication to, the educational enrichment of their students. An additional thanks is extended to the Bureau of Archaeological Research in Tallahassee, Florida. I also wish to express my sincere gratitude to the Muskogee Creek nation in Florida and their kind hospitality on several occasions. I especially want to thank Dan Penton and Emv, who have provided excellent instruction and assistance on several occasions. *Mvto!*

Notes

1. The dates Jones (1994, table 1) ran through Teledyne Isctopes (New Jersey) in 1977 and used for temporal estimations were based on phase-estimates that lasted 19.7 years on average. Marrinan and White (2007, table 4) report calibrated dates collected from Mound 3 and provide the most reliable estimates to date.
2. Joby Kidd was a field assistant recruited by B. Calvin Jones from a local Tallahassee High School (Jones 1982, 7). The author visited his house to see his personal collection from Mound 3 and hear his eye-witness accounts.

Bibliography

Alt, S. (2002) Identities, traditions, and diversity in Cahokia's uplands. *Midcontinental Journal of Archaeology* 27(2), 217–235.

Blakely, R.L. (1995) Social organization at Etowah, a reconsideration of paleodemographic and paleonutritional evidence. *Southeastern Archaeology* 14(1), 46–59.

Blitz, J.H. and Livingood, P. (2004) Sociopolitical implications of Mississippian mound volume. *American Antiquity* 69(2), 291–301.

Blitz, J.H., and Lorenz, K.G. (2006) *The Chattahoochee Chiefdoms*. University of Alabama Press, Tuscaloosa AL.

Bloch, L.J. (2014) The unthinkable and the unseen. Community archaeology and decolonizing social imagination at Okeeheepkee, or the Lake Jackson Site. *Journal of the World Archaeological Congress* 10(1), 70–106.

Bohannon, C.F. (1972) *Excavations at the Pharr Mounds, Prentiss and Itawamba Counties, Mississippi and Excavations at the Bear Creek Site, Tishomingo County Mississippi.* United States Department of the Interior, National Park Service. Washington DC.

Brose, D.S. (1984) Mississippian Period cultures in Northwestern Florida. In *Perspectives on Gulf Coast Prehistory*, D.D. Davis and R.P. Bullen (eds), 165–97. University of Florida Press, Monographs in Anthropology and History 5. Gainesville FL.

Brose, D.S. and Percy, G.W. (1978) Fort Walton settlement patterns. In *Mississippian Settlement Patterns*, B. Smith (ed.), 81–114. Academic Press, New York.

Brown, J.A. (1979) Charnel houses and mortuary crypts, Disposal of the dead in the Middle Woodland Period. In *Hopewell Archaeology*, D. Brose and N. Greber (eds), 211–19. Kent State University Press, Kent OH.

Brown, J.A. (1986) The Mississippian Period. In *Ancient Art of the American Woodland Indians*. D.S. Brose, J.A. Brown and D.W. Penney (eds), 93–129. Harry N. Abrams, New York.

Brown, J.A. (1997) The archaeology of ancient religions in the Eastern Woodlands. *Annual Reviews in Anthropology* 26, 465–85.

Brown, J.A. (2004) The Cahokian expression, creating court and cult. In *Hero, Hawk, and Open Hand, American Indian Art of the Ancient Midwest and South*, R.F. Townsend and

R.V. Sharp (eds), 105–24. Yale University Press/The Art Institute of Chicago, New Haven CT and London.

Caldwell, J. (1964) Interaction spheres in prehistory. *Illinois State Museum Scientific Papers* 12(6), 133–93.

Christensen, L.B. (2009) "Cult" in the study of religion and archaeology. In *Aspects of Ancient Greek Cult, Context, Ritual and Iconography*, J.T. Jensen, G. Hinge, P. Schultz, and B. Wickkiser (eds), 13–28. Aarhus University Press, Langelandsgade.

Cobb, C.R., and King, A. (2005) Re-Inventing Mississippian tradition at Etowah, Georgia. *Journal of Archaeological Method and Theory* 12(3), 167–92.

Coe, J.L. (1995) *Town Creek Indian Mound, a Native American legacy.* University of North Carolina Press, Chapel Hill NC.

Colvin, M. (2012) Old-Woman-Who-Never-Dies, A Mississippian survival in the Hidatsa world. Unpublished Master's thesis, Texas State University, San Marcos TX.

Cotter, J.L. and Corbett J.M. (1951) *Archaeology of the Bynum Mounds, Mississippi.* United States Department of the Interior, National Park Service, Archaeological Research Series 1. Washington DC.

Duffield, L. (1973) The Oklahoma Craig Mound, another look at an old problem. *Bulletin of The Oklahoma Anthropological Society* 22, 1–10.

Ford, J.A. (1965) *Hopewell Culture Burial Mounds near Helena, Arkansas. Anthropological Papers of the American Museum of Natural History* 50(1).

Fowler, M.L. (1991) Mound 72 and Early Mississippian at Cahokia. In *New Perspectives on Cahokia, Views from the Periphery*, J.B. Stoltman (ed.), 1–28. Prehistory Press, Madison WI.

Hally, D.J. (2004) Mortuary patterns at a sixteenth-century town in northwestern Georgia. *Southeastern Archaeology* 23(2), 166–77.

Hann, J. (1988) *Apalachee, the Land between the Rivers.* University Presses of Florida, Gainesville FL.

Hultkrantz, Å. (1967) *The Religions of the American Indians.* University of California Press, Berkeley CA.

Jeffries, R.W. (1994) The Swift Creek Site and Woodland platform mounds in the Southeastern United States. In *Ocmulgee Archaeology 1936–1986*, D.J. Hally (ed.), 71–83. University of Georgia Press, Athens GA.

Jones, B.C. (1982) Southern Cult manifestations at the Lake Jackson Site, Leon County, Florida, salvage excavation of Mound 3. *Midcontinental Journal of Archaeology* 7(1), 3–44.

Jones, B.C. (1991) High status burials in Mound 3 at Florida's Lake Jackson Complex, Stability and Change in Fort Walton Culture. Unpublished paper presented at the 48th Annual Southeastern Archaeological Conference, Jackson. Manuscript on file at the Bureau of Archaeological Research, Tallahassee FL.

Jones, B.C. (1992) November 1992 septic tank survey at Lake Jackson Mounds State archaeological site, Leon County, Florida. Unpublished document on file at the Bureau of Archaeological Resources, Florida Department of State, Tallahassee FL.

Jones, B.C. (1994) The Lake Jackson Mound Complex (8LE1), stability and change in Fort Walton Culture. *The Florida Anthropologist* 47(2), 120–46.

Keel, B.C. (1972) Woodland Phases of the Appalachian Summit Area. Unpublished Ph.D. dissertation, University of North Carolina, Chapel Hill NC.

Kelly, J.E. (1991) The evidence for prehistoric exchange and its implications for the development at Cahokia. In *New Perspectives on Cahokia, Views from the Periphery*, J.B. Stoltman (ed.), 65–92. Prehistory Press, Madison WI.

Kelly, J.E. (1996) Redefining Cahokia, principles and elements of community organization. *Wisconsin Archaeologist* 77, 97–119.

Kelly, J.E. (2003) The context of the post pit and meaning of the Sacred Pole at the East St. Louis Mound Group. *Wisconsin Archaeologist* 84, 107–25.

Kimball, L.R., Thomas R.W. and Crites, G.D. (2010) The Biltmore Mound and Hopewellian mound use in the southern Appalachians. *Southeastern Archaeology* 29(1), 44–58.

King, A. (2004) Deciphering Etowah's Mound C, the construction history and mortuary record of a Mississippian burial mound. *Southeastern Archaeology* 23(2), 153–65.

King, A. (2007a) The Southeastern Ceremonial Complex, from cult to complex. In *Southeastern Ceremonial Complex, Chronology, Content, Context*. A. King (ed.), 1–14. University of Alabama Press, Tuscaloosa AL.

King, A. (2007b) Mound C and the Southeastern Ceremonial Complex in the history of the Etowah Site. In *Southeastern Ceremonial Complex, Chronology, Content, Context*, A. King (ed.), 107–33. University of Alabama Press, Tuscaloosa AL.

King, A., Walker, C.P., Sharp, R.V., Reilly, F.K. III and McKinnon, D.P. (2011) Remote sensing data from Etowah's Mound A, architecture and the recreation of Mississippian tradition. *American Antiquity* 76(2), 355–71.

King, M.E. (1974) Current research. *American Antiquity* 39(4), 621–42.

Klingle, D. (2006) Burial in Florida, Culture, Ritual, Health, and Status, the Archaic to Seminole Periods. Unpublished Master's thesis, Florida State University, Tallahassee FL.

Knight, V.J. (1986) The institutional organization of Mississippian religion. *American Antiquity* 51, 675–87.

Knight, V.J. (2001) Feasting and the emergence of platform mound ceremonialism in Eastern North America. In *Feasts, Archaeological and Ethnographic Perspectives on Food, Politics, and Power*, M. Dietler and B. Hayden (eds), 311–33. Smithsonian Institution Press, Washington DC.

Knight, V.J. (2006) Symbolism of Mississippian mounds. In *Powhatan's Mantle, Indians in the Colonial Southeast*, G.A. Waselkov, P.H. Wood, and T. Hatley (eds), 421–34. University of Nebraska Press, Lincoln NE.

Knight, V.J. (2010) *Mound Excavations at Moundville: Architecture, Elites, and Social Order*. University of Alabama Press, Tuscaloosa AL.

Lankford, G.E. (2007) The "Path of Souls", some death imagery in the Southeastern Ceremonial Complex. In Reilly and Garber (eds) 2007, 174–212.

Lankford, G.E. (2008) *Looking for Lost Lore, Studies in Folklore, Ethnology, and Iconography*. University of Alabama Press, Tuscaloosa AL.

Lankford, G.E. (2011a) *Native American Legends of the Southeast, Tales from the Natchez, Caddo, Biloxi, Chickasaw, and Other Nations*. University of Alabama Press, Tuscaloosa AL.

Lankford, G.E. (2011b) The swirl-cross and the center. In *Visualizing the Sacred, Cosmic Visions, Regionalism, and the Art of the Mississippian World*, G.E. Lankford, F.K. Reilly III and J.F. Garber (eds) 251–75. University of Texas Press, Austin TX.

Larson, L.H. (1971) Archaeological implications of social stratification at the Etowah Site, Georgia. *Memoirs of the Society for American Archaeology* 25, 58–67.

Ledoux, S.C. (2009) Embodying the Sacred, Temporal Changes in the Cosmological Function of Art and Symbolism in the Mississippian Period, AD 1250–1400. Unpublished honors Thesis. Texas State University, San Marcos TX.

Lévi-Strauss, C. (1981) Four Winnebago myths, a structural sketch. In *Culture in History, Essays in Honor of Paul Radin*, S. Diamond (ed.), 351–62. Octagon Books, New York.

Lewis, B.R., Stout, C. and Wesson, C. (eds) (1998) The Design of Mississippian Towns. In *Mississippian Towns and Sacred Spaces, Searching for an Architectural Grammar*, B.R. Lewis and C. Stout (eds), 1–21. University of Alabama Press, Tuscaloosa AL.

Lindauer, O. and Blitz, J.H. (1997) Higher ground: the archaeology of North American platform mounds. *Journal of Archaeology* 5(2), 169–207.

Mainfort, R.C., Shannon, G.W. and Tyler, J.E. (1985) 1983 Excavations at Pinson Mounds, The Twin Mounds. *Midcontinental Journal of Archaeology*, 10(1), 49–75.

Mainfort, R.C., Cogswell, J.W., O'Brien, M.J., Neff, H. and Glascock, M.D. (1997) Neutron activation analysis of pottery from Pinson Mounds and nearby sites in western Tennessee, local production vs. long-distance importation. *Midcontinental Journal of Archaeology* 22, 43–68.

Marrinan, R.A. and White, N.M (2007) Modeling Fort Walton Culture in northwest Florida. *Southeastern Archaeology* 26(2), 292–318.

McGlynn, S. (2006) *Lake Jackson Watershed Piping the Sink, Porter Hole Sink 1999*. Unpublished report, McGlynn Labs. Tallahassee FL.

Milanich, J.T., Cordell, A.S. Knight V.J., Kohler, T.A. and Sigler-Lavelle, B.J. (1997) *Archaeology of Northern Florida, A.D. 200–900, The McKeithen Weeden Island Culture*. University Presses of Florida, Gainesville FL.

Milner, G.R. (2004) *The Moundbuilders, Ancient Peoples of Eastern North America*. Thames and Hudson, London.

Payne, C. (1994) Mississippian Capitals, An Archaeological Investigation of Precolumbian Political Structure. Unpublished Ph.D. dissertation, University of Florida, Gainesville FL.

Payne, C. (2002) Architectural reflections of power and authority in Mississippian towns. In *The Dynamics of Power*, M. O'Donovan (ed.), 188–213. Center for Archaeological Investigations Occasional Paper 30, Southern Illinois University, Carbondale IL.

Payne, C. (2006) The foundations of leadership in Mississippian Chiefdoms, perspectives from Lake Jackson and Upper Nodena. In *Leadership and Polity in Mississippian Society*, B.M. Butler and P.D. Welch (eds), 91–111. Center for Archaeological Investigations Occasional Paper 33, Southern Illinois University, Carbondale IL.

Payne, C. (2010) Disposal of Heirlooms and the End of Memory at Lake Jackson. Unpublished paper presented at the 75th Annual Meeting of the Society for American Archaeology, St Louis, Missouri.

Payne, C. and Scarry, J.F. (1998) Town structure at the edge of the Mississippian world. In *Mississippian Towns and Sacred Spaces, Searching for an Architectural Grammar*, R.B. Lewis and C. Stout (eds), 22–47. University of Alabama Press, Tuscaloosa AL.

Pluckhahn, T.J. (2003) *Kolomoki, Settlement, Ceremony, and Status A.D. 350 to 750*. University of Alabama Press, Tuscaloosa AL.

Prentice, G. (1986) An analysis of the symbolism expressed by the Birger Figurine. *American Antiquity* 51(2), 239–66.

Reilly, F.K. III (2004) People of earth, people of sky, visualizing the sacred in Native American art of the Mississippian Period. In *Hero, Hawk, and Open Hand, American Indian Art of the Ancient Midwest and South*, R.F. Townsend and R.V. Sharp (eds), 124–37. Yale University Press/Art Institute of Chicago, New Haven CO and London.

Reilly, F.K. III, and Garber, J.F. (eds) (2007) *Ancient Objects and Sacred Realms, Interpretations of Mississippian Iconography*. University of Texas Press, Austin TX.

Reilly, F.K. III and Garber, J.F. (eds) (2011) *Visualizing the Sacred: Cosmic Visions, Regionalism, and the Art of the Mississippian World*. University of Texas Press, Austin TX.

Scarry, J.F. (1985) A proposed revision of the Fort Walton ceramic typology: a type-variety system. *Florida Anthropologist* 38(3), 199–233.

Scarry, J.F. (2007) Connections between the Etowah and Lake Jackson Chiefdoms, Patterns in the Iconographic and Material Evidence. In *Southeastern Ceremonial Complex, Chronology, Content, Context*, A. King (ed.), 134–50. University of Alabama Press, Tuscaloosa, AL.

Sears, W.H. (1953) Kolomoki burial mounds and the Weeden Island Mortuary Complex. *American Antiquity* 18(3), 223–9.

Seinfeld, D.M., Bigman, D.P., Stauffer, J.G. and Nowak, J.C. (2015) Mound Building at Lake Jackson (8LE1), Tallahassee, Florida: New Insights from Ground Penetrating Radar. *Southeastern Archaeology* 34(3), 220–36.

Shahramfar, G. (2008) Determining Fort Walton Burial Patterns and Their Relationship within the Greater Mississippian World. Unpublished Master's thesis, University of South Florida, Tampa FL.

Shapiro, G. (1987) Working text to accompany CARL acquisition proposal for the Letchworth site. July 28, 1987. On file at the Bureau of Archaeological Research and/or the Department of Historical Resources, both in Tallahassee (Florida).

Steadman, L.B., Palmer, C.T. and Tilley, C.F. (1996) The universality of ancestor worship. *Ethnology* 35(1), 63–76.

Stephenson, K., Bense, J.A. and Snow, F. (2002) Aspects of Deptford and Swift Creek on the south Atlantic and Gulf coastal plains. In *The Woodland Southeast*,.G. Anderson and R.C. Mainfort (eds), 318–51. University of Alabama Press, Tuscaloosa AL.

Storey, R. (1993) Catalog of the Lake Jackson Mound 3 Skeletons. Unpublished manuscript on file, Florida Master Site File, Tallahassee FL.

Storey, R. (2005) Notes on Lake Jackson Pathologies. Copies of email correspondence between R. Storey and D.A. Klingle. On file in the Department of Anthropology, Florida State University, Tallahassee FL.

Sundstrom, L. (1996) Mirror of heaven: cross-cultural transference of the sacred geography of the Black Hills. *World Archaeology* 28(2), 177–89.

Swanton, J.R. (1928) Religious beliefs and medical practices of the Creek Indians. *Forty-Second Annual Report of the Bureau of American Ethnology to the Secretary of the Smithsonian Institution 1924–1925*, 473–672.

Swanton, J.R. (1995) [1929] *Myths and Tales of the Southeastern Indians*. University of Oklahoma Press, Norman OK.

Tesar, L.D. (1980) *The Leon County Bicentennial Survey Report: An Archaeological Survey of Selected Portions of Leon County, Florida*. Bureau of Historic Sites and Properties, Miscellaneous Project Report Series 49, Tallahassee FL.

Tesar, L.D. (2012) Apalachee Fort Walton, the Lake Jackson Mounds Site Complex (8LE1) and beyond. Unpublished manuscript on file, Florida Master Site File, Tallahassee FL.

Thornock, C.L, King, A., Stephenson, K. and Corsi, A. (2015) The Hollywood Site (9RI1) and the foundations of Mississippian in the middle Savannah River valley. Unpublished manuscript on file at the University of South Carolina, Columbia SC.

Turner, B.L., Kingston, J.D. and Milanich, J.T. (2005) Isotopic evidence of immigration linked to status during the Weeden Island and Suwannee Valley Periods in north Florida. *Southeastern Archaeology* 24(2), 121–36.

Wallis, N.J. (2007) Defining swift creek Interactions, Earthenware Variability at Ring Middens and Burial Mounds. *Southeastern Archaeology* 26(2), 212–31.

Waring, A.J. (1968a) The Southern Cult and Muskhogean Ceremonial, General Considerations. In *The Waring Papers. Papers of the Peabody Museum of Archaeology and Ethnology*, S. Williams (ed.) 58, 30–69. Harvard University, Cambridge MA.

Waring, A.J. (1968b) Some recent thoughts on the cult. In *The Waring Papers. Papers of the Peabody Museum of Archaeology and Ethnology*, S. Williams (ed.) 58, 87–93. Harvard University, Cambridge MA.

Waring, A.J. and Holder, P. (1945) A Prehistoric ceremonial complex in the Southeastern United States. *American Anthropologist* 47, 1–34.

Watson, P.J. (1990) Trend and tradition in Southeastern archaeology, *Southeastern Archaeology* 9(1), 43–54.

Willey, G.R. (1949) *Archaeology of the Florida Gulf Coast*. Smithsonian Miscellaneous Collections 113, US Government Printing Office, Washington DC.

Willey, G.R. and Woodbury, R. (1942) A chronological outline for the northwest Florida coast. *American Antiquity* 7(3), 232–52.

5

Effigy mounds and rock art of Midcontinental North America: shared iconography, shared stories

Bradley T. Lepper, Robert F. Boszhardt, James R. Duncan, and Carol Diaz-Granados

(This chapter was first published in North American Archaeologist *43(1), 2022, 3–48 and is republished here with permission. The original is accompanied by a comprehensive (22 pp) table of Effigy Mound groups with Lower World forms in apparent paired association with conical, oval or other vulvar mounds. For reasons of economy and space this is not reproduced here but is available at* https://doi.org.10.1177/0197693121996728*)*

The Great Serpent Mound (33AD1) is one of the largest geoglyphs in the world. Located in southern Ohio on a prominent bluff that projects into the Ohio Brush Creek valley (Figs 5.1 and 5.2) it consists of three distinct components: a long,

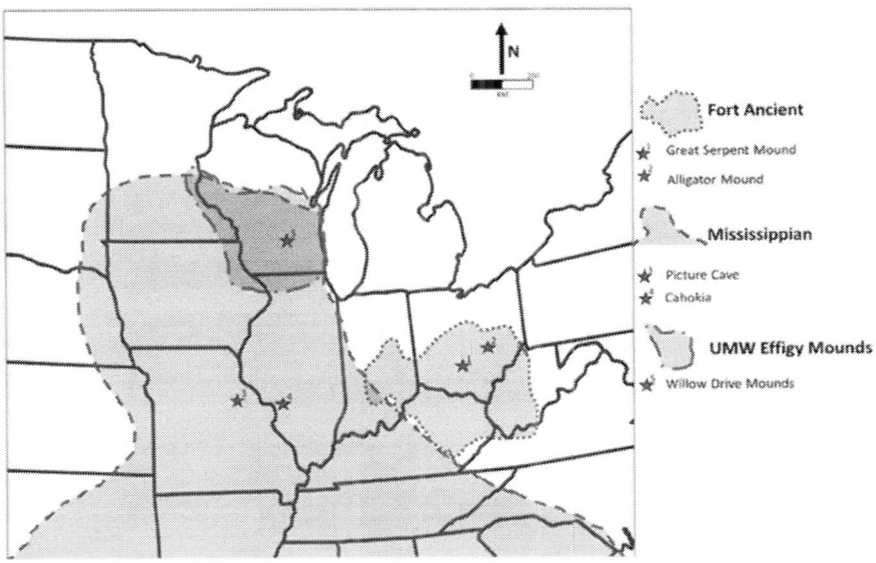

Fig. 5.1 The North American Midcontinent showing key sites and culture areas mentioned in the text.

serpentine embankment ending in a spiral, an oval enclosure, and a wishbone-shaped earthwork (Lepper *et al.* 2018 [this vol. Chapter 8]). The total length of this ensemble is 435 m. It was first brought to the attention of the scientific community in 1848 when Ephraim Squier and Edwin Davis published their map and description in the first volume of the Smithsonian Institution's *Contributions to Knowledge* series. They also surveyed the so-called "Alligator" Mound (33LI5) in central Ohio (Fig. 5.1). It is an effigy of a quadruped with a small, round head and a long, curled tail (Lepper and Frolking 2003).

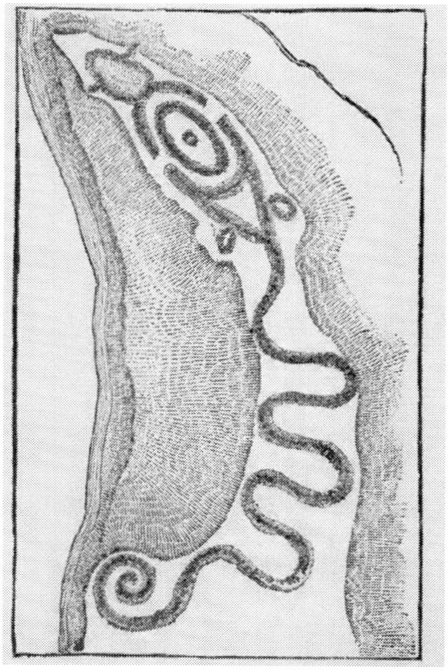

Fig. 5.2 The John P. MacLean (1885) map of Serpent Mound shows a wishbone-shaped earthwork between the oval enclosure (sometimes identified almost certainly incorrectly as an "egg") and the edge of the cliff. This earthwork was omitted from the earlier and more widely reproduced map by Ephraim Squier and Edwin Davis (1848), but it does appear on maps by Putman (n.d.), Holmes (1886), and Willoughby (1918). MacLean interpreted the wishbone as a separate effigy of a frog. We concur that it is a separate effigy, but we interpret it in the light of American Indian oral traditions as a depiction of First Woman engaged in sexual intercourse with the Great Serpent (see also Chapter 8). Courtesy, Ohio History Connection.

Squier and Davis (1848, 124–35) also devoted a separate section of their monograph to documenting several effigy mounds in Wisconsin, which they felt had "few features in common" with Ohio's effigies. Actually, the Upper Midwest (UMW) effigy mounds share a number of important characteristics with Ohio's Serpent and Alligator. Robert Birmingham and Leslie Eisenberg (2000, 111) observed that most effigy mound groups in the UMW are "located on high ground, bluffs, or terraces overlooking major rivers, streams, lakes, and large wetlands" and the same is true for Ohio's effigy mounds. Lynne Goldstein (1995, 106) noted that one of the most common features of Midwestern effigy mounds is the "fireplace or altar" made from stone and often occurring "in prominent parts of the effigy form, such as the heart or head area". At least one small stone mound was uncovered at the base of Alligator Mound on the left side of its body (Lepper and Frolking 2003); and both the Alligator and Serpent mounds had associated exterior stone altars exhibiting evidence of repeated fires (Lepper and Frolking 2003; Lepper 2020a).

In spite of these shared features, the conviction that the effigy mounds of Ohio and Wisconsin are unrelated persists among many archaeologists. Indeed, when Lepper (2018, 69) suggested that the effigy mounds of the UMW may have provided a source of inspiration for the builders of Ohio's Serpent Mound, William Romain and Edward Herrmann (2018, 85) responded that such a claim was comparable to "the arguments employed by ancient alien theorists".

We reject the implied assertion that the Effigy Mound societies of the UMW and the effigy mound builders of the Ohio Valley could not have influenced one another's cultural expressions. In this paper, we offer examples of specific sets of symbols expressed as effigy mounds or rock art glyphs that support the hypothesis that the Ohio effigies are representations of characters and stories that figure prominently in the oral traditions of the Siouan speaking groups that are historically associated with both regions. Although particular symbols may be expressions of a more widespread and ancient religious/cultural tradition (Power 2004, 177), we argue that the consistent co-occurrence of symbols, their modes of expression, media employed, and the historical circumstances associated with the timing of their appearance together indicate active interchange between the UMW and the Ohio Valley at a particular moment in time (Lepper 2020a).

Squier and Davis (1848, 125) observed that the UMW effigy mounds frequently occurred "in groups or ranges, sometimes, though not always, placed with apparent design in respect to each other". Lepper *et al.*'s (2018 [Chapter 8]) interpretation of Ohio's Great Serpent Mound suggests that it, too, is a grouping of three discrete mounds forming a coherent design, which they interpreted as a representation of a key episode in an important Siouan oral tradition (Lepper *et al.* 2018 [Chapter 8]). Reviewing the UMW effigy mounds in this light, Boszhardt identified the Willow Drive Mound Group in Madison, Wisconsin (Fig. 5.3) as consisting of earthworks reminiscent of those at Serpent Mound, possibly indicating

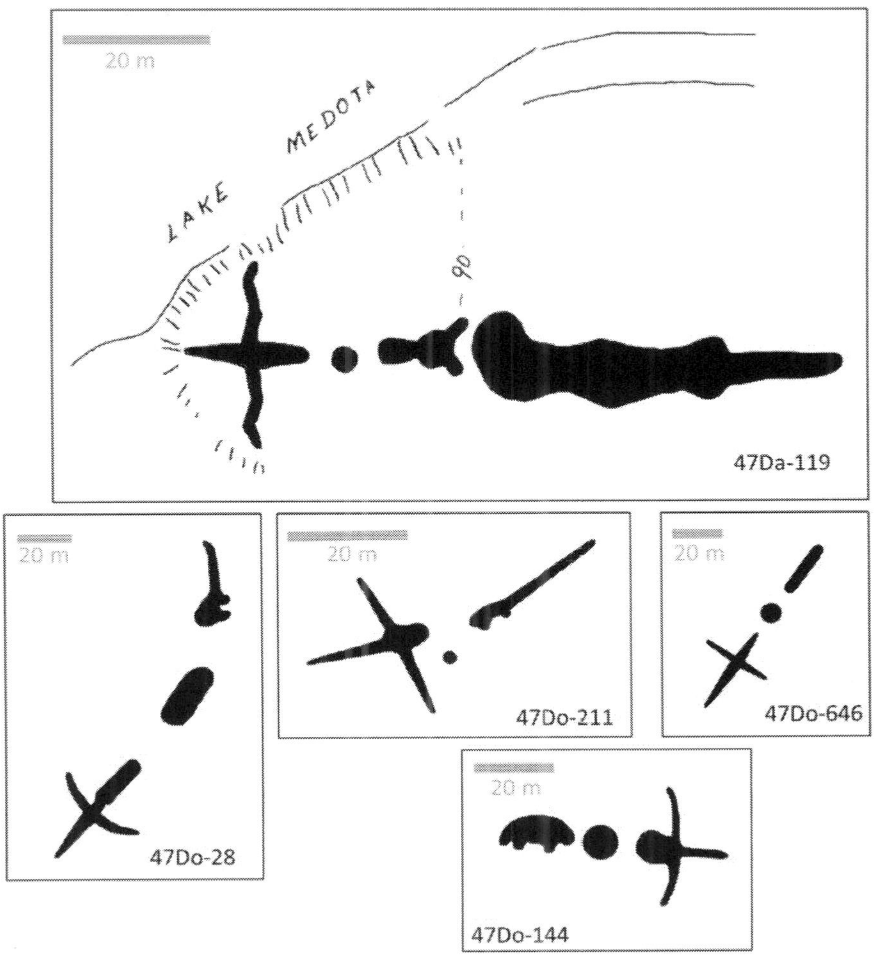

Fig. 5.3 Sketch of Willow Drive Mound Group in Madison, Wisconsin showing effigy arrangements that may correlate with Ohio's Great Serpent Mound complex and the oral traditions of the Great Serpent engaging in coitus with First Woman (top). Also, comparable examples of UMW effigy mound arrangements that suggest Lower World beings procreating, including conical/oval vulvar mounds behind bird-shaped mounds (bottom) (all redrawn by Boszhardt from maps in Rosebrough (2010). Scales are approximate).

that these might be telling a version of the same story. In addition, comparable motifs appear in rock art of this region, suggesting a widespread and consistent symbolic vocabulary used to tell the same corpus of stories.

Understanding the nature of the relationship between the mounds in these two regions requires, as a first step, accurately determining their respective ages. Although, there are relatively few radiocarbon dates for the thousands of UMW effigy mounds it is widely accepted that the majority were constructed during the Late Woodland period (*c.* AD 700–1150) (e.g., Birmingham and Rosebrough 2017, 154). On the other hand, the age of Serpent Mound is debated (see discussion below). Nevertheless, we argue here that iconic motifs shared among the effigy mounds of the Ohio Valley and the UMW, the parietal art of the Midcontinent, and imagery engraved on portable objects, along with the available radiocarbon dates, allow us to encompass all of these cultural expressions within the same relatively narrow window of time.

Effigy mounds of the Ohio river valley

Serpent Mound is the pre-eminent effigy mound in North America yet the age of its original construction is the subject of ongoing debate (Herrmann *et al.* 2014; Lepper 2018; 2020a; 2020b; Lepper *et al.* 2018 [Chapter 8]; 2019; Monaghan and Herrmann, 2019; Romain *et al.* 2017; Romain and Herrmann, 2018; Romain 2019). Attempts to obtain chronometric dates for the mound have, so far, yielded only *terminus post quem* dates, because none of the dated samples can be reliably linked to its original construction.

In 1991, Robert Fletcher *et al.* (1996) conducted limited excavations into Serpent Mound and obtained wood charcoal from different sections of undisturbed mound deposits, which yielded two identical AMS radiocarbon dates of 920±70 BP (Beta-55277/CAMS-3566 and Beta-55278/CAMS-3567).

The team interpreted these dates as evidence for the construction of Serpent Mound during the early Late Pre-contact period (Fletcher *et al.*,1996, 133) indicating a Fort Ancient cultural affiliation. Fletcher's team also recovered a small fragment of charcoal from a soil core, which yielded a date of 2920±55 BP (Beta-47212, ETH-8520). The depth of the sample would place it more than 60 cm beneath the projected original surface on which the mound was built (Fletcher *et al.* 1996, 132). It therefore likely represents a charcoal fragment displaced from the mound fill either by the coring operation or by bioturbation and therefore provides only a *terminus post quem* date.

In 2011, Herrmann *et al.* (2014, 119) collected 18 "continuous solid-earth cores" from various points along Serpent Mound from which they extracted small sediment samples for dating purposes. The samples included material from what they asserted was a buried A horizon as well as material incorporated into the mound fill. The resulting dates on "organic sediment" ranged from 2320±30 BP (Beta-337168) to 2170±30 BP (Beta-337163) for the supposed paleosol (2014, 119). Samples from the mound fill yielded a similar range of from 2530±80 BP (Beta-337136) to 2180±30 BP (Beta-337167) (2014, 119).

Based on these data, Herrmann's *et al.* team (2014, 124) concluded that Serpent Mound was "initially constructed 2,300 years ago during the Early Woodland (Adena) period". In a series of responses to these claims, Lepper and various colleagues have disputed the conclusion that the Early Woodland dates reported provide an accurate determination of the age of Serpent Mound (Lepper 2018; 2020a; 2020b; Lepper *et al.* 2018 [Chapter 8]; 2019). We argue, as Herrmann *et al.* (2014, 121) originally acknowledged, the radiocarbon dates they obtained from Serpent Mound can demonstrate only that "the mound could have been constructed any time *after* 300 BC" (emphasis added).

Another set of dates for the construction of Serpent Mound was obtained during the 2017 removal of CCC-era stone stairs that extended over the tail of Serpent Mound (Pickard *et al.* 2018; Lepper *et al.* 2019). The removal of the steps exposed what Pickard *et al.* interpreted as intact mound strata from which they obtained two AMS radiocarbon dates on two fragments of oak charcoal: 1263±22 BP (AA-110452) and 1300±30 BP (Beta-473077) as well as a radiocarbon date on soil humates of 720±30 BP (Beta-470763). The dates on particulate wood charcoal, which overlap at one standard deviation, can provide only a maximum age estimate for the mound. The charcoal may be from old wood or it may have come from Late Woodland features that were inadvertently disturbed by the Fort Ancient inhabitants of the site and incorporated into the mound fill. The soil humates date is more problematic (Lepper 2020b), but it does provide a *terminus ante quem* date for the construction of Serpent Mound.

Ohio's other definite effigy mound, Alligator Mound, long was thought to be a Hopewell culture effigy due to its proximity to the Newark Earthworks. Excavations undertaken in 1999 resulted in the recovery of wood charcoal embedded in the floor of the mound, which yielded radiocarbon dates that averaged between AD 1170 and 1270 (Beta-134236, Beta-134237) (Lepper and Frolking 2003, 158). This established that the Alligator was constructed by the Fort Ancient culture during the Late Pre-contact period; and Lepper and Frolking (2003, 159) suggested that it represented an underwater panther similar to the long-tailed quadruped mounds of the UMW.

There is a stone serpent effigy, or petroform, along the Big Sandy River in eastern Kentucky that shares features with Ohio's Serpent Mound (Sanders 1991, 277). The Stone Serpent Mound (15Bd6) is made entirely from sandstone cobbles and has a "well-defined serpent outline" (Sanders 1991, 277). It is 191.4 m long and is 0.9 m high at its highest point. A short distance to the east of the eastern end of the serpent there is a "semicircular ring of stone, 5.2 m in diameter and 0.5 m in height" (Sanders 1991, 274), which is similar to the oval earthwork at Serpent Mound (Sanders 1991, 277). Test excavations at the Stone Serpent Mound yielded neither diagnostic artifacts nor dateable materials. It is, however, similar to the Kern Effigy (33WA372), a smaller petroform serpent effigy along the Little Miami River in southwestern Ohio, which has been reliably dated to *c.* AD 1200 and attributed to the Fort Ancient culture (White 1986). Therefore, the Kern Effigy provides corroborative evidence for the importance of serpent iconography as well as the existence of effigy mounds in the Ohio Valley during the Late Pre-contact period. The Kentucky Stone Serpent Mound, based on its similarities to both Ohio's Serpent Mound and the Kern Effigy, offers additional support for these conclusions.

The iconography of effigy mounds

In the absence of an undisputed chronometric age for Serpent Mound, Lepper and colleagues (Lepper 2018; 2020a; Lepper *et al.* 2018 [Chapter 8]; 2019) have sought to assign an age to the effigy through a thematic and stylistic analysis. According to Meyer Schapiro (1953), style is derived from icons/symbols that are repeated in the same form, manner, and expression across time and space. Icons that have been associated with specific time periods through radiocarbon dating, dendrochronology, or other widely accepted chronometric dating techniques, can be used to date similar motifs and symbols at other sites. This method has been used successfully by many researchers including Deetz (1965), Brown (1989; 2007; 2011), Conkey and Hastorf (1990), Diaz-Granados and Duncan (2000), Diaz-Granados (2015), Duncan (2015) and others. Therefore, this method provides an alternate line of evidence for placing Serpent Mound in its cultural and temporal context.

During the Early and Middle Woodland Periods, serpent imagery is uncommon; and when serpents are depicted, they tend to be relatively naturalistic representations (Lepper 2018: 65–6; Lepper *et al.* 2018 [Chapter 8], 442; but see Carr and McCord, 2013, 13–28 for examples of non-naturalistic Middle Woodland serpents). In contrast, during the Mississippian Period, serpent imagery became more common, more elaborate, and expressed in an increasing variety of media (e.g., Griffin 1952, 236; Drooker 1997, 326; Phillips and Brown 1978, 137–9; Diaz-Granados and Duncan 2004b, 156; Reilly 2011, 123–30). Moreover, Mississippian depictions of serpents included "often-bizarre configurations of dragon-like creatures whose images invoke mystery and hidden knowledge" (Reilly and Garber 2007, 2). For example, a Stirling phase flint clay statuette, the Birger Figurine, depicts a snake with a felid head (Mueller and Fritz 2016, 122). Another elaborate image of the Great Serpent (or Underwater Spirit) is a shell engraving of a winged being with a combination of cervid, avian, and serpentine parts including a long serpentine tail ending in a rattlesnake's rattle (Duncan 2015, 232). Both are from Cahokia and date to around AD 1050.

Lepper *et al.* (2018) proposed that the iconic imagery of Serpent Mound, as depicted in the James P. MacLean map (Fig. 5.2), invoked the same "mystery and hidden knowledge", which it shared with contemporary pictographs on the walls of Picture Cave in Missouri (Diaz-Granados *et al.* 2001; Duncan *et al.* 2015, 125–32). Ephraim Squier and Edwin Davis's 1848 map of Serpent Mound has been the accepted representation of the serpent for more than a century, but there are reasons for doubting its accuracy.

Lepper *et al.* (2018, 440–1) argued that Squier and Davis's map and Frederic Putnam's (1890) restoration of Serpent Mound were influenced by their interpretation of the mound as a serpent with an egg in its mouth and so ignored the therefore enigmatic wishbone-shaped mound that partially encompassed the "egg". This design element was, however, independently documented by Putnam himself (e.g., American Antiquarian Society 1884, 11), as well as by MacLean (1885), whose surveys pre-dated Putnam's restorations, William H. Holmes (1886), and Charles Willoughby (1918; 1919).

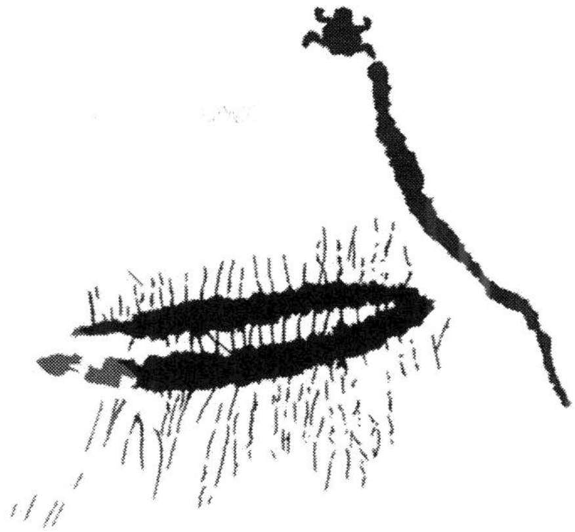

Fig. 5.4 Drawing of a portion of Panel 3 from Picture Cave, Missouri, showing the tableau comprised of three glyphs that correspond to the three principal elements of Serpent Mound as mapped by MacLean: the Great Serpent (Glyph 67), First Woman (Glyph 64), and the large oval that has been interpreted as a the vulva of First Woman (Glyph 59) (Diaz-Granados *et al.* 2015). We interpret these three images as a tableau both because of their proximity to one another, but also because they appear to have been painted with the same pigment and application technique (drawing by Peter Lepper).

It was not until Lepper *et al.* (2018) recognized this same set of motifs at Picture Cave that they concluded that MacLean's, Putnam's, Holmes's, and Willoughby's maps should be taken seriously. Specifically, they argued that the three design elements comprising the Serpent Mound ensemble, the serpent, oval, and wishbone-shaped mound, corresponded to three associated motifs on Panel 3 at Picture Cave, which Duncan and Diaz-Granados previously had identified as a stylized First Woman, her vulva, and the Great Serpent (Fig. 5.4; compare with Fig. 5.2). Lepper *et al.* (2018, 446–7) argued that this tableau depicted the pivotal moment of the Dhegihan Sioux genesis story. The Kentucky Stone Serpent, with its associated ring of stones, may be another symbolic depiction of the Great Serpent and the vulva of First Woman.

The use of these specific motifs and the ways they are brought together in varying but recognizably similar tableaus, are established features of the Braden art tradition, which arose near the confluence of the Missouri and Mississippi rivers during the Terminal Late Woodland (or Emergent Mississippian) Period (Brown 2007; 2011). The Braden art style is characterized by the depiction of spirit beings in a relatively naturalistic, and often kinetic, format – most often, but not always, in profile and usually with other diagnostic details, such as fine line graphic depictions of ritual paraphernalia.

The Great Serpent and the Braden art tradition

Sometime between AD 750 and AD 950 a religious re-awakening began in the lower Missouri River valley. This occurred among rapidly developing Late Woodland societies roughly contemporaneous with the Mature period of effigy mound construction in the UMW (see below). Siouan linguistic groups appear to have been at the center of this revival, but religious themes shared by Siouan speaking societies also are found among some of their neighbors, especially Caddoan speakers (Bowers 1950, 8–22, 1992, 47–50; Fletcher and La Flesche 1992, 5–8; Parks 1991 Vol. 3, 90–101).

Much of humanity shares a common concern: what happens after death? The Dhegihan Sioux linguistic groups, the builders of Cahokia, formulated their answer long before they constructed the largest mound center in North America. It involved three premises: 1) all matter shared an animating or spirit force originating from a mysterious sacred, eternal being; 2) this force could not be destroyed and could migrate from one entity to another; 3) some entities became particular repositories for this force, possessing more of it than others.

For the Dhegiha, this spirit force came to human beings from two ancestral, supernatural parents, First Man and First Woman. The Dhegihan people constructed dwellings for these spirits, which could be made by simply sharing one's body with the spirit at a feast, making a small bundle for the spirit to live in, or by purifying and consecrating a natural place for the spirit. A special dwelling or shrine also could be built for the spirit, such as a great mound of earth, in which the spirit could dwell and be closer to its realm. But the size was not as important as was the degree of respect it showed for the spirit inhabiting the shrine. One thing that First Man's and First Woman's spirits most enjoyed was the telling of stories about their adventures and prowess. This was the ultimate form of respect – sharing oral traditions. Among these stories, none were more important than those which told how First Woman became the source for the rebirth of First Man and his descendants, the Dhegihan Sioux. This is the "Making of the Earth" rite mentioned by Alice Fletcher and Francis La Flesche (1992) and reconstructed by Duncan from oral traditions shared with him by Osage elders and recorded in various ethnographies (e.g., Bowers 1950; 1992) and from the sequence of elaborate panels of pictographs at Picture Cave (Duncan 2015, 209–240).

The earliest expression of the Braden art tradition is found on the walls of Picture Cave in eastern Missouri (Fig. 5.1). Beginning about AD 850 and culminating around AD 1025, a complex storyboard of paintings and drawings, graphic expressions of elaborate oral traditions, transformed this cave into a shrine, a sacred focal point for telling the stories of First Man, First Woman, the Great Serpent, and the creation of all life on the Earth (Diaz-Granados *et al.* 2015, 47–56, 106).

The genesis traditions of the Siouan speakers and their neighbors guaranteed not only their own rebirth, but the rebirth of all good things, including the Sun and Morning Star through First Woman's powers of regeneration. This ability was transferred to First Woman by the Great Serpent through sexual intercourse. It was a transformational event that is at the heart of the Making of the Earth Rite – a ceremony of world renewal (Fletcher and La Flesche 1992, 171).

The Making of the Earth Rite and the Great Serpent Mound

The Making of the Earth Rite begins with a stick ball game between the Water Spirits of the Lower World and First Man and his followers from the Upper World. The Water Spirits win, and First Man is decapitated. His spirit (the Sun) descends beneath the western horizon into the Lower World. First Woman, the Earth, has lost her husband's shining face. Without his presence she grows old and barren and all living things wither and die. Her two grandsons, The Stone and The Dark Wolf come to their Grandmother's aid. She feeds them and gives them powerful weapons. She paints and dresses her grandsons for war, and they descend into the lower worlds. The two grandsons attack and overcome the Underwater Spirits with the help of their gifted weapons. They confront the chief of the Underwater Spirits, the Great Serpent, and wound him with their arrows.

After the epic battle, The Dark Wolf and The Stone gather the trophies that attest to their bravery and prowess in battle. Among these are the Great Serpent himself as a captive. He is feasted and adopted by First Woman. After the feast, the most important moment arrives, the "Walking with the Buffalo" rite. First Woman accepts the Great Serpent into her bed, and they engage in sexual intercourse. The Great Serpent allows his power of resurrection to flow into First Woman's body. She becomes a sacred vessel containing his power to resurrect. This culminating event is an integral part of many North American Indian oral traditions and it is recorded in a variety of media across the midcontinent, including the pictographs of Picture Cave and at Serpent Mound (Figs 5.2 and 5.4).

Interconnected by the great rivers, the Missouri, the Mississippi and the Ohio, the many Siouan speaking groups employed earth, First Woman's body, to construct memorials, earthen mounds of many shapes, including the Great Serpent, to remind them of First Woman's powers of rebirth (Griffin 1960, 809–65; Morse and Morse 1983, 233; Lepper *et al.* 2018 [Chapter 8]). But these sacred places did not just commemorate how First Woman acquired her powers; they were the focus of ceremonies intended "to insure the continuance of that which had been created" (Fletcher and La Flesche 1992, 171; see also Birmingham 2010, 202).

Effigy mounds of the Upper Midwest

Between *c.* AD 700 and 1150, Native people constructed more than 3000 effigy mounds across that portion of the UMW lying between southern Lake Michigan and the upper Mississippi River valley (Fig. 5.1; Birmingham and Rosebrough 2017, 118). This area conforms to present day southern Wisconsin, and contiguous portions of northern Illinois, northeast Iowa, and southeastern Minnesota.

Due to their distinctive shapes, southern Wisconsin's effigy mounds have been studied for nearly 200 years, beginning with surveys undertaken prior to statehood (e.g., Taylor 1838; Squier and Davis 1848, 124–7). Increase Lapham (1855) conducted the first systematic survey of "imitative" mounds for his classic *Antiquities of Wisconsin*. As of the first decade of the 21st century, the Wisconsin Historical Society had documented over 3200 animal-shaped earthen mounds that were constructed in over 1000 locations in the UMW (Birmingham 2010, 6). Since then, LiDAR studies have identified nearly 100 more in just two medium sized Driftless Area valleys (e.g., Boszhardt *et al.* 2018).

The UMW effigies are dominated by varieties of birds (e.g., raptors and long-necked geese), mammals (e.g., bears and deer), long-tailed quadrupeds, and some serpents. The long-tailed quadrupeds historically have been identified as panthers, turtles, or lizards though they are now referred to as water spirits or water panthers based on Ho-Chunk and Menominee beliefs respectively (Birmingham 2010; Rosebrough 2010; Birmingham and Rosebrough 2017). These reflect a tripartite cosmology with an Upper World (sky), Middle World (land) and Lower World (caves and water) (Birmingham and Rosebrough 2017, 128–39); and the mounds were built in conjunction with regional world renewal ceremonies (Birmingham 2010; Birmingham and Rosebrough 2017).

Effigy mound shapes vary across the UMW heartland with bears (quadrupeds lacking tails) most common in the rugged southwestern region and long-tailed quadrupeds (water spirits) in the glaciated east. Rosebrough (2010) undertook a comprehensive analysis of effigy mound form distributions and associated Late Woodland ceramics, identifying nearly 25 sub-regions, each interpreted as a social landscape. In her study, she identified only three definite serpent effigies (Fig. 5.5, top) on the basis of their clearly defined heads, sinuous bodies, and tapering or rattle tails (Rosebrough 2010, 369, fig. 8.10). She also noted that "forked linears" (linears with bifurcated ends) also have been identified as snakes perhaps with horns or antlers (2010, 366, fig. 8.2). Some of these linear mounds have conical heads, a style sometimes referred to as club or tadpole (Rosebrough 2010, 356). There also are mounds that appear to represent snakes in the act of transforming to water spirits or water panthers. For example, at the Draves effigy mound site in southeastern Wisconsin, a longtailed water spirit mound has a wavy serpentine body (Fig. 5.5).

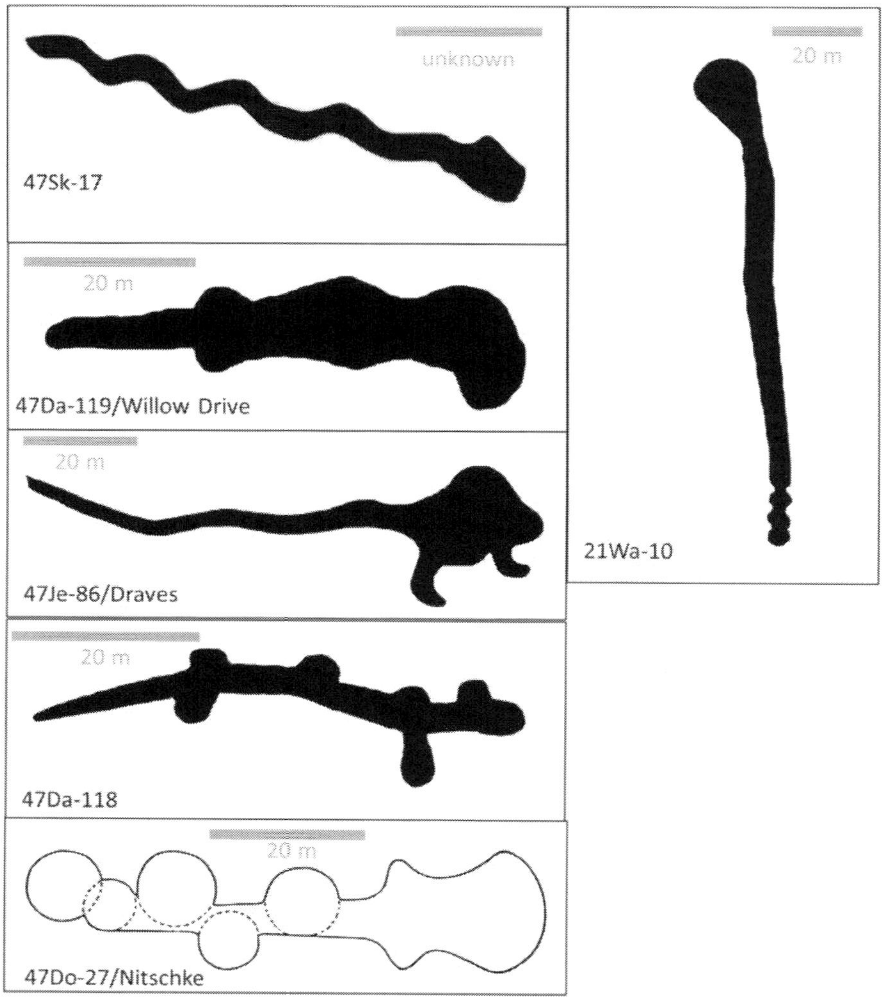

Fig. 5.5 Examples of UMW serpent effigy mounds and quadrupeds with undulating bodies (redrawn by Boszhardt from maps in Rosebrough (2010). Scales are approximate).

There are indigenous stories that shed light on the various shapes of serpentine mounds, such as the Ho-Chunk story *The Woman Who Married a Snake*, in which Black Dog dives into the river, but the people watching do not see him come back up. "They were about to give him up for drowned, when unexpectedly, the water began to roar like a waterfall and to swirl. Soon he emerged from the depths, only now he had horns, four legs, and a body like that of a snake" (Dieterle, n.d.). Furthermore, some Ho-Chunk creation stories (e.g., Radin 1965, 120, 164) tell of Earthmaker stabilizing a spinning primordial world by piercing four corners with snakes (or water spirits), which led Robert Hall (1993, 44) to interpret linear mounds as abstract snake effigies.

The Late Woodland stage in southern Wisconsin has been divided into three periods based on nearly 100 radiocarbon dates from mounds and associated habitation sites (Stoltman and Boszhardt 2019; Stoltman and Christensen 2000). The Initial period (AD 500–700) represents the transition from Middle to Late Woodland ceramic styles and no effigy mounds are known to have been built during this period.

The Mature period (AD 700–1050) represents the climax of effigy mound construction. Due to increasing populations and evidence for landscape packing over time, it is possible that most of the numerous interior effigy mounds were constructed between *c.* AD 900–1050 (Theler and Boszhardt 2006).

The Final period (AD 1050–1150) is marked by interactions with southern groups. Beginning at AD 1050 and coinciding with Cahokia's "Big Bang", Middle Mississippian colonists established settlements along the upper Mississippi River in western Wisconsin (Pauketat *et al.* 2015; Boszhardt and Benden 2017).

After AD 1100, in conjunction with Cahokia's Stirling phase, a second wave of Middle Mississippian contact ("Ramey horizon") swept over and beyond the effigy mound region to northern Wisconsin, central Minnesota and northwestern Iowa (Fig. 5.1). This included the construction of palisaded villages such as Aztalan, Fred Edwards, and Hartley Fort. Within these remote, defensive settlements, hybridization occurred that blended Late Woodland and Middle Mississippian themes and material culture; notably ceramics. Thus, during the Final period of effigy mound building in the UMW, local societies were interacting with external groups over distances of hundreds of kilometers. This period overlaps the construction of Ohio's Serpent Mound, Alligator Mound, and the creation of the parietal art of Picture Cave in Missouri (Lepper *et al.* 2018 [Chapter 8]). We propose that this confluence of events is not coincidental.

The Making of the Earth Rite and the Willow Drive Mounds

One of the densest concentrations of UMW effigy mounds is situated along the chain of glacial lakes in south-central Wisconsin where the city of Madison now exists. Birmingham (2010) considers this to be the center of the Effigy Mound world and documented over 1200 mounds along the five lakes. One of the groups along the south shore of Lake Mendota is the Willow Drive Mounds (Fig. 5.1). This group was built on a low peninsula with a marsh and minor creek to the west

(Boszhardt 2014). It originally consisted of four mounds arranged in an east–west linear configuration.

This group was first mapped by Theodore Lewis in 1888 (Fig. 5.3, top) who recorded a "goose" mound at the west end, the head of which pointed to the marsh. The bird's body was approximately 30 m long with a wingspan of 35 m. A small, 6–7 m diameter, conical mound was situated east of the bird's tail.

Just beyond the conical mound was an unusual wishbone-shaped effigy. This 20–25 m long mound consisted of a slightly flared stem coming out of a round center from which two prongs opened eastward. The prongs partially wrapped around the head of an odd, undulating effigy that was nearly 50 m long.

In 2014, Boszhardt proposed that the Willow Drive Mound Group might represent an undulating serpent/panther impregnating a woman (the wishbone-shaped effigy) who thereby produced a conical egg, which hatched into the bird (Boszhardt 2014). Independently, Lepper *et al.* (2018) proposed a strikingly similar interpretation of the elements comprising Ohio's Great Serpent Mound based on iconographic comparisons to Mississippian pictographs at Picture Cave in Missouri and Dhegihan Sioux oral traditions. These insights suggest an alternative interpretation of the Willow Drive Mound Group. As at Serpent Mound, the wishbone-shaped effigy represents First Woman being impregnated by the Great Serpent, depicted here as an undulating serpent/panther. The conical mound near the head of First Woman may be the Willow Drive version of Serpent Mound's "egg", which Lepper (2020a) suggested served as a portal connecting this world with the Lower World. These two mound groups, separated by approximately 800 km, might therefore be telling versions of the Making of the Earth, or a closely related genesis story.

Related iconography at other UMW effigy mound groups

We have identified other potential examples of UMW effigy mound groups that include some of the same *dramatis personae* in similar arrangements, which corroborate the idea that effigy mounds in both of these regions may be embodiments of the same corpus of oral traditions (Fig. 5.3, bottom half). Indeed, nearly 300 UMW effigy mound groups include Lower World forms paired with conicals or ovals suggesting, per Hall (1979, 262), Lower World spirit beings in the act of procreation (Fig. 5.6).

At the Nitschke group (47Do-27) in eastern Wisconsin there is a long-tailed quadruped (Mound 10) upon which were added a series of small conical mounds resulting in a sinuous body (McKern 1930, 501–6) (Fig. 5.5, bottom). In addition, a few effigy mound groups include double oval embankments (e.g. 47Wn-12), that strongly resemble the oval at the head of Ohio's Great Serpent (Fig. 5.6, top; compare with Fig. 5.2).

Contemporaneous rock art tells the same stories

Although the imagery of effigy mounds and rock art often have been characterized as naturalistic, Sigfried Giedion (1962, 18) has asserted that indigenous art "is never naturalistic". Jill Cook made the same point:

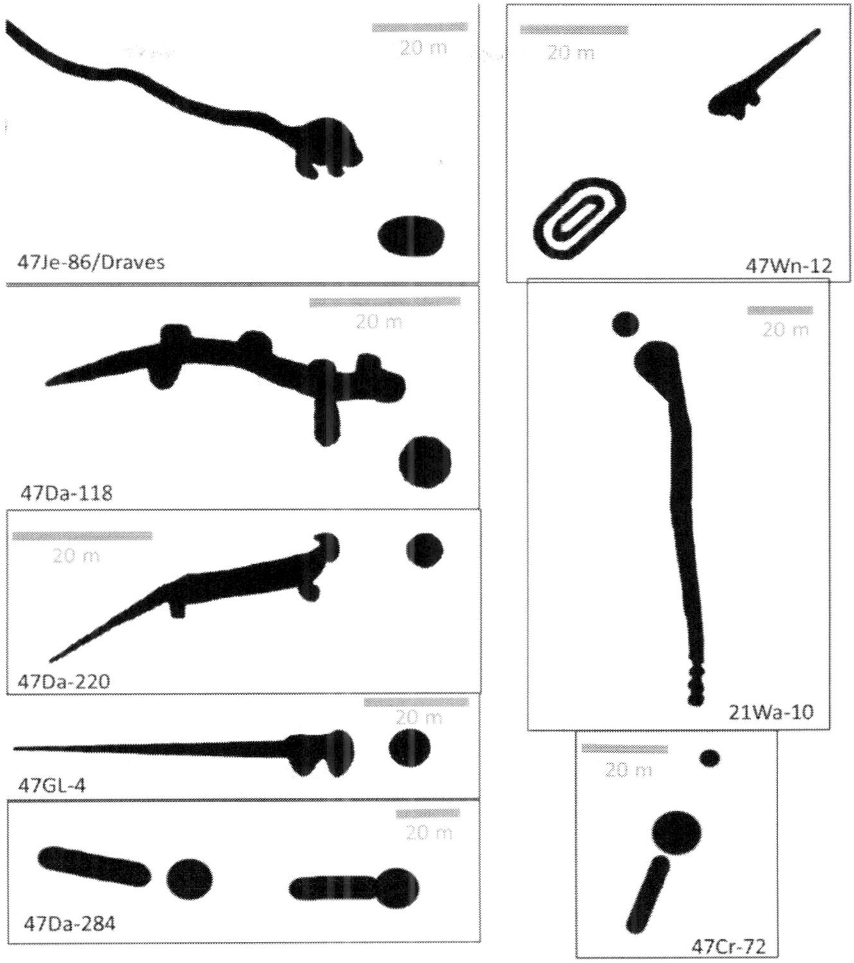

Fig. 5.6 Examples of UMW effigy mound pairings of Lower World beings with conical/oval mounds suggesting procreation following Hall's (1979; 1997) association of Earth Diver stories with world renewal (all redrawn from maps in Rosebrough's (2010) dissertation. Scales are approximate. See Table 1 in the original publication of this paper (Lepper *et al.* 2022) at https://doi.org.10.1177/0197693121996728 for a comprehensive list of such mound pairings.

> ... realism was not the goal. The artists were simplifying, exaggerating and distorting to engage the mind of the viewer. Abstraction, caricature, metaphor, grouping, contrast, balance and isolation are all used to intrigue and stimulate the viewer's attention to a virtual reality with meaningful implications for the real lifestyle. (Cook 2013, 17)

Moreover, forms used to represent spiritual beings are, of necessity, abstractions; and creating images of that which is inexpressible, "raised the power of the representation to a higher level of potency, transforming it into a magical symbol" (Giedion 1962, 24). Furthermore, the media used in creating this imagery, whether mounded earth or markings on stone, partially restricted the artist to relying on simple outlines to convey their message (Duncan and Diaz-Granados 2018, 35). Regardless of the reasons for the iconic, abstract imagery, the use of same symbolism and configurations of motifs in the effigy mounds and in the petroglyphs and pictographs, indicate a shared symbolic vocabulary; and suggest that, despite the different media, the same or closely-related stories were being told.

Related iconography in the rock art of the Upper Midwest

Rock art imagery in the UMW includes many of the same motifs depicted in the Central Midwest and in the effigy mounds, including examples of apparent procreation symbolism that may relate to genesis stories featuring the Great Serpent and First Woman. Images of Lower World snakes or long-tailed quadrupeds are relatively rare in UMW area rock art. Lewis (2006, 224–5) recorded four snakes at Carvers Cave (21Ra-27) and another eight at La Moille Cave (21Wn-1) both along the Mississippi River in eastern Minnesota, some of which had distinct rattles on their tails (Winchell 1911, 560–2 and pls ii–iv). La Moille also had several long-tailed quadrupeds, one with a spiral tail, in addition to raptors, humans, and abstract symbols, including a wishbone-shaped glyph (Fig. 5.7) suggestive of the wishbone-shaped mounds we interpret as images of First Woman.

In 1929, W.C. McKern of the Milwaukee Public Museum drew and photographed a series of petroglyphs at Samuel's Cave (47Lc-5) near La Crosse, Wisconsin (Boszhardt 1995, appendix B). The drawings include a snake-like petroglyph that angles upward and connects to an oval, which is superimposed over a U-shaped crescent (Fig. 5.7).

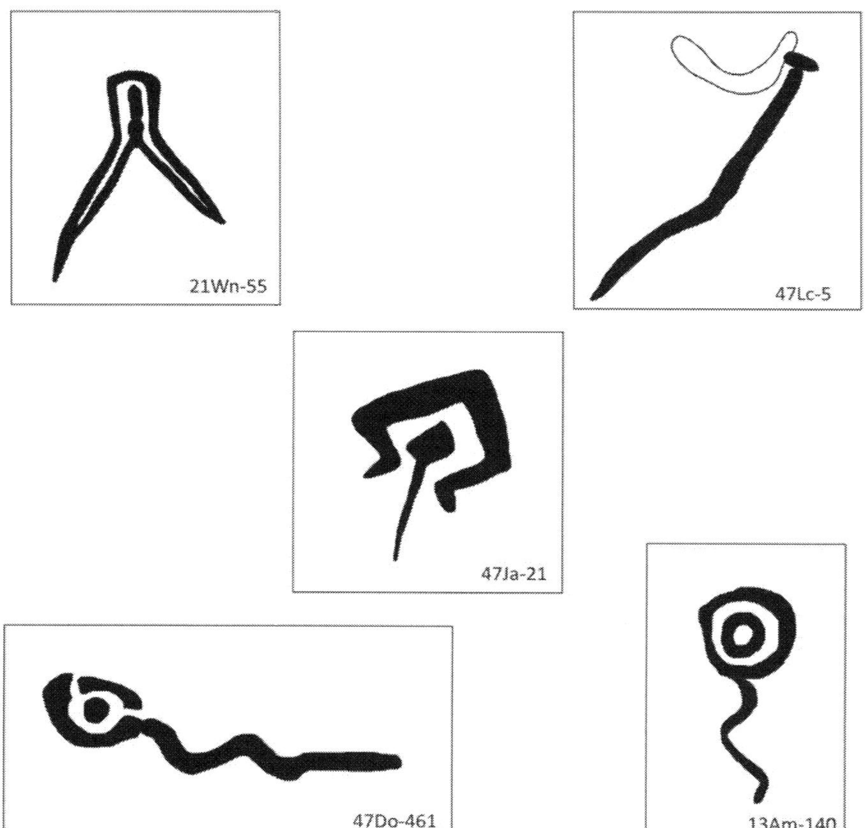

Fig. 5.7 UMW rock art images of vulvar forms including one with a wishbone shape from La Moille Rockshelter (21WN-55) and several examples with serpentine associations, suggesting procreation (all redrawn by Boszhardt from published images. Not to scale).

Jack Steinbring and Franklin Farvour (1987) recorded an ogee-like concentric circle within an oblique rectangle combination at the Hensler petroglyph site (47Do–461) in eastern Wisconsin (Face 1, Glyph 16). Goldstein (1983, 181) believed this glyph was connected to a snake glyph. Steinbring and Farvour (1987, 407–8) dismissed this snake, but the undulating glyph is clearly visible in Steinbring's published photographs of Glyph 16 (Fig. 5.7, lower left). The ogee motif is widespread in Mississippian iconography (Phillips and Brown, 1978: Plate 16). It is associated with serpents and represents a portal between levels of the Mississippian cosmos (Reilly, 2004: 130–131).

In addition to the serpent on Face 1 at Hensler, a petroglyph composition on Face 3 (Fig. 5.8) has elements that likely reference First Man, First Woman and the Great Serpent. At one end of this panel, a serpent appears to emerge from a relatively large circle and is adjacent to a moon-like crescent. This serpent's head points past a set of four wavy perpendicular lines and a spiral; a set that may conform to the Ho-Chunk creation story of Earthmaker using snakes to hold down a spinning world. The Hensler spiral is strongly reminiscent of the tail of Ohio's Great Serpent Mound and may be a *pars pro toto* representation of the Great Serpent.

Hensler's Face 3 panel continues to a set of three anthropomorphic glyphs. The one nearest the spiral has a line emerging from the midsection, perhaps indicating a penis, turned downward toward a second female figure with a circle/ vulva between her legs. We suggest these figures represent the Great Serpent in human form and First Woman; and the two sets of serpent-and-circle glyphs at this site bear a strong resemblance to the numerous pairings of Lower World effigies and conical mounds in the UMW.

Among UMW rock art motifs are various styles of vulva forms that include diamonds and ovals with central dots or vertical lines. (e.g., Boszhardt 2003, 37; Schrab and Boszhardt 2016; Baldner 2020, 52–5 and 58). Some vulvas have a long vertical line extending below them (Fig. 5.7) and resemble so-called "tadpole" or aligned linear-conical/oval mounds. These may be more abstract representations of stories like the Great Serpent impregnating First Woman and are comparable to concentric vulvas coupled with serpent or phallic motifs observed in Missouri rock art (Diaz-Granados and Duncan 2004b, 156; Edging and Ahler 2004, 100–2).

Along the upper Iowa River, a rock fall known as Sacred Rock (13Am-140) was carved with a double oval over a sinuous curved line (Baldner 2017, 78–80; 2020, 60–1; Stanley 2004, 402). This glyph suggests a snake impregnating a vulva (a *pars pro toto* representation of First Woman) and Baldner (2020, 60) has compared it

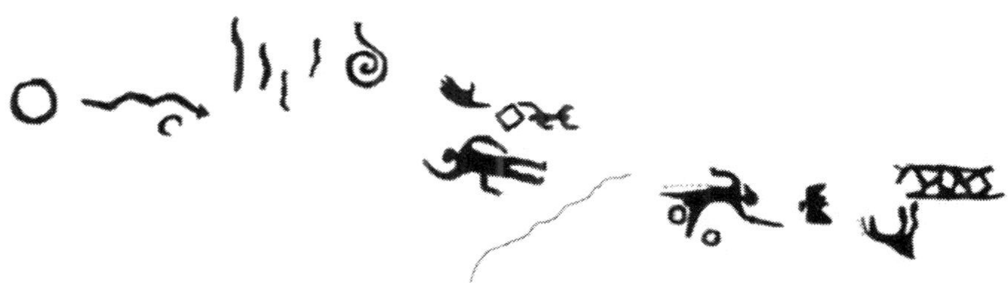

Fig. 5.8 Petroglyph panel on Face 3 of the Hensler site in southeast Wisconsin showing figures that may correlate with versions of the First Woman, First Man, and Great Serpent stories. Note the glyph that resembles the spiral tail of Serpent Mound and the anthropomorph on the right with a circular figure between its legs, which is reminiscent of the wishbone-shaped mound associated with the oval earthwork at Serpent Mound (redrawn by Boszhardt from Steinbring and Farvour (1987, fig. 6).

to Ohio's Great Serpent Mound as well as to copper snake pendants. The copper serpents are rare, but widespread at Late Pre-contact and protohistoric Oneota sites (Benn 1989, 250; Pozza 2019; Baldner 2020, 60). Several are recorded from the Fort Ancient site of Madisonville in Ohio (Drooker 1997) and some of these bear a marked resemblance to Serpent Mound (Lepper 2018, 66).

Corroborative iconography in the rock art of Missouri

In addition to the extensive series of pictographs from Picture Cave, which provided a key to the interpretation of the components of Serpent Mound (Lepper *et al.* 2018 [Chapter 8]), there are a number of other rock art sites in Missouri with related imagery. The Wallen Creek Petroglyph site (Fig. 5.9) depicts a double headed, meandering serpent associated with a wishbone-shaped anthropomorphic figure. A graphic phallus and a "pit" representing First Woman's vulva are in a position indicating coitus, which resulted in the transferal of powers, including those of procreation, rebirth, and resurrection. This depiction of coitus between the Great Serpent and First Woman, takes place in the Lower World at night and, as with the Picture Cave panel, Serpent Mound, and the Willow Drive Mound Group, represents First Woman and the Great Serpent engaged in the transfer of power that will allow her to resurrect the Sun so that it can reappear in the daytime sky (Diaz-Granados *et al.* 2018).

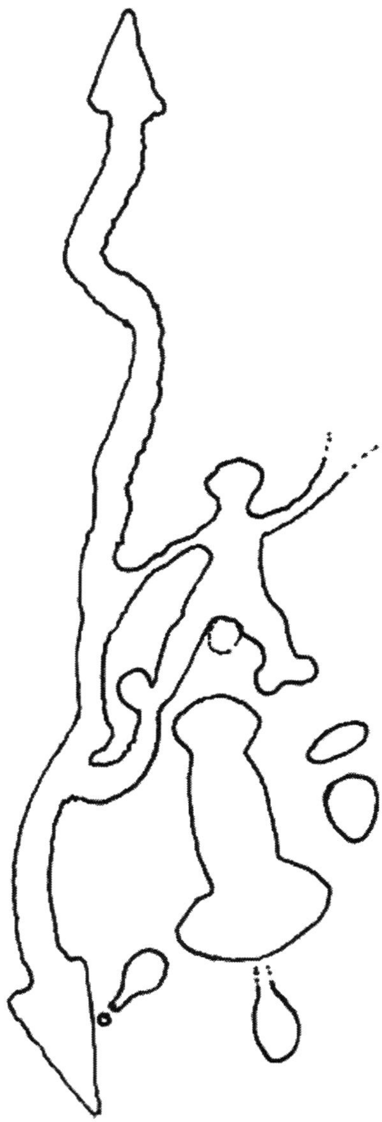

Fig. 5.9 Drawing of the Wallen Creek petroglyph by Jim Duncan. A graphic depiction of First Woman engaged in coitus with the Great Serpent. As with the Picture Cave panel (Fig. 5.5), Serpent Mound (Fig. 5.2), and the Willow Drive Mound Group (Fig. 5.4), it represents the moment when she acquired the power to resurrect the Sun and create all life on Earth.

The Three Hills Creek petroglyph site in southeastern Missouri includes at least two groupings of vulvar motifs (Fig. 5.10). One of these is associated with a wishbone-shaped motif, which here may represent a phallus (Fig. 5.10, right); however, it could encompass multiple meanings. We interpret both panels of glyphs as *pars pro toto* representations of coitus between First Woman and the Great Serpent. These motifs are essential

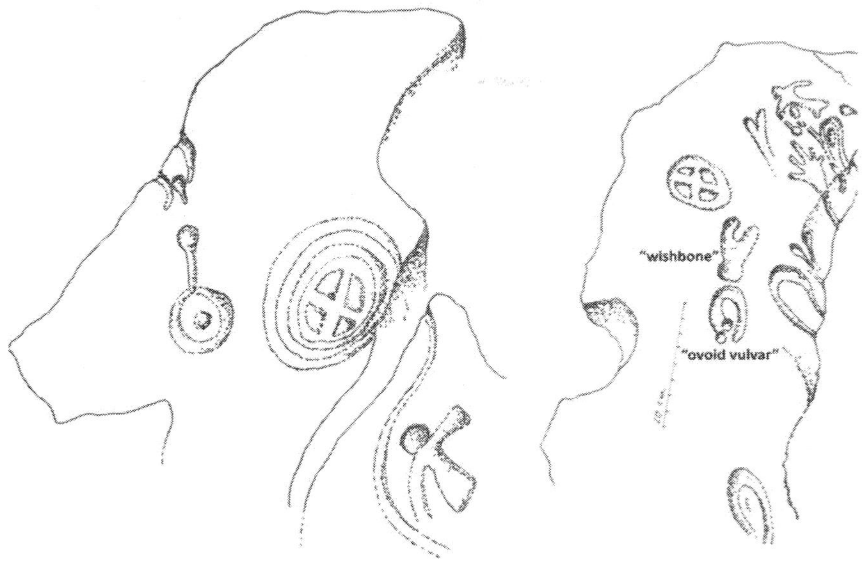

Fig. 5.10 Drawings of two portions of the Three Hills Creek petroglyph by Jim Duncan depicting coitus (*pars pro toto*) between First Woman and the Great Serpent in association with cross-in-circle motifs, which represent the Earth. In the section on the right, the ovoid vulva of First Woman is associated with a wishbone-shaped motif. This pairing of motifs also is found at Picture Cave, Serpent Mound, the Willow Drive Mound Group, and possibly the Hensler petroglyphs. In each case, these vignettes represent enactments of the Dhegihan Sioux "Making of the Earth Rite".

elements in the Making of the Earth Rite, the principal Dhegihan genesis narration (Fletcher and La Flesche 1992, 171).

The Washington State Park Petroglyph site in Missouri includes a three-dimensional representation of a vulva associated with a serpent, and a bird (Diaz-Granados *et al.* 2018, 61). This bird can be associated with Hawk or Morning Star. The arrangement of the motifs duplicates features of a tableau from Picture Cave: a large raptor just to the right of First Woman's vulva and the Great Serpent, with his right wing on the Great Serpent's back (Diaz-Granados *et al.* 2015, 224).

There are a number of other petroglyph sites that include motifs representing coitus between First Woman (represented as a vulvaform) in close proximity with the Great Serpent. These include the Maddin Creek Site, Rocky Hollow Site, Thousand Hills State Park Site, and others in the state (Diaz-Granados and Duncan 2000; 2004a; Diaz-Granados *et al.* 2018). Two Missouri sites include long-tailed quadrupeds with spiral tails (Diaz-Granados and Duncan 2000, fig. 5.2, pl. 23) that are comparable to one at La Moille Rockshelter in eastern Minnesota. Likewise, the Washington State Park A site has a spiral with a serpent head (Diaz-Granados and Duncan 2000, fig. 5.2; pl. 28). Duncan and Diaz-Granados (2008, 62, fig. 3.2) associate such spirals with the Great Serpent; and the imagery is reminiscent of the spiral tail of Ohio's Great Serpent Mound as well as the spiral glyph on the Hensler petroglyph panel in eastern Wisconsin (compare Figs 5.2 and 5.8).

The avian or bird symbol is the most common of all the symbols found in Missouri's petroglyphs. The migration of birds from the south in the spring, bringing the spirit of First Woman, heralded the beginning of the planting season among the sedentary First Nation farmers. After the harvest, First Woman returns to the south with the birds, taking the corn spirits with her because she has to care for them until spring (Diaz-Granados and Duncan 2004a, 194–5). Likewise, bird effigies in the UMW reflect seasonal migration and world renewal, as do some avian rock art depictions in this region, such as the bird adjacent to the female figure at Hensler (Fig. 5.8).

The presence of these three important symbols: the vulvaform, the serpent, and the bird, evokes the annual cycle, the rebirth of all plant and animal life, including human life. It was during the spring planting, summer growing season, and the fall harvest that we find these rites revolving around migrating birds, as well as First Woman and her consort, the Great Serpent. First Woman's presence was the catalyst needed for a successful farming season. It is, therefore, not surprising to see these iconic motifs co-occurring again and again over a wide area expressed in mound forms and imagery on rock faces, pottery, and shell. These various co-occurrences of serpent and vulvar motifs, but also birds, are suggestive of the same series of Great Serpent/First Woman genesis stories that we have identified at other petroglyph and effigy mound sites in the UMW and the Ohio Valley. Together, they offer evidence of a widespread series of related oral traditions and a consistent vocabulary of motifs used to represent those stories.

Shared icons and shared stories of the Late Woodland/Mississippian Periods in Midcontinental North America

Contrary to Squier and Davis's (1848, 135) tentative assessment that the effigy mounds in Ohio and Wisconsin seemed to have "few features in common", we submit that the effigies in these geographically separated locations actually have many shared attributes that attest to a significant cultural connection between them. Rosebrough (2010, 560) concluded in her study of the Effigy Mound "Culture" (the scare quotes are Rosebrough's) that "Late Woodland social networks should have readily allowed material goods, ideas, and marriage partners to move across the study area [UMW] and beyond". During the Terminal Woodland Period, Late Woodland people in the UMW were increasingly involved in wider spheres of interaction.

Douglas Price and colleagues, through a study of strontium isotopes in the teeth of the ancient inhabitants of Aztalan, determined that "the general picture is one of substantial human movement at this critical juncture in North American prehistory when Mississippian groups and influences were expanding across the upper Midwest" (Price *et al.* 2007, 536). Rosebrough (2010) considered how the specialized world renewal knowledge of effigy mound ritual specialists might have been transformed through contact with new people and ideas.

One factor potentially contributing to this Mississippian expansion was a period of severe droughts in the central Mississippi valley between AD 1100 and 1250 that coincided with an abrupt appearance of Mississippian influence into the Fort Ancient region, which was not experiencing drought conditions (Cook 2017, 137; Comstock and Cook 2018, 96–9). Robert Cook (2017, 107) suggests that this "may well have acted as a pull for Mississippians to come into the region". These droughts also may be partly responsible for the movement of Mississippian peoples into the upper Mississippi Valley.

In this light, we view Ohio's Serpent Mound, Alligator Mound, and likely the Kentucky Stone Serpent Mound as ultimately emerging from a confluence of the Mississippian artistic florescence that reached its peak between AD 850 and 1025, the simultaneous surge of effigy mound construction in the UMW and central Mississippi valley, and the droughts that began around AD 1100. The result was a rapid spread of people and ideas into the central Ohio Valley where those ideas coalesced with the beliefs and traditions of the local people; and the Great Serpent Mound represents the grand synthesis of that historic confluence. A reviewer of a previous version of this paper asked why this dramatic confluence of events did not result in more than these few effigy mounds in the Ohio Valley. That's a question worth asking, but regardless of which time period Serpent Mound finally is determined to inhabit, its near singularity in the Ohio Valley still will be a conundrum. We suggest, however, that since the creation of these few Ohio Valley effigies coincided with the very end of the UMV effigy mound tradition, the construction of earthen effigies commemorating this shared cultural ideology already was going out of style and being replaced with regionally variable renderings of key stories in alternative media.

The symbolism of First Woman, and the Great Serpent continued to be invoked in Late Pre-contact Oneota rock art in the UMW, and it persisted into the Contact period when ethnographers recorded related stories from diverse tribes. And, as demonstrated by Duncan's and Diaz-Granados's personal acquaintances with Osage elders, some of those traditions survive to this day. The meanings we have attached to the iconography of the mounds and petroglyphs are not always self-evident. We have, for example, identified wishbone-shaped mounds and rock art motifs as First Woman; and oval earthworks, conical mounds, and oval/diamond-shaped rock art motifs as vulvas that served as *pars pro toto* representations of First Woman. These interpretations are supported by Dhegihan Sioux associations of First Woman with horseshoe-shaped mounds, earth circles, or small conical piles of earth all with vulva symbolism (Fletcher and La Flesche 1992, 254–5).

Writing about the cryptic deep cave imagery of the European Upper Paleolithic, Giedion (1962, 241) maintained that such "great abstract symbols which have no counterparts in the world of reality" could be understood fully only by the holy men and women and the privileged few who had been initiated into their mysteries. Such symbols therefore require a key in order to decipher their meaning. Our key has been the corpus of oral traditions recorded for the indigenous tribes with an historically documented presence in these regions and especially the Siouan speaking groups whose traditions are particularly well documented.

The iconic symbolism in the effigy mounds and rock art of Midcontinental North America relates to the stories the Native Americans of this region told each other about where they came from; but the symbols weren't simply static reminders of those stories. Fletcher and La Flesche (1992, 171) wrote that the Making of the Earth Rites were not just about dramatizing the Omaha creation stories, their enactment was intended "to insure the continuance of that which had been created". The symbols, whether shaped from the earth or depicted on stone surfaces, were "identified with the ... the prayer ... to be fulfilled. The symbol itself was reality, for it was believed to possess the power of ... directly affecting the course of events" (Giedion 1962, 91–2).

Acknowledgements

The authors thank Peter Lepper for his rendering of Figure 5.4. Lepper thanks his current and former colleagues at the Ohio History Connection, especially Meghan Marley, Linda Pansing, and William Pickard for their active participation in the archaeological research at Serpent Mound and for the times they took on some of his workload, which allowed him to spend time on this project. He also thanks Tod Frolking, emeritus professor of geosciences at Denison University, for his assistance with the archaeological investigations of both Serpent and Alligator mounds. Boszhardt is indebted to Robert Birmingham, William Green, Amy Rosebrough, James Stoltman, and James Theler for insights regarding UMW effigy mounds; and the late Robert Salzer and Jack Steinbring along with Geri Schrab and Danielle Benden regarding rock art inspirations. Among many Native American acquaintances, Mike and Karen Ann Hoffman, Truman and Cloris Lowe I and II, and the late Merlin Red Cloud shared eye-opening cultural experiences. Duncan and Diaz-Granados would like to acknowledge a number of late elders with whom they became friends on the Osage Reservation. These Osage elders provided invaluable information and insight for over a period of two decades. Their passings constitute a great loss to Osage knowledge: Louis Burns, Raymond Red Corn, Sr, Andrew (Bud) Red Corn, Charles Red Corn, Frances Holding, Preston Morrell, Leonard Maker, Alma Jean Maker, Harry Maker, Charles Pratt, Jake Waller, Robert (Bob) Smith, and Cora Jean Big Elk. We treasure the continued input of our many Osage friends and relatives. Finally, we thank two anonymous reviews of a previous version of this manuscript for their insightful comments and suggestions. We understand the reason for anonymity in the peer review process, but regret that we cannot acknowledge these individuals by name.

Bibliography

American Antiquarian Society (1884) *Proceedings. Annual Meeting*, October 22, 1883, at the hall of the Society in Worcester. *Proceedings of the American Antiquarian Society* 3(1), 1–35.

Baldner, R.P. (2017) In sculpted valleys: revisiting the native American rock art legacy in northeast Iowa – Part II. *Journal of the Iowa Archaeological Society* 64, 61–97.

Baldner, R.P. (2020) Indigenous equations: exploring iconography and meaning in rock art of northeastern Iowa. *Journal of the Iowa Archaeological Society* 67, 36–67.

Benn, D.A. (1989) Hawks, serpents, and bird-men: emergence of the oneota mode of production. *Plains Anthropologist* 34(125), 233–60.

Birmingham, R.A. (2010) *Spirits of the Earth: The Effigy Mound Landscape of Madison and the Four Lakes*. University of Wisconsin Press, Madison WI.

Birmingham, R.A. and Eisenberg, L.E. (2000) *Indian Mounds of Wisconsin*. University of Wisconsin Press, Madison WI.

Birmingham, R.A. and Rosebrough, A.L. (2017) *Indian Mounds of Wisconsin* (2nd edn). University of Wisconsin Press, Madison WI.

Boszhardt, R.F. (1995) *Rock Art Research in Western Wisconsin 1994–1995*. Reports of Investigations 201, La Crosse: Mississippi Valley Archaeology Center, University of Wisconsin-La Crosse WI.

Boszhardt, R.F. (2003) *Deep Cave Rock Art in the Upper Mississippi Valley*. Prairie Smoke Press St. Paul MN.

Boszhardt, R.F. (2014) The Willow Drive Mounds (47Da-0119) and Willow Creek Habitation (47Da-0124) Sites. Report submitted to the Wisconsin State Archaeologist's Office, Wisconsin Historical Society, Madison MN.

Boszhardt, R.F. and Benden, D.M. (2017) *Beneath Your Feet: Archaeology at Trempealeau*. Driftless Pathways LLC, Lodi CA.

Boszhardt, R.F., Harris, S., Schmitt, C., Theler, J.L., Wyse, T. and Bendon, D.M. (2018) A lidar survey for effigy mounds in the Bad Axe River Valley, Vernon County, Wisconsin. *The Wisconsin Archeologist* 99(2), 5–24.

Bowers, A.W. (1950) *Mandan Social and Ceremonial Organization*. University of Chicago Press, Chicago IL.

Bowers, A.W. (1992) *Hidatsa Social & Ceremonial Organization*. University of Nebraska Press, Lincoln NE.

Brown, J.A. (1989) On style divisions of the southeastern ceremonial complex: a revisionist perspective. In *The Southeastern Ceremonial Complex*, P. Galloway (ed.), 183–204. University of Texas Press, Austin TX.

Brown, J.A. (2007) Sequencing the Braden style within Mississippian period art. In *Ancient Objects and Sacred Realms*, F.K. Reilly III and J.F. Garber (eds) 213–45. University of Texas Press, Austin TX.

Brown, J.A. (2011) The regional culture signature of the Braden art style. In *Visualizing the Sacred, Cosmic Visions, Regionalism, and the Art of the Mississippian World*, G.E. Lankford, F.K. Reilly III and J.F. Garber (eds), 37–63. University of Texas Press, Austin TX.

Carr, C. and McCord, R. (2013) Ohio Hopewell descriptions of composite creatures. Part I – biological identification and ethnohistorical insights. *Midcontinental Journal of Archaeology* 38, 5–81.

Comstock, A.R. and Cook, R.A. (2018) Climate change and migration along a Mississippian periphery: a Fort Ancient example. *American Antiquity* 83, 91–108.

Conkey, M. and Hastorf, C. (1990) *The Uses of Style in Archaeology*. Cambridge University Press, Cambridge.

Cook, J. (2013) *Ice Age Art: The Arrival of the Modern Mind*. British Museum Press, London.

Cook, R.A. (2017) *"Continuity and Change in the Native American Village" Multicultural Origins and Descendants of the Fort Ancient Culture*. Cambridge University Press, Cambridge.

Deetz, J. (1965) *The Dynamics of Stylistic Change in Arikara Ceramics*. University of Illinois Press, Champaign IL.

Diaz-Granados, C. (2015) Symbolism and preliminary assessment of styles in Picture Cave. In Diaz-Granados *et al.* (eds) 2015, 189–208.

Diaz-Granados, C. and Duncan, J.R. (2000) *The Petroglyphs and Pictographs of Missouri*. University of Alabama Press, Tuscaloosa AL.

Diaz-Granados, C. and Duncan, J.R. (2004a) Empowering the SECC: The "Old Woman" and oral tradition. In Diaz-Granados and Duncan (eds) 2004b, 190–215.

Diaz-Granados, C. and Duncan, J.R. (2004b) *The Rock-Art of Eastern North America: Capturing Images and Insight*. University of Alabama Press, Tuscaloosa AL.

Diaz-Granados, C., Duncan, J.R. and Reilly, F.K. III (eds) (2015) *Picture Cave: Unraveling the Mysteries of the Mississippian Cosmos*. University of Texas Press, Austin TX.

Diaz-Granados, C., Simek, J., Sabo, G. III and Wagner, M. (eds) (2018) *Transforming the Landscape: Rock Art and the Mississippian Cosmos*. American Landscapes 4, Oxford.

Diaz-Granados, C., Rowe, M., Hyman, J.R., Duncan, J.R. and Southon, J.R. (2001) AMS radiocarbon dates for charcoal from three Missouri pictographs and their associated iconography. *American Antiquity* 66, 481–92.

Dieterle, R. (n.d.) The woman who married a snake. Story collected by Paul Radin, retold by Richard Dieterle. Available at: https://hotcakencyclopedia.com/ho.WomanWhoMarriedSnake.html (accessed 22 June 2020)

Drooker, P.B. (1997) *The View From Madisonville: Protohistoric Western Fort Ancient Interaction Patterns. Memoirs of the Museum of Anthropology*. Memoir 31, University of Michigan, Ann Arbor MI.

Duncan, J.R. (2015) Identifying the characters on the walls of Picture Cave. In Diaz-Granados *et al.* (eds) 2015, 209–40.

Duncan, J.R. and Diaz-Granados, C. (2018) The Big Five petroglyph sites: Their place on the landscape and relation to their creators. In Diaz-Granados *et al.* (eds) 2018, 30–56.

Duncan, J.R., Rowe, M.W., Diaz-Granados, C., Steelman, K.L. and Guilderson, T. (2015) The black warrior pictograph: dating and interpretation. In Diaz-Granados *et al.* (eds) 2015, 125–32.

Edging, R. and Ahler, S.R. (2004) Rock-art and late woodland settlement in the Northern Ozarks. In Diaz-Granados and Duncan (eds) 2004b, 90–109.

Fletcher, A.C. and La Flesche, F. (1992) *The Omaha Tribe*. University of Nebraska Press, Lincoln NE.

Fletcher, R., Cameron, T., Lepper, B.T., Wymer, D.A. and Pickard, W. (1996) Serpent Mound: a Fort Ancient icon? *Midcontinental Journal of Archaeology* 21, 105–43.

Giedion, S. (1962) *The Eternal Present: A Contribution on Constancy and Change*. Pantheon Books, New York.

Goldstein, L. (1983) *The Southeast Wisconsin Archaeological Project: 1982–83. Report of Investigations No. 68.* Milwaukee: Archaeological Research Laboratory, University of Wisconsin-Milwaukee WI.

Goldstein, L. (1995) Landscapes and mortuary practices: a case for regional perspectives. In *Regional Approaches to Mortuary Analysis* L.A. Beck (ed.), 100–21. Plenum Press, New York.

Griffin, J.B. (1952) Prehistoric cultures of the central Mississippi valley. In *Archaeology of Eastern United States*, J.B. Griffin (ed.), 226–38. University of Chicago Press, Chicago IL.

Griffin, J.B. (1960) A hypothesis for the prehistory of the Winnebago. *Culture in History* S. Diamond (ed.), 809–65. Columbia University Press, New York.

Hall, R.L. (1979) In search of the ideology of the Adena-Hopewell climax. In *Hopewell Archaeology: The Chillecothe Conference*, D.S. Brose and N. Greber (eds) 258–65. Kent State University Press, Kent OH.

Hall, R.L. (1993) Red Banks, Oneota, and the Winnebago: views from a distant rock. *The Wisconsin Archeologist:* 74, 10–79.

Hall, R.L. (1997) *An Archaeology of the Soul: North American Indian Belief and Ritual.* University of Illinois Press, Urbana IL.

Herrmann, E.W., Monaghan, G.W., Romain, W.F., Schilling, T.M., Burks, J., Leone, K.L., Purtill, M.P. and Tonetti, A.C. (2014) A new multistage construction chronology for the Great Serpent Mound. *Journal of Archaeological Science* 50, 117–125.

Holmes, W.H. (1886) A sketch of the Great Serpent Mound. *Science* 8, 624–8.

Lapham, I.A. (1855) *The Antiquities of Wisconsin.* Smithsonian Contributions to Knowledge 7. Government Printing Office, Washington DC.

Lepper, B.T. (2018 [Chapter 8]) On the age of Serpent Mound: a reply to Romain and colleagues. *Midcontinental Journal of Archaeology* 43, 62–75.

Lepper, B.T. (2020a) The Mississippian iconography of Serpent Mound. *Journal of Ohio Archaeology* 7, 38–55.

Lepper, B.T. (2020b) Why radiocarbon dates on bulk sediment from Serpent Mound are problematic. *Current Research in Ohio Archaeology* 2020 [https://ohioarchaeology.org/146-resources/research/articles-and-abstracts-2020/587-why-radiocarbon-dates-on-bulk-sediment-from-serpent-mound-are-problematic] (accessed 16 October 2020).

Lepper, B.T. and Frolking, T.A. (2003) Alligator Mound: geoarchaeological and iconographical interpretations of a late prehistoric effigy mound in central Ohio, USA. *Cambridge Archaeological Journal* 13, 147–67.

Lepper, B.T., Frolking, T.A. and Pickard, W.H. (2019) Debating the age of Serpent Mound: a reply to Romain and Herrmann's rejoinder to Lepper concerning Serpent Mound. *Midcontinental Journal of Archaeology* 44, 42–56.

Lepper, B.T., Duncan, J.R., Diaz-Granados, C., and Frolking, T.A. (2018) Arguments for the age of Serpent Mound. *Cambridge Archaeological Journal* 28, 433–50.

Lewis, T.H. (2006) Sculptures in Carver's Cave, St. Paul, Minn. *The Wisconsin Archeologist* 87(1/2), 223–25 (report from original 1898 *The Macalaster Monthly* 1–2, 37–42).

MacLean, J.P. (1885) The Great Serpent Mound. *American Antiquarian* 7, 44–7.

McKern, W.C. (1930) The Kletzien and Nitschke Mound Groups. *Bulletin of the Public Museum of the City of Milwaukee* 3–4, 417–572.

Monaghan, G.W. and Herrmann, E.W. (2019) Serpent Mound: still built by the Adena, and still rebuilt during the Fort Ancient period. *Midcontinental Journal of Archaeology* 44, 84–93.

Morse, D.F. and Morse, P.A. (1983) *Archaeology of the Central Mississippi Valley*. Academic Press, New York.

Mueller, N.G. and Fritz, G.J. (2016) Women as symbols and actors in the Mississippi Valley: evidence from female flint-clay statues and vessels. In *Native American Landscapes: An Engendered Perspective*, C. Claassen (ed), 109–48. University of Tennessee Press, Knoxville TE.

Parks, D.R. (1991) *Traditional Narratives of the Arikara Indians*. University of Nebraska Press, Lincoln NE.

Pauketat, T.R., Boszhardt, R.F. and Benden, D.M. (2015) Trempealeau entanglements: an ancient colony's causes and effects. *American Antiquity* 80, 260–89.

Phillips, P. and Brown, J.A. (1978) *Pre-Columbian shell engravings from the Craig Mound At Spiro, Oklahoma* Peabody Museum Press, Harvard University, Cambridge MA.

Pickard, W., Marley, M., Pansing, L. *et al.* (2018) Stone Steps Removal at Serpent Mound: Site Maintenance Provides Additional Radiocarbon Dates. On File, Ohio History Connection, Department of Archaeology, Columbus OH.

Power, S.C. (2004) *Early Art of the Southeastern Indians: Feathered Serpents & Winged Beings*. University of Georgia Press, Athens GA.

Pozza, J.M. (2019) Approaching a vast and varied copper collection: an analysis of Oneota copper artifacts of the Lake Koshkonong region in southeastern Wisconsin. *Journal of Archaeological Science Reports* 25, 632–47.

Price, T.D., Burton, J.H. and Stoltman, J.B. (2007) Place of origin of prehistoric inhabitants of Aztalan, Jefferson Co., Wisconsin. *American Antiquity* 72, 524–38.

Putnam, F.W. (1890) The Serpent Mound of Ohio. *The Century* 39, 871–88.

Putnam, F.W. (n.d.) Sketch of Serpent Mound by F.W. Putnam. Peabody Museum of Archaeology and Ethnology, Harvard University; Image number 2004.24.32579A. On-line collections. Available at: https://pmem.unix.fas.harvard.edu:8443/peabody/ view/objects/asitem/search$0040/1/title-desc?t:state:flow=9fda5a71-fb58-4ad3-974016a3e51ad035 (accessed 5 September 2018).

Radin, P. (1965) *The Winnebago Tribe*. University of Nebraska Press, Lincoln NE.

Reilly, F.K. III (2004) People of the earth, people of the sky: visualizing the sacred in native American art of the Mississippian period. In *Hero, Hawk and Open Hand: American Indian Art of the Ancient Midwest and South*, R.F. Townsend and R.V. Sharp (eds), 125–37. Yale University Press/Art Institute of Chicago, New Haven CT and London.

Reilly, F.K. III (2011) The great serpent in the Lower Mississippi Valley. In *Visualizing the Sacred, Cosmic Visions, Regicnalism, and the Art of the Mississippian World*, G.E. Lankford, F.K. Reilly III and J.F. Garber (eds), 118–36. University of Texas Press, Austin TX.

Reilly, F.K. III and Garber, J.F. (2007) Introduction. In *Ancient Objects and Sacred Realms*, F.K. Reilly III and J. F. Garber (eds), 1–7. University of Texas Press, Austin TX7.

Romain, W.F. (2019) Serpent Mound in its Woodland period context: second rejoinder to Lepper. Midcontinental Journal of Archaeology 44, 57–83.

Romain, W.F. and Herrmann, E.W. (2018) Rejoinder to Lepper concerning Serpent Mound. *Midcontinental Journal of Archaeology* 43, 76–88.

Romain, W.F., Herrmann, E.W., Monaghan, G.W. and Burkes, J. (2017) Radiocarbon dates reveal Serpent Mound is more than two thousand years old. *Midcontinental Journal of Archaeology* 42, 201–22.

Rosebrough, A.L. (2010) Every Family a Nation: A Deconstruction and Reconstruction of the Effigy Mound "Culture" of the Western Great Lakes of North America. Unpublished Ph.D. Dissertation, University of Wisconsin-Madison WI.

Sanders, S.L. (1991) The stone Serpent Mound of Boyd County, Kentucky: an investigation of a stone effigy structure. *Midcontinential Journal of Archaeology* 16, 272–84.

Schapiro, M. (1953) Style. In *Anthropology Today* A.L. Kroeber (ed.), 283–311.University of Chicago Press, Chicago IL.

Schrab, G. and Boszhardt, R.F. (2016) *Hidden Thunder Rock Art of the Upper Midwest*. Wisconsin Historical Society Press, Madison WI.

Squier, E. and Davis, E. (1848) *Ancient Monuments of the Mississippi Valley.* Contributions to Knowledge 1, Smithsonian Institution, Washington DC.

Stanley, L.A. (2004) Ratcliffe sacred rock and the seven sacred stones. In Diaz-Granados and Duncan (eds) 2004b, 145–58.

Steinbring. J. and Farvour, F. (1987) The Hensler petroglyph Site, Dodge County, Wisconsin. *The Wisconsin Archeologist* 68(4), 396–411.

Stoltman, J.B. and Boszhardt, R.F. (2019) An overview of driftless area prehistory. In *Physical Geography and Geology of the Driftless Area: The Career and Contributions of James C. Knox*, E.C. Carson, J. Elmo Rawling III, J. Michael Daniels and J.W. Attig (eds), 93–118. The Geological Society of America Special Paper 543, Denver CO.

Stoltman, J.B. and Christensen, G.C. (2000) The Late Woodland stage in the driftless area of the Upper Mississippi Valley. In *Late Woodland Societies: Tradition and Transformation Across the Midcontinent*, T.E. Emerson, D.L. McElrath and A.C. Fortier (eds), 497–524. The University of Nebraska Press, Lincoln, NE.

Taylor, R.C. (1838) Notes respecting certain Indian mounds and earthworks in the form of animal effigies, chiefly in the Wisconsin territory. *U.S. Silliman's American Journal of Science and Art* 34, 88–104.

Theler, J.L. and Boszhardt, R. (2006) Collapse of crucial resources and cultural change: a model for the Woodland to Oneota transformation. *American Antiquity* 71(3), 433–72.

White, J.R. (1986) The Kern Effigy: evidence for a prehistoric Fort Ancient summer solstice marker. *North American Archaeologist* 7(2), 137–65.

Willoughby, C.C. (1918) Hand drawn map of Serpent Mound. Peabody Museum of Archaeology and Ethnology, Harvard University; Image number 2010.1.30.146. Available at: https://pmem.unix.fas.harvard.edu:8443/peabody/view/objects/asitem/ search$0040/4/title-desc?t:state:flow=8a50112c-9c65-4a83-8d38-b1b18e39ba9c (accessed 18 January 2020).

Willoughby, C.C. (1919) The Serpent Mound of Adams County, Ohio. *America Anthropologist* 21, 153–63.

Winchell, N.H. (1911) *The Aborigines of Minnesota.*: Minnesota Historical Society St Paul MN.

6

"Paired Figures Confronting a Forked Pole": so what's up with the Forked Pole?

George Sabo III and Alex W. Barker

In their monumental examination of pre-Columbian shell engravings from the Craig Mound at Spiro, Phillips and Brown recognize a distinctive set of compositions within the Craig C series, described as "Paired Figures Confronting a Forked Pole" (Phillips and Brown 1984, pls 314–23). Persisting for decades as one of many compositional themes, this particular set acquires elevated significance in relation to ongoing re-assessment of the internal structure of the Craig Mound. This chapter takes a closer look at the Forked Pole element of the paired figure compositions. What, specifically, is the role of the Forked Pole in these compositions? It clearly serves an artistic function as a central axial element integral to the symmetrical, bilateral image structure, but is there more? Is there, perchance, a symbolic referent at work that contributes decisively to expression of an overall narrative? Our goal is to provide an answer to this question, but *en route* to that end we must establish an interpretive framework by addressing, briefly, two prior topics: revised interpretations of archaeological features within the Craig Mound, and the salience of the Paired Figures Confronting a Forked Pole theme within the Craig C corpus.

Archaeology of the Craig Mound

Brown's paired volumes on *The Spiro Ceremonial Center* (Brown 1996) provide a convenient point of departure, eliminating the need to reprise a series of earlier and far less rigorous assessments (e.g., Clements 1945; Orr 1946; Hamilton 1952; Duffield 1973). His discussion of the Great Mortuary outlines a sequence of events that begin with creation of an ossuary of commingled human bones and artifacts disinterred from other contexts and redeposited within the confines of a square or rectangular bermed earthwork – now identified as a low platform mound with most of the interior sediments removed – erected at the base of what later became the primary or largest element of the four-lobed Craig Mound. Next, three rows of cedar pole crib works or litters, in sizes graduated by row, were laid down over the ossuary to receive subsequent sets of remains. To make room for new ossuary additions, some earlier-deposited remains were periodically removed and reburied in the platform mound flanks. Finally, a specially prepared floor area was created, encircled by upright posts embedded into a portion of the underlying ossuary deposit. This floor area was covered by a variety of sacred objects, discussed below. The upright posts contributed to the subsequent formation of a hollow chamber that protected objects placed on the floor, accounting for the preservation of perishable items including carved wood, engraved shell, split cane basketry and matting, and fabric woven of plant fibers, feathers, and animal fur. Brown referred to the whole as the Great Mortuary, construction of which he put around AD 1400 (Brown 1996, 85–103).

In a book chapter published four years later, Brown (2010) turned to consideration of the symbolic importance of secondary burials using remains deposited in the Craig Mound ossuary and crib works as a primary data set. This analysis continued to make use of an undifferentiated Great Mortuary context, comparing that material with secondary burials in Mound 72 at Cahokia. Brown argued that in both cases, secondary treatments of human bones served as instruments for representing cosmological visions central to the organization of the living community, noting differences between Spiro and Cahokia in underlying principles and conventions. A new inference Brown proposes for the Great Mortuary is its potential association with structural change in Spiroan society involving a turn to collective representation of ancestral communities, from earlier mortuary practices that incorporated expressions of individual status categories (Brown 2010, 34).

Sacred objects placed on the floor of the hollow chamber are interpreted as a display of "artifacts of collective representation", but here, too, items from separate depositional contexts – ossuary, crib works, and hollow chamber floor – are examined as a single analytic unit (Brown 2010, 43–5). Even so, another significant advancement comes from the derivation of five cosmological principles reflected in the display: subordination of individual identities within a collective whole; quadrilateral spatial organization mirroring cosmological orientations; size categorization reflected in crib works positioning; reflection of historicity by intermingling of older and newer burial formats; and reflection of social order in the multi-layered deposit. These principles correspond, in turn, to a larger cosmographic order represented by the arrangement of mounds and other features across the Spiro site (Brown 2010, 46–8).

Brown (2012) presents further exploration of the aggregate Great Mortuary contents as a cosmological "center of the universe" display. An important feature of this presentation is an explicit focus on the arrangement of artifacts specially placed on the hollow chamber floor. This arrangement will be summarized below, but artifact categories include carved wood and stone statuary, woven fabrics, carved shell beads, decorated basketry boxes containing regalia items and other sacred objects (but not human remains, *contra* Brown 1996; 2010; cf. Brown 2010, 43), ceramic vessels, socio-technic weapons (i.e., weapons whose role is primarily social and symbolic rather than functional), and other ritual equipment including embossed copper plates, and, most important to this discussion, shell cups engraved with what are best described as "scenes" from narrative traditions that must have possessed great importance at the time.

While here, too, the material contents of the crib works remain unseparated from the hollow chamber floor arrangement, the analysis presented focuses narrowly on the latter as the product of a discrete event, created as the product of a "devotional economy" (Brown 2012, 133–6). Within this cultural framework, communities near and far gathered at Spiro to add their own sacred objects to a locally produced set in an overall effort to produce a cosmographic tableau representing component elements of a regionally shared belief system with accompanying ritual practices. Representing this belief system are the justly celebrated sacra comprising the Southeastern Ceremonial Complex (Krieger 1945; Williams 1968; cf. Galloway 1989; King 2007).

About the time Brown's 2010 and 2012 book chapters appeared, another set of revised ideas coalesced around discussion taking place during a series of Mississippian iconography workshops convened by F. Kent Reilly III at Texas State University (e.g. Reilly and Garber 2007; Lankford *et al.* 2011). There, conversations involving Brown, the late Robert Hall, Alex Barker, and George Sabo catalyzed a new perspective that separated the ossuary formation and crib works addition – perceived as a historically connected series of events motivated by the same set of underlying schemas (cf. Beck *et al.* 2007) – from the subsequent creation of a specially demarcated floor area encircled by upright posts. Within these newly established confines, a ritually charged cosmographic tableau emerged via placement of sacred objects in relation to a *different* schema. This tableau, along with its protective hollow chamber – henceforth referred to as the Spirit Lodge – was preserved, until the 1934–5 assault by looters, within the central core of the Craig Mound. Notably, review of photos from the University of Oklahoma/WPA excavations of the Craig Mound in the years following the looting indicate that a new layer of sediments was added to cover (thereby putting to a close) the ossuary/crib works deposit, prior to construction of the hollow chamber floor. Adding to the confusion, creation of the floor within the upright pole circle involved Spiroan excavations through the newly added sediments to expose a portion of the underlying ossuary/crib works deposits, on top of which the Spirit Lodge tableau was arranged. This penetration into the underlying ossuary deposit by 15th century excavations to create the Spirit Lodge is but one of several circumstances accounting for the persistent conflation of ossuary, crib works, and hollow chamber features and their contents within the Great Mortuary rubric.

A more detailed overview the separation of Great Mortuary (ossuary and crib works) and Spirit Lodge (hollow chamber) features and their chronological sequencing is provided by Brown *et al.* (2020). A forthcoming, multi-authored volume based on the Mississippian iconography workshop discussions will provide a comprehensive presentation of our current views on early 15th century events at Spiro that stimulated completion of internal Craig Mound features. Here, we briefly summarize the primary components of the cosmogram preserved on the Spirit Lodge floor.

Dominating the center of the tableau is the carved stone figure of a female identified as First Woman, or Earth Mother. To the southwest, the disarticulated remains of an individual – represented by a skull to which adhered a partially preserved, woven headband – had been placed alongside a large chunk of galena, nine oval bowls, a large number of long flint bifaces or "swords", and several copper plates. A stone carving depicting a vulture pecking on the head of a recumbent human was placed alongside this assemblage.

Another major component consists of a set of decoratively woven basketry boxes that appear to have contained ceremonial regalia (Horton and Sabo 2011; Horton 2020). These were arranged along the eastern side of the tableau. Some had specially bundled, embossed copper plates set on top of their closed lids. Weaponry in the form of copper bitted axes and arrowheads were arranged on opposite ends of this row of boxes. Also in this area sat three carved wooden figurines. At the north end, possibly embedded in the Spirit Lodge wall, sat another figurine facing outward – the famed "Resting Warrior" carved stone statue. Seven chipped and polished stone maces and another carved pipe decorated with a rattlesnake image were placed near this statue. Other items placed around the tableau surrounding the Earth Mother carving included additional carved statues, woven textiles, and carved marine shell beads, T-shaped smoking pipes, and sundry food offerings. Brown's contribution to this volume provides the supporting argument, but, in brief, our overall interpretation is that the tableau represents the stage setting for a rite of renewal performed as a re-enactment of the primordial creation of the world (Brown *et al.* 2020, 106).

The coherence of the Forked Pole theme

The remaining group of items arranged within the Spirit Lodge is a set of slightly more than 100 engraved shell cups rendered in the Craig C style. Unlike the many hundreds of carved shell cups and fragments from other Craig Mound contexts, one distinctive property of this Craig C series is that they are all whole or nearly whole, and they exhibit a far better state of preservation. Phillips and Brown also make note of the "unique features" of the Paired Figures Confronting a Forked Pole that sets this group "somewhat apart" from other Craig C examples (Phillips and Brown 1984, x). One plausible interpretation is that Craig C materials incorporated into the Spirit House tableau were produced specifically for the ritual activities resulting in the creation of that feature. Supporting this inference is our finding that these cups are also decorated with what we interpret as storytelling scenes, most if not all of which cohere around a single narrative arc linked thematically with the just described layout of sacred items within the Spirit Lodge.

The canonical series of Paired Figures compositions that we examine in this chapter consists of ten closely rendered versions of a single composition in which one figure – sporting a "Wedgemouth" facial design in profile view – is positioned to the left of a Forked Pole that is grasped by the figure on the right, who exhibits a "T-Bar" facial design.[1] Both figures have three-pronged "tongues" protruding from their mouths that we interpret as speech scrolls (Fig. 6.1). Both also are characteristically depicted with an anatomically anomalous convention of both

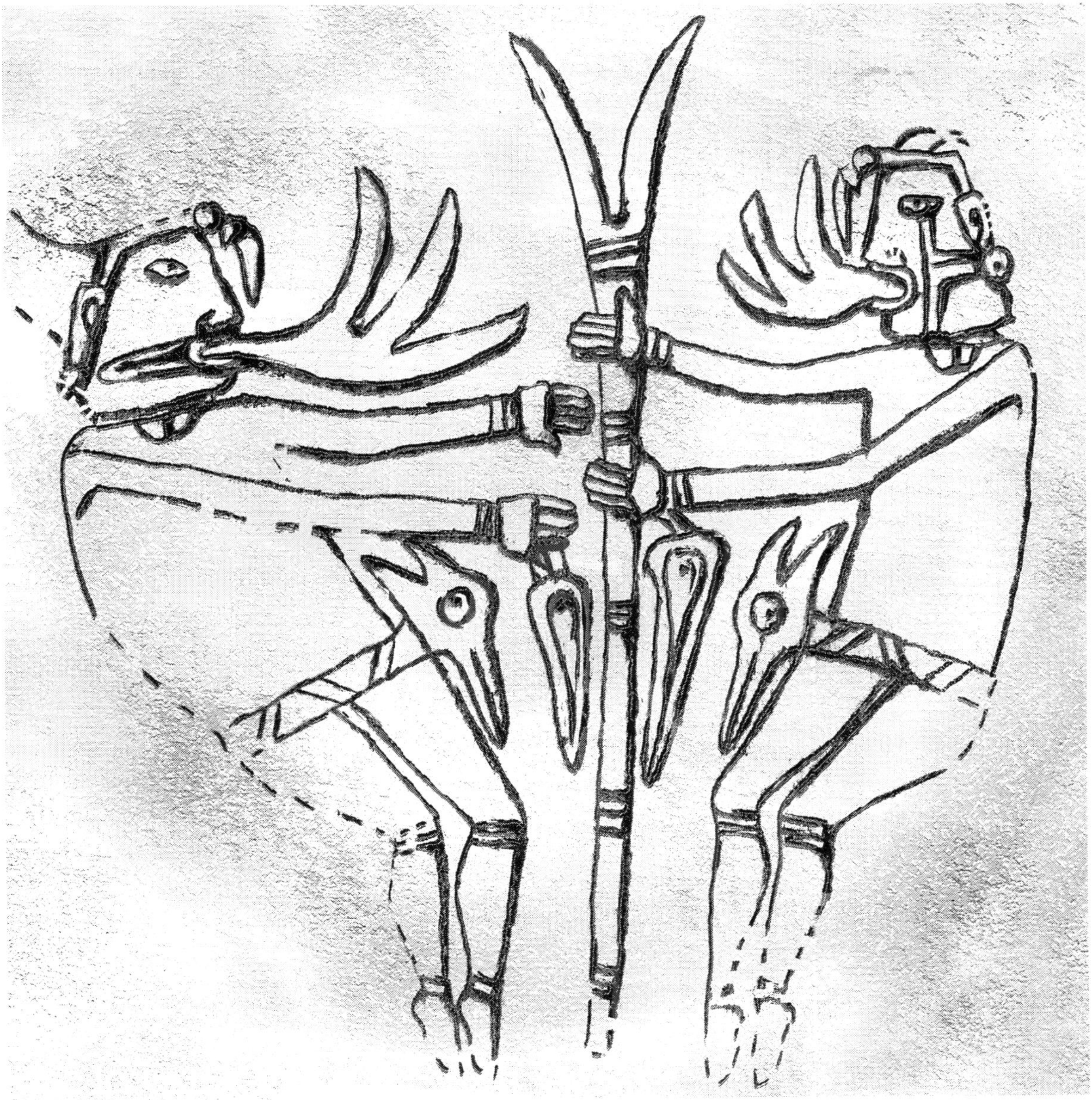

Fig. 6.1 Example of *Paired Figures Confronting a Forked Pole* (Phillips and Brown 1984, pl. 315; drawn by M. Jane Kellett, Arkansas Archeological Survey).

hands shown with palms facing the viewer and both thumbs pointing in the same direction, either facing up or facing down.

Before proceeding with further assessment of this composition, it is necessary to establish a crucial element of the identities of Wedgemouth and T-Bar. The Wedgemouth figure appears in alternative guises in addition to his standard anthropomorphic form, including a Janus-faced figure, a Birdman, and an antlered Snake Man (Fig. 6.2). From an iconographic perspective, there are thus

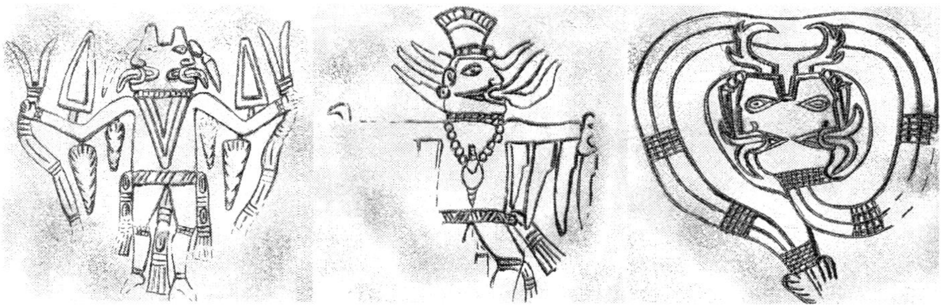

Fig. 6.2 Wedgemouth in alternate guises suggesting identity as a deity or supernatural (left to right, Janus-faced figure; Birdman; antlered Snake Man; Phillips and Brown 1984, pls 289, 300, 307; drawn by M. Jane Kellett, Arkansas Archeological Survey).

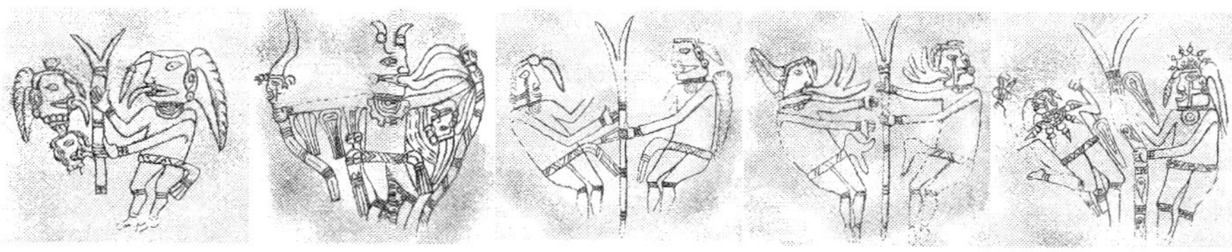

Fig. 6.3 Barker's core sequence of the Forked Pole theme (left to right, Phillips and Brown 1984, pls 286.1, 279, 313, 322, 309; drawn by M. Jane Kellett, Arkansas Archeological Survey).

a range of forms associated with a single actant denoted by the Wedgemouth surround. In cultural terms, he is likely a shape-shifter – a deity or spirit being. This inference seems consistent with the "ogee" or portal symbol rendering of the Wedgemouth design when viewed from a full face perspective. In contrast, the T-Bar character appears only in standard anthropomorphic form. The front view cross-in-circle rendering of the facial design furthermore can be interpreted as a symbolic indicator of earthly or human identity (Reilly 2004, 129–30). Thus, the compositions may be interpreted as depicting the transfer of a Forked Pole from a deity or supernatural to a human. Alex Barker (2020; see also Brown *et al.* 2020, 106–12) places this canonical series within a larger sequence that comprises the overarching narrative, consisting of five individual scenes (Fig. 6.3).

The first scene is illustrated by a composition showing Wedgemouth grasping the Forked Pole in presentation mode before two detached heads that also illustrate the Wedgemouth facial design. Within the larger corpus of Spiroan artistic renderings, detached heads are often exhibited in contexts suggesting symbolic reference to ancestry, or earlier representatives of an ongoing lineage. In the next scene, a central Wedgemouth figure grasps recurved "serpent staffs" at the ends of both outstretched arms, each staff surmounted by a T-Bar head. Speech scrolls indicate an utterance reaching the ear of one of the T-Bar figures.

In the third scene, Wedgemouth on the right presents the Forked Pole to T-Bar on the left, but with no indication of a speech act. This is the sole composition on which the standard left–right positioning of Wedgemouth and T-Bar is reversed.

The fourth scene consists of our canonical series (Phillips and Brown 1984, pls 314–23) in which the transference of the Forked Pole is accompanied by speech acts on the part of both Wedgemouth and T-Bar. One possible interpretation is that the Forked Pole serves as a material referent to the act of transference, and what is actually being transferred from the deity to the human is knowledge or information – perhaps in the form of a sacred text – presented as a song, chant, or spoken formula. In these depictions, where the transfer has already taken place, the Wedgemouth figure is characteristically shown with thumbs facing down after releasing the pole.

The final scene is depicted in the fifth composition, in which one T-Bar figure grasps a recurved Forked Pole while the other T-Bar figure performs a celebratory dance. This composition and that representing Scene 3 are the only ones that depict T-Bar in poses different from those comprising the canonical set.

In sum, the overall theme is a transfer of some sort from the collectivity of Wedgemouth deities to the figure of T-Bar, symbolized by hand-off of the Forked Pole. As suggested above, a sacred text in the form of a song, chant, or other utterance is one likely candidate for what is being transferred. A final inference advanced by Barker is that the Wedgemouth figure represents ancestors or another category of spirit being associated with a specific cultural tradition that T-Bar overturns, transforms, or uniquely inflects through the actions which are the core subject of the Craig C corpus.

We turn now to an exploration of what those actions might have been.

Forked Poles as sacred power symbols

A key element of our interpretations is the suggestion that the Wedgemouth figure represents the deity or perhaps a lineage of deities or supernaturals from whom a sacred gift is bequeathed to the human community, represented by T-Bar. The Forked Pole, portrayed as a hand-off from Wedgemouth to T-Bar, appears as a representation of the transferred gift. The prominent use of what we regard as speech symbols in these compositions suggest that the sacred gift takes form as a text or formula conveyed by speech act, song performance, chant, or some other utterance. Viewed within the context of the Spirit Lodge tableau, which we regard as a set piece for ritual performance of an act of renewal, the transferred gift very likely embodies or, at least, is associated with creative powers derived from the spiritual realm. How does the Forked Pole motif fit into to this narrative?

There is another example of the Forked Pole motif that bears upon this investigation. At an Arkansas rock shelter located about 45 miles (28 km) east of Spiro, a petroglyph tableau features two ranks of anthropomorphic figures arranged in what may plausibly be interpreted as a dance circle (Fig. 6.4). Nearby, positioned to suggest a role as leader or conductor of the dance, is a larger individual wearing a

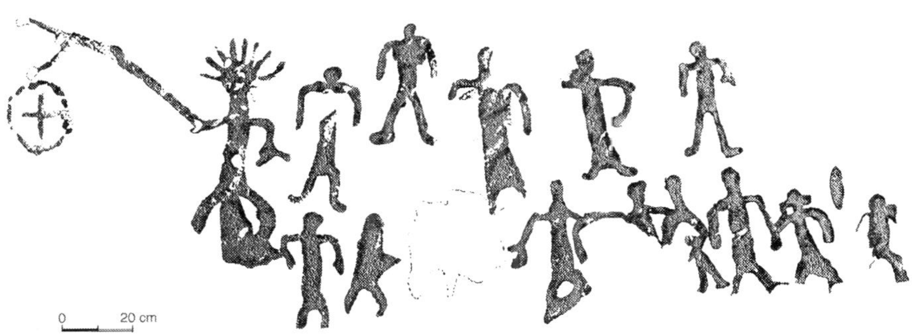

Fig. 6.4. Forked Pole rock art scene from The Narrows archaeological site (drawn by Leslie C. Walker, Arkansas Archeological Survey).

headdress and grasping a Forked Pole. The Forked Pole terminus extends above a cross-in-circle (or, world center) motif. The formal similarity of this tableau with a historic Osage dance celebrating a creation story provides further support for interpretation of the Forked Pole is a material indicator of the transfer of intangible cosmogonic power from deities to humans (cf. Mathews 1961, 10–15). In this case, the transferred power enabled primordial Osage communities to explore and establish their first communities on This (the Middle) World. Cosmogonic power enables humans to accomplish extraordinary tasks in the Middle World, often employing otherwise conventional means.

Another observation is that sets of three parallel lines encircling the Forked Pole shaft in all examples of our canonical set may represent the three-layered cosmos, providing symbolic reference to the concept of an *axis mundi* linking vertically separate dimensions of existence (Lankford 2007, 29–30). This *axis mundi* association may be identified as one element of Forked Pole symbolism compatible with the ogee as a portal symbol and the cross-in-circle as a world-center symbol. Filling out the cosmological linkage is the Wedgemouth figure in the guise of a deity associated with the unseen spirit world.

In sum, the Forked Pole motif is plausibly identified as an index of interactions that link deities or supernaturals and humans – residents of separate realms or domains within a multi-dimensional cosmos – in relationships appropriate to the transference of gifts across those domains, including knowledge or information about, or access to, cosmogonic power.

Next, we turn our attention to additional correspondences found in sacred narratives. Our purpose is not to assume any sort of historical continuity linking ancient Forked Poles to specific referents that appear in historic texts, but rather to explore if symbolic references appearing in recorded native testimony might plausibly be used as guides for inferring cognate forms reflected in Spiroan imagery, based on assumption of a shared cultural ancestry or, at least, thematic sharing among neighboring ancestral groups (Knight 2013, 140).

We begin with a Skidi Pawnee story that takes place following events through which *Tirawa* and the star-gods placed people on earth and bequeathed to them the goods and knowledge necessary to make their way through life, including sacred bundles and associated ceremonies. In one story (*Death of the Flint-Monster: Origin of Birds*, in Dorsey 1904, 24–30), that takes place a long time ago when there were people and animals but no birds, a boy and his sister live in the wilderness between two villages. The boy, aware of a mysterious animal suspected of carrying people off from one of the villages, resolves to find out if the animal might carry him off as well. He and his sister travel a great distance to visit the village. Shortly after their arrival, the mysterious animal carries off a warrior during a night-time victory dance following the return of a war party. This prompts the boy to go into the forest to ponder the event, after which he returns with a Forked Pole cut from a willow tree. Implanting the pole in the ground by his dwelling, he asks the young women of the village to guess its purpose. He marries the only woman able read his thoughts, leaving her with his sister (who transforms her from an ugly and sickly girl to a beautiful woman) while he goes in search of the animal, taking with him the Forked Pole. Soon he encounters the animal, a fearsome creature covered in flint, and both he and the animal understand that they will fight to the death. As the animal prepares to attack, the boy unwraps and displays his Forked Pole, immobilizing the animal so he can then shoot it dead with his bow and arrow. Upon his return to the village, the animal's severed paw is mounted on the Forked Pole for all to see. This empowers the rest of the villagers to transform into birds, animals, or anything else they wish to be. The boy – a child of the Sun – turns into a red bird.

A central theme, or *leitmotif*, of this story is the instrumental power of the Forked Pole. Though events clearly indicate that the boy and his sister are extraordinary individuals, to achieve his objective of defeating the monstrous animal the boy relies on additional powers conveyed via the Forked Pole that he crafts following inspiration received from his lonely sojourn into the forest. In the confrontation with his foe, the agency of the Forked Pole combines with that of the boy's own actions and conventional weaponry to produce a victory. This victory enables further world-changing events to take place, in which the villagers are transformed into the many animals and birds found in the present world.

This story and its "instrumental power of the Forked Pole" theme is one of a larger corpus of texts concerning sacred poles and sacred trees (Hall 1995, 102–8). These, in turn, are related to an even wider corpus Native American narratives that tell how humans, newly placed on the earth's surface shortly after creation, acquired the wherewithal to make their way – to create and maintain their distinctive societies – using cosmogonic powers manifest in sacred bundles and a wide array of other objects and manufactures bequeathed or inspired by deities, including pipes, musical instruments, weapons, and symbolic imagery.

An example of the latter is reflected in another Pawnee story about the *Origin of the Pipe-Stick Ceremony* (Dorsey 1906, 52–6). A young man dreams about a water monster and, upon waking, travels to the river revealed in his dream. He meets the monster in its underwater abode, where he learns the mysteries of animals and is instructed to return to his home and make an image of the monster. He is mostly successful, but unsure how to get a feather to decorate the image's headpiece. In a second dream, the monster gives the young man instructions on how to capture eagles. So, the young man goes to a high hill, digs a deep hole in the top, covers the hole with branches, and places skinned rabbits on top of the branches. Crouching in the hole beneath the branches, he is able to grab eagles as they alight to feed on the rabbits. Plucking their feathers, he completes the image of the water monster, who then gives him the Pipe-Stick, which the young man decorates with additional feathers. He is then instructed to make Forked Poles from the wood of a talking plum bush. Many birds and animals help the young man produce the Forked Poles and they teach him songs, through which the poles acquire power to make rain and influence other elements of nature for the benefit of the people.

Here again, an important *leitmotif* is the power of crafted objects (Forked Poles, again), inspired by suggestion of spirit beings and culture heroes, to empower humans to undertake world-altering actions. The larger purpose of these stories is to account for the creation of circumstances, institutions, or other apparatus or structures necessary for the success of human action in the world. These themes are widespread across the Southeast (Urban and Jackson 2004) and Plains (DeMallie and Parks 2001), suggesting the Spiroan imagery represents cognate versions of very widespread symbolic referents that persisted among many groups and transcended language group boundaries.

The traditions clearly spell out interconnections between human and spirit realms, in which extraordinary powers are bequeathed to extraordinary individuals, enabling them to accomplish tasks that benefit all of humanity. In historically recorded stories the fork pole serves as a material indicator of the transfer of knowledge and intangible power from deities to humans. The Forked Pole as an *axis mundi*, along with ogee and cross-in-circle motifs as cosmological portal and world-center, comprise the symbolic apparatus enabling select individuals to wield cosmogonic power, through which dangerous worlds are transformed into places safe and supportive of human prosperity.

In this world of gods and monsters, ritual acts performed in combination with the proper instruments provide a means through which humans, via social agency, can act like gods (Barth 1987). Among ancient Spiroans and their neighbors, the Forked Pole appears to have been one such instrument.

Note

1. Barker (2020) suggests use of the Wedgemouth and T-Bar designations as neutral labels for what are clearly two distinct characters whose images, distinguished by facial tattooing, are rendered on several Craig C compositions.

Bibliiography

Barker, A.W. (2020) Craig-Style iconography. In *Recovering Ancient Spiro: Native American Art, Ritual, and Cosmic Renewal*, E.D. Singleton and F.K. Reilly III (ed), 236–51. National Cowboy & Western Heritage Museum, Oklahoma City OK.

Barth, F. (1987) *Cosmologies in the Making: A Generative Approach to Cultural Variation in Inner New Guinea*. Cambridge University Press, Cambridge.

Beck, R.A., Bollander, D.J., Brown, J.A. and Earle, T.K. (2007) Eventful archaeology: the place of space in structural transformation. *Current Anthropology* 48, 833–60.

Brown, J.A. (1996) *The Spiro Ceremonial Center: The Archaeology of Arkansas Valley Caddoan Culture in Eastern Oklahoma*. Memoirs of the Museum of Anthropology 29. University of Michigan, Ann Arbor MI.

Brown, J.A. (2010) Cosmological layouts of secondary burials as political instruments. In *Mississippian Mortuary Practices: Beyond Hierarchy and the Representationist Perspective*, L.P. Sullivan and R.C. Mainfort Jr (eds), 30–53. University Press of Florida, Gainesville FL

Brown, J.A. (2012) Spiro reconsidered: sacred economy at the western frontier of the Eastern Woodlands. In *The Archaeology of the Caddo*, T.K. Perttula and C.P. Walker (eds), 117–38. University of Nebraska Press, Lincoln NE.

Brown, J.A., Barker, A.W. and Sabo, G. III (2020) The Spirit Lodge, Spiro renewal, and cosmic renewal. In *Recovering Ancient Spiro: Native American Art, Ritual, and Cosmic Renewal*, E.D. Singleton and F.K. Reilly III (eds), 92–113. National Cowboy & Western Heritage Museum, Oklahoma City OK.

Clements, F.E. (1945) Historical sketch of the Spiro Mound. *Contributions to the Museum of American Indian, Heye Foundation* 14, 48–68.

DeMallie, R.J. and Parks, D.R. (2001) Tribal traditions and records. In *Handbook of North American Indians, Vol. 13, Plains*, R.J. DeMallie (ed.), 1062–73. Smithsonian Institution, Washington DC.

Dorsey, G. (1904) *Traditions of the Skidi Pawnee*. Memoirs of the American Folklore Society 8, Houghton, Mifflin, Boston.

Dorsey, G. (1906) *The Pawnee Mythology*. Carnegie Institution, Washington DC.

Duffield, L.F. (1973) The Oklahoma Craig Mound: another look at an old problem. *Bulletin of the Oklahoma Anthropological Society* 22, 1–10.

Galloway, P. (ed.) (1989) *The Southeastern Ceremonial Complex: Artifacts and Analysis*. University of Nebraska Press, Lincoln NE.

Hall, R.L. (1995) *An Archaeology of the Soul: North American Indian Belief and Ritual*. University of Illinois Press, Urbana IL.

Hamilton, H.W. (1952) The Spiro Mound. *Missouri Archaeologist* 14, 17–106.

Horton, E. (2020) Sacred bundles in the Craig Mound Spirit Lodge at Spiro. In *Recovering Ancient Spiro: Native American Art, Ritual, and Cosmic Renewal*, E.D. Singleton and F.K. Reilly III (eds), 136–49. National Cowboy & Western Heritage Museum, Oklahoma City OK.

Horton, E. and Sabo, G. III (2011) Spiro Perishable Project makes exciting new discovery. *Field Notes: Newsletter of the Arkansas Archeological Society* 358, 9–13.

King, A. (ed.) (2007) *Southeastern Ceremonial Complex: Chronology, Content, Context*. The University of Alabama Press, Tuscaloosa AL.

Knight, V.J. Jr (2013) *Iconographic Method in New World Prehistory*. Cambridge University Press, Cambridge.

Krieger, A.D. (1945) An inquiry into supposed Mexican influence on a prehistoric cult in the Southern United States. *American Anthropologist* 47, 483–515.

Lankford, G.E. (2007) Some cosmological motifs in the Southeastern Ceremonial Complex. In Reilly and Garber (eds) 2007, 8–38.

Lankford, G.E., Reilly, F.K. III and Garber, J.F. (2011) *Visualizing the Sacred: Cosmic Visions, Regionalism, and the Art of the Mississippian World*. University of Texas Press, Austin TX.

Mathews, J.J. (1961) *The Osage: Children of the Middle Waters*. University of Oklahoma Press, Norman OK.

Orr, K.G. (1946) The archaeological situation at Spiro, Oklahoma: a preliminary report. *American Antiquity* 11, 228–55.

Phillips, P. and Brown, J.A. (1984) *Pre-Columbian Shell Engravings from the Craig Mound at Spiro, Oklahoma*. Part 2. Peabody Museum Press, Harvard University, Cambridge MA.

Reilly, F.K. III (2004) People of earth, people of sky: visualizing the sacred in Native American art of the Mississippian Period. In *Hero, Hawk, and Open Hand: American Indian Art of the Ancient Midwest and South*, R.F. Townsend and R.V. Sharp (eds), 125–37. Yale University Press and The Art Institute of Chicago, New Haven CT and London.

Reilly, F.K. III and Garber, J.F. (eds) (2007) *Ancient Objects and Sacred Realms: Interpretations of Mississippian Iconography*. University of Texas Press, Austin TX.

Urban, G. and Jackson, J.B. (2004) Mythology and folklore. In *Handbook of North American Indians, Vol. 14, Southeast*, R.D. Fogelson (ed.), 707–19. Smithsonian Institution, Washington DC.

Williams. S. (ed.) (1968) *The Waring Papers: The Collected Works of Antonio J. Waring, Jr.* Papers of the Peabody Museum of Archaeology and Ethnology 58, Cambridge MA.

7

The Hero Twins in the Lower Mississippi Valley

David H. Dye

Religious narratives centering on the Hero Twins comprise an integral component of Indigenous New World belief systems (Lévi-Strauss 1995). As Divine Beings, the Hero Twins have ancient origins in eastern North America and beliefs concerning them are widespread throughout North America (Radin 1915; 1945; 1948; 1949; 1954; Sumner 1951; Hultkrantz 1979; Lankford 1987; 2008, 2011; Hall 1989; 1997; Myers 2002). In fact, Paul Radin (1949) characterizes the Hero Twins' narratives as the basic North American myth. Mississippian iconography supports the presence of Twins imagery in eastern North America (King 2007; Reilly and Garber 2007; Lankford *et al.* 2011; Diaz-Granados *et al.* 2015; Dye 2017).

Margaret Sumner (1951) has suggested these mythic narratives extolling the Twins diffused westward from the Eastern Woodlands to the Great Plains (Sumner 1951, 74), but it is doubtful that an "origin" for the Twins' narratives and associated institutions will be found or that beliefs concerning them diffused or were independently invented across eastern North America. The basic Twins story almost certainly arrived with the earliest migrants into the New World, and over time morphed into myriad versions due to ritual sodality distinctions, rather than diffusing from one area to another. Thus, ritual sodalities venerating the Twins circulated through ritual transfer from polity to polity, and region to region, perhaps in a manner similar to the movement through ritual purchase of historically documented Thunder medicine lodges. It is more likely that religious institutions such as medicine societies (ritual sodalities) venerating the Twins cut across kinship lines and in this sense Twins-associated rituals could be adopted, appropriated, purchased, or transferred by individuals who cross-cut kin lines in other polities as well, resulting in numerous differences and distinctions in conceptualizing the Twins. Thus, movement would have taken place within the context of an institution such as a medicine society or ritual sodality, being transferred through gifting or purchase.

In this paper I follow an iconographic approach in outlining linkages between Tunican polities of the northern Lower Mississippi Valley (nLMV) and ritual paraphernalia used in honoring and supplicating the Hero Twins, referred to here as *Lightning Boy* (Thrown Away) and *Thunder Boy* (Lodge Boy). The epithets Lightning Boy and Thunder Boy reference lightning motifs and thunder producing symbolic weaponry, such as exaggerated bifaces and exotic war clubs. In numerous allegorical stories and charter myths, the Twins avenge their father/uncle's death by killing his murderers and then resurrecting him (Radin 1945; 1949; Hall 1997, 162). Such events were re-enacted in legerdemain theatrics employing symbolic weaponry that showcased the Twins' power of requickening (i.e., re-awakening or rejuvenating) the dead (Dye 2020). In addition, *Datura* (jimsonweed) use may have been a crucial component in the widespread creation and circulation of novel Hero Twins sodalities with their beliefs in flight and demonstrations of healing, miracles, and resurrection, as well as employment of raptor regalia.

The Hero Twins may shape-shift, taking on varying forms, especially crested birds in the Mississippian iconographic corpus (Lankford 2008, 155). Chartering narratives detailing the Twin's powers were crucial for explaining how death and mourning came into existence and how death could be overcome through re-awakening or requickening. At their core Twin's sacred narratives are recitations of death's defeat and charters for religious sodalities that venerated the Twins as capable of resurrecting the dead. These cosmological models comprised apodictic principles employed by an aristocratic cohort of suppliants organized as ritual institutions, especially medicine lodges, which furthered their member's interests and thus provided access to and holds on offices, power, titles, and wealth. These restrictive and secretive institutions formed a web of entangled and interconnected relationships among clans, ritual sodalities, and social houses that underpinned the ability of a few to hold authority over the majority.

The Hero Twins in eastern North America

Throughout eastern North America the Twins are associated with deadly gaming, death, fire, lightning, mortal combat, rain, sun, thunder, and warfare. For example, according to the Cherokee, the Twins are envisioned as Thunderers who, through their possession of lightning, brought Sacred Fire to This (the Middle) World from the Upper World (Mooney 1900, 240–2), as weather deities they could summon rain (Hann 1988, 343). The Lenape believe "man-like beings with wings produce the thunder and bring the storms; the lightning-flashes are their arrows" (Harrington 1913, 227, 233). The Apalachee culture hero, Thunder, is known as "Ray of the Sun", a euphemism for lightning, reflecting the belief that lightning originates from the Sun (Van Horne 1993, 137). Lightning is represented in the Apalachee charter myth as the descendant of the Sun, and the Twins in general are often thought of as Children of the Sun (Duncan and Diaz-Granados 2000), who are invested with divine powers symbolized by thunder and lightning. Thunder, as a culture hero, is the ultimate warrior who defeats enemies through his prowess and power, and the force which sustains society by providing rain (Van Horne 1993, 141–2). As mythical warriors the Twins could strike mortal blows upon their enemies, typically cannibalistic giants, on behalf of humankind (Swanton 1929, 7–9; Hudson 1976, 127).

In a Choctaw narrative, the Sun rubs off the Twin's skin and then places them in boiling water. After surviving the test, Sun then instructs a large buzzard to carry the two brothers from his home in the sky to their home on earth (Bushnell 1909, 35). Unfortunately, many of these post-16th century stories lack the chartering elements for political, religious, and social institutions, which they originally possessed (Keyes 1994). As the Hero Twins mythic narratives have a well-documented presence in eastern North America (Radin 1948; Sumner 1951; Hultkrantz 1979; Lankford 1987; Hall 1989; 1997; Myers 2002), such archetypal and etiological explanations would have been important in justifying and legitimizing elite claims to offices, regalia, and titles, and behaviors, such as contraries.

Mythic narratives of the Hero Twins provide a cornerstone for religious beliefs with their emphasis on the cyclical nature of life and death through rebirth, reincarnation, and requickening (Hankoff 1977). Myth allows the suppliant to exist or remain in the sacred realm, or "true reality", by being associated with and imitating the actions of culture heroes (Eliade 1971). Ritual sodality members conjured and supplicated the Twins for their powers of lightning and thunder. Their depictions as Thunder beings with tail feathers, talon feet and wings, and grasping hawk moths (Knight and Franke 2007), provides a convincing association with *Datura* and its ability to provide one with the sensation of flight. Their dreams/visions from ingesting magical plants, especially *Datura*, gives one the sensation of being a bird. Raptor claws and feathers have been associated with *Datura* in ancient Mexico, from which the plant originated and spread (Froese 2020). By theatrical imitation of the Hero Twins, warriors entered the sacred world and through dreams/visions and supplication garnered the Twins' apotropaic powers.

Decapitation may have been conducted to commemorate the Hero Twins' combat with cannibalistic giants who killed their father/uncle. In an Ojibwa story, the Twins reveal their powers by playing a deadly game known as "cutting off heads" (Sumner 1951, 54). In mortal contests, as an example of high-stakes gambling, the Hero Twins defeat the giants, thus providing a metaphor for the ability to overcome death. Decapitation is often the result of high-stakes gaming in dawn time contests involving the Twins (Curtin and Hewitt 1918; Lankford 2008; 163–90) and plays an important role in charter myth recitations and legerdemain theatrics (Petrovich 2009; Chacon and Dye 2011). Thus, charter narratives often require emulation of culture hero behaviors and exhibitions of decapitation and dismemberment as important components of ritual violence, demonstrating powers derived from other-than-human beings (Brown and Dye 2007; Dye 2017).

By manipulating ritual, charismatic individuals emerge who harness political power through their involvement in religious institutions, especially ritual sodalities (Hayden 2001; 2011; 2018). The promotion and stabilization of hereditary inequalities inherent in medicine societies aids its members in gaining some degree of control and influence over the political economy through ritual means (Earle 2021). Religious practitioners, through force of personality, establish and legitimize their holds over a core constituency through charter myths, dreams/visions, esoteric practices, legerdemain theatrics, religious performance, restrictive secret societies, and witchcraft accusations (Fortune 1932; Radin 1945; Hayden 2001; 2011; 2014, 2018; Emerson 2003; Dye 2021a).

Narrations, re-enacted through performances, involve complex ritual acts. For example, the Oglala Sioux artist, Kills Two, in his pictorial vignette *Horse Dance*, depicts the ceremonial re-enactment of a warrior's vision of Thunder Beings and Thunder Horses with painted streaks of lightning (Alexander 1938, pl. 9). Thunder Beings are also represented in Black Hawk's pictorial representation of his personal spiritual vision (Berlo 2000, 26–32). A person's dreams or visions provide an important means of obtaining gifts, knowledge, and power in Lakota society, and Black Hawk's arresting imagery of powerful other-than-human beings conveys the transformative power of the vision experience. The Hero Twins as Thunder beings are often portrayed as supernatural animal composites. Black Hawk's drawings illustrate human-like figures with bison horns, raptor talon feet and "hands", and round eyes (Berlo 2000, pls 1 and 2). The talon hands of Black Hawk's Thunder Beings grasp or emit lightning bolts. As the Lakota believe Thunder Beings shoot lightning from their eyes, dancers impersonate such figures, wearing bison horn head coverings with mirrors that flash in the same manner as "lightning-eyed Spirit Beings" (Wissler 1912, 98).

Religious sodalities cycled over time as a result of the turn-over in charismatically charged authority figures who regularly instituted new medicine societies (Golla 1975). Prairie and Plains polities repeatedly formed new societies upon the demise of older sodalities (Howard 1965, 113), allowing political changes and adjustments to take place as needed by aristocratic congregations. Thus, the lifespan of medicine societies honoring and revering the Twins may have been relatively short-lived, giving rise to contemporary and competitive variations of Twins ritual institutions over only a few generations. Headed by emerging leaders, novel Mississippian religious societies would have arisen in the face of changing political and social structures in an atmosphere of conflict, factionalism, and rivalry.

The Mississippian Hero Twins

The ritual organization of Twins supplication was structured through charter narratives, with their dramatic characters, plots, and scenes, which extoll the Twins as preternatural beings. Charter myths direct the foundation for human agency in creating and perpetuating specific religious sodalities and their articulation with the political and ritual economy. Twin myths recount and substantiate social origins, emphasizing one of the basic Mississippian structural principles: the duality of essential, complementary opposites. Mississippian rituals functioned to conjure, control, placate, or supplicate ancestors and culture heroes, such as the Hero Twins (Townsend and Sharp 2004; Reilly and Garber 2007; Lankford *et al.* 2011; Dye 2012; 2020; Pauketat 2013).

As principal Mississippian culture heroes, the Hero Twins possessed extraordinary and miraculous powers associated with bundles and sacra, especially revitalizing and resurrecting the dead (Radin 1945; 1949; Duncan and Diaz-Granados 2000;

Weeks 2009; Dye 2012; 2018; 2020; Lankford and Dye 2014). The primary protagonist of the Twins charter myth is the "wild" brother (aka Lightning Boy or Thrown Away), raised in the watery Beneath World (Underworld) and possessing a suite of attributes and powers associated with that realm: death, rain, and warfare. The Twins bestowed to humans valuable ceremonial regalia and ritual institutions, such as religious sodalities, which imbued members with lightning and thunder powers. The Twins' adversaries and antagonists include animals, cannibalistic giants, monsters, and Symplegades-like (clashing rocks) dangers in the cosmoscape, in addition to a host of other powerful beings, including Thunderbirds and water spirits (Sumner 1951, 64–5). Garnering such powers by humans from the Twins required appropriate dreams/visions, fasting, purification, and supplication, but these requests also provided remarkable benefits such as defeating one's enemies, healing the sick, overcoming death, and precipitating changes in weather, especially droughts and pluvial events.

In addition to being revenant culture heroes, the Twins are also acknowledged for their transformative powers. They could escape from or discomfit an antagonist by shape-shifting into arrows that could be shot over long distances. At other times they might assume the form of down or feathers to float wherever they wished to travel (Sumner 1951; Lankford 2008; 157) or they might transform into crested birds (Lankford 2008). It is interesting to note in this regard that birds and raccoons are consistent iconographic motifs associated with the Mississippian Twins. During their adventures, the Twins often brought back power gifts for their father/uncle: antlers stolen from Beneath World water spirits, feathers plucked from Thunderbirds, horns cut from buffalo bulls, and scalp locks taken from other-than-human-persons (Sumner 1951). These items, in addition to animal and human body parts, became ritual paraphernalia worn as regalia during ritual sodality performances that demonstrated and venerated a person's connections with the powerful Hero Twins and visualized their sources of power. Such objects and regalia were imbued with agency, animism, and sentiency, being called upon by the owner for aid, health, power, and success.

Combating or engaging death through high stakes gaming was crucial to the enterprise of ritual sodalities. Charter myths frequently extolled the Twins' legendary abilities to bring one another back to life after having been killed, often as a result of death through combat or gambling with powerful enemies. For example, mutual ritual decapitation and legerdemain is vividly materialized in Hightower-style mortal combat theme gorgets (Dye 2004, fig. 6; Marceaux and Dye 2007; Reilly and Garber 2011, 301). Replicating such events, recounted through mythic charters by secret society members, showcased their ability to heal and to revive the dead via dramatic demonstrations of prestidigitation by replacing severed body parts, especially heads removed through decapitation.

Reviving the dead revealed the power of initiated society members and demonstrated how life forces could be allocated and controlled based on the widespread belief in the capture and deployment of life forces (Dye 2016). The Twins' ritual death and revival constituted an important Mississippian religious theme, often the primary focus of ritual institutions such as medicine lodges. Ethnohistoric accounts relate how religious practitioners not only employed sacred bundles to conjure or summon powerful culture heroes for the supplication of personal spiritual power, but how these medicine people also manipulated animal pelt bundles, through acts of legerdemain, to "kill" and then requicken society members. Finally, ritual actors could destroy their antagonists or enemies through magical death with these bundles (Gangloff 1995, 64).

Perhaps the earliest Mississippian imagery of the Twins is found at Picture Cave, dating to the early 11th century (Duncan and Diaz-Granados 2000, 12–16; Diaz-Granados *et al.* 2015; Duncan 2015, fig. 17.11). These images appear as discrete, pictorial vignettes, one component of a complex oral narrative, an *aide-mémoire*, depicting cosmic events in which the Twins, as powerful spirits, assume human-like form, perhaps during drug-induced states from magical plants such as *Datura* or tobacco. Picture Cave is important for contextualizing the Hero Twins in Mississippian artistic imagery and religious narratives as well as ritual regalia and paraphernalia. The Twins are also represented at Gottschall Rockshelter in southwest Wisconsin (Dieterle 2005), which is roughly contemporary with the Picture Cave images (Salzer and Rajnovich 2001, fig. 23).

By the 13th century the Hero Twins were depicted on ceramics, copper, and shell throughout the Midwest and Midsouth. While narratives of the Twins undoubtedly found popularity prior to the Mississippian period, it is with the transformation of ritual institutions that Twins imagery flourishes as crucial and integral components of medicine societies. Figural images of the Twins are found in eastern Oklahoma, the nLMV, the Middle Cumberland Valley, and the southern Appalachians at about the same time.

The Braden style was introduced from the Mississippian world into eastern Oklahoma at the northern Caddoan Spiro site in the early to mid-13th century, where it is found engraved on shell cups and gorgets (Brown 2004). The Braden-style Lightner Cup from Spiro (Phillips and Brown 1978, 19–20, pl. 20) illustrates the Twins, accompanied by a third party, in proximity with a water spirit, which may serve as a locative for the watery realm. The Craig style, a local inspiration crafted at Spiro and apparently influenced by the imported Braden style, also incorporates Twins imagery (Phillips and Brown 1984; Townsend 2004, 30–1; Barker 2020). Craig-style shell gorgets portraying the Twins often employ two accompanying animals that play important roles in Twins charter myths: raccoons, as hindquarter motifs, and birds, as feather or whole body headdress elements (Dye 2017; Phillips and Brown 1978, 154–5; 1984, pls 127, 128, 132, 136, and 142).

Likewise, the Hero Twins are visualized in the Middle Cumberland Valley, including ceramic adorno rims with double braids and rattle heads (Smith and Beahm 2011; Lankford and Dye 2014), "Chacmool-like" figures (Smith *et al.* 2019), and figurines (Smith and Sharp 2021), as well as rock art and shell gorgets (Beahm and Smith 2012; Beahm 2013, 367; Sharp *et al.* 2020). The Thruston Tablet, an irregular limestone slab engraved between about AD 1250 and 1325, comprises a palimpsest or story board that includes the mythic portrayal of the Twins (Steponaitis *et al.* 2011; Sharp *et al.* 2020). Although stylistically dissimilar, the tablet comprises human-like figural art representing the Twins (Willoughby 1932, fig. 29; Phillips and Brown 1978, figs 177–8, 232; Power 2004, fig. 16) that bears a striking resemblance to the Braden-style Spiro Lightner Cup (Steponaitis *et al.* 2011, 164). As is the case with Craig-style gorgets from Spiro, the Twins on the Thruston Tablet wear raccoon hindquarters and bird feathers as headdress regalia. The images also include woodpecker head clubs and serpent staffs, in addition to other ceremonial accoutrements. Shell gorgets illustrating the Hero Twins have also been found in the Middle Cumberland Valley, where they represent rebirth and renewal (Smith and Beahm 2011; Beahm 2013).

Found throughout the Mississippi–Ohio rivers confluence region (MORCR) and up the Cumberland River and into the southern Appalachian polities, marine-shell crafting constituted a flourishing tradition (Smith and Smith 1989; Brain and Phillips 1996; Hoffman 1997; Smith 1997; 2017; King 2003; Hally 2007; Sullivan 2007; Rodning 2012). An artistic repertoire representing the Twins arrived in the Appalachian Highlands during mid-13th century, giving rise to a long period of marine-shell crafting that lasted until approximately AD 1650. The Twins may be identified in four sequential Appalachian shell art styles: Hightower, Cartersville, Williams Island, and face mask gorgets.

Hightower shell gorgets, which date between approximately AD 1250 and 1325 (Brain and Phillips 1996; Dye 2004, 195; Hally 2007; King 2011, 283), comprise characteristics of the Hightower style, and regalia specific to the Twins, deer antler and raccoon pelt headdress elements (Dye 2017), both of which are shared with the Middle Cumberland Valley Thruston Tablet (Steponaitis *et al.* 2011) and the eastern Oklahoma Craig style (Barker 2020). The second expression of the Twins is found in Cartersville-style shell gorgets (AD 1300–1375). A third style, Williams Island, dates between AD 1425 and 1525 (Lankford 2008, 156; King 2011, 284). The fourth Twins imagery is the face-mask-style, which enjoyed great popularly from about AD 1575 to 1650 (Smith and Smith 1989; King 2011, 285; Smith 2017). Marvin and Julie Smith (1989) argue that face mask gorgets represent the Thunderers (i.e., the Twins).

In eastern North America key celestial deities and culture heroes are often characterized by specific ritual regalia. The Twins are associated with distinctive ritual paraphernalia in the form of headdress regalia: the bladder headdress and double paired braids in the Cumberland and Mississippi Valleys (Lankford and Dye 2014; Smith *et al.* 2019), raccoon pelts in the Craig style at Spiro (Phillips and Brown 1984; Barker 2020), and the combination of deer antlers and raccoon pelts in the Hightower-style of the Appalachian Highlands (Marceaux and Dye 2007; Dye 2017). The bladder headdress is found at Picture Cave (Duncan 2015), the Middle Cumberland Valley (Sharp *et al.* 2020), and the nLMV (Lankford and Dye 2014). For example, "Line Face" in the Thruston Tablet possesses, in varying scenes, bladder, feather, and raccoon headdress elements (Steponaitis *et al.* 2011).

Based on the Thruston Tablet imagery and mythic narratives, bladder headdresses may either appear with the wild twin (Lightning Boy or Thrown Away) or both Twins (Lankford and Dye 2014; Steponaitis *et al.* 2011). For example, Picture Cave has two identical figures identified as the Twins, both wearing bladder headgear and carrying exaggerated arrows (Diaz-Granados and Duncan 2000, fig. 5.48; Duncan and Diaz-Granados 2000, 14–15; Duncan 2015). A similar interpretation for both Twins adorned with bladder headgear has been suggested for a rim-effigy form found in the nLMV (Lankford and Dye 2014). Here, the mythic reference is based on the use of bladders by the father/uncle of Lodge Boy and Thrown Away, who attempts to prevent the wild boy from escaping into the Beneath World waters by attaching an inflated bladder-float to his head. Bladder-float headdress regalia are elements of ritual accoutrements in the Hidatsa Naxpike Sun Dance, in which those who undergo self-inflicted torture are painted red and white and wear bladders as headdress regalia (Lowie 1919, 429). The Hidatsa link the Twins with the Sun Dance in their chartering myth, and Twins iconography has been associated with early forms of Sun Dance-like rituals among nLMV Tunican speakers (Lankford and Dye 2014).

Three figural art styles are associated with raccoon hindquarters in the depiction of the Hero Twins: Craig, Hightower, and Middle Cumberland (Thruston Tablet). The combination of deer antlers and raccoon hindquarters as components of pelt headdresses has a long tradition of association with the Twins in the Appalachian Highlands from approximately AD 1250 to 1600 (Marceaux and Dye 2007; King 2011; Dye 2017). There is some temporal overlap in the Twins pelt headdress regalia, especially in the Craig, Hightower, and Middle Cumberland (Thruston) styles. In virtually every instance, the Twins are rendered as wearing ritual head gear. In some nLMV imagery they don the same headdress regalia, while in other contexts they wear differing ceremonial accoutrements and headdress regalia, presumably reflecting different mythic plot motifs.

The Hero Twins in the northern Lower Mississippi Valley

Based on linguistic analysis of indigenous polity names recorded by members of the mid-16th century Hernando de Soto expedition (Rankin 1993), the nLMV from the mouth of the Ohio River south to the mouth of the Arkansas River, was home to Tunican speaking people organized as competitive, chiefly polities (Hoffman 1993; 1994; Hudson 1997; Jeter 2002). Significant differences existed among these regional polities as reflected in the Spanish accounts (Hoffman 1993; Hudson 1997; Young and Hoffman 1993). Archaeological phase designations, mapped by ceramic frequency distributions, provide additional support for Tunican political provinces recorded by the Iberian explorers (Phillips 1970; Young and Hoffman 1993). Figural portrayals of the Hero Twins had become prominent in the Tunican iconographic record as early as the mid-13th century as people migrated southward upon the breakup of Cahokia (Burnette *et al.* 2020).

The pre-1650 Tunican ceramic assemblages are significantly different from those of the later post-1650 Siouan (Quapaw) who settled in the Lower Arkansas Valley and the nLMV (Hoffman 1994; House 2013). Early contact period Tunicans, prior to their collapse, possessed religious structures best understood through their materialized beliefs: marine shell gorgets, ritual ceramic wares, and symbolic weaponry. While continuities are evident in traditional forms of ritual as expressed in ceramic production and practice, novel sacra appear in the late 16th century in the form of new ceramic design elements, motifs, and shapes, as well

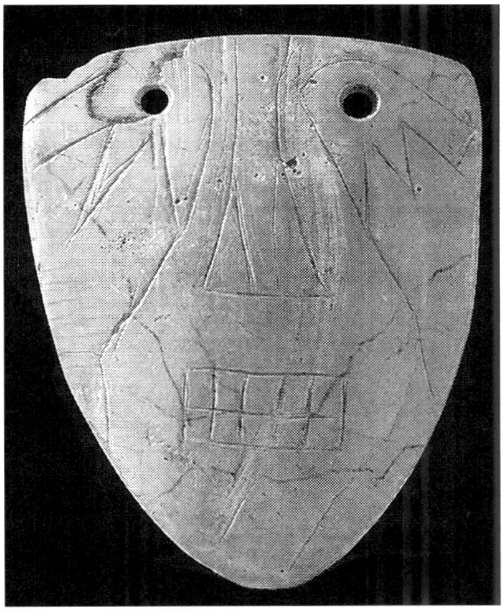

Fig. 7.1 Face Mask Gorget, Campbell Site (23PM5, photograph by David H. Dye).

as face mask gorgets and symbolic weaponry, signaling improvisations and innovations of extant ritual practices as well as transformations in linkages between political and ritual economies (Fig. 7.1). The re-alignment of religious sodalities, based on the re-organization of rituals and changes in attendant motifs and sacra, reflects structural disjunctions in political and religious practice and reveals disarticulations in ritual behavior and religious sodality cycling. The Hero Twins's imagery as recorded as ceramic and shell media occupy a pivotal role in these nLMV restructured and transformed religious institutions. While the Hero Twins may be recognized as two individuals, it is typically the wild twin who is depicted in Mississippian iconography. In addition to their panoply of ritual regalia (bellows-shaped aprons, bird feathers, bi-lobed arrows, deer antlers, and raccoon pelts), they are also shown holding symbolic weaponry: arrows, bifacial knives, crown-form maces, raptor talon hooks, and spatulate celts (Marceaux and Dye 2007). Mississippian iconography also depicts the Twins in association with anthropomorphic heads, chunkey stones, hawk moths, and human-headed serpents.

The Twins are expressed in the Eddyville-style of marine shell gorgets, which is at "home in the Central Mississippi Valley" and their close correspondence with the gorgets suggests they are from the same workshop (Brain and Phillips 1996, 52). The Eddyville-style (aka Big Toco), with its beginning in the mid-13th century (Hally 2007, fig. 10.3), illustrates the Hero Twins, both singly and together. In both cases they are adorned with bellows-shaped aprons as scalp pouches, bi-lobed arrows, and marine shell beads. They either brandish weaponry and carry a human head, or they hurl chunkey stones. Such depictions are part of a central mythic narrative that communicates a cosmological allegory of the instauration and transfer of sacred powers, as well as resurrection of the dead (Brown and Dye 2007). Symbolic weaponry is crucial ritual gear for legerdemain performances honoring and supplicating the Hero Twins (Dye 2020). And the chunkey player theme illustrates deadly gaming with mythic monsters.

The chunkey game is a salient gambling contest in the Midwest and Southeast (Zych 2017). The essential feature of a match centers around a player who rolls a clay or stone disk along the hard-packed surface of a chunkey ground or yard, sometimes aided by a chunkey stick, while an opponent (or both players) hurls a pole after the chunkey roller with the object of hitting or coming as close as possible to the disk at its point of rest (DeBoer 1993). Elite sponsored, institutional based chunkey game rituals, perhaps conducted under the purview of ritual sodalities, began in the mid-11th century with the rise of Cahokia (Pauketat 2013).

The Mississippian chunkey game was based on widely accepted and well-known protocols that included artistic representations, ceremonial regalia, charter myths, a gambling ethos, regulations and rules, and ritual practices. Charter myths include descriptions of primordial contests in which the Hero Twins challenged cannibalistic giants to deadly contests, often with unfortunate outcomes. A recurring mythic motif finds the losers often being decapitated (Lankford 2008, 163–90). That ritual chunkey games played a crucial role in the Mississippian belief system is underscored by Charles Hudson (1976, 425), who suggests the chunkey game's popularity declined after European contact as a result of its being "bound up with traditional Southeastern beliefs and social alignments, and after these beliefs and social alignments changed, the game lost most of its meaning".

James Brown and John Kelly (2000) connect the chunkey player theme with Cahokia in the second half of the 11th century, with the game's emphasis on a close set of ritual paraphernalia: chunkey equipment, long-nosed maskettes, and symbolic weaponry. The Twins, visualized as chunkey players, are associated with crested birds, which are attached to chunkey poles or staffs. George Lankford (2004; 2007; 2008) identifies crested birds as weather powers and suggests they are alternative forms of the Hero Twins, one of their transformative guises. The Hero Twins also hold decapitated human heads with ellipsoidal eye surrounds and hair braids in the chunkey player theme gorgets. The concentric circles on the chest of the Douglass Gorget are interpreted as chunkey stones, reflecting the Hero Twins' connection with the chunkey game (Sharp *et al.* 2020, 339) (Fig. 7.2).

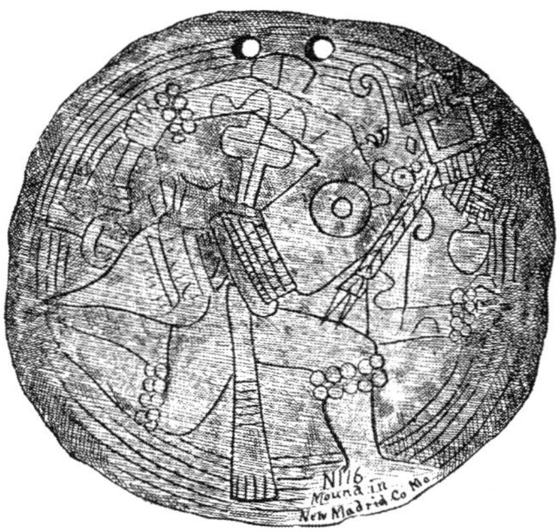

Fig. 7.2 Rendering of the incised design on the Douglass Gorget, New Madrid County, Missouri (from Thruston 1897, pl. 17).

Distinctive ceramic effigies – often termed "corn god" figures, but more recently designated "coneheads" – adorn bowl rims (Fig. 7.3) and comprise a tradition of Twins imagery that began about AD 1250, although the conehead motif is evident at Picture Cave in the early 11th century. Based on the distinctive bladder headdress element discussed in the charter narratives (Lankford and Dye 2014), the ceramic imagery may only represent the wild twin, Lightning Boy, although in artistic imagery and mythic narratives both Twins at times wear bladder headdresses. This artistic expression was also widely employed on hooded bottles.

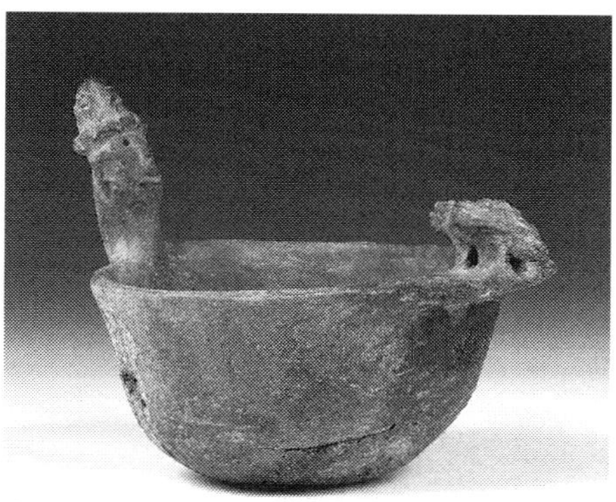

Fig. 7.3 Lightning Boy Bowl with Snapping Turtle Rim Rider, Bradley Site (3CT7, courtesy of the Memphis Museum of Science and History, photograph by David H. Dye).

An additional feature of the Twins mythic narratives is the ability to remove one's brains and replace them with pebbles. This is reflected in the construction of a hollow adorno head that is filled with pebbles, so the head will rattle when shaken. In one of the opening episodes in the Lodge Boy/Thrown Away oicotype for the Caddoan/Siouan myth cluster, a small plot element describes how Thrown-Away emerges from the water and plays with his brother but flees when their father appears. When Lodge-Boy informs his father about his twin brother, the father tells Lodge-Boy to either seize Thrown-Away (the wild twin) by the hair or tie an inflated animal bladder to his head. In one Pawnee episode, the father "returns with two bladders blown up and containing rattles, one of which he directs his son [Lodge-Boy] to tie to the hair of his younger brother" (Dorsey 1906, 494–5). The bladder prevents Thrown-Away from escaping into the water. The association of Lightning Boy with the snapping turtle in Fig. 7.3 further emphasizes the connection with water-spirit power, and perhaps Lightning Boy's ability to transform as a water spirit.

The many examples of ceramic conehead rattles alert us to the widespread identity of the wild twin and the form itself represents a mythic narrative that charters ritual institutions, especially ritual sodalities, supplicating and venerating the Hero Twins for personal power. The Hidatsa Naxpike (Lowie 1919, 429), for example, wear inflated bladders as ritual headgear and a Menomini charter myth relates how the Hero Twins sing medicine lodge songs while rattling the small stones in their heads. Thus, the rattle-head motif in ceramics, mythic narratives, and ritual sodalities may represent an eastern variant of a later ritual that became known as the Sun Dance (Skinner and Satterlee 1915, 341; Lankford and Dye 2014, 46–8; Sharp *et al.* 2020, 333–4).

Face-mask gorgets were introduced into the nLMV sometime in the late 16th or early 17th century from the Appalachian Highlands, perhaps as a new religious institution that venerated the Twins (Lankford and Dye 2014). One prior form of early to mid-16th century shell gorgets, Citico-style rattlesnake gorgets, are absent from the nLMV, and the arrival of face-mask gorgets in this region signals an important political event, tied into a major transformation of the existing entanglements of aristocratic cohorts. Although introduced late, face-mask gorgets became the most widely circulated type of marine-shell gorgets and may represent the rapid expansion of Twins religious sodalities among competing medicine lodges extending from the Atlantic Coast to the western edge of the northern plains, perhaps associated with the early fur trade in the first half of the 17th century (Dye 2022).

Artistic depictions of the Hero Twins in the nLMV possess continuity in theme, but stylistic differences as institutional and ritual transformations. Widespread circulation of Twins sacra begins in the decades after people move southward from the American Bottom during the Cahokia diaspora. Early portrayals of the Twins may be seen at Picture Cave (Diaz-Granados *et al.* 2015) and in the widely circulated long-nosed maskettes (Duncan and Diaz-Granados 2000), suggesting Twins institutions and narratives were deeply embedded in Mississippian religion and ritual. Renditions of the Twins in ceramic and shell media were crafted by people in the nLMV beginning in the mid-13th century and continuing within ritual institutions such as the medicine lodge with imagery in ceramic and shell media.

The Hero Twins, legerdemain, and symbolic weaponry

The ability of the Hero Twins to revive the dead is a central religious theme that underlies the charter narratives of ritual sodalities. Supplication for magical powers continued until recent times among Plains polities. For example, the Pawnee Hero Twin, Long-Tooth-Boy, possesses a flint stone, which had magic powers, having been formed after lightning struck water (Dorsey 1904a, 89–90, 344). These supernatural powers allowed Long-Tooth-Boy to foretell or predict impending dangers. He often demonstrated his ability to revive the dead by bringing his brother back to life through the recitation of the magical incantation, "Brother, you have been sleeping long enough; awake", upon which the brother is returned from death to life (Dorsey 1904a, 93). Menominee narratives also feature the wild boy reviving the dead (Sumner 1951, 56).

The Twins are often associated with the powers of lightning and thunder. In Caddo narratives the Twins travel to the sky to become Lightning and Thunder beings (Dorsey 1905, 31–6). In Caddo cosmology Lightning Boy's tongue resembles a flash of lightning. The Cherokee Wild Boy is assisted by a bolt of lightning with which he destroys his enemies (Mooney 1888, 104–5). For the Osage, Lightning (Boy) struck a tree and created a club. Lightning then informed the man to use it to free his wife. When the man hit the chain that bound his wife, "it seemed as though lightning struck it" (Dorsey 1904a, 27). Each Twin appears to have had separate ritual functions, which perhaps also played out in differing religious sodalities, based on ethnographic accounts of 19th century narratives. Lightning Boy and Thunder Boy bundles had multiple roles, being used in various ritual functions, and differing ritual regalia associated with Lightning Boy and Thunder Boy. While both Twins share a common emphasis on symbolic weaponry and ritual utilitarian wares – bottles and bowls with transformative motifs – weaponry and ceramics differ in fundamental and significant ways.

As noted above, based on an historic example of shell mask use by the Kansa, Marvin and Julie Smith (1989) argue that face-mask gorgets represent the Twins. I take this a step further and suggest face-mask gorgets are specifically associated with Lightning Boy, based on five key attributes identified with the iconography of the wild twin. First, face-mask gorgets have round eyes, which typically are associated with watery realm spirits of the Beneath World. Second, the shell's surface is scraped and abraded to create a long nose, a key attribute of the wild boy. In some mythic narratives his nose is also cut to civilize him. Third, some gorgets exhibit long, sharp teeth. As a watery realm person, wild boy's sharp-pointed teeth are broken or ground to make him a human-like person. Fourth, the masks often have zig-zag eye-surrounds, similar to the lightning motifs in Plains art. For example, Reo Fortune (1932, 192) observed the use of zig-zag body markings by the Omaha to represent lightning. Likewise, Black Hawk drew pictures of his vision of Thunder Beings with zig-zag lightning motifs (Berlo 2000). Reginal and Gladys Laubin (1977, pl. 18) note how red zig-zags painted by Chief One Bull memorialized how he "struck like lightning" at the battle of the Little Big Horn. Finally, Wild Boy has animal-like hair that is long and matted. On face-mask gorgets, hair is represented by parallel, engraved lines at the top of the gorget.

Lightning Boy had a long tradition of veneration in the Mississippian world. James Duncan and Carol Diaz-Granados identify copper and shell long-nosed maskettes as the Twins (Duncan and Diaz-Granados 2000), circulating throughout much of the Caddoan and Mississippian worlds (Williams and Goggin 1956; Muller 1989; Brown and Kelly 2000; Brown and Muller 2015). Long-nosed maskettes represent an early Mississippian artistic horizon, with the shell maskettes dating from AD 900 to 1200, and the copper maskettes dating from approximately AD 1150 to 1250. The long- and short-nosed versions may reflect mythic narratives, with the long nose being associated with Lightning Boy and the short nose with Thunder Boy. They are also depicted as cave art in Picture Cave in the early 11th century (Diaz-Granados *et al.* 2015). By the early 17th century nLMV ceramic vessels and face-mask gorgets still retained many of the key attributes of the wild twin, including bladder-floats, long noses, round eyes, and sharp teeth. Northern Lower Mississippi Valley vessels depicted Lightning Boy for some 400 years or more (Lankford and Dye 2014). Ritual practices employed Lightning Boy adorno rim bowls and hooded bottles for purification necessary for vision quests and supplicating personal guardian spirits. These rituals were in part related to the supplication of Lightning Boy for personal power, success in warfare, and appeals for rain through weather magic.

In the nLMV Tunican homeland, face-mask gorgets are found only on early contact period sites based on their restricted association with late 16th and early 17th century horizon markers: astragalus dice, "Siouan" disk pipes, specific ceramic motifs and types (e.g., Campbell Applique, "helmet" bowls, Campbell-style "cat serpents", late open top female effigies), early 17th century European goods, short-handle spatulate celts, and thumbnail scrapers. Lower Mississippi Valley face-mask gorgets appear to have been imported from the Appalachian Highlands, circulated through the region from Virginia to Montana. The route into the northern Plains appears to have taken place along the Missouri River (Beery 1998). A few face-mask gorgets were curated over a considerable time period, such as the one associated with a Kansa war bundle (Howard 1956), but the majority were in use for a short period of time, perhaps limited to the first half of the 17th century (Smith 2017).

One of the many names for Lightning Boy is Flint, and Mississippian symbolic weaponry, often reflected in shell gorget imagery, includes chunkey stones and ritual biface blades such as Duck River swords (Dye 2004, fig. 6; 2021b) (Fig. 7.4). As inalienable objects, chunkey stones were gifted within the context of ritual sodalities as veneration of the Hero Twins, who played the chunkey game as a deadly contest of life and death (Brown and Dye 2007; Dye and Bartholomew 2017). Late 19th century Osage rituals juxtaposed flint knives with war clubs in warfare rituals, perhaps suggesting a dual opposition between Lightning Boy (flint knives) and Thunder Boy (war clubs) (La Flesche 1939).

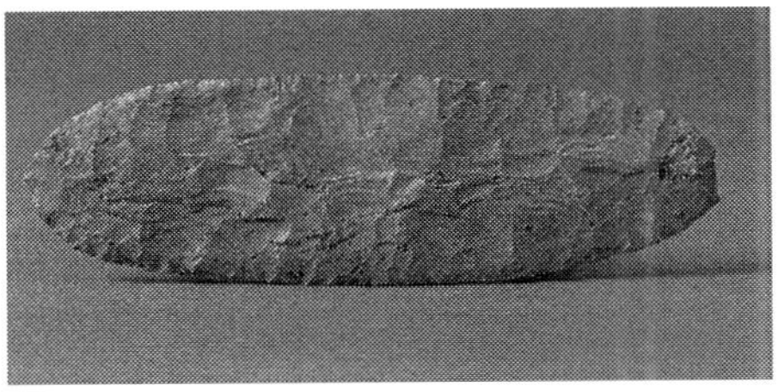

Fig. 7.4 Symbolic weaponry, biface, Chickasawba Site (3MS5, photograph by David H. Dye).

The association of flint bifaces with the Wild Boy is also illustrated in the Hidatsa Sun Dance ritual, where Lightning Boy, known as Spring Boy, overcomes his adversary, Long Arm, by cutting off his hand and thereby opening the Orion portal for the passage of souls to travel along the Milky Way (Path of Souls). Spring Boy's encounter with Long Arm is memorialized through ritual performances in which Lighting Boy impersonators dance with human hands and scalps attached to their wrists (Bowers 1965, 317). George Lankford (2016) suggests hand imagery at Moundville reflects rituals associated with the Path of Souls; similar hand imagery in the nLMV may also reflect such concerns as well.

The combination of ritual wares (bowls and hooded bottles) and regalia (face-mask gorgets and symbolic weaponry) as ceremonial paraphernalia in the nLMV suggests important linkages to religious sodalities. The Hidatsa Sun Dance, with its Lightning Boy impersonator, exemplifies the ritual role of the Hero Twins, and specifically Lightning Boy (Bowers 1965). Lightning Boy rituals may have been restructured into various "shell societies", which emphasized shooting shells from otter skin bundles to demonstrate the ability of society members to overcome death and to destroy one's enemies through legerdemain (Gangloff 1995). Marine shells in the form of face-mask gorgets link the Twins with shell society bundles and regalia. The act of shooting assumed a crucial role in rituals: shell society members shooting beads with society bundles, and warrior society members shooting lightning with Lightning Boy war bundles. These bundles had many functions, but the basic premise rested on their destructive power for killing and their restorative or revivifying capabilities for healing and resurrecting society members (Hoffman 1891; Howard 1965; Skinner 1920; Gangloff 1995, 66; Young 2001, 996–7; Weeks 2009).

In the nLMV ceramic bottles and bowls also illustrate the presence of a Thunder Boy ritual sodality. Symbolic war clubs are found as painted motifs on bottles and as adorno rims on bowls (Hathcock 1983). Symbolic forms of war clubs in the late 16th and early 17th centuries are also materialized as short-pole, spatulate celts and rectangular polished blades, both of which appear in the nLMV during the early contact period (Moore 1911, fig. 64; Mainfort *et al.* 2006; Mainfort 2008) (Fig. 7.5). As is the case with Lightning Boy societies, Tunican religious institutions dedicated to Thunder Boy also may have been transformed along the Missouri River into religious and social institutions such as the various Thunder societies,

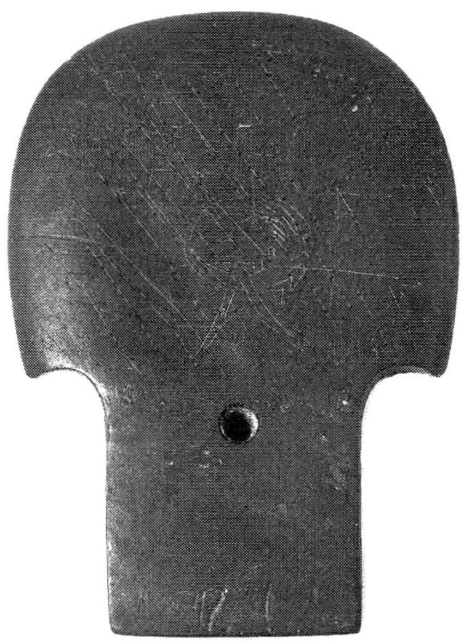

Fig. 7.5 Symbolic weaponry, short pole spatulate celt, Clay Hill Site (3LE11, photograph by David H. Dye).

which emphasized war clubs, objects associated with Thunder Boy, as primary components of Thunder bundles (Harrington 1914; Skinner 1911; Foster 1994).

Alice Fletcher and Francis La Flesche (1911, 490–3) note the importance of symbolic weaponry among the Omaha, for whom the club serves as "the weapon of the Thunder beings". War clubs symbolized the Thunder deity, who was able to transform into a falcon (Hudson 1976, 127; Van Horne 1993), evoking the metaphor of raptors attacking and killing with deadly force. As falcons the Thunderers ascend to the Upper World after completing their missions of bringing rain or killing their enemies (Dorsey 1904b; Swanton 1929, 7–8). Muskogee war bundles sometimes included falcon skins to evoke the power of the Thunderers (Gatschet 1969, II, 52). Thunder charter myths embody prototypical warrior attributes (Keyes 1994). Thunder and Lightning are often conflated, with the Twins being jointly referred to as Thunderers. Mississippian chiefs carried war clubs to proclaim they were the living incarnation of the Thunder deity (Hann 1988, 343; Van Horne 1993, 144) and war clubs were imbued with animistic power in charter myths (Gatschet 1969, 244–6). Thus, the social role of Thunder is linked with the war club, which is symbolized by falcons and visualized as symbolic weaponry (Willoughby 1932; Burnett 1945; Phillips and Brown 1978; 1984; Brown 1996).

The Hero Twins and ritual sodalities

Hero Twins art in the nLMV Tunican homeland had a long tradition in local ceramic crafting that began in the mid-13th century and continued until the mid-17th. The Twins portrayal in Early Mississippian iconographic form should not be construed as their initial appearance in the Mississippian belief system, but rather as a transformation of prior and existing cosmological beliefs and ideas, which were re-articulated as elite offices and positions of rank changed through the structure of religious sodalities. That the Hero Twins became materialized in ceramic form suggests important transformations were taking place in the belief system during the 13th century, perhaps prompted by structural alterations in the political and ritual economy. Interred sacra representing the Twins would have embodied their sacred power for deceased sodality members. Accordingly, as political offices became increasingly reinforced through religious sodalities, ceramics began to assume roles based on sacred imagery that had previously been materialized in cave art, rock art, shell engravings, and stone sculptures.

A transformation in early contact Tunican religious structures resulted from a new focus and increased intensity stemming from internal and external forces and stresses. With the growth of rival corporate groups, often based on interrelated families articulated as medicine societies or social houses, transformations in religious sodalities emphasizing changes in the belief system and political economy become evident (Weeks 2009; Lankford 2016; Dye 2017). For example, James Brown (2007, 241) argues that Etowah's Mound C burial configuration reflects a society whose "top tier was composed of a multiplicity of rival, yet interrelated families" organized as social houses or ritual sodalities. George Lankford (2016) suggests that Moundville was home to a sodality of shamans structured as a medicine/healing lodge with its own artistic symbols, mythological charters, and ritual activities. The Moundville sodality's focus relied on esoteric knowledge and rituals connected to successful access to and safe passage along the Path of Souls, emphasizing mortuary ceremonialism and spiritual healing. One component of the ritual paraphernalia employed by medicine societies at Moundville is the noteworthy increase in engraved ceramics bearing religious imagery (Phillips 2012).

Mississippian religious sodalities are discernible in the nLMV in the various sets of ceramic vessels similar to those found at Moundville. Religious sodalities are defined here as specific forms of belief, ritual, and worship conducted or pursued by an exclusive, social community of practitioners, often composed of a closed, secretive group or sect, who support and express devotion to a specific ancestor, culture hero, deity, idea, or spirit. Ritual sodality members typically embrace, abide by, and share a general set of goals explicitly rationalized by related or similar beliefs (Wallace 1966, 75; Bertemes and Biehl 2001; Malone *et al.* 2007, 2; Ware 2014; Hayden 2018). Ritual sodalities empowered aristocratic cohorts of Mississippian polities, who, as high-born members of elite families, authorized, promoted, and sponsored communal feasts, religious protocols, and ritual performances. Noble families perpetuated positions of political authority through their investment and involvement in the ritual economy and associated religious institutions (Fortune 1932; Knight 1989; 2011; Beck 2007; Brown 2007; Thompson 2011; Beck and Brown 2012).

Historic period sodality recruitment and survival rested on a society's promises of a continued line of descendants, long life for its members, and rebirth/reincarnation upon death. These would have been powerful incentives and rewards for membership and participation in religious sodalities (Radin 1945, 70; Bailey 1995). Among the Omaha, for example, ritual sodality enrollment and privileges were restricted to a hereditary aristocracy (Fortune 1932). Medicine society membership was predicated on the applicant experiencing a vision of the sodality deity, learning sleight-of-hand and other magical feats, memorizing esoteric knowledge, and paying onerous fees. Acts of legerdemain were taught to the initiate and demonstrated before the uninitiated as a powerful message of how members could defeat death and control and manipulate life forces. In addition, conjuring the appearance or manifestation of the society avatar, culture hero, or spiritual being, such as one or both of the Twins, served to return the world to its original cosmic and social order, and placed the suppliant in a sacred reality through imitation, performance, supplication, and veneration.

Those who wished to become members of the lodge applied for instruction and once accepted they were initiated through a sequence of stages of varying complexity that provided the novitiate with increased power. For most secret societies a significant amount of wealth must be paid for the privilege of joining the lodge. Such onerous dues and the prerequisites for private instruction, which required considerable financing, served to restrict membership to the wealthy. Often a ritual "father" instructed and tutored a ritual "son" in the process of advancement through the various grades of membership. Semi-public rituals include recitations and recitals of the sodality charter myth, often conducted in the context of complex performances. A central theme of such performances includes finessed acts of dramatic legerdemain, in which the initiate is "killed" by being "shot" with small pellets or shells propelled from an otter skin medicine bundle or pouch (Hoffman 1891; Fortune 1932; Golla 1975; Gangloff 1995; Weeks 2009: Lankford 2016).

Religious and social sodalities were once widespread in eastern North American and have been recorded ethnographically along the Atlantic Seaboard, the Midwest, and Great Plains. The Mississippi Valley, based on archaeological and iconographic evidence, also had numerous religious sodalities that venerated specific culture heroes, including the Hero Twins. Ceramic art suggests their importance in Tunican cosmology as early as the 13th century and continuing into the early 17th century (Lankford and Dye 2014). The Twins may have been venerated as individual and separate sodalities based on Lightning Boy imagery as ceramic bottles and bowls, shell gorgets, and symbolic weaponry as knives and Thunder Boy visualized as ceramic imagery and symbolic weaponry in the form of war clubs.

The Twins association with supernatural ability and strength, especially lightning and thunder powers, made them a major object of supplication. That the Twins could requicken the dead would have been powerful incentives for joining a religious sodality. Lower Mississippi Valley ritual lodges appear to have assumed central importance in the organization of ritual practice, which included the veneration of specific culture heroes, especially the Hero Twins, who, when supplicated, provided success through supernatural powers, as well as possessing the ability to revive the dead.

Conclusion

The Twins are both central protagonists in mythic narratives concerned with death, rebirth, revivification, warfare, and weather. Associated rituals showcase the Twins' ability to defeat death and to revive the dead, feats ritually replicated through legerdemain. Visions based on magical plants, especially *Datura* and tobacco, were essential for membership in such ritual sodalities. The rise of Mississippian figural art signals the transformation of religious sodalities that competed with one another and sought innovative forms of artistic expression as key religious paraphernalia. The Hero Twins were important Mississippian culture heroes associated with the dawn time and their mythic charters legitimized and underwrote religious and social institutions.

Mississippian Twins imagery is represented earliest in the Cahokia area, by the mid-13th century Lightning Boy and Thunder Boy ritual sodalities become increasingly popular in the nLMV embodying distinctive ceramic effigies featuring human-like figures wearing bladder-float headdresses. The presence of symbolic weaponry such as exaggerated lithic bifaces and hypertrophic stone clubs, suggests people in nLMV engaged in legerdemain theatrics. During the early contact period Lightning Boy and Thunder Boy sacra signal a novel restructuring of ritual sodalities that is revealed in the archaeological record. Such dualistic forces are symbolized by the Twins who serve as metaphors for mortal combat between the forces of the Above World and the Beneath World actualized by high-stakes gaming and mortal combat in the dawn time that rids the world of enemies and monsters before initiating social order and structure. Ritual performances employing symbolic weaponry strengthened ritual sodalities through re-enactments of these dramatic events.

Acknowledgements

My thanks to Carol Diaz-Granados for her invitation to contribute to this volume and to Robert Sharp and Kevin Smith for their sage advice and support in our many discussions of the Hero Twins over the years. I am appreciative of the help from Sean Cotner, Jerry Davis, Jim Duncan, and Jeff Wilkes in locating and making available the various objects photographed for this chapter.

Bibliography

Alexander, H.B. (1938) *Sioux Indian Painting.* C. Szwedzicki, Nice.

Bailey, G. (ed.) (1995) *The Osage and the Invisible World: From the Works of Francis La Flesche.* University of Oklahoma Press, Norman OK.

Barker, A.W. (2020) Craig-style Iconography. In *Recovering Ancient Spiro: Native American Art, Ritual, and Cosmic Renewal,* E.D. Singleton and F.K. Reilly III (eds), 236–51. National Cowboy & Western Heritage Museum, Oklahoma City OK.

Beahm, E.L. (2013) Mississippian polities in the Middle Cumberland region of Tennessee. Unpublished Ph.D. dissertation, University of Georgia, Athens GA.

Beahm, E.L. and Smith, K.E. (2012) Twins and Grandmother Spider: mythic themes of community creation, maintenance, and reproduction in Middle Cumberland iconography. Unpublished paper presented at the 77th Annual Meeting of the Society for American Archaeology, Memphis TN.

Beck, R.A. Jr (ed.) (2007) *The Durable House: House Society Models in Archaeology.* Center for Archaeological Investigations Occasional Paper 35, Southern Illinois University, Carbondale IL.

Beck, R.A. Jr and Brown, J.A. (2012) Political economy and the routinization of religious movements: a view from the Eastern Woodlands. In *Beyond Belief: The Archaeology of Religion and Ritual,* Y.M. Rowan (eds), 72–88. American Anthropological Association Archaeological Paper 21, Washington DC.

Beery, D.S. (1998) The Implications of Shell Mask Gorgets to Trade Between the Plains and Southeast. Unpublished Master's thesis, University of Montana, Missoula MT.

Berlo, J.C. (2000) *Spirit Beings and Sun Dancers: Black Hawk's Vision of the Lakota World.* George Braziller, New York.

Bertemes, F. and Biehl, P.F. (2001) The archaeology of cult and religion: an introduction. In *The Archaeology of Cult and Religion,* P.F. Biehl and F. Bertemes (eds), 11–24. Archaeolingua, Budapest.

Bowers, A.W. (1965) *Hidatsa Social and Ceremonial Organization.* Bureau of American Ethnology Bulletin 194, Smithsonian Institution, Washington DC.

Brain, J.P., and Philips P. (1996) *Shell Gorgets: Styles of the Late Prehistoric and Protohistoric Southeast.* Peabody Museum of Archaeology and Ethnology, Cambridge MA.

Brown, J.A. (1996) *The Spiro Ceremonial Center: The Archaeology of Arkansas Valley Caddoan Culture in Eastern Oklahoma*. Museum of Anthropology Memoir 29, University of Michigan, Ann Arbor MI.

Brown, J.A. (2004) The Cahokian expression: creating court and cult. In Townsend and Sharp (eds) 2004, 105–23.

Brown, J.A. (2007) The social house in Southeastern archaeology. In Beck (ed) 2007, 227–47.

Brown, J.A. and Dye, D.H. (2007) Severed heads and sacred scalplocks: Mississippian iconographic trophies. In Chacon and Dye (eds) 2007, 278–98.

Brown, J.A. and Kelly, J. (2000) Cahokia and the Southeastern Ceremonial Complex. In *Mounds, Modoc, and Mesoamerica: Papers in Honor of Melvin L. Fowler*, S.R. Ahler (ed.), 469–510. Illinois State Museum, Scientific Papers 28. Springfield IL.

Brown, J.A. and Muller, J. (2015) Tradition and horizons in Southeastern representation: lessons from Picture Cave. In Diaz-Granados *et al.* (eds) 2015, 113–24.

Burnett, E.K. (1945) The Spiro Mound collection in the Museum. In *Contributions from the Museum of the American Indian, Heye Foundation* 1, 1–47.

Burnette, D.J., Dye, D.H. and Hill, A.A. (2020) Climate change, ritual practice, and weather deities at Spiro. In *Recovering Ancient Spiro: Native American Art, Ritual, and Cosmic Renewal*, E.D. Singleton and F.K. Reilly III (eds), 77–89. National Cowboy & Western Art Museum, Oklahoma City OK.

Bushnell, D.I. Jr (1909) *The Choctaw of Bayou Lacomb, St. Tammany Parish, Louisiana*. Bureau of American Ethnology Bulletin 48, Smithsonian Institution, Washington DC.

Chacon, R.J. and Dye, D.H. (eds) (2011) *The Taking and Display of Human Body Parts as Trophies by Amerindians*. Springer, New York.

Curtin, J. and Hewitt, J.N.B. (1918) *Seneca Fictions, Legends, and Myths. Bureau of American Ethnology Annual Report* 13. Smithsonian Institution, Washington DC.

DeBoer, W.R. (1993) Like a Rolling stone: the chunkey game and political organization in Eastern North America. *Southeastern Archaeology* 12(2), 83–92.

Diaz-Granados, C. and Duncan, J.R. (2000) *The Petroglyphs and Pictographs of Missouri*. University of Alabama Press, Tuscaloosa AL.

Diaz-Granados, C, Duncan, J.R. and Reilly, F.K. III (eds) (2015) *Picture Cave: Unravelling the Mysteries of the Mississippian Cosmos*. University of Texas Press, Austin TX.

Dieterle, R.L. (2005) Gottschall: a new interpretation. In *The Encyclopedia of Hočąk (Winnebago) Mythology*. http://www.hotcakencyclopedia.com/ho.Gottschall.html (accessed 29 December 2015.

Dorsey, G.A. (1904a) *Traditions of the Skidi Pawnee*. American Folklore Society Memoir 8. New York.

Dorsey, G.A. (1904b) *The Mythology of the Witchita*. Carnegie Institution Publication 21. Washington DC.

Dorsey, G.A. (1905) *Traditions of the Caddo*. Carnegie Institution of Washington Publication 41, Washington, DC.

Dorsey, G.A. (1906) *Pawnee Mythology*. Carnegie Institution of Washington. Washington DC.

Duncan, J.R. (2015) Identifying the characters on the walls of Picture Cave. In Diaz-Granados *et al.* (eds), 201–37. University of Texas Press, Austin TX.

Duncan, J.R. and Diaz-Granados, C. (2000) Of Masks and myths. *Midcontinental Journal of Archaeology* 25(1), 1–26.

Dye, D.H. (2004) Art, ritual, and chiefly warfare in the Mississippian world. In Townsend and Sharp (eds) 2004, 190–205.

Dye, D.H. (2012) Mississippian religious traditions. In *The Cambridge History of Religions in America, Vol. 1: Pre-Columbian Times to 1790*, S.J. Stein (ed.), 137–55. Cambridge University Press, New York.

Dye, D.H. (2016) *Ancient Mississippian Trophy-Taking*. Oxford Handbooks Online Doi: 10.1093/oxfordhb/9780199935420.013.30.

Dye, D.H. (2017) Animal pelt caps and Mississippian ritual sodalities. *North American Archaeologist* 38(1), 63–97.

Dye, D.H. (2018) Identifying Lower Mississippi Valley protohistoric water spirit cults. In *Ceramics of Ancient America: Multidisciplinary Approaches*, Y.P. Huntington, D.E. Arnold and J. Minich (eds), 29–61. University Press of Florida, Gainesville FL.

Dye, D.H. (2020) Mississippian symbolic weaponry at Spiro. In *Recovering Ancient Spiro: Native American Art, Ritual, and Cosmic Renewal*, E.D. Singleton and F.K. Reilly III (eds), 153–73. National Cowboy & Western Art Museum, Oklahoma City OK.

Dye, D.H. (2021a) Fire burn and caldron bubble: Mississippian witchcraft agency, animism, and materiality. In *New Methods and Theories for Analyzing Mississippian Imagery*, B.T. Giles and S.P. Lambert (eds), 131–61. University Press of Florida, Gainesville FL.

Dye, D.H. (2021b) The Link Farm Cache: invoking the ancestors and supplicating the Hero Twins. In *Mississippian Culture Heroes, Ritual Regalia, and Sacred Bundles*, D.H. Dye (ed.), 161–210. Lexington Books, New York.

Dye, D.H. (2022) Culture heroes, inalienable goods, and religious sodalities: long distance exchange in Eastern North America at European contact. In *Trade Before Civilization: Long-Distance Exchange and the Rise of Social Complexity*, K. Kristiansen, J. Ling and R. Chacon (eds), 142–72. Cambridge University Press, New York.

Dye, D.H. and Bartholomew, M.J. (2017) Tennessee-Style Double-Cup Chunkey Stones as Inalienable Goods. Unpublished paper presented at the 29th Annual Meeting of Current Research in Tennessee Archaeology, Burns (TN).

Earle, T. (2021) *A Primer on Chiefs and Chiefdoms*. Eliot Werner, Clifton Corners, NY.

Eliade, M. (1971) *The Myth of the Eternal Return: Cosmos and History*. Princeton University Press, Princeton NJ.

Emerson, T.E. (2003) Materializing Cahokia shamans. *Southeastern Archaeology* 22(2), 135–54.

Fletcher, A.C. and La Flesche, F. (1911) The Omaha Tribe. *Bureau of American Ethnology, 27th Annual Report*, 17–654. Smithsonian Institution, Washington DC.

Fortune, R.F. (1932) *Omaha Secret Societies*. Columbia University Contributions to Anthropology 14. Columbia University Press, New York.

Foster, L.M. (1994) Sacred Bundles of the Ioway Indians. Unpublished Master's thesis, Iowa State University, Ames IO.

Froese, T. (2020) A mural of psychoactive thorn apples (*Datura* spp.) in the ancient urban center of Teotihuacan, Central Mexico. *Economic Botany* 74(1), 92–9.

Gangloff, D. (1995) Dual Organization: A Symbolic Analysis of the Omaha Shell Society. Unpublished Ph.D. dissertation, Rutgers University, New Brunswick NJ.

Gatschet, A.S. (1969) [Vol. 1: 1884, Vol. 2: 1888] *A Migration Legend of the Creek Indians*. Kraus Reprint, New York.

Golla, S.M.J. (1975) Skidi Pawnee Religion: A Structural Analysis. Unpublished Master's thesis, George Washington University, Washington DC.

Hall, R.L. (1989) The cultural background of Mississippian symbolism. In *The Southeastern Ceremonial Complex: Artifacts and Analysis*, P. Galloway (eds), 239–78. University of Nebraska Press, Lincoln NE.

Hall, R.L. (1997) *An Archaeology of the Soul: North American Indian Belief and Ritual*. University of Illinois Press, Chicago IL.

Hally, D.J. (2007) Mississippian shell gorgets in regional perspective. In A. King (ed.) 2007, 185–231.

Hankoff, L.D. (1977) Why the healing gods are Twins. *Yale Journal of Biology and Medicine* 50(3), 307–19.

Hann, J.H. (1988) *Apalachee: The Land Between the Rivers*. University Press of Florida, Gainesville FL.

Harrington, M.R. (1913) A preliminary sketch of Lenápe Culture. *American Anthropologist* 15(2), 208–35.

Harrington, M.R. (1914) *Sacred Bundles of the Sac and Fox Indians*. University Museum Anthropological Publication 4(2), 123–238. University of Pennsylvania, Philadelphia PA.

Hathcock, R. (1983) *The Quapaw and Their Pottery: A Pictorial Study of Proto-historic Pottery of the Quapaw Indians, 1650–1750*. Hurley Press, Camden AR.

Hayden, B. (2001) Rich Man, poor man, beggerman, chief: the dynamics of social inequality. In *Archaeology at the Millennium: A Sourcebook*, G.M. Feinman and T.D. Price (eds), 231–72. Kluwer Academic/Plenum, New York.

Hayden, B. (2011) Big Man, big heart? The political role of aggrandizers in egalitarian and transegalitarian societies. In *For the Greater Good of All: Perspectives on Individualism, Society and Leadership*, D.R. Forsyth and C.L. Hoyt (eds), 101–18. Palgrave Macmillan, New York.

Hayden, B. (2014) *The Power of Feasts: From Prehistory to the Present*. Cambridge University Press, New York.

Hayden, B. (2018) *The Power of Ritual in Prehistory: Secret Societies and Origins of Social Complexity*. Cambridge University Press, New York.

Hoffman, D.S. (1997) From the southeast to Fort Ancient: a survey of shell gorgets in West Virginia. *West Virginia Archeologist* 49, 1–40.

Hoffman, M.P. (1993) Identification of ethnic groups contacted by the de Soto Expedition in Arkansas. In Young and Hoffman (eds) 1993, 132–42.

Hoffman, M.P. (1994) Ethnic identities and cultural change in the protohistoric period of eastern Arkansas. In *Perspectives on the Southeast: Linguistics, Archaeology, and Ethnohistory*, P.B. Kwachka (ed.), 61–70. University of Georgia Press, Athens GA.

Hoffman, W.J. (1891) The Mide'wiwin, or "Grand Medicine Society" of the Ojibwa. *Smithsonian Institution, Bureau of Ethnology, Annual Report* 7, 149–300. Washington DC.

House, J.H. (2013) Native American material culture from the Wallace Bottom Site, southeastern Arkansas. *Southeastern Archaeology* 32(1), 54–69.

Howard, J.H. (1956) The persistence of Southern Cult gorgets among the Historic Kansa. *American Antiquity* 21(3), 301–3.

Howard, J.H. (1965) *The Ponca Tribe*. Bureau of American Ethnology Bulletin 195, Smithsonian Institution, Washington DC.

Hudson, C. (1976) *The Southeastern Indians*. University of Tennessee Press, Knoxville TN.

Hudson, C. (1997) *Knights of Spain, Warriors of the Sun: Hernando de Soto and the South's Ancient Chiefdoms*. University of Georgia Press, Athens GA.

Hultkrantz, Å. (1979) *The Religions of the American Indians*. University of California Press, Berkeley CA.

Jeter, M.D. (2002) From prehistory through protohistory to ethnohistory in and near the northern Lower Mississippi Valley. In *The Transformation of the Southeastern Indians, 1540–1760*, R. Ethridge and C. Hudson (eds), 177–223. University Press of Mississippi, Jackson MS.

Keyes, G. (1994) Myth and social history in the early Southeast. In *Perspectives on the Southeast: Linguistics, Archaeology, and Ethnohistory*, P.B. Kwachka (ed.), 106–15. University of Georgia Press, Athens GA.

King, A. (2003) *Etowah: The Political History of a Chiefdom Capital*. University of Alabama, Tuscaloosa AL.

King, A. (ed.) (2007) *Southeastern Ceremonial Complex: Chronology, Content, Context*. University of Alabama Press, Tuscaloosa AL.

King, A. (2011) Iconography of the Hightower Region of Eastern Tennessee and Northern Georgia. In Lankford *et al.* (eds) 2011, 279–93.

Knight, V.J. (1989) Some speculations on Mississippian monsters. In *The Southeastern Ceremonial Complex: Artifacts and Analysis*, P. Galloway (ed.), 205–10. University of Nebraska Press, Lincoln NE.

Knight, K.V. (2011) North America: Eastern Woodlands. In *The Archaeology of Ritual and Religion*, T. Insoll (ed.), 623–38. Oxford University Press, New York.

Knight, V.J. and Franke, J.A. (2007) Identification of a moth/butterfly supernatural in Mississippian art. In Reilly and Garber (eds) 2007, 136–51.

La Flesche, F. (1928) The Osage Tribe: two versions of the child naming rite. *Bureau of American Ethnology, 43rd Annual Report*, 23–164. Smithsonian Institution, Washington DC.

La Flesche, F. (1939) *War Ceremony and Peace Ceremony of the Osage Indians*. Bureau of American Ethnology Bulletin 101, Smithsonian Institution, Washington DC.

Lankford, G.E. (1987) *Native American Legends: Tales from the Natchez, Caddo, Chickasaw, and Other Nations*. August House, Little Rock AR.

Lankford, G.E. (2004) World on a string: some cosmological components of the Southeastern Ceremonial Complex. In Townsend and Sharp (eds), 207–17.

Lankford, G.E. (2007) Some cosmological motifs in the Southeastern Ceremonial Complex. In Reilly and Garber (eds) 2007, 8–38.

Lankford, G.E. (2008) *Looking for Lost Lore: Studies in Folklore, Ethnology, and Iconography*. University of Alabama Press, Tuscaloosa AL.

Lankford, G.E. (ed.) (2011) *Native American Legends of the Southeast: Tales from the Natchez, Caddo, Biloxi, Chickasaw, and Other Nations*. University of Alabama Press, Tuscaloosa AL.

Lankford, G.E. (2016) Was there a Moundville Medicine Society? In *Rethinking Moundville and its Hinterland*, V.P. Steponaitis and C.M. Scarry (eds), 74–98. University Press of Florida, Gainesville FL.

Lankford, G.E. and Dye, D.H. (2014) Conehead effigies: a distinctive art form of the Mississippi Valley. *The Arkansas Archeologist* 53, 37–50.

Lankford, G.E., Reilly, F.K. III, and Garber, J.F. (eds) (2011) *Visualizing the Sacred: Cosmic Visions, Regionalism, and the Art of the Mississippian World*. University of Texas Press, Austin TX.

Laubin, R. and Laubin, G. (1977) *Indian Dances of North America*. University of Oklahoma Press, Norman OK.

Lévi-Strauss, C. (1995) *Myth and Meaning: Cracking the Code of Culture*. Schocken, New York.

Lowie, R.H. (1919) The Hidatsa Sun Dance. *Anthropological Papers* 16, 411–21. American Museum of Natural History, New York.

Mainfort, R.C. Jr (2008) *Sam Dellinger: Raiders of the Lost Arkansas*. University of Arkansas Press, Fayetteville AR.

Mainfort, R.C. Jr, Fisher-Carroll, R. and Gall, D.G. (2006) Sociotechnic celts from the Upper Nodena Site, northeast Arkansas. *Midcontinental Journal of Archaeology* 31(2), 323–43.

Malone, C., Barrowclough, D.A. and Stoddart, S. (2007) Introduction: cult in context. In *Cult in Context: Reconsidering Ritual in Archaeology*, D.A. Barrowclough and C. Malone (eds), 1–7. Oxbow Books, Oxford.

Marceaux, S. and Dye, D.H. (2007) Hightower anthropomorphic marine shell gorgets and Duck River sword-form bifaces: Middle Mississippian ritual regalia in the southern Appalachians. In King (ed.) 2007, 165–84.

Mooney, J. (1888) Myths of the Cherokees. *Journal of American Folk-Lore* 1(2), 97–108.

Mooney, J. (1900) *Myths of the Cherokee. Nineteenth Annual Report of the Bureau of American Ethnology*. Smithsonian Institution, Washington DC.

Moore, C.B. (1911) Some Aboriginal sites on Mississippi River. *Journal of the Academy of Natural Sciences of Philadelphia* 14, 265–480.

Muller, J. (1989) The Southern Cult. In *The Southeastern Ceremonial Complex: Artifacts and Analysis*, P. Galloway (ed.), 11–26. University of Nebraska Press, Lincoln NE.

Myers, B.J. (2002) Hero Twins: Explorations of Mythic and Historical Dichotomies. Unpublished Honors Thesis, Southern Illinois University, Carbondale IL.

Pauketat, T.R. (2013) *An Archaeology of the Cosmos: Rethinking Agency and Religion in Ancient America*. Routledge, New York.

Petrovich, S.M. (2009) The Severed Head in Native American Myth and Image. Unpublished Master's thesis, University of Houston, Clear Lake TX.

Phillips, E. (2012) Social Contexts of Production and Use of Pottery Engraved in the Hemphill Style at Moundville. Unpublished Ph.D. dissertation, University of Alabama, Tuscaloosa AL.

Phillips, P. (1970) *Archaeological Survey in the Lower Yazoo Basin, Mississippi, 1949–1955.* Papers of the Peabody Museum of Archaeology and Ethnology 60(1–2). Peabody Museum, Cambridge MA.

Phillips, P. and Brown, J.A. (1978) *Pre-Columbian Shell Engravings from the Craig Mound at Spiro, Oklahoma.* Part 1. Peabody Museum Press, Cambridge MA.

Phillips, P. and Brown, J.A. (1984) *Pre-Columbian Shell Engravings from the Craig Mound at Spiro, Oklahoma.* Part 2. Peabody Museum Press, Cambridge MA.

Power, S.C. (2004) *Early Art of the Southeastern Indians: Feathered Serpents and Winged-Beings.* University of Georgia Press, Athens GA.

Radin, P. (1915) *The Winnebago Myth of the Twins: A Comparative Study.* University of California, Berkeley CA.

Radin, P. (1945) *The Road of Life and Death: A Ritual Drama of the American Indians.* Princeton University Press, Princeton NJ.

Radin, P. (1948) *Winnebago Hero Cycles: A Study in Aboriginal Literature.* Waverly Press, Baltimore MD.

Radin, P. (1949) The basic myth of the North American Indians. *Eranos-Jahrbuch* 17, 359–419.

Radin, P. (1954 *The Evolution of an American Indian Prose Epic.* Special Publication 3. Bollingen Foundation, Princeton NJ.

Rankin, R. (1993) Language affiliations of some de Soto place names in Arkansas. In Young and Hoffman (eds) 1993, 210–21.

Reilly, F.K. III, and Garber, J.A. (eds) (2007) *Ancient Objects and Sacred Realms: Interpretations of Mississippian Iconography.* University of Texas Press, Austin TX.

Reilly, F.K. III, and Garber, J.A. (2011) Dancing in the Otherworld: the human figural art of the Hightower Style revisited. In Lankford *et al.* (eds) 2011, 294–312.

Rodning, C.B. (2012) Late prehistoric and protohistoric shell gorgets from southwestern North Carolina. *Southeastern Archaeology* 31(1), 33–56.

Salzer, R.J. and Rajnovich, G. (2001) *The Gottschall Rockshelter: An Archaeological Mystery.* Prairie Smoke Press, St Paul MN.

Sharp, R.V., Smith, K.E. and Dye, D.H. (2020) Cahokia and the legacy of the Classic Braden Style in the Nashville Basin. In *Cahokia in Context: Hegemony and Diaspora*, C.H. McNutt and R.M. Parish (eds), 319–51. University Press of Florida, Gainesville FL.

Skinner, A. (1911) War customs of the Menomini Indians. *American Anthropologist* 13(2), 299–313.

Skinner, A. (1920) *Medicine Ceremony of the Menomimi, Iowa, and Wahpeton Dakota, with Notes on the Ceremony of the Menomimi, Iowa, and Wahpeton Dakota, with Notes on the Ceremony among the Ponca, Bungi Ojibwa, and Potawatomi.* Indian Notes and Monographs 4, Museum of the American Indian, Heye Foundation, New York.

Skinner, A. and Satterlee, J.V. (1915) Folklore of the Menomini Indians. *Anthropological Paper* 13(3), 217–546. American Museum of Natural History, New York.

Smith, K.E. and Beahm, E.L. (2011) Through the Looking Glass: Mississippian Iconography Through the Lens of the Castalian Spring Mounds, Sumner County, Tennessee. Unpublished aper presented at the 68th Annual Southeastern Archaeological Conference, Jacksonville TN.

Smith, Kevin E. and Sharp, R.V. (2021) "Cradleboard figurines" or icons of sacred bundles? In *Mississippian Culture Heroes, Ritual Regalia, and Sacred Bundles*, D.H. Dye (ed.), 107–21. Lexington Books, New York.

Smith, K.E., Sharp, R.V. and Dye, D.H. (2019) Iconographic Depictions of the Middle Cumberland "Hero Twins". Un published paper presented at the 31st annual meeting of Current Research in Tennessee Archaeology, Middle Tennessee State University, Murfreesboro TN.

Smith, M.T. (1997) Shell from the Plains: a Southeastern perspective. *Central Plains Archeology* 5, 1105–7.

Smith, M.T. (2017) Marine shell trade in the post-Mississippian Southeast. In *Forging Southeastern Identities: Social Archaeology, Ethnohistory, and Folklore of the Mississippian to Early Historic South*, G.A. Waselkov and M.T. Smith (eds), 85–98. University of Alabama Press, Tuscaloosa AL.

Smith, M.T. and Smith, J.B. (1989) Engraved shell masks in North America. *Southeastern Archaeology* 8(1), 9–18.

Steponaitis, V.P., Knight, V.J. Jr, Lankford, G.E., Sharp, R.V. and Dye, D.H. (2011) Iconography of the Thruston Tablet. In Lankford *et al.* (eds) 2011, 137–76.

Sullivan, L.P. (2007) Shell gorgets, time, and the Southeastern Ceremonial Complex in southeastern Tennessee. In King (ed.) 2007, 88–106.

Sumner, M.L. (1951) Lodge-Boy and Thrown-Away: An Analytic Study of an American Indian Folktale. Unpublished Master's thesis, Stanford University, Stanford CA.

Swanton, J.R. (1929) *Myths and Tales of the Southeastern Indians*. Bureau of American Ethnology, Bulletin 88, Smithsonian Institution, Washington DC.

Thompson, C.E. (2011) Ritual and Power: Examining the Economy of Moundville's Residential Population. Unpublished Ph.D. dissertation, University of Alabama, Tuscaloosa AL.

Thruston, G.P. (1897) *Antiquities of Tennessee and the Adjacent States* (2nd edn). Robert Clarke, Cincinnati OH.

Townsend, R.F. (2004) American landscapes, seen and unseen. In Townsend and Sharp (eds) 2004, 15–35.

Townsend, R.F. and Sharp, R.V. (eds) (2004) *Hero, Hawk, and Open Hand: American Indian Art of the Ancient Midwest and South*. Yale University Press and Art Institute of Chicago, New Haven CT and London.

Van Horne, W.W. (1993) The Warclub: Weapon and Symbol in Southeastern Indian Societies. Unpublished Ph.D. dissertation, University of Georgia, Athens GA.

Wallace, A.F.C. (1966) *Religion: An Anthropological View*. Random House, New York.

Ware, J.A. (2014) *A Pueblo Social History: Kinship, Sodality, and Community in the Northern Southwest*. School for Advanced Research Press, Santa Fe NM.

Weeks, W.R. Jr (2009) Antiquity of the Midewiwin: An Examination of Early Documents, Origin Stories, Archaeological Remains, and Rock Paintings from the Northern Woodlands of North America. Unpublished Ph.D. dissertation, Arizona State University, Tempe AZ.

Williams, S, and Goggin, J.M. (1956) The long nosed god mask in Eastern United States. *Missouri Archaeologist* 18(3), 3–72.

Willoughby, C.C. (1932) Notes on the history and symbolism of the Muskhogeans and the people of Etowah. In *Etowah Papers: Exploration of the Etowah Site in Georgia*, W.K. Moorehead (ed.), 1–105. Yale University Press, New Haven CT.

Wissler, C. (1912) Societies and Ceremonial Associations in the Oglala Division of the Teton-Dakota. *Anthropological Paper* 11, 1–99. American Museum of Natural History, New York.

Young, G.A. (2001) Intertribal religious movements. In *Handbook of North American Indians, Plains*, R.J. DeMallie (ed.) 13(2), 996–1010. Smithsonian Institution, Washington DC.

Young, G.A. and Hoffman, M.P. (eds) (1993) *The Expedition of Hernando de Soto West of the Mississippi River, 1541–1543*. University of Arkansas Press, Fayetteville AR.

Zych, T.J. (2017) Chunkey and the historic experience in the Mississippian world. In *Prehistoric Games of North American Indians: Subarctic to Mesoamerica*, B. Voorhies (ed.), 63–86. University of Utah Press, Salt Lake City UT.

8

Arguments for the age of Serpent Mound

Bradley T. Lepper, James R. Duncan, Carol Diaz-Granados, and Tod A. Frolking

(This chapter was first published in Cambridge Archaeological Journal *28(3), 2018, 433–50 and is republished here with permission)*

Serpent Mound (site code 33AD1), located in northern Adams County, Ohio, is one of the largest prehistoric effigy mounds, or geoglyphs, in the world (Fig. 8.1). It is a sinuous earthen embankment 435 m (1427 ft) long when measured along the winding course of its body from the tip of the tail to the farthest anterior extremity of the earthwork. Ephraim Squier and Edwin Davis (1848, 97), the first scholars to survey the mound, reported its original height as "upwards of five feet" (1.5 m).

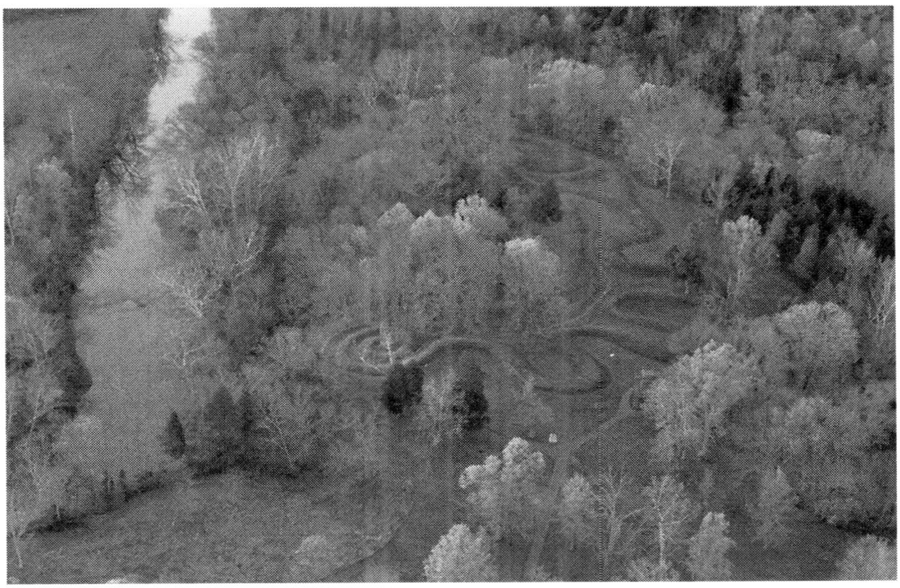

Fig. 8.1 Aerial photograph of Serpent Mound (photograph by Timothy E. Black, Newark Earthworks Center).

Serpent Mound is one of the most iconic symbols of ancient America. It is a National Historic Landmark and is currently on the United States Department of the Interior's Tentative List of sites to be considered for nomination to the UNESCO World Heritage List. It has been and remains the focus of a great deal of interest and speculation, but surprisingly little scientific inquiry.

The most intensive investigation of the site was undertaken by Frederic W. Putnam (1890) between 1887 and 1889. His work revealed the presence of three components at the site, which now are identified as an Adena culture occupation consisting of two conical burial mounds and a small area of habitation remains, a terminal Late Woodland (so-called "Intrusive Mound" culture) component consisting of burials added to the Adena burial mounds, and a Fort Ancient culture component including a small, oblong burial mound and a relatively large habitation area that overlaid the more restricted Adena occupation (Fig. 8.2). Putnam's excavations did not recover any culturally diagnostic artefacts within the effigy mound itself that might link it to one or another of the major periods of site use, and archaeologists are divided as to whether they attribute the original construction of Serpent Mound to the Adena or Fort Ancient cultures.

Prior to the advent of radiocarbon dating and in the absence of culturally diagnostic artifacts in direct association with Serpent Mound, efforts to place the effigy within a cultural or temporal context appear to have been based mainly on arguments from association. More recently, three separate teams of researchers have undertaken limited efforts to locate and extract samples of organic material from the mound for use in obtaining reliable radiocarbon dates for its construction. Finally, arguments from iconography, or style, have been used in attempts to establish which culture has the closest relationship to the effigy. The purpose

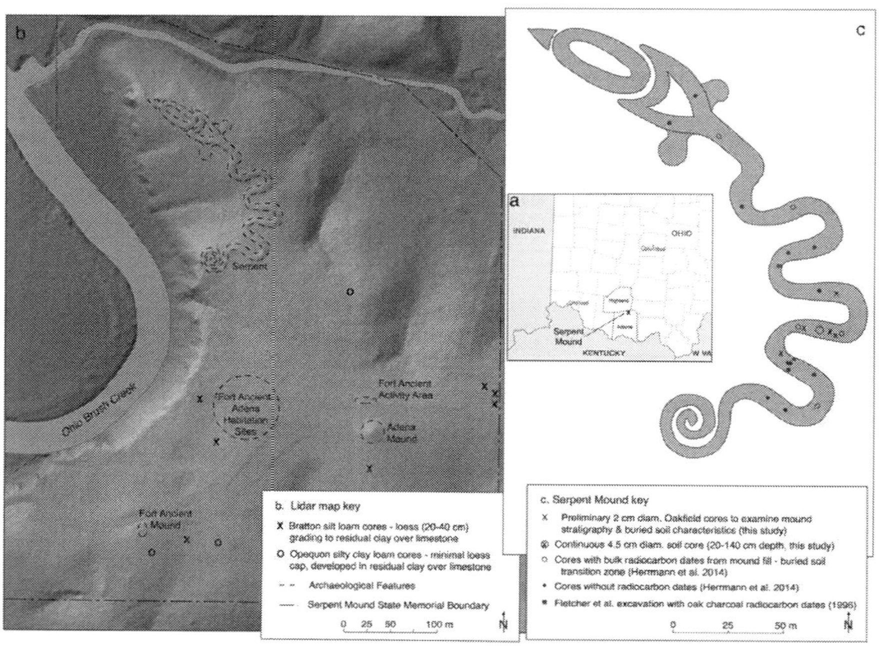

Fig. 8.2 Maps of Serpent Mound showing: a. general location in southwestern Ohio; b. grey-scale LiDAR elevation map of the Serpent Mound area showing topography, soil core locations, and outlines of selected archaeological structures and features; c. outline of Serpent Mound showing locations of excavations and cores from this and previous investigations.

of this paper is to review and evaluate the evidence and arguments for the age and cultural affiliation of Serpent Mound and offer new evidence and arguments to contribute to a resolution of this important debate.

Argument from association

Putnam (1888, 51) believed, for reasons that he did not make explicit, that Serpent Mound was built by what later archaeologists would refer to as the Adena culture, the same culture responsible for the earliest habitation remains and the two conical burial mounds at the site. He asserted only that "everything relating to the construction of the great earthwork points to antiquity".

Henry Shetrone (1920, 153) expressed the opinion that Serpent Mound had been built by "the Fort Ancient peoples". Subsequently, however, in an unpublished manuscript, he decided that "on the assumption that the builders of the adjacent burial mounds also constructed the effigy, the origin of Serpent Mound, for the time at least, may be attributed to the Adena culture" (Shetrone 1947, 162).

William Webb and Charles Snow (1974 [1945], 341) stated that Serpent Mound "is now believed to be of Adena origin", but they listed it as an element of the "Southeastern ceremonial complex appearing in Hopewell-Adena" (1974 [1945], 340). Webb and Raymond Baby (1957, 106) included Serpent Mound as an Adena motif in their tabulation of artistic motifs and other traits that suggested a relationship between Adena-Hopewell and the "Southern Cult" (1957, 104). It was the only example they could provide of serpent iconography associated with the Adena culture.

Emerson Greenman (1967, 17) recognized that, on the basis of the available information, Serpent Mound could not be assigned to "a particular culture ... with certainty" but offered his opinion that Serpent Mound was likely to have been built by the Adena culture. His argument was that, since the Adena burial mounds appear to have included the interments of "priests or medicine men" and Serpent Mound appeared to have a "ceremonial or religious" function, there was therefore a plausible connection between the effigy mound and the religious specialists buried in such close proximity.

James Griffin (1966, 57) believed that "although the artifacts taken by Putnam from the conical mound south of the serpent and from the lower level of the near-by village site cannot be positively assigned to the builders of the effigy, it is considerably less likely that the later Fort Ancient occupants built the serpent". He presented no substantive evidence in support of his conclusion though, in a later article, the likelihood that the effigy mound had been built by the Adena culture had hardened into a certainty: "Serpent Mound, the burial mound near it, and the lower levels of the village site are Adena" (Griffin 1978, 242).

Attempts to provide an age for the original construction of Serpent Mound based merely on its association with nearby documented features cannot be definitive, due to the presence of multiple components at the site. An argument from association therefore could support either an Adena or Fort Ancient affiliation.

Argument from chronometric dating

Fort Ancient culture affiliation

There have been three attempts to resolve the question of the age of Serpent Mound by obtaining radiocarbon dates on materials recovered from within and below Serpent Mound. In 1991, Robert Fletcher *et al.* (1996) sought to relocate deposits of "clay, mixed with ashes" that Putnam (1890, 875) described as having been used in the construction of Serpent Mound. Fletcher and colleagues extracted a systematic series of soil cores from along the axis of the effigy mound in order to locate one of Putnam's old trenches. Once the team identified disturbed stratigraphy consistent with expectations for a back-filled trench, they excavated a narrow trench into the disturbed fill and continued excavating laterally until undisturbed deposits were encountered. No clay-and-ash layer was observed at the base of the mound, so the team extracted bulk soil samples from undisturbed portions of the mound in an attempt to recover dateable charcoal through flotation analysis.

Fletcher and colleagues successfully recovered charcoal fragments from two sediment samples separated by approximately 23 cm (Fletcher *et al.* 1996, 119). The charcoal was identified as white oak and the two samples produced identical AMS radiocarbon dates of 920±70 BP (Beta-55277/CAMS-3566 and Beta55278/CAMS-3567). They interpreted these dates as evidence for the construction of Serpent Mound by the Fort Ancient culture during the early Late Prehistoric period (Fletcher *et al.* 1996, 133). Particulate charcoal within the matrix of a mound, however, may or may not derive from fires burning during the construction of the mound. It is possible that younger or older charcoal fragments might have been mechanically introduced into the mound strata through subsequent bioturbation. On the other hand, the samples were obtained from clearly defined stratigraphic contexts without apparent evidence for later intrusions.

Adena culture affiliation

In 2011, Herrmann *et al.* (2014, 119) initiated a multidisciplinary investigation to "reevaluate when and how Serpent Mound was built". The team extracted 18 "continuous solid-earth cores" from which they obtained samples of dispersed organics in mineral sediment or soil. They obtained nine AMS radiocarbon dates on this material. The samples were taken from various depths and include material from a palaeosol beneath the mound, as well as material incorporated into the mound fill. The resulting dates ranged from 2530±80 BP (Beta-337166) to 2170±30 BP (Beta-337163) (Herrmann *et al.* 2014, 119).

On the basis of these dates, Herrmann *et al.* (2014, 124) concluded that Serpent Mound was "initially constructed 2,300 years ago during the Early Woodland (Adena) period". The team attributed the dates that were "200–300 years older" than their proposed date for the initial construction of the mound to "charcoal from deeper, older horizons that were borrowed from their original context in order to be placed on the mound" (Herrmann *et al.* 2014, 121). Herrmann *et al.* (2014, 124) cited the "complete lack of post-Adena charcoal" in the soil cores they analyzed as "the strongest evidence for when the sub-mound paleosol was buried and Serpent Mound construction began". They attempted (2014, 122) to resolve the apparent discrepancy between the dates they obtained for the Serpent and the much later dates obtained by Fletcher and colleagues by postulating that the portion of the Early Woodland mound investigated by the latter had been repaired or refurbished by the Fort Ancient culture.

Issues with Herrmann et al.*'s interpretations of soils and radiocarbon dates*

Herrmann *et al.* (2014, 119) described their cores in terms of colour, texture, horizon contacts, and inclusions, but they conducted no physical or chemical analyses to provide support for their interpretations. Nowhere in their discussion of the supposed sub-mound palaeosol do they acknowledge the very different parent materials (aeolian and residual) that actually comprise the Bratton silt loam soil that is present on the Serpent Mound ridgetop and other upland sites nearby (Williams and Kerr 1977; Lucht and Brown 1994). This apparent lack of understanding of the nature of the surface beneath the mound becomes problematic when assigning horizons to this extensively disturbed surface. None of their core descriptions, either presented in their paper or recorded in their field notes deposited at the Ohio History Connection, reveals the sequence of silty horizons (A/E/B1) that would be present overlying a redder, more clay-rich residual subsoil (2Bt2) if the basal mound fill had been loaded directly onto the A horizon of an undisturbed Bratton silt loam soil.

The absence of an intact palaeosol is not surprising, since Putnam (1890, 875) stated that the builders of Serpent Mound stripped off the upper, organic levels of the soil prior to initiating mound construction. This observation was, in fact, the only explicit, empirical argument Griffin (1966, 57) offered in support of his firmly expressed belief that Serpent Mound was built by the Adena-Hopewell, since "the removal of the topsoil preparatory to constructing such an earthwork is a fairly consistent Hopewellian trait". Putnam's observation that the builders of the mound had stripped the "black soil"/A horizon prior to constructing the effigy is supported by the profile exposed by his excavation of the sides of the effigy "throughout" its length (Putnam 1890, 875) as illustrated in a contemporary photograph of the serpent's tail immediately after the excavation, which clearly shows dark-coloured mound fill in contact with a light-coloured subsoil (Fletcher *et al.* 1996, 120). Further confirmation is provided by the stratigraphic profile exposed in Fletcher *et al.*'s (1996, 118–19) re-excavation of one of Putnam's trenches, as well as by the lack of identifiable buried silty A and E horizons in field examinations of eight soil cores extracted by Frolking and Lepper in 2014 from locations in close proximity to the cores removed by Herrmann *et al.* (2014, 118; see Fig. 8.2c for core locations).

To illustrate the textural changes between topsoil and subsoil, average soil horizon texture data from five Bratton silt loam profiles in Adams County are presented in Table 8.1. The silty zone comprising the A/E or Ap horizons averaged

Table 8.1 Average horizon depths and textures for five Bratton silt loam profiles in Adams County, Ohio*

Horizon	Depth (cm)	Sand %	Silt %	Clay %	SD Clay**
Ap	0–23	4	77	19	3.3
Bt1	23–36	3	64	33	4.5
2Bt21	36–48	3	55	42	10.8
2Bt22	48–65	4	49	47	13.1
2Bt23	65–80	4	38	58	17.2

* Ohio State University Soil Testing Lab data, profiles ad-s03 (1955), ad-s06 (1957), ad-s15 (1961), ad-s23 (1962), ad-032 (1982).
** Standard deviations of clay contents for each horizon.

23±4.4 cm thickness with 19% clay. The clay content increases to about 30–35% in the upper B horizon and increases further to 40–70% in the residual subsoil. Because loess is predominantly silt with a relatively constant clay content when deposited, the clay content itself provides a useful horizon indicator when differentiating loessial topsoil from illuvial clay-enriched loess Bt horizons and the underlying clayey residuum 2Bt and 2C horizons.

To gain a clearer picture of the horizons and parent material transitions of the Bratton silt loam soil within the Serpent Mound National Historic Landmark property, 14 locations at varying distances from the mound were cored with an Oakfield soil tube (2 cm diameter) and briefly described (Fig. 8.2b). Ten of the 14 cores revealed Bratton profiles with a silty topsoil having a shallow 5 cm weak A horizon developed since the cessation of agricultural activity and occasionally traces of a thicker 20 cm degraded Ap horizon. Unlike the cores taken from Serpent Mound discussed below, all of these cores showed a smooth transition from the silty 8.5–10YR top soil to a significantly heavier, silty clay loam to clay loam 8.5–5YR subsoil. The thickness of what could be considered a loess cap varied widely from perhaps 20 to 68 cm (8–27 in). Some of this variation was undoubtedly due to erosion subsequent to post-European settlement agriculture. Cores taken on the sloping flanks of the upland lacked a significant silty cover and revealed a darker A horizon developed in silty clay with a substantial residual contribution (Opequon silty clay loam soil series).

On Serpent Mound itself, we examined eight Oakfield cores from three coils of the serpent to find a site with the expected buried soil horizonation of a Bratton silt loam profile (Fig. 2.2c). None of these revealed a clearly identifiable buried silty A horizon lying directly below the mound fill. Texturally, there was no clear silt loam surface horizon that graded into the silty clay loam (Bt1) and silty clay (2Bt2) of the buried subsoil. In terms of colour, there was no apparent melanization, darkening of a horizon from humification of organic material, which would indicate a stable soil surface upon which the mound had been constructed. We ultimately selected a site in the centre of the coil between Herrmann *et al.*'s (2014) sites C-6 and C-7. Here we extracted a 120 cm long, 4.5 cm diameter core from 20 cm below surface to 140 cmbs. Based on Herrmann *et al.*'s (2014) descriptions and what we observed in our preliminary cores, the contact between mound fill and buried soil probably occurred at a depth of 90–100 cmbs.

Both loess and clay-rich residual soil materials were used in mound construction. The upper 33 cm of the mound was dominantly silt loam with a few pebbles present, likely fill from Putnam's or a later reconstruction (Table 8.2). Below this was a 20 cm thick variegated zone, perhaps taken from the E/2B1 transitional zone of an excavated Bratton profile. Below this, extending to 90 cm, were irregular zones of 10YR silt and 5–7.5YR silty clay loam to silty clay material, perhaps suggesting successive dumps of basket loads drawn from different portions of an excavated profile. The zone from 90–102 cm, the likely contact region, appeared to be looser, and perhaps slightly more granular, than the zones above and below, but there was no apparent change in organic matter content or degree of melanization that would suggest a buried A horizon. There was also no clear contact between mound fill and the underlying soil. Based on this core, we cannot explain the apparent physical disturbance of what we interpret to be subsoil material, but there is no question that much of any silty topsoil that should have been present had been truncated.

Laboratory analyses support the field observations that the sub-mound surface was disturbed and the topsoil stripped prior to mound construction. The 30–32% clay content in the zone of the buried surface (90–110 cmbs) refutes the presence

Table 8.2 Textures and organic carbon content of samples from core into Serpent Mound fill and underlying soil*

Sample depth (cm)	Pre-Mound depth (cm)**	Sand %	Silt %	Clay %***	OC %
20–30	–	6.9	74.8	18.3	0.11
38–45	–	5.7	68.8	25.5	0.98
50–57	–	4.0	61.6	34.4	1.24
63–68	–	2.6	55.2	42.2	1.54
71–78	–	2.8	58.3	38.9	1.28
81–87	–	3.2	61.1	35.7	1.72
90–95	–	2.8	64.6	32.6	1.16
96–101	0–5	2.7	66.6	30.7	1.06
104–109	8–13	2.4	67.3	30.2	1.14
112–118	16–22	1.8	67.0	31.3	1.12
122–128	26–32	1.9	63.0	35.1	1.25
132–138	36–42	2.5	62.0	35.5	1.20

* Particle-size data determined by the pipette method (Gee and Bauder 1986) and oxidizable soil organic carbon measured gravimetrically by loss on ignition (450°C for 4 hours) following Hoskins (2002).

** Assumes 96 cm below surface represents ground surface for mound construction.

*** The increase in clay toward the base of the core reflects an increased contribution of silty clay residuum. Even excluding the silty surface sample with low carbon content, there is a weak positive linear correlation between carbon content and % clay (OC = 0.0348 clay(p)+0.0684; $r^2 = 0.534$), suggesting much of the organic matter resides in stable clay-humus complexes (Duchaufour 1982). This conclusion was supported by the microscopic examination of the sand fraction (0.064–2.0 mm) and the coarse fraction (>2 mm) isolated by wet sieving in the pipette process. The transitional zone of basal mound fill and underlying soil (90–110 cmbs), i.e. the putative buried A horizon, revealed at most a few minuscule specks of charcoal per 20 g soil sample.

of an eluviated loess-based buried silty A/E horizon (Table 8.2). These results suggest that the radiocarbon dates of Herrmann *et al.* (2014) more likely reflect the age distribution of finely disseminated carbon rather than charcoal that might date a singular event.

Mean carbon radiometric age increases down through a soil profile from A to E to upper B horizons because annual additions of labile carbon are concentrated near the soil surface, whereas predominantly older, more resistant pools of carbon dominate the subsoil. In a review of several papers analyzing modern forest and prairie soils, Oades (1989, fig. 3–21) showed a mean bulk radiocarbon age of 1000 years at a 20 cm depth increasing to 2000 years at 35 cm. Thus the loss or removal of topsoil prior to burial would skew the radiocarbon age of the buried surface toward even older dates.

From these studies, it follows that if the topsoil at the Serpent Mound was removed prior to mound construction, then the dating of dispersed soil carbon at the truncated surface would yield ages considerably older than the date of mound construction. Indeed, Herrmann *et al.* (2014, 121) correctly conceded that the dates they obtained on dispersed organic material could provide only a maximum age for the effigy: "the mound could have been constructed any time after 300 BC".

A final point of consideration is Herrmann *et al.*'s claim that the Fletcher *et al.* profile indicates that the original mound in this location, as well as at least 0.70 m of underlying sediment, might have been completely eroded by "long-term processes associated with gully formation" (Herrmann *et al.* 2014, 123). Their interpretation of the Fletcher *et al.* profile is based principally on the assertion that there is no A_b/E_b horizon present (Herrmann *et al.* 2014, 123); however, they offer no objective evidence in support of this claim. It is important to note that Hermann *et al.*'s topographic map, while commendable for the level of detail revealed by 10 cm contours, visually exaggerates the apparent steepness of slopes near the mound. The steep slope to the west of the mound coil with the two Putnam trenches, which lacks the "V" contours typical of a gully, has a maximum slope of about 20% decreasing to 10% adjacent to the mound, suggesting that any focused long-term slope erosion had not extended headward to the mound itself. Particularly problematic for their argument is that this steep area is to the west of the mound axis, whereas Fletcher *et al.*'s trench was on the east side of the divide. Gullies do not tend to extend headward across divides where there would be no contributing water flow.

There is no evidence in the stratigraphy revealed in the cross-section exposed by Fletcher and colleagues of gully incision or of soil material washing in or slumping in to fill the supposed gully. Indeed, the clay-rich 2Bt horizon of the palaeosol was present along the extent of the Fletcher trench, clearly indicating a lack of extensive erosion. Therefore, the notion that erosion destroyed this portion of an Adena effigy that was later repaired by the Fort Ancient culture appears to be an *ad hoc* explanation to account for the otherwise anomalous Late Prehistoric radiocarbon dates on charcoal recovered from mound fill in this location.

In spite of the apparent consistency in five of the seven dates that Herrmann and colleagues obtained for the surface beneath Serpent Mound, their claim that these five dates provide a reliable estimate for the age of the original construction of the effigy is compromised by their inability to demonstrate that these samples are directly associated with that construction event. Rather, as they state, these dates simply provide an earliest possible construction date for the mound.

A new radiocarbon date supporting a Fort Ancient culture affiliation

In 2017, the Ohio History Connection (OHC) removed stone steps that had been installed across the tail of Serpent Mound by the Civilian Conservation Corps (CCC). In so doing, two artificially shaped sandstone slabs were exposed, which appear to be remnants of a previously undocumented stone stairway that had been partially dismantled and buried by the CCC in the course of building a more elaborate stairway in the same location. In the course of removing the CCC fill around the stone slabs, the OHC archaeologists exposed a portion of the surface of the intact earthwork. The original mound fill consists of brown (10YR 5/6) silty clay loam with minute, scattered flecks of charcoal (around 0.18 mm in diameter). In contrast to the loose CCC fill, the mound fill was very firm and showed no signs of bioturbation. OHC archaeologists extracted a bulk soil sample, which subsequently yielded an AMS radiocarbon date on the organic material of 720±30 BP (Beta-470763; cal AD 1246–1302). Because the date was run on soil humates rather than solely charcoal, the association of the date with mound construction is likely to be imprecise; however, a radiocarbon date on soil humates from the fill of Alligator Mound was found to be broadly corroborative of a date obtained on charcoal from the base of the mound (Lepper and Frolking 2003, 159). Therefore, the soil humates date for Serpent Mound likely does reflect the approximate date of mound construction. This third Fort Ancient-era radiocarbon date for Serpent Mound, obtained from a segment of the earthwork far from the area suggested by Herrmann and colleagues to have been subject to damage and later repair, provides additional support for the argument that the Fort Ancient culture constructed Serpent Mound.

Argument from iconography

George Kubler (1962, 9) argued that a "shape in time" emerges from a study of the history of things: "all materials worked by human hands under the guidance of connected ideas developed in temporal sequence". One of the implications of this observation is that a monumental earthwork constructed in the shape of a serpent is not likely to have existed in a cultural vacuum. It may, therefore, be possible to link Serpent Mound either to the Adena or the Fort Ancient cultures, or indeed some other culture, based on whether or not effigy mounds were an important part of their cultural repertoire, as well as on the overall importance and the specific characteristics of serpent iconography in those cultures.

Original configuration of Serpent Mound

Squier and Davis produced the first published map of Serpent Mound and, because it was the first, it has been assumed that it represents the mound in its most

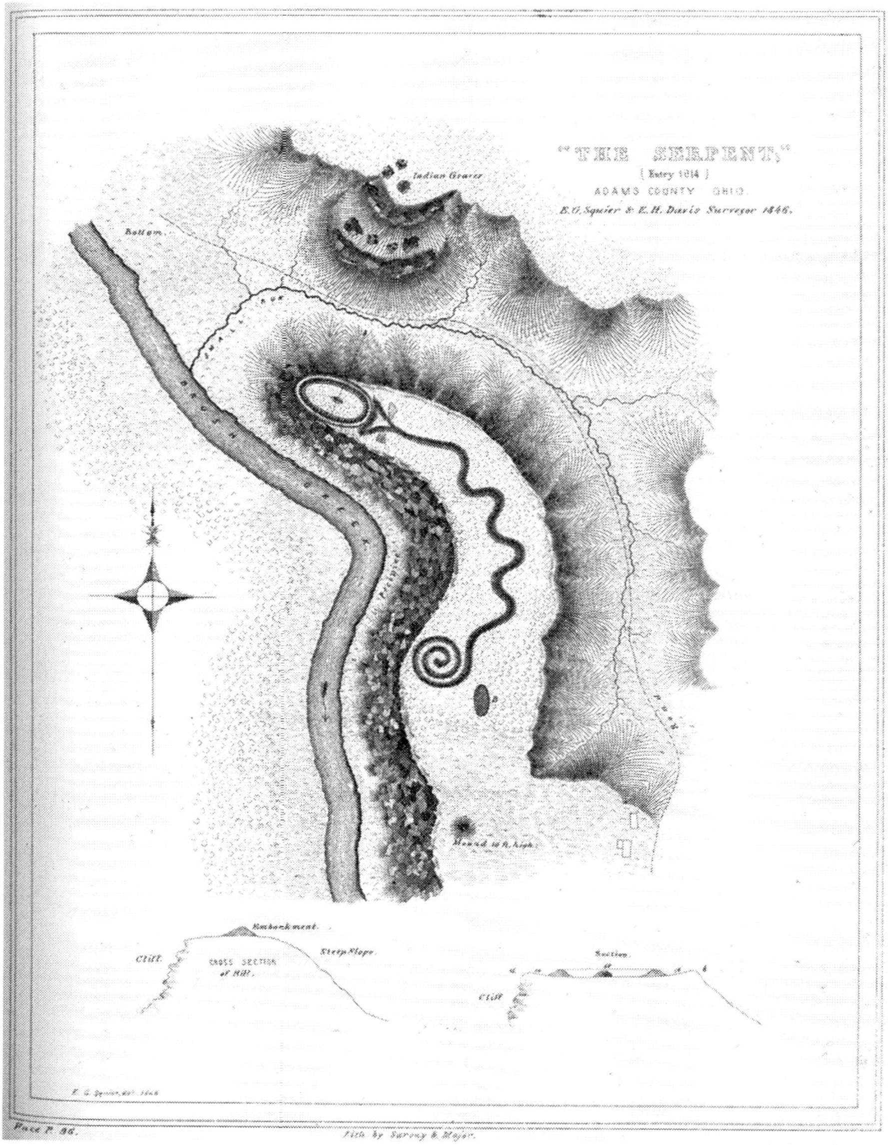

Fig. 8.3 Squier and Davis's (1848) map of Serpent Mound. The earliest published map of Serpent Mound (courtesy of Ohio History Connection).

pristine state (Fig. 8.3). Their map shows two distinct elements: the serpent itself and an oval embankment with a "small circular elevation of large stones much burned" (Squier and Davis 1848, 97) at its centre. But Squier and Davis, particularly Squier, had preconceptions about the Serpent that may have influenced how they perceived and depicted the effigy.

According to Squier, Serpent Mound represented a serpent with an egg gripped in its gaping jaws. He believed that "the Serpent and Egg of Ohio are distinctly allusive to the specific notions of cosmogony which prevailed among the nations of the East" (Squier 1851, 251).

Putnam, in his early surveys of Serpent Mound, documented the same two elements, but he also observed a "slightly raised circular ridge of earth, from either side of which a curved ridge extends towards the sides of the oval figure" located between the oval figure and the edge of the bluff (American Antiquarian Society 1884, 11; Willoughby 1919, 159). Ultimately, like Squier and Davis, he disregarded that earthwork and did not include it in his restorations of the Serpent. He also agreed with Squier's interpretation and rhetorically asked whether it would be "forcing the facts to argue ... that in the oval embankment, with its central pile of burnt stones, in combination with the serpent, we have the three symbols everywhere regarded in the Old World as emblems of those primitive faiths?" (Putnam 1890, 876).

William H. Holmes (1886, 627) thought it certainly was forcing the facts. He rejected Squier and Davis's speculations, arguing that "it is manifestly wrong to go thus out of our way to seek a symbolism for the oval enclosure, as do Squier and Davis, who liken it to the symbolic egg of old-world philosophy". He surveyed Serpent Mound in 1886 and his map included the wishbone-shaped earthwork (Holmes 1886).

John P. MacLean conducted two independent surveys of Serpent Mound in 1884, two years prior to Putnam's investigations and subsequent restoration (Fig. 8.4). He argued that the wishbone-shaped earthwork, which Putnam had observed but dismissed, actually was a separate effigy of a frog. He described it as "in the act of leaping; the hind legs stretched backward, the fore legs outward and forward, the body drawn up at the back, and the head depressed" (MacLean 1885, 45).

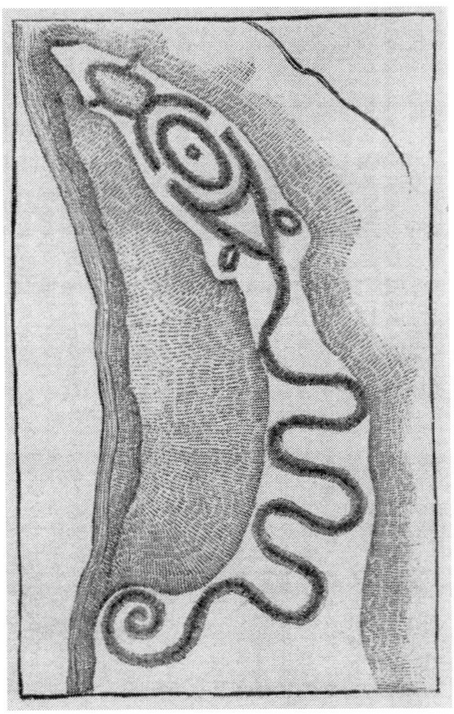

Fig. 8.4 John P. MacLean's (1885) map of Serpent Mound showing the wishbone-shaped earthwork, which he interpreted as a frog (courtesy of Ohio History Connection).

Holmes's 1886 survey and map confirmed MacLean's observation that the embankment forming the body of the serpent continued around the oval enclosure terminating in "a rounded and slightly widened point" (Holmes 1886, 626). Holmes was not, however, convinced by MacLean's argument that the earthwork was a frog effigy. He noted that the appendages of the alleged frog were "too obscure to be identified with absolute certainty", but, regardless of its interpretation, the main part of the frog-like earthwork was "distinctly traceable" leaving "no doubt" as to its artificial character (Holmes 1886, 626).

Charles Willoughby visited the Serpent Mound in 1919, after Putnam's restorations. He stated that the wishbone-shaped earthwork, though unrestored, was nonetheless unmistakably present and he felt it should have been considered part of the original earthwork and restored (Willoughby 1919, 159).

This extended discussion of the original configuration of the anterior portion of Serpent Mound has been necessary in order to provide a more secure basis on which to build an iconographic interpretation of the entire effigy. This, in turn, will facilitate comparisons with other depictions of serpents in the archaeological and ethnohistoric records of the Eastern Woodlands.

The age of effigy mounds in Eastern North America

Naturalistic effigy mounds are a particular class of geoglyph, which, in Eastern North America, include a limited number of motifs. For the effigy mounds of the Upper Midwest, Robert Birmingham (2010, 29) has observed that "bears, water spirits, and snakes loom especially important". He identified the general period of effigy mound construction as between AD 700 and 1100, though he notes (2010, 203) that this range "is based on comparatively few precise radiocarbon dates from the mounds themselves".

A few mounds from earlier periods have been claimed to be effigy mounds, but all of these are more or less problematic, due either to issues with their identification as effigy mounds, or to the determinations of their age. For example, Mound A at the Late Archaic site of Poverty Point is thought by some to represent a bird. Diana Greenlee, however, concluded that "there is no way to know ... if that's what the builders of Mound A intended. We can only speculate" (Ellerbe and Greenlee 2015, 59). Similarly, Cath Oberholtzer (2013, 163) acknowledged "the ambiguity of the zigzag shape" of the Middle Woodland Ontario Serpent Mound.

The only other well-documented naturalistic effigy mound in Ohio is the so-called Alligator Mound (Squier and Davis 1848, 98–100). It has been securely dated to the Late Prehistoric period with two AMS radiocarbon dates of 820±40 BP (Beta-134236) and 840±40 BP (Beta-134237) (Lepper and Frolking 2003, 159).

There are two relatively small stone serpent effigies in the valley below Fort Ancient (White 1986; 1987). Known as the Kern Effigies, they lack the sinuous naturalism of Serpent Mound and some question whether they are indeed serpent effigies. John White, however, argued that their configurations were dictated by astronomical alignments, rather than a commitment to strict naturalism. Kern Effigy 1 is aligned to the summer solstice sunrise, whereas Kern Effigy 2 is aligned to the winter solstice sunrise. Kern Effigy 1 yielded two radiocarbon dates: 530±95 BP (SI-6267) and 765±80 BP (SI-6268) (White 1986, 150), which correspond to the age of the nearby Anderson Village (White 1986, 151).

There are, therefore, no effigy mounds in Eastern North American that have been chronometrically dated to the Early Woodland period. All of the securely dated effigy mounds in this region were built in the Late Woodland and Late Prehistoric periods.

Serpent iconography in the Eastern Woodlands

Serpent imagery is virtually absent in the iconography of the Adena culture, apart from the apparently serpentine pattern on the loincloth of the male human depicted on the Adena Effigy Pipe (Lepper 2010). There are occasional serpents in Hopewell art, but a wide variety of other species, especially birds and mammals, are more frequently depicted.

In stark contrast, during the Late Prehistoric period in Ohio, as well as throughout the broader Mississippian world, serpents were one of the most frequently depicted creatures. James Howard (1968) observed that "gorgets showing the rattlesnake, in either realistic or highly conventionalized form, are among the most common of items" associated with the Southeastern Ceremonial Complex.

Penelope Drooker (1997, 326) presented numerous examples of serpent imagery from Madisonville and other Fort Ancient culture sites, including the "snakelike intertwining of the guilloche motifs that decorate ceramic vessels during Early–Middle Fort Ancient times" as well as "the serpents engraved in stone ..., carved in antler ..., and formed of metal ... during Late Fort Ancient times". Three copper serpent effigy pendants from a single burial at Madisonville are of particular interest in this regard, because they bear a marked resemblance to Serpent Mound (Drooker 1997, 273).

Fletcher *et al.* (1996, 134–8) drew particular attention to similarities between the iconography of the head of Serpent Mound and the way rattlesnake heads are depicted on the late Mississippian Citico-style shell gorgets. Fletcher *et al.* (1996, 138) noted that, although these gorgets "appear to have originated in the eastern Tennessee-northern Georgia region", similar gorgets have been documented in "late Fort Ancient burials" (see also Sharp 1996, 173; Spencer 2016, 27).

The Birger figurine is a richly evocative sculpture of a woman and a large serpent with the teeth of a mammalian carnivore, which was found at the BBB Motor Site, a Middle Mississippian ceremonial location associated with Cahokia. Natalie Mueller and Gayle Fritz (2016, 122–3, 242) argue that the woman is the Siouan Grandmother, First Woman, or "Old-Woman-Who-Never-Dies".

The numerous examples of serpents in Mississippian iconography, coupled with the virtual absence of serpents in Adena art, suggest that Serpent Mound fits more comfortably within a Fort Ancient cultural context and it is within this time frame that clues to its purpose and meaning might more fruitfully be sought.

Iconography of Picture Cave: a "Rosetta Stone" for the interpretation of Serpent Mound

Picture Cave in Missouri contains a remarkable series of pictographs that appear to be "discrete vignettes depicting a series of important cosmic events" in the beliefs of the ancestors of the Dhegihans (Duncan 2015, 209) (Fig. 8.5). The images provide rich insights into the Mississippian Ideological Interaction Sphere (Reilly and Garber 2007, 3). Serpent iconography is especially prominent in the corpus of images and includes a large black serpent confronting a figure variously thought to represent either a frog (Townsend 2015, 156) or a humanoid female

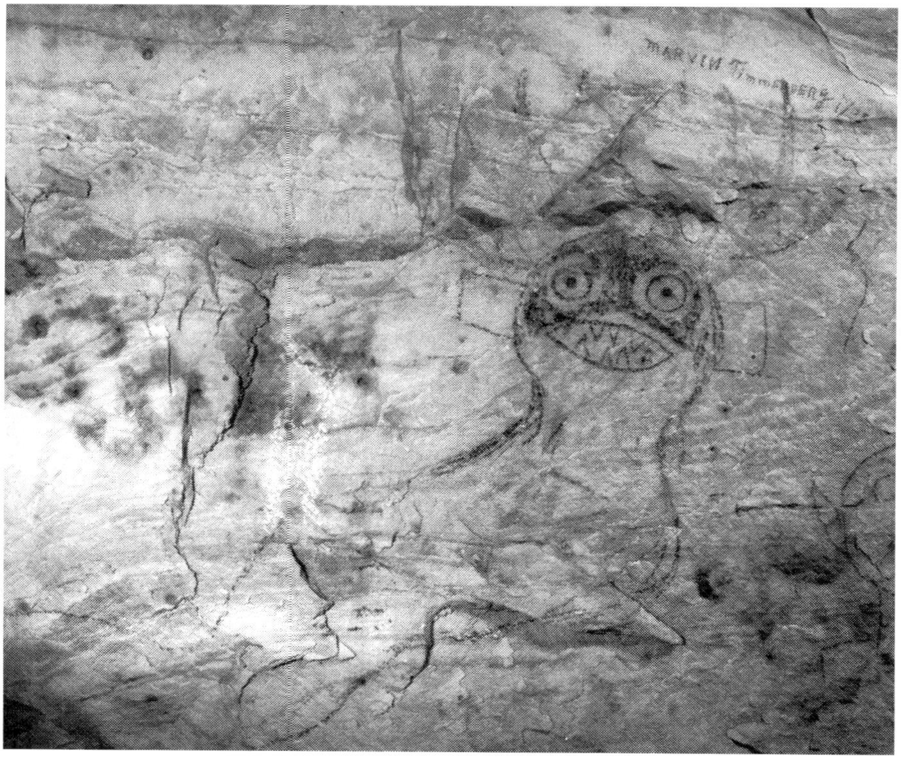

Fig. 8.5 Beneath World Spirit. Glyph 43 from Panel 3 at Picture Cave. The similarity between its "toothy mouth" and the bi-convex Glyph 59 suggested to Reilly (2007, 137) that Glyph 59 was a *pars pro toto* representation of the same supernatural being. The blocky projections extending from each side of the creature's head have analogues in the projections extending from the head of Serpent Mound (Figs 8.2 and 8.3).

that James Duncan (2015, 224) identified specifically as "First Woman on her back with legs drawn up and with a prominent pudendum, in a coital position" (Fig. 8.6). According to Siouan oral traditions referenced by Duncan, First Woman is intimately connected with serpents: "she is the consort of First Man, but she is also the consort of the Snakes, the Lower World water spirits" (Duncan 2015, 224).

Associated with the Picture Cave images of the serpent and the frog/First Woman is a large, biconvex figure that F.K. Reilly (2015, 137–8) interprets as a "toothy mouth", a "*pars pro toto* representation" of the Great Serpent, the "Lord of the Beneath World and Guardian of the Realm of the Dead" (Fig. 8.7). Richard Townsend (2015, 156) identifies the glyph not as a mouth, but as a vulva, or the "Old Woman Earth Deity Vagina". These three elements of this panel of pictographs at Picture Cave bear a striking resemblance to the three principal elements that comprise Serpent Mound and we suggest that this vignette may provide a sort of Rosetta Stone for the interpretation of the iconography of the serpent, "egg" and "frog" at Serpent Mound (Fig. 8.8; compare with Fig. 8.4). When read in this light, the serpent effigy would be the Lord of the Beneath World, the "frog" would be First Woman with spread legs in a coital position, and the "egg" would be the "toothy mouth" of the Great Serpent or First Woman's symbolically enlarged vulva. In support of the interpretation of the ovals at both Serpent Mound and Picture Cave as vulvae, Carol Diaz-Granádos (2011, 83) noted that there is "a variety of vulva forms" in Missouri rock art and "at times the vulva is portrayed in conjunction with ... serpents".

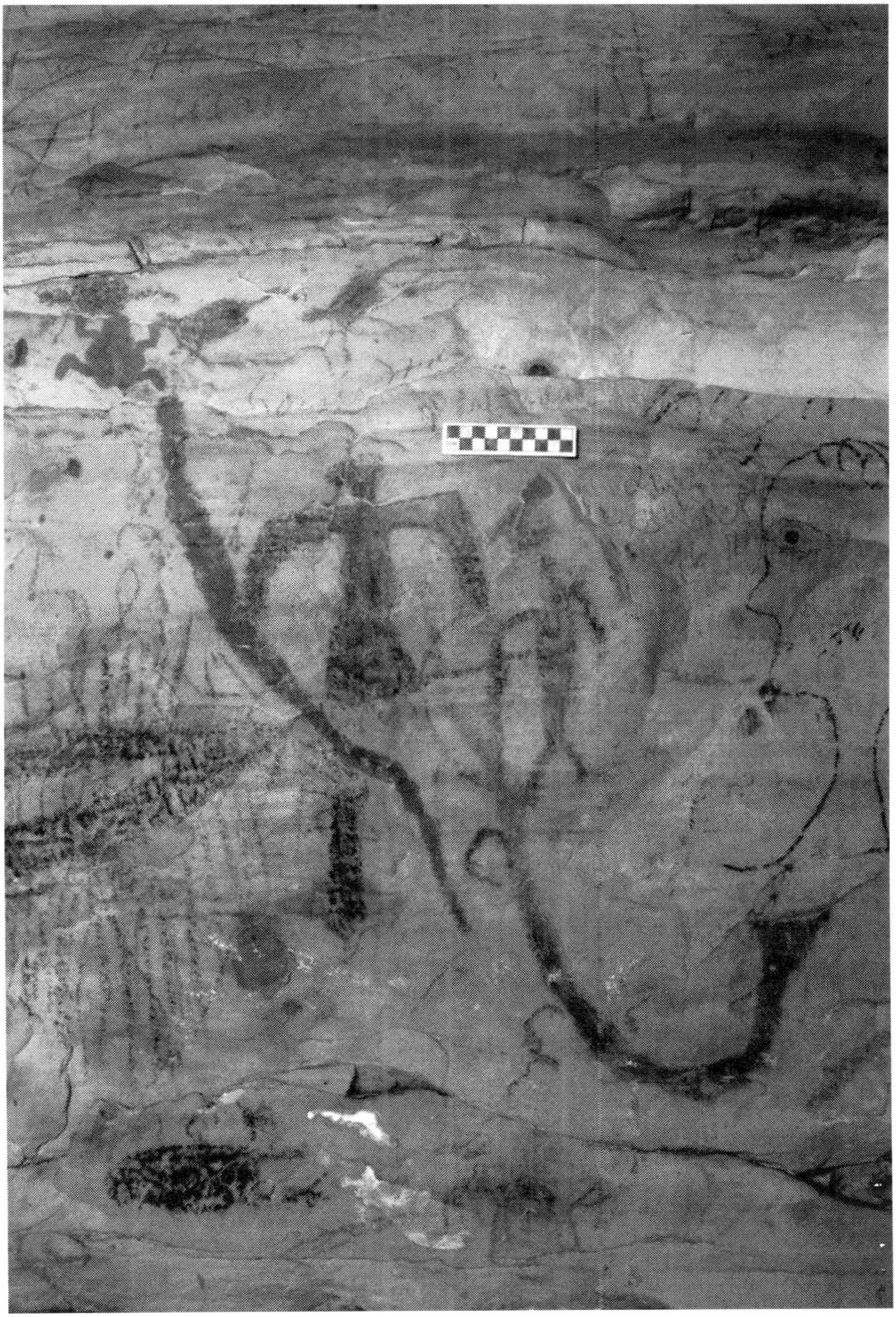

Fig. 8.6 Serpent (Glyph 67), woman (Glyph 64,) and a small part of the bi-convex vulvoid (Glyph 59) pictographs from Panel 3 at Picture Cave. These three glyphs appear to have been painted onto the rock face using the same pigment and technique.

If an antlered serpent pictograph at Picture Cave, referred to by Reilly (2015, 135) as "Beneath World Spirit I" (Fig. 8.5) represents the same character depicted in the tableau with First Woman and the enlarged vulva/toothy mouth (Fig. 8.6), then there is another important connection with the iconography of Serpent

Mound. Beneath World Spirit I has large, blocky projections extending from the side of its head.

One suggestion is that these projections represent earspools (Diaz-Granádos *et al.* 2001, 52; Reilly 2015, 136). There are similar projections extending from the head of Serpent Mound. They appear on both the Squier and Davis (Fig. 8.3) and MacLean (Fig. 8.4) maps but, although Putnam observed these features (American Antiquarian Society 1884, 12), he did not include them in his restorations of the effigy. They have been interpreted variously as "wings" (MacLean 1887, 56) or "horns" (Willoughby 1919, 162), but in the context of the Picture Cave iconography, they can be understood as the earspools of the great Beneath World Spirit. The Beneath World Spirit I pictograph produced an AMS radiocarbon date of 950±100 BP (CAMS-41465) (Diaz-Granádos *et al.* 2001, 489), which interestingly, though not, we think, coincidentally, is virtually identical to the dates of 920±70 BP obtained by Fletcher *et al.* (1996) for Serpent Mound.

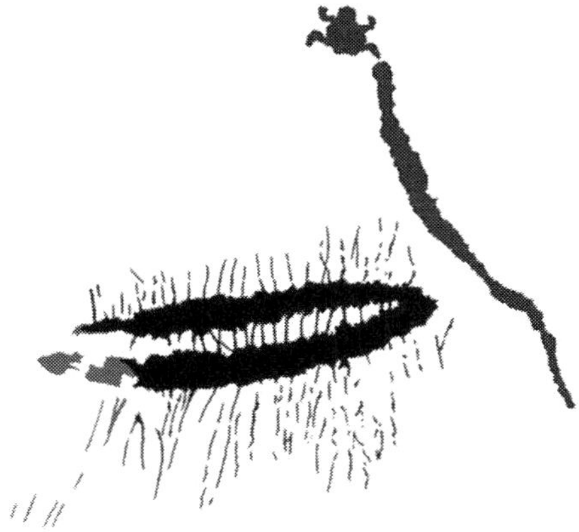

Fig. 8.7 Serpent, woman and vulvoid group from Panel 3 at Picture Cave (drawing by Peter Lepper).

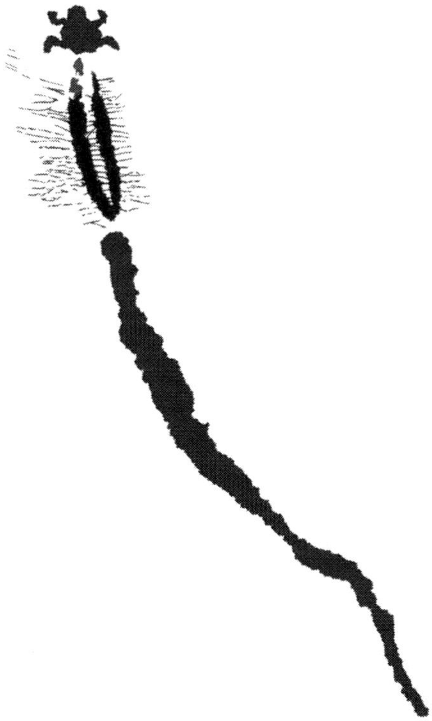

Fig. 8.8 Serpent, woman and vulvoid group from Panel 3 at Picture Cave re-arranged and with the size of Glyph 59 adjusted to show the resemblance of the group to the three elements comprising Serpent Mound (drawing by Peter Lepper).

Picture Cave and Dhegihan oral traditions

Based on more than 50 years of style analysis and dating in the Western Mississippian region, co-authors Duncan and Diaz-Granádos have concluded that the Picture Cave serpent, vulva and coital figure were created between AD 950 and 1025. Jon Muller (1966, 25–39; 1989, 23–4) first recognized a distinct and naturalistic style of shell engraving and repoussé copper plates from around the confluence of the Ohio River and the Mississippi River. Meanwhile, in the late 1960s and early 1970s, Philip Phillips and James Brown (1978, 69–102) had begun the monumental task of describing the hundreds of shell engravings from Spiro and subjecting them to style analysis. Brown (1989, 193–8) continued this task by assigning the oldest and most realistic style, Braden, to the Cahokia area. Continuing work by the Linda Schele Workshop, led by F. Kent Reilly III, has anchored this Classic Braden style to the Cahokia region and its southern environ, the Ohio/Mississippi confluence (Reilly and Garber 2007).

In 2011, Brown (2011) and Diaz-Granádos (2011) assigned the Cahokia region and the Braden art style to the ancient Dhegihans, ancestors of the modern day Quapaw, Osage, Kansas, Ponca and Omaha. Finally, in 2015, Brown and Muller (2015, 114–24) identified Picture Cave as the seminal expression of the Braden art style, firmly placing the beginnings of a religious resurgence in the prairie/plains adjacent to the lower Missouri River and its confluence with the Mississippi.

There is little doubt that the Western Mississippian region was the focal point of long-enduring religious traditions between AD 1050 and 1250. Evidence for shared religious and ritual knowledge over a large part of eastern North America long has been key to defining what is now referred to as the Mississippian Ideological Interaction Sphere (Reilly and Garber 2007). The core elements of these interacting, yet regionally distinctive, belief systems remained surprisingly steady over time; and we argue that the meaning of Ohio's Serpent Mound and the corresponding glyphs from Picture Cave may be found in the oral traditions of groups whose ancestors were a part of that interaction sphere.

According to Alice Fletcher, Putnam's colleague who greatly assisted in the fund-raising that allowed Harvard University to purchase Serpent Mound, and Francis La Flesche (e.g. Fletcher and La Flesche 1992, 171), the Dhegiha had a shared oral tradition of the creation of the earth (Middle World). After long years of searching for and recovering bits and pieces of this lore, La Flesche was able to identify components of one of what had been two paramount Dhegihan rites.

Comparing three templates from similar oral traditions, "medicine rites" collected by Alfred W. Bowers (1950; 1992), Alanson Skinner (1926) and Paul Radin (1948, 115–36), along with John Matthews' (1961, 735–70) descriptions of the Osage Native American Church rites, La Flesche's vast ethnographic collections (Bailey 1995, 276–305) and the images from Picture Cave, co-authors Duncan and Diaz-Granádos have constructed a coherent narrative of what we believe to be the essential elements of the genesis story of the Dhegiha, the *Mon-Thin-Ka-Ga'-Xe*, "The Making of the Earth Rite". What follows is a brief version of that reconstructed story.

The Making of the Earth Rite

Long before time began, the Water Spirits, the Great Serpent and his children the snakes, coerced First Man's eldest son, Morning Star, the one who would succeed First Man as the Sun, and some companions into coming down to the Beneath World and engaging in some friendly competitive games of chance. The final game, the single stick-ball game, involved high stakes – the losers' heads. The Water Spirits won and the Great Serpent, the chief of the Water Spirits, cut off their heads. One of the Water Spirits, a particularly greedy, bloated, and eyeless creature representing death, swallowed all but Morning Star's head.

The Upper Worlds were thrown into darkness, there being no shining Sun to rise into the sky. Morning Star's sister, Evening Star, had two sons, Stone and the Grey Wolf, whom Morning Star had helped to raise. These two young men went to visit their grandmother, First Woman or Old-Woman-Who-Never-Dies.

First Woman lived in her lodge at the top of the Beneath Worlds, the Moon. She fed the two young men and gave them several powerful sacred weapons to defeat the Water Spirits. First Woman also painted her grandsons: Grey Wolf was painted black, a signal to all that he would kill all foes and take no prisoners; Stone was painted red and white and he was given a holy bull snake's hide, to tie on the left arm of a vanquished enemy to make him a prisoner.

Grey Wolf was sent to scout and find the town of the Water Spirits. First Woman changed into a spider and carried her grandson Stone down into the Beneath World to help Grey Wolf attack and defeat the Water Spirits. The two boys, Stone and Grey Wolf, gave a whoop and attacked the town of the Water Spirits. They quickly shot the bloated Water Spirit, Death, and he vomited up Morning Star's companions in his death throes. These resurrected companions joined in the fight with Stone and Grey Wolf.

The two boys and their companions attacked the Water Spirits. They shot the Great Serpent, wounding him and causing him to fall. Stone rushed up to him and tied the holy bull snakeskin to his upper left arm; Grey Wolf picked up the war club that the Great Serpent had taken from Morning Star after beheading him. Walking among the writhing and bleeding snakes, Grey Wolf collected their scalps and weapons, while Stone made the Great Serpent lead him to the centre of the town to retrieve Morning Star's head. Singing their victory songs, Stone, Grey Wolf and their companions danced into the sky, taking the head of Morning Star to his mother, First Woman.

First Woman and her grandsons made a feast at which the Great Serpent was given gifts and First Woman adopted him as a husband to replace her loss. As her adopted husband, the Great Serpent then had intercourse with First Woman and she gained his ability to resurrect or reincarnate and rejuvenate herself. In this crucial event, First Woman became a holy or sacred vessel, receiving from the Great Serpent his unique power of resurrection. This is the image rendered in black pigment on the wall at Picture Cave (Duncan 2015, 224). This graphic and salient image mirrors the Serpent Mound as mapped by MacLean in 1885.

This imagery records the moment when First Woman bridges the cosmos, bringing the life-giving powers from the Beneath Worlds to the Middle World, the Earth. With this crucial acquisition, First Woman becomes the sacred receptacle of these vital, animating powers.

First Woman again became Grandmother Spider and wove a holy web of life, the Earth, the snare where all life takes on a bodily form. Into this web Stone and the Grey Wolf placed the head and body of Morning Star, who then burst forth from this snare as the *axis mundi* or sacred tree with the risen (resurrected) Sun. The Middle World was then ready for all living things, including humans. The Great Serpent coils around the sacred tree or axis and becomes the rainbow in the daytime sky and the Milky Way in the night sky.

What has just been narrated is a widespread genesis tradition: while differing in details, its central or core theme is amazingly similar across many nations. This genesis rite is widespread in the eastern United States and it is known by some as the Great Medicine Rite (Hall 1997, 59–74; Weeks 2009). The culmination of this great rite is the adoption ritual where Stone and the Grey Wolf gave the war captive, the Great Serpent, as a replacement husband to First Woman (Hall 1997, 10–13, 32–5, 50–58). This adoption ritual was the foundation for the next rite, the most important, *Mon-Thin-Ka-Ga'-Xe*, "The Making of the Earth".

This ritual, the coital act between First Woman, the spirit of the Earth, and the Great Serpent has enormous symbolic significance throughout North America. Alice Kehoe (1970) and Alfred Bowers (1950) have extensively documented these sexual rites known as "Walking with the buffalo". The participating women passed this power directly to their husbands through intercourse and indirectly to their people, enabling them to enjoy increased power in warfare and hunting (Bowers 1950, 284).

Conclusions

> ... we always may be sure that every man-made thing arises from a problem as a purposeful solution. (Kubler 1962, 8)

Determining the age of Serpent Mound is an important goal, because of the necessity of having a cultural context in which to situate the largest effigy mound in North America. Previous efforts to assign an age and cultural affiliation to the mound have been unsuccessful, for a variety of reasons.

If Serpent Mound represents the solution to a problem, as Kubler suggests, then it is a Fort Ancient solution to a Mississippian problem. Early Fort Ancient communities were becoming larger, more sedentary, and frequently organized around a central plaza (Henderson *et al.* 1992, 261; see also Cook 2008). These changes coincided with the development of new leadership roles, and such nascent elites would have benefited from grander expressions of unifying religious beliefs coupled with a more consistent iconography. Susan Power (2004, 177) has observed that "while the snake was an ancient image, new serpentine expressions were created in the Mississippian period, often distinguished by their unique size, placement, elaboration, and at times function".

A Fort Ancient Serpent Mound fits well within the context of Robert Cook's (2008) research indicating that there were significant interactions between Fort Ancient peoples and Mississippians. A further implication of our interpretation of Serpent Mound as a symbolic representation of a key moment in the Dhegihan creation story is that the Fort Ancient culture may have included some Dhegihan groups. This possibility is affirmed by the migration stories of some Dhegihan tribes (Henning 1993). Alternatively, elements of the Dhegihan creation story may have been a part of the cosmologies of other groups that subsequently lost them due to the catastrophic cultural disruptions following European contact.

If Serpent Mound was created by the Adena culture, then it existed in a splendid isolation that persisted for nearly a thousand years before anything else like it appeared in eastern North America. If it was created by the Fort Ancient culture, then it has a clear cultural context in the cosmology of contemporary Mississippian and related groups, including the Fort Ancient culture.

The similarities between the iconography of Picture Cave and Serpent Mound suggest that they are telling the same or a closely related story. The Dhegihan oral traditions appear to contain these same elements and provide the rest of that story. Fletcher and La Flesche (1911, 171) wrote that the Omaha's Making of the Earth Rites "not only dramatized the myth of Creation, but were believed to insure the continuance of that which had been created". Similarly, Birmingham (2010, 202) has proposed that "the effigy mound landscape did not merely *symbolize* periodic recreation of the world and its people in the form of their animal and spirit-being ancestors, but the landscape itself was perceived by the mound builders as creation in progress". Therefore, if we are correct, that the same iconography is represented both at Picture Cave and at Serpent Mound and that this iconography represents the Dhegihan Creation story, then Serpent Mound would not have been conceived as a static monument, but rather as an instrument through which the world could be actively renewed. That would provide a compelling reason for the construction of such a monumental earthwork – a reason that makes the most sense in a Mississippian context.

Acknowledgements

The 2014 field crews that assisted Frolking and Lepper in the extraction of soil cores included, on 16 September: Steven Forman with the Department of Geology at Baylor University, Ohio History Connection staff Linda Pansing, Bill Pickard, Kellie Locke Rogers, and Logan Miller; and on 16 October: Ohio History Connection staff Kellie Locke Rogers and Logan Miller and Denison University student Logan Eyer. We thank William Romain and William Monaghan for sharing raw data recorded during the Herrmann *et al.* (2014) investigation. We thank Peter Lepper for creating Figs 8.7 and 8.8. Finally, we thank two anonymous reviewers [for the original paper] for their helpful suggestions for improving this paper.

Bibliography

American Antiquarian Society (1884) *Proceedings of the American Antiquarian Society at the Annual Meeting held at Worcester, October 22, 1883.*

Bailey, G.A. (1995) *The Osage and the Invisible World: From the Works of Francis La Flesche.* University of Oklahoma Press Norman OK.

Birmingham, R.A. (2010) *Spirits of the Earth: The Effigy Mound Landscape of Madison and the Four Lakes.* University of Wisconsin Press, Madison WI.

Bowers, A.W. (1950) *Mandan Social and Ceremonial Organization.* University of Chicago Press, Chicago IL.

Bowers, A.W. (1992) *Hidatsa Social and Ceremonial Organization*. University of Nebraska Press, Lincoln NE.

Brown, J.A. (1989) On style divisions of the Southeastern Ceremonial Complex – a revisionist perspective. In *Southern Ceremonial Complex, Artifacts and Analysis: The Cottonlandia conference*, P. Galloway (ed.), 183–204. University of Nebraska Press, Lincoln NE.

Brown, J.A. (2011) The regional cultural signature of the Braden Art Style. In *Visualizing the Sacred: Cosmic visions, regionalism, and the art of the Mississippian world*, G.E. Lankford, F.K. Reilly III and J.E. Garber (eds), 37–63. University of Texas Press, Austin TX.

Brown, J.A. and Muller, J. (2015) Tradition and horizons in southeastern representation: lessons from Picture Cave, In *Picture Cave, Unraveling the Mysteries of the Mississippian Cosmos*, C. Diaz-Granádos, J.R. Duncan and F.K. Reilly III (eds), 113–24. University of Texas Press, Austin TX.

Cook, R. (2008) *SunWatch: Fort Ancient Development in the Mississippian World*. University of Alabama Press, Tuscaloosa AL.

Diaz-Granádos, C. (2011) Early manifestations of Mississippian iconography in Middle Mississippi Valley rock-art. In *Visualizing the Sacred: Cosmic visions, regionalism, and the art of the Mississippian world*, G.E. Lankford, F.K. Reilly III and J.E. Garber (eds), 64–95. University of Texas Press, Austin TX.

Diaz-Granádos, C., Rowe, M.W. Hyman, M., Duncan, J.R. and Southon, J.R. (2001) Radiocarbon dates for charcoal from three Missouri pictographs and their associated iconography. *American Antiquity* 66, 481–92.

Drooker, P.B. (1997) *The View from Madisonville: Protohistoric Western Fort Ancient Interaction Patterns*. Memoirs of the Museum of Anthropology 31, University of Michigan, Ann Arbor MI.

Duchaufour, P. (1982) *Pedology, Pedogenesis and Classification* (trans. T.R. Paton). George Allen & Unwin, London.

Duncan, J.R. (2015) Identifying the characters on the walls of Picture Cave. In *Picture Cave: Unraveling the Mysteries of the Mississippian Cosmos*, C. Diaz-Granádos, J.R. Duncan and F.K. Reilly III (eds), 209–37. University of Texas Press, Austin TX.

Ellerbee, J. and Greenlee, D.M. (2015) *Poverty Point: Revealing the Forgotten City*. Louisiana State University Press, Baton Rouge LA.

Fletcher, A.C. and La Flesche, F. (1911) *The Omaha Tribe*. Twenty-seventh Annual Report of the Bureau of American Ethnology, 1905–1906. US Government Printing Office, Washington DC.

Fletcher, A.C. and La Flesche, F. (1992) *The Omaha Tribe*, Vol. 2. University of Nebraska Press, Lincoln NE.

Fletcher, R., Cameron, T., Lepper, P.T., Wymer, D.A. and Pickard, W. (1996) Serpent Mound: a Fort Ancient icon? *Midcontinental Journal of Archaeology* 21, 105–43.

Gee, G.W. and Bauder, J.W. (1986) Particle-size analysis. In *Methods of Soil Analysis, Part 1: Physical and Mineralogical Methods*, A. Klute (ed.), 383–411. Agronomy Monograph 9, American Society of Agronomy, Madison WI.

Greenman, E.F. (1967) *Serpent Mound*. Ohio Historical Society, Columbus OH.

Griffin, J.B. (1966) *The Fort Ancient Aspect: its Cultural and Chronological Position in Mississippi Valley Archaeology*. Museum of Anthropology, Anthropological Papers 28, University of Michigan, Ann Arbor MI.

Griffin, J.B. (19780 The Midlands and Northeastern United States. In *Ancient Native Americans*, J.D. Jennings (ed.), 221–79. W.H. Freeman, San Francisco CA.

Hall, R.L. (1997) *An Archaeology of the Soul: North American Indian Belief and Ritual*. University of Illinois Press, Urbana IL.

Henderson, A.G., Pollack, D. and Turnbow, C.A. (1992) Chronology and cultural patterns. In *Fort Ancient Cultural Dynamics in the Middle Ohio Valley*, A.G. Henderson (ed.), 253–79. Monographs in World Archaeology 8, Madison WI.

Henning, D.R. (1993) The adaptive patterning of the Dhegiha Sioux. *Plains Anthropologist* 38, 253–64.

Herrmann, E.W., Monaghan, G.W., Romain, W.F., Schilling, T.M., Burks, J., Leone, K.L., Purtill, M.P. and Tonetti, A.C. (2014) A new multistage construction chronology for the Great Serpent Mound, USA. *Journal of Archaeological Science* 50, 117–25.

Holmes, W.H. (1886) A sketch of the Great Serpent Mound. *Science* 8, 624–8.

Hoskins, B. (2002) *Organic Matter by Loss on Ignition*. University of Maine, Soil Testing Lab., Orono ME.

Howard, J.H. (1968) *The Southeastern Ceremonial Complex and Its Interpretation*. Memoir 6, Missouri Archaeological Society, Columbia MO.

Kehoe, A. (1970) The function of ceremonial sexual intercourse among the Northern Plains Indians. *Plains Anthropologist* 15, 99–103.

Kubler, G. (1962) *The Shape of Time: Remarks on the History of Things*. Yale University Press, New Haven CT.

Lepper, B.T. (2010) The Adena Pipe: icon of ancient Ohio. *Timeline* 27(1), 2–15.

Lepper, B.T. and Frolking, T.A. (2003) Alligator Mound: geoarchaeological and iconographical interpretations of a Late Prehistoric effigy mound in central Ohio, USA. *Cambridge Archaeological Journal* 13, 147–67.

Lucht, T.E. and Brown, D.L. (1994) *Soil Survey of Adams County, Ohio*. Soil Conservation Service, US Department of Agriculture & Ohio Department of Natural Resources, Columbus OH.

MacLean, J.P. (1885) The Great Serpent Mound. *American Antiquarian* 7, 44–7.

MacLean, J.P. (1887) *The Mound Builders*. Robert Clarke & Co, Cincinnati OH.

Matthews, J.J. (1961) *The Osages: Children of the Middle Waters*. University of Oklahoma Press, Norman OK.

Mueller, N.G. and Fritz, G.J. (2016) Women as symbols and actors in the Mississippi Valley: evidence from female flint-clay statues and effigy vessels. In *Native American Landscape: An Engendered Perspective*, C. Claassen (ed.), 109–50. University of Tennessee Press, Knoxville TN.

Muller, J. (1966) An Experimental Theory of Stylistic Analysis. Unpublished PhD dissertation, Harvard University.

Muller, J. (1989) The Southern Cult. In *Southern Ceremonial Complex, Artifacts and Analysis: the Cottonlandia Conference* P. Galloway (ed.), 11–26. University of Nebraska Press, Lincoln NE.

Oades, J.M. (1989) An introduction to organic matter in mineral soils. In *Minerals in Soil Environments* (2nd edn), J.B. Dixon and S.S. Weed (eds) 89–159. SSSA Book Series 1, Soil Science Society of America, Madison WI.

Oberholtzer, C. (2013) The living landscape. In *Before Ontario: The Archaeology of a Province*, M.K. Munson and S.M. Jamieson (eds), 152–64. McGill-Queens University Press, Montreal.

Phillips, P. and Brown, JA. (1978) *Pre-Columbian Shell Engravings from the Craig Mound at Spiro, Oklahoma, Part 1*. Harvard University, Peabody Museum of Archaeology and Ethnology, Cambridge MA.

Power, S.C. (2004) *Early Art of the Southeastern Indians: Feathered Serpents & Winged Beings*. University of Georgia Press, Athens GA.

Putnam, F.W. (1888) *Twenty-Second Report of the Trustees of the Peabody Museum of American Archaeology and Ethnology* 4(2), 49–52.

Putnam, F.W. (1890) The Serpent Mound of Ohio. *The Century* 39, 871–88.

Radin, P. (1948) *Winnebago Hero Cycles: A Study in Aboriginal Literature*. Indiana University Publications in Anthropology and Linguistics Memoir 1, Baltimore MD.

Reilly, F.K. III (2015) The cave and the Beneath World spirit: mythic dragons from the North American past. In *Picture Cave: Unraveling the Mysteries of the Mississippian Cosmos*, C. Diaz-Granádos, J.R. Duncan and F.K. Reilly III (eds), 133–43. University of Texas Press, Austin TX.

Reilly, F.K. III and Garber, J.F. (2007) Introduction. In *Ancient Objects and Sacred Realms: Interpretations of Mississippian Iconography*, F.K. Reilly III and J.F. Garber (eds) 1–7. University of Texas Press, Austin TX.

Sharp, W.E. (1996) Fort Ancient farmers. In *Kentucky Archaeology*, R.B. Lewis (ed.), 161–82. University of Kentucky Press, Lexington KY.

Shetrone, H.C. (1920) The culture problem in Ohio archaeology. *American Anthropologist* 22, 144–72.

Shetrone, H.C. (1947) Ohio Archaeology and Archaeologists. Unpublished manuscript VFM 3174, Ohio History Connection, Columbus OH).

Skinner, A. (1926) Ethnology of the Iowan Indians. *Bulletin of the Public Museum of Milwaukee* 5(4).

Spencer, D. (2016) *Early Native Americans in West Virginia: The Fort Ancient Culture*. History Press, Charleston SC.

Squier, E.G. (1851) *The Serpent Symbol and the Worship of the Reciprocal Principles of Nature in America*. George P. Putnam, New York.

Squier, E. and Davis, E. (1848) *Ancient Monuments of the Mississippi Valley*. Smithsonian Institution, Washington DC.

Townsend, R.F. (2015) The Cave, Cahokia, and the Omaha Tribe. In *Picture Cave: Unraveling the Mysteries of the Mississippian Cosmos*, C. Diaz-Granádos, J.R. Duncan and F.K. Reilly III (eds), 145–65. University of Texas Press, Austin TX.

Webb, W.S. and Baby, R.S. (1957) *The Adena People*, No. 2. Ohio Historical Society, Columbus OH.

Webb, W.S. and Snow, C.E. (1974) [1945] *The Adena People*. University of Tennessee Press, Knoxville TN.

Weeks, W.R. Jr (2009) Antiquity of the Midewiwin: An Examination of Early Documents, Origin Stories, Archaeological Remains, and Rock Paintings from the Northern Woodlands of North America. Unpublished PhD dissertation, Arizona State University.

White, J.R. (1986) The Kern Effigy: evidence for a prehistoric Fort Ancient summer solstice marker. *North American Archaeologist* 7, 137–65.

White, J.R. (1987) Kern Effigy #2: a Fort Ancient winter solstice marker? *Midcontinental Journal of Archaeology* 12, 233–42.

Williams, N.L. and Kerr, J.W. (1977) *Soil Survey of Highland County, Ohio*. Soil Conservation Service, US Department of Agriculture & Ohio Department of Natural Resources, Columbus OH.

Willoughby, C.C. (1919) The Serpent Mound of Adams County, Ohio. *American Anthropologist* 21, 153–63.

9

Contextualizing Mississippian statuary from the Mississippi–Ohio River confluence

Steven L. Boles

This chapter is devoted to five Mississippian Period (AD 1050–1450) statues and their ties to Cahokia. Cahokia was the largest Pre-contact site in North America and located near modern-day St Louis, Missouri (for recent summaries, see Pauketat and Alt 2015; Emerson *et al.* 2018). Briefly, the suite contains four previously known statues and one statue recovered in recent years that has not been widely reported (Boles 2014). The discussion of these statues combines various interpretative methods including iconography, archaeological contexts, and ethno-historical accounts. While use of the latter is not without critics, its use here is to provide possible correlates and/or to provoke thought. Combined, these lines of study allow an approach that moves us past looking at many Pre-contact American Indian cultural items as works of art and as such highly valued trade items; instead, it allows for another way of interpreting these items as representations of mythological personas, culture heroes, or perhaps even portraits of an individual. Such items are more appropriately viewed as religious sacra or sacred belongings (Emerson 1989).

The movement of these sacred cultural materials outside the area of production and use, then, is far more complex than trade, elite exchange, and merely items associated with political economies. Various theories for the movement and deposition of these sacred objects have been suggested and include missionizing groups, fictive adoption ceremonies associated with alliance building events, and migration (Emerson and Girard 2004; Pauketat 2004; 2013; Boles 2020; 2022a). The latter is informed by looking at the use and ritual deposition of religious sacra via archaeological contexts and by comparing how similar objects were used, transferred, and eventually decommissioned by American Indians according to accounts recorded primarily during the late 19th and early 20th centuries.

As mentioned above, five Mississippian stone sculptures are discussed herein and will be used to explore the various aspects and movement of Cahokian religious sacra. Specifically, four of the statues were either made at Cahokia or likely influenced by Cahokians but recovered outside of Cahokia, and the fifth was likely made along the Lower Ohio River but ended up at Cahokia (Fig. 9.1, nos 1, 2, 6, 8, 9). For two of the four previously known statues, contextual details are not widely known, and for another, there is some debate on provenance or duplicate reporting (Smith and Miller 2009, 149–50).

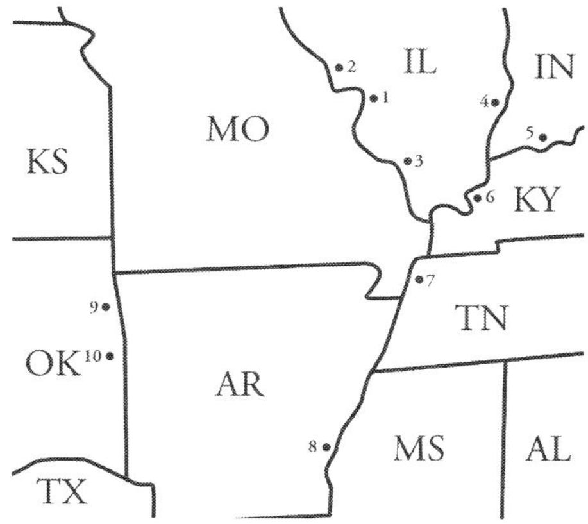

Fig. 9.1 Sites discussed with Cahokia-style or Tennessee-Cumberland style statues: 1. Cahokia, Madison/St Clair Counties, Illinois; 2. unreported, Greene County, Illinois; 3. Ware, Union County, Illinois; 4. unreported, Edwards County, Illinois; 5. Angel, Vanderburgh County, Indiana; 6. unreported, near Tolu, Kentucky; 7. Obion County, Tennessee; 8. Opossum Bayou ("Westbrook" statue), Desha County, Arkansas; 9. Harlan, Cherokee County, Oklahoma; 10. Spiro, Le Flore County, Oklahoma.

Two definitive styles are recognized among the five statues and have been researched and written about extensively. The previously reported statues include two Tennessee-Cumberland style statues (Tolu, Cahokia) and two Cahokia style statues (Westbrook and Harlan); the unreported statue is also of the Cahokia style. Following Smith and Miller's criteria in separating statues (<3 in/76 mm) from figurines (>3 in), the sculptures discussed here will be referred to as statues (Smith and Miller 2009, 17–18).

The older of the two statuary styles is referred to as the Cahokia style and it originated in the Cahokia area (near modern-day St Louis, Missouri) during the late 11th or early 12th century (Emerson and Hughes 2000; Emerson *et al.* 2002; 2003; Boles *et al.* 2018). Earlier effigy pipes have been recovered from Terminal Late Woodland (TLW) or Merrell phase (AD 975–1050) contexts in the uplands adjacent to the American Bottom (Emerson 1982; Koldehoff 1996; 2016). These large animal effigy pipes are a dramatic invention from the preceding small clay pipes common in Late Woodland assemblages and infer changes to pipe-smoking rituals. This new form of effigy pipes seemingly served as the precursor to the more refined Cahokia statuary and figure pipes as originally defined by Emerson (1982). Emerson describes the Cahokia style statues as highly developed, realistic portrayals of human or near-human figures and typically engaged in specific acts or deeds. Many of these statues have been interpreted as representations of mythological beings. Dark red flint clay mined from sinkholes within the Greater Cahokia region was the favored material for the carving of Cahokia statues although a few made from sandstone and limestone have been recorded (Emerson 1982, 18; 1989, 54–6; Boles 2022a).

In contrast, the later Tennessee-Cumberland style statues as originally defined by Engle (1957) and later refined by Smith and Miller (2009), are exclusively human figures with a focus on facial features and less attention to torso and body. These statues were made during the 13th and 14th centuries throughout a wider geographic area from near the Mississippi–Ohio River confluence region on the northwest perimeter down to as far away as Georgia to the southeast perimeter. Given the wide extent of production, a variety of raw materials were used for their production and include sandstone, limestone, marble, fluorite, and even wood. The Tennessee-Cumberland statues were often deposited in male/female pairs and the uniqueness of facial characteristics has been interpreted as expressions or likenesses of specific individuals although singular male or females are thought to represent mythological ancestral personas.

Deposition for both statuary styles include mounds, shrines/special-use features, and as mortuary accompaniments. Both statuary styles have also been recovered outside of their cultural production areas and these are of special interest in delineating interactions between distinct and often distant groups.

The outline for the chapter includes details for each statue followed by a discussion on the re-analysis of the statues with a focus on contexts and iconography and informed by ethno-histories. Noteworthy in the discussion are the introduction of a newly discovered Cahokia-style statue, the discussion on a poorly known Cahokia statue-pipe, the argument for the discovery of a Tennessee-Cumberland statue attributed to Cahokia, the likelihood of a TLW origin for the Cahokia style statuary and figure pipes, and an argument for Cahokia's religious sacra (statues and figure pipes) entering the archaeological record with Cahokia migrants or their descendants.

Westbrook statue, Opossum Bayou, Desha County, Arkansas

The Westbrook statue, the name by which it most commonly referred to in archaeological literature, was actually discovered by Harvey McGehee of McGehee, Arkansas and pictured in his collection in 1972 (Parks and Thompson 1972, 222–3). McGehee recovered the statue in Desha County, Arkansas (Fig. 9.1, 8) in 1969 and two years later Greg Perino first mentioned it in a summary of known flint clay (then thought to be bauxite) statues (1971, 117). This statue has been written about and pictured many times since and has also been commonly referred to as the Corn Goddess in the collecting community.

As for description, the Westbrook statue is kneeling and appears to be emerging from a basket or sacred bundle (Fig. 9.2A). The back of the basket was drilled for the pipe stem hole with the bowl drilled through the top of the basket. She is kneeling with her hands resting on the platform or ground. Sunflower stalks as well as what appears to be corn stalks are sprouting from her upturned palms and arch over her head enshrouding her. She is 17.8 cm long by 17.8 cm tall by 14 cm wide and weighs approximately 1.8 kg.

Much of the contextual information presented here was obtained from interviewing J.T. Ross, Harvey's son-in-law. The Westbrook statue was recovered from the Opossum Fork Bayou Mound (also known as the Richland Mound and the DeSoto Mound) 3DE24, which is situated near the Arkansas River roughly 20 km above its confluence with the Mississippi River. The site was farmed at the time of discovery and the field contained one small conical mound, approximately 20m in diameter and roughly 1 m tall. It reportedly contained five layers of burials with the oldest being Tchefuncte (*c.* 600–200 BC) located at the water table followed by Marksville (*c.* 200 BC–AD 400) and then Coles Creek (*c.* AD 700–1200). Harvey also mentioned that some Mississippian shell-tempered sherds were found on the surface of the mound as well as a Cahokia-style discoidal (Fig. 9.23). Mortuary offerings were sparse amongst the approximated 200 excavated burials. However, nine pipes were recovered from burials at the site and include the Westbrook pipe, several limestone effigy pipes including a bound captive effigy, a deteriorated human effigy, a bear effigy, and a frog effigy, as well as two pipes made from clay including another frog effigy and a plain elbow pipe. A handful of pots were also encountered including two early Caddo grit tempered Smithport Plain Bottles.

The Westbrook statue was found with what McGehee identified as an adult female in an intrusive shaft tomb burial approximately 9 ft (2.74 m) below the mound's surface (Fig. 9.2C). Burials of this type are generally associated with the early Caddo period (Girard *et al.* 2014, 41, 46–50). Of interest, flint clay statues were also recovered from Caddo shaft burials at Gahagan (Emerson and Girard 2004).

Typical funerary objects associated with early Caddo shaft burials were also recovered with the Westbrook burial (Girard *et al.* 2014, 50–1, 97). Over 200 Marine shell beads were recovered on the chest and arms of the Westbrook individual (Fig. 9.2D). A necklace with four large marine shell beads was recovered from the neck. Near the left arm was a 9.5 kg cobble of minimally worked galena with the broken Westbrook statue nearby (Fig. 9.3A). The 9.53 kg (21 lb) galena cobble, reminiscent of the galena human effigy recovered at Spiro, was possibly used to smash the Westbrook statue *in situ* as nearly all the pieces were recovered in a small area.

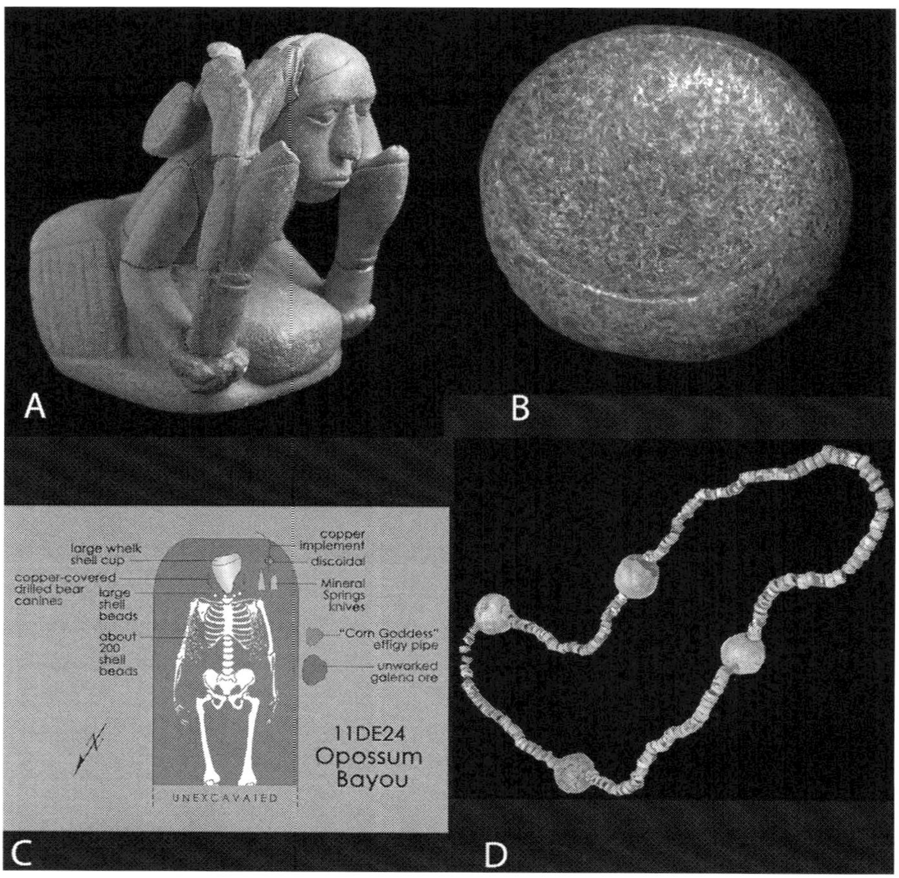

Fig. 9.2 Mortuary belongings and sketch of Westbrook burial: A. flint clay statue; B. Cahokia-style discoidal recovered at Opossum Bayou; C. sketch of burial based on interview with Harvey McGehee; D. shell beads.

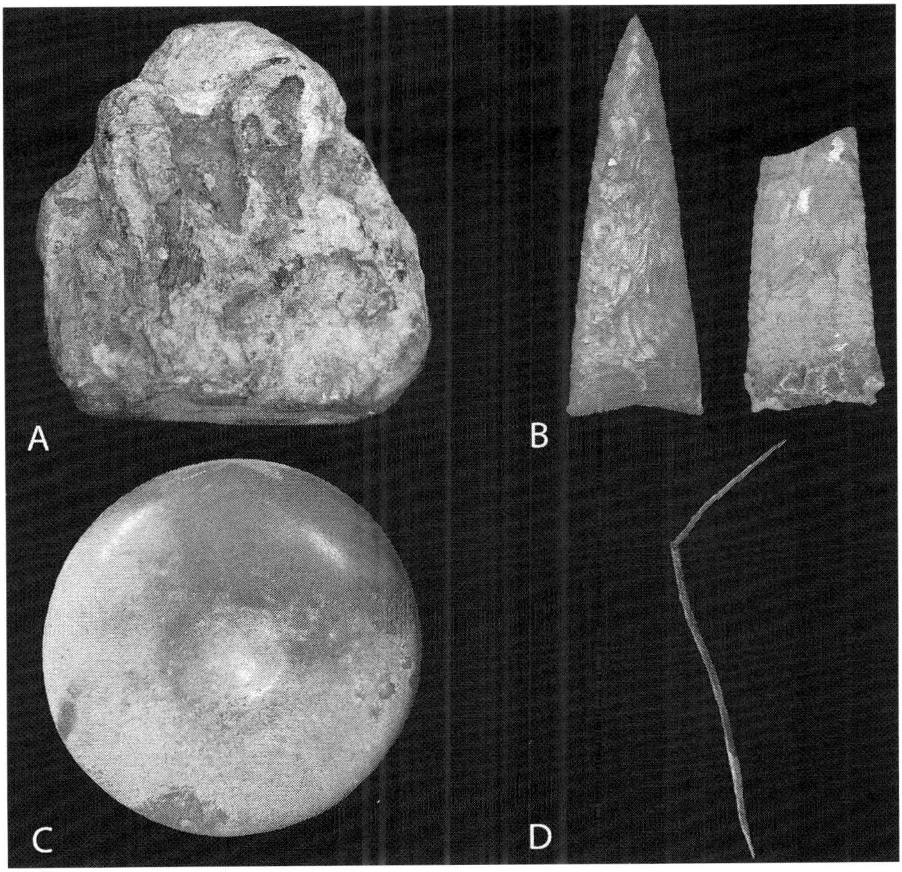

Fig. 9.3 Mortuary belongings of Westbrook burial: A. galena cobble; B. two Mineral Springs knives; C. dolomite discoidal; D. copper pin.

Above the left shoulder were two Caddo-related Mineral Springs or Gahagan knives (Fig. 9.3B). One knife was complete and the other broken and burned and it also has white kaolin clay residue adhering to it (see discussion below). Above the knives was a large limestone or dolomite discoidal with a copper pin resting upon it (Fig. 9.3C, D). The copper pin is identical to bent hair pins recovered from Caddo burials at Harlan (Bell 1972, see pls 5 c, f; 23 e) The skull had been removed and a large plain conch shell dipper put in its place (Fig. 9.4A). The inverted shell was positioned with the long axis perpendicular to the skeleton with the tapered end closest to the skeleton. On either side of the shell cup were copper covered drilled wooden bear canine effigy ear adornments (Fig. 9.4B). The individual had been placed on a slab of white Kaolin clay approximately 7–10 cm thick that extended from the waist to above the cup; a similar burial lining was noted at the Washington Square Mound site (Corbin and Hart 1998, 47–78; Girard *et al.* 2014, 80).

The Westbrook Caddo knives and discoidal have been erroneously referred to as Cahokia style items by Leon Tucker, McGehee's collecting partner, who was present when the Westbrook burial was discovered (Jeter *et al.* 2020). Ramey knives from Cahokia are bi-pointed not triangular in shape like the Caddo Gahagan/Mineral Springs knife form. Cahokia style discoidals are typically small in diameter (5–9 cm) and have cups that encompass the diameter with relatively

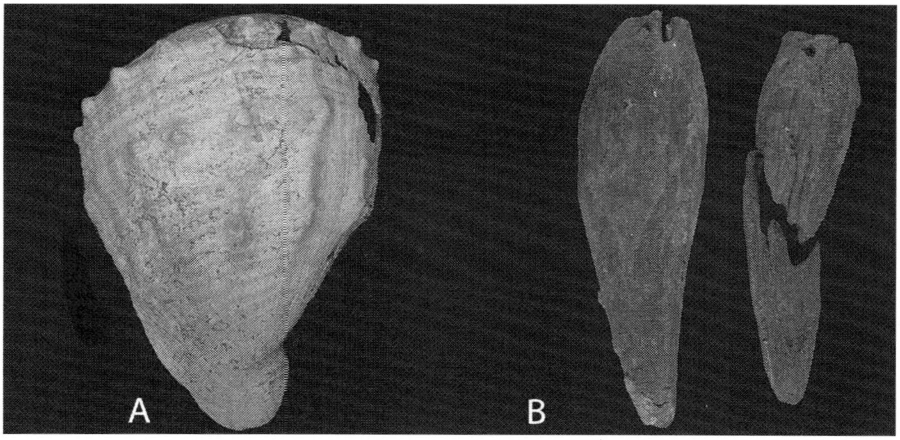

Fig. 9.4 Mortuary belongings of Westbrook burial and another burial in the same mound: A. whelk shell cup; B. copper covered wooden bear canine effigy ear adornments recovered from a different burial within the same mound as the Westbrook burial and identical to those found with the Westbrook burial.

flat or vertical edges (Fig. 9.2B). The Westbrook discoidal is much larger with small diameter, shallow cups and has a rounded edge and roller track (Fig. 9.3C). This style is often referred to as a Bradley style and is consistent with discoidals produced in the Arkansas region (Perino 1971, 112–16).

The Westbrook burial was discovered lying slightly below the water table, thus limiting complete excavation and observations. The burial was not opened up much beyond the width of the skeleton and not below the knees therefore it is possible that not all the funerary objects were recovered. Of interest, McGehee also encountered a wooden covering over the burial and speculated that it was part of an old canoe. The wooden surface had been charred and only vestiges of the wood remained. Cyrus Thomas noted a similar burial in a mound located in Roane County, Tennessee. There, a 9 ft (2.74 m) long sun-dried canoe contained one individual buried with a Tennessee-Cumberland statue placed near the head. Four other burials were placed in sitting positions at the cardinal directions and facing the central "canoe" burial. One had a clay pipe and two discoidals, one a large shell, a third was with two celts, and the fourth did not have any associated non-perishable artifacts (Thomas 1985, 358–61).

The Westbrook burial was found in a part of Arkansas that lies outside the defined "Caddo Area" and in a region defined as the "Lower Mississippi Valley Culture Area" (Girard *et al.* 2014). However, the Arkansas River, via the Mississippi River, connects both cultural areas and thus the discovery of an important burial that appears to follow Caddo mortuary traditions outside the Caddo core is less troubling as a result. Caddo and Cahokia interactions are also well documented thus it is within reason to minimally speculate that a Cahokian(s) traveling with Caddoans died *en route* between the two regions.

Harlan female, Cherokee County, Oklahoma

The Cahokia style Harlan female statue-pipe was recovered in 1950 at the Harlan Site (CK-6) in Cherokee County, Oklahoma (Bell 1972; Fig. 9.1, 9). The site covers *c.* 20 acres/8.1 ha and includes seven mounds. It was located on a tributary of the Grand or Neosho River and roughly 5 miles/8 km above the confluence of the Grand and Arkansas rivers.

The Harlan figure is carved from a soft and weathered piece of sedimentary stone. In its current state, it stands 17.5 cm tall with a maximum diameter of 13 cm (Fig. 9.5). The female figure is standing on a flat circular or oval disk and is depicted in a forward leaning, walking position. She is wearing a kilt-like skirt and is carrying a small, strapped pouch in her left hand (Fig. 9.5A). There is a long cylindrical shaped object placed vertically along her right side. At the base of this object are three bulbous rings giving the object the appearance of a large rattlesnake (Fig. 9.5B). The snake appears to come down her back and wrap around her right leg (Fig. 9.5C). There is also what appears to be the lower leg of another human to the right of the snake but the detail is too eroded or marred to discern anything else (Fig. 9.5D). The hole for the pipe stem is above the female's right shoulder and the bowl comes down into the indefinable mass from above (Fig. 9.5C). It is unclear if the pipe function was part of its original design or added later.

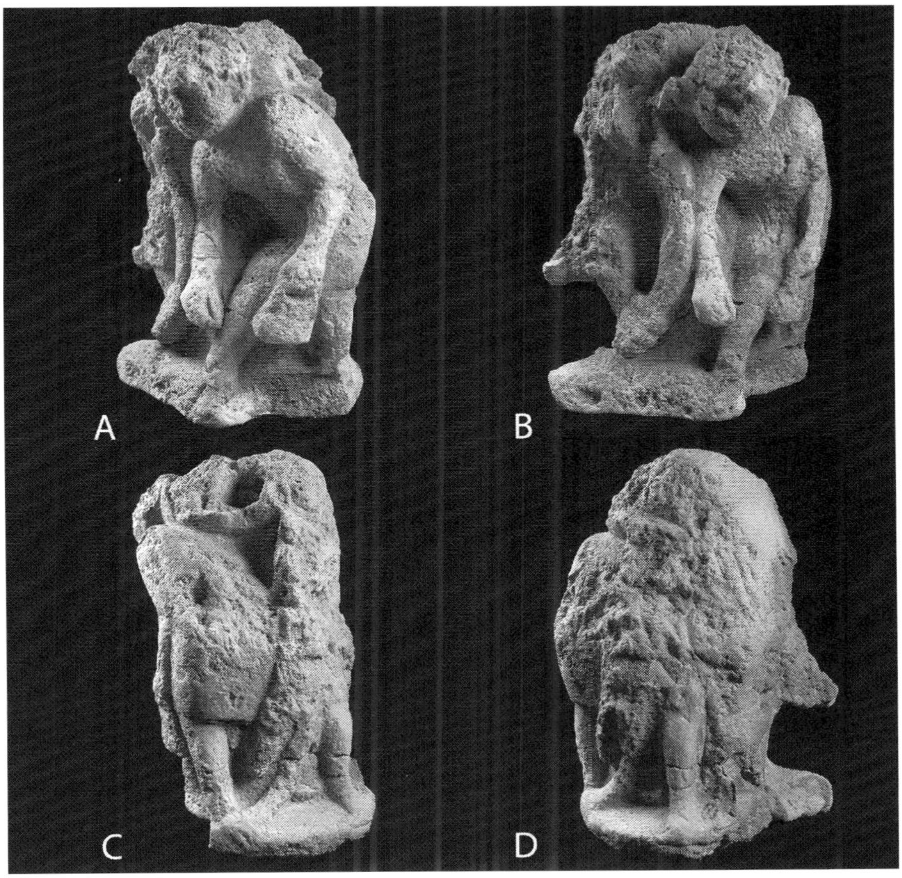

Fig. 9.5 Siltstone Cahokia-style statue recovered from the Harlan site, Oklahoma.

Emerson *et al.* briefly mentions the Harlan figure in their article regarding the sourcing of the material for the Cahokia style statues. They note that the Harlan figure was made from claystone and not from Missouri flint clay, as are nearly all the identified figures (2002, 325).

The Harlan statue was recovered from the center mound (Bell's "1B") of three conjoined low conical burial mounds with Mound 1A being 7 ft (2.13 m) tall and 50 ft (15.24 m) in diameter, the other two (1B, 1C) being 4 ft (1.22 m) and 3½ ft (1.07 m) tall respectively and both 35 ft (10.7 m) in diameter (Bell 1972, 18–19, fig. 4). This mound configuration is similar to that of the Spiro Craig Mound (Hamilton 1952). Unlike Spiro, Bell's continuation long profile through the center of all three mounds showed no superpositioning and thus he assumed that all three mounds were built at the same time and then connected with the same homogenous soil creating saddles in between the mounds. Collectively, the three mounds contained 124 burials with a minimum number of 195 individuals. Burial types included flexed, semi-flexed, secondary/bundle, cremations, and extended. The cremation burials are of particular interest as they were noted by Bell as being the most likely of the burial types to contain funerary objects (90%).

The Harlan statue was associated with Burial #41, which was one of ten cremation burials. Burial #41 contained parts of eight skulls and various long bone fragments scattered along a charcoal and ash deposit covering an approximate area of 9 × 6½ ft (2.74 × 1.98 m (Bell 1972, 48–9). Six of the skulls were grouped together while the other two were placed apart with one being 2 ft (0.61 m) to the west and one 5 ft (1.52 m) to the northeast. The statue-pipe was close to the northeast skull along with the remains of two conch shells. Other funerary objects in the cremation area include another conch shell, two sets of stone earspools, two small pieces of copper (one with raised ridges), several isolated pottery sherds, an engraved Caddo bottle, parts of a crushed jar, and 11 projectile points (Hayes and Reed types).

Three other burials are of particular interest as they also contained Cahokia related funerary objects and were interred in the central mound (1B). Burial #114 was another cremation burial that was divided between areas A and B based on concentrations of ash, charcoal, and bits of burned bone. Bell states that no bone was recoverable and thus the number of individuals present was not known (1972, 91). Area A was oval-shaped and approximately 5 ft (1.52 m) long by 2½ ft (0.76 m) wide. Associated funerary objects were placed at each end of Area A and include a mano, an acorn-shaped concretion, a mass of colored clay, five pottery vessels with three identifiable as Caddo types, and two chert knives made from Oklahoma Kay County chert. Based on Plate 28, the knives are both bi-pointed and similar to Cahokia Ramey knives. Ramey knives were typically made from southern Illinois Mill Creek chert, which is very similar in grain and color to Kay County chert. Without first-hand examination, the chert type for these knives cannot be discerned from the black and white plate, but it is possible that they are made from Mill Creek. Regardless, the bi-pointed style and workmanship is consistent with Ramey knives but not with bi-pointed Caddo Friendship blades, which are much more refined and typically have rounded blade ends (Perino 1963; Early 1988).

Area B was larger: *c.* 7 ft × 4 ft (2.13 × 1.22 m). This cremation area underlay Burial# 41 with the Cahokia style statue-pipe. Funerary objects in Area B were placed in three concentrations and included three conch shells, six pottery vessels, two caches of arrow points, a stone earspool, a stone celt, and a stone spud. Bell describes the spud as being made from granite, 17.8 cm long, 6.3 cm wide at the bit, and 3 cm thick. Judging from Plate 29, the spud is identical to the style of spuds produced in the Cahokia area and often made from basalt or diabase (Boles *et al.* 2018). The spud was placed near the three conch shells and the pulley-shaped earspool. The earspool had a veneer of copper sheeting on one spool, which was adhered to reed matting (Bell 1972, 91).

The last interment of note is Burial #37, also in Mound 1B. Bell describes the burial as a single individual represented by a skull, two femurs, a tibia, a humerus, and some finger bones (1972, 43). He further states that the poorly preserved individual was either buried in a tightly flexed position with leg bones close to the skull or it was possibly a secondary bundle burial. Funerary objects included a pottery bottle, a stone earspool, and two long-nosed copper god masks. The masks are often associated with Cahokia and appear in rock art at Picture Cave, located along Cahokia's western periphery.

Based on the positioning of burials within the mound, Bell placed Burials 37 and 114 as Middle Gibson Aspect and Burial 41 as Late Gibson Aspect. Bell's Gibson Aspect was later redefined as the Harlan phase and spanning AD 1000–1250. This time frame is contemporaneous with Cahokia's Terminal Late Woodland phase (AD 975–1050) through Cahokia's Mississippian Lohmann phase (AD 1050–1100), Stirling Phase (AD 1000–1200) and into the early Moorehead phase (AD 1200–1275). The recovery of the Cahokia style statue-pipe, spud, god masks, and bi-pointed knives are not only important in showing a connection to Cahokia but are particular noteworthy in that the time of deposition is contemporaneous with their production at Cahokia and also during a time in which a major depopulation of Cahokia began. This is an important observation that we will return to in the discussion.

Unreported, Bear-Cape male statue, Greene County, Illinois

In 2010, a surface collector recovered the male sandstone statue in the Illinois River floodplain in Greene County, Illinois (Fig. 9.1, 2). The nearest known Mississippian site to the find location is the Schild Site, also located in the floodplain and roughly 3 km east of the Illinois River and 8 km north of its confluence with the Mississippi River. According to an interview with the finder (via the collector who purchased the object), the statue was found in the bank of a deep channelized branch within 18 in (45 cm) of the surface. It was lying on its side with the base protruding slightly. According to the collector, the impression was still visible a week later when he visited the discovery site with the finder. Unfortunately, neither individual noticed if feature fill was present, therefore, it is not known if the statue was in a pit or a structure basin. It may be safe to assume, however, that it was not placed in a burial, as human remains were not present in the cut-bank or in the ditch below.

Decades earlier, in 1962, Greg Perino conducted excavations into a nearby burial mound and two cemeteries on a bluff above the Schild Site. There he recovered a flint clay female pipe from a female and infant burial (Perino 1971; Goldstein 1980). Perino excavated hundreds of burials dating from the Terminal Late Woodland Period through the Early Mississippian Lohmann and Stirling phases. Perino mentions that a flat-topped rectangular mound with evidence of a burned temple structure was located in the nearby floodplain. He suggested that a village located around the mound may have been silted over. However, most of this area was destroyed about 1940 for highway fill.

The Bear-Cape male is carved from a red, ferruginous piece of sandstone that also appears to have been coated in red ochre (Fig. 9.6). The figure is *c.* 16.7 cm tall by 12. 5 cm long by 6.7 cm wide and weighs 1.5 kg. The figure is kneeling and is adorned with a number of accoutrements. He has a top hair knot and a crenulated headdress or braids that wrap above the forehead over the ears and down the back of the head. He is also wearing ear spools (Fig. 9.6A). He has a flattened nose, protruding lips and an overall ominous or intent expression (Fig. 9.6B). He is wearing a bearskin cape with the bear's paws gripping his shoulders. The bear's

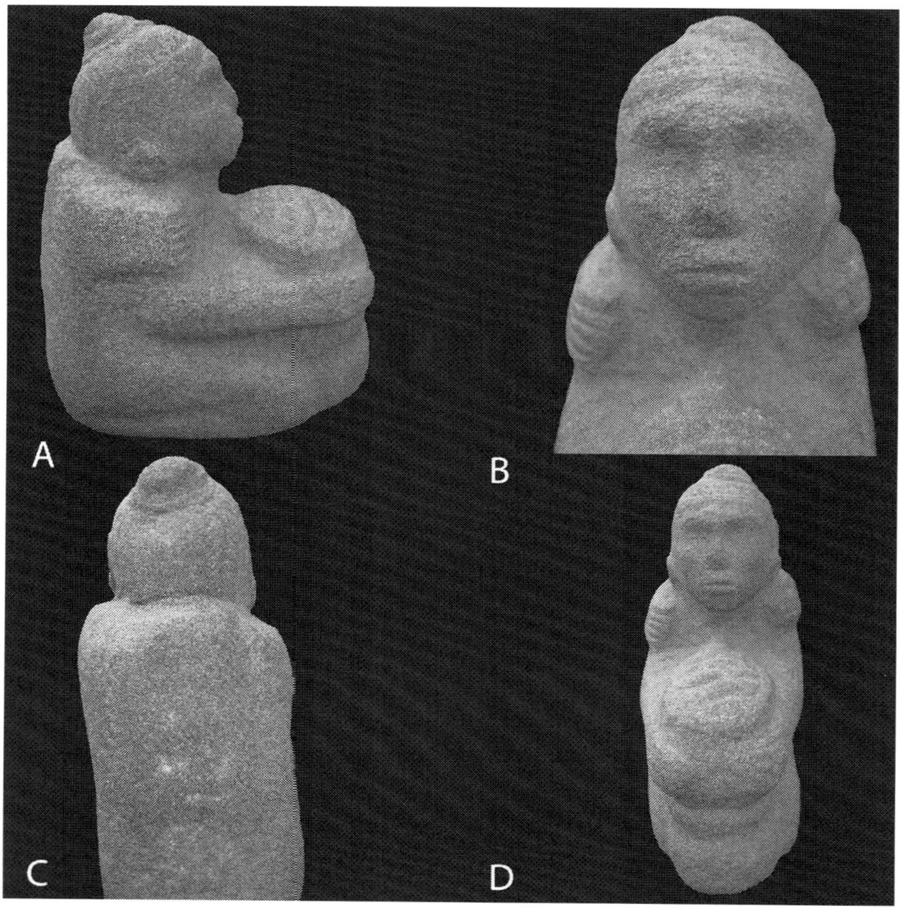

Fig. 9.6 Bear-Cape male sandstone statue, Greene County, Illinois.

head is draped down his back (Fig. 9.6C). His arms appear to have bands or possibly beaded bracelets on the forearms. His hands are gripping a compound jar that is resting on his knees (Fig. 9.6D). His hands are disproportionate and oversized. Fingers are visible but overall the hands appear more like paws than anatomically correct human hands.

Employing Emerson's philosophy about statue detail, when a detail is present it is there for a reason, and when absent, also for a specific reason (Emerson 1989, 52; Smith and Miller 2009, 21); the lack of detail or alteration to anatomical detail should not be correlated to the level of artistic talent. With this in mind, the oversized paw-like hands may then be demonstrating authoritative possession similar to the Keesee statue (Phillips County, Arkansas) whose right hand and oversized fingers are gripping what appears to be a bundle (Sharp 2011; 2012; 2013; Boles 2020). The jar is mounded over with what appears to be ears of maize. The bottom of the statue has a series of fine grooves or slots running mostly perpendicular to the long axis.

Though made from sandstone, the Bear-Cape figure is carved in the Cahokia style and similar to some of the Cahokian flint clay male statues (Emerson 1983). The Bear-Cape male has numerous accoutrements as do a few of the males recovered at Spiro (Resting Warrior, Conquering Warrior, and WPA Warrior; Fig. 9.1, 10) and the Guy Smith pipe from southern Illinois (West 1934; Hamilton 1952; Brown 1996). The Bear-Cape male also shares the associated pot or jar with two flint clay statues, the Keesee statue with the jar placed in front of a kneeling male and the Schild female statue with a jar used as the pipe bowl behind her and a snake wrapped around the jar (Perino 1971, 116–17; Sharp 2011; 2012; 2013; Boles 2022a). The Bear-Cape male was not broken when decommissioned similar to the deposition for a number of flint clay males but he may have been burned; ferruginous sandstone will often turn red when heated.

Correct data: Tolu statue, Crittenden County, Kentucky

The Tolu statue was pictured in 1957 and reported to be from the bottomland of the Ohio River near Tolu, Kentucky (Fig. 9.7A; Fundaburk and Fundaburk 1957, pls 97 and 98). The statue was then referred to as the Tolu statue in various publications and by default associated with the Late Mississippian Period Tolu Site (15CN1), located 4 km upstream and investigated in the 1930s by Webb and Funkhouser (1931). The statue could have just as easily been associated with other nearby Mississippian mound and village sites such as Carrsville, 8 km southwest on the Kentucky side of the Ohio River or the even closer, Orr-Herl Site, 3.3 km to the north in Hardin County, Illinois (Fig. 9.1, 6). As these other locales illustrate, naming a statue as having been discovered "nearby", but not from an actual find site, can be misleading.

Although Smith and Miller (2009, 146) correctly noted the actual find spot, an interview with the finder's son and other locals provide additional details about the discovery of the statue and the find site location (Jim Marlen pers. comm. 2010). The fluorite statue was found on the Mildred Orange farm in Crittenden

County, Kentucky in 1954. The find site, as previously noted, is actually 4 km downstream from the Tolu mound site and located on a high bluff above the Ohio River floodplain and *c.* 0.8 km from the river. In 1954, Willard Johnson farmed the Orange farm and reportedly unearthed the statue while plowing the site (Smith and Miller 2009, 146). However, according to family and local informants, Johnson allowed two men access to dig at the site for a "fee" of having first pick of whatever was found. This fact was kept quiet, as Mrs Orange was not fond of people digging for artifacts. The two locals discovered the fluorite statue while excavating a burial and may have struck the statue with a shovel (Fig. 9.7B). Johnson reportedly took the statue as his fee and was able to find one of the missing arms. The other arm either shattered when struck or was broken off at the time of burial and not interred with the statue. A visit to the site in 2011 revealed a small, looted, conical, stone box burial mound, adding credence to the informant's account. Additionally, fluorite is soft and brittle, had Johnson actually hit the statue with farm equipment, it would have likely sustained considerable damage beyond breakage to the arms. The site is currently grass covered but, when tilled, was noted to contain a small Mississippian village site approximately 0.2 ha in size (Rip Wheeler and Tony Perryman pers. comm. 2010). This unassuming site

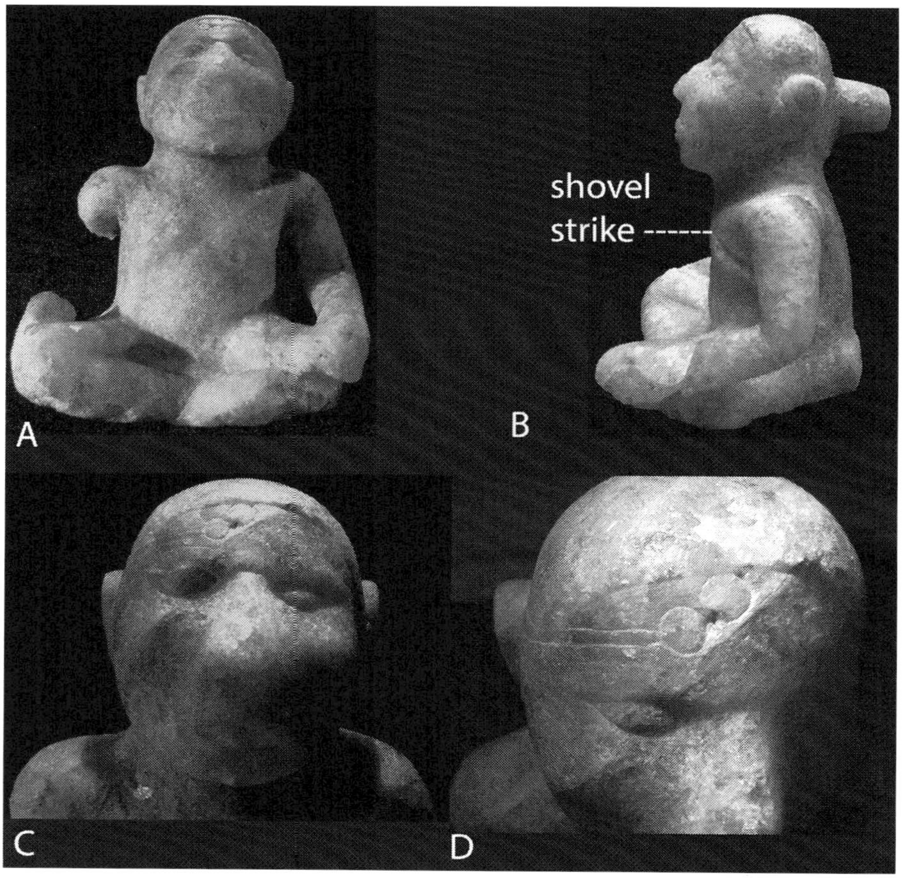

Fig. 9.7 Fluorite Tennessee-Cumberland statue recovered south of Tolu, Kentucky.

is similar to other such sites where Tennessee-Cumberland statues have been recovered (Smith and Miller 2009).

The Tolu statue is 25.4 cm tall with a width and depth of 19 cm (Fig. 9.7). It is made from blue fluorite with yellow and white banding and weighs 8.16 kg (18 lb). Fluorite is a soft, colorful mineral that was used to produce personal adornment items as well as statues during the Mississippian Period (Boles 2012). In the confluence region, large deposits of fluorite are located in Hardin and Pope Counties in Illinois and across the Ohio River in Crittenden County, Kentucky. Fluorite from this source area was most likely used for production of the Tolu figure (Boles 2011, 239). More specifically, the only locale for banded blue fluorite is reportedly located in small area near Cave-In-Rock, in Hardin County (Buddy Davis of Marion, Kentucky, 3rd generation fluorite driller, pers. comm. 2011).

The only accoutrements on the Crittenden County figure are two engraved beads located in his forelock (Fig. 9.7C, D). He is largely carved in what has been described as the Tennessee-Cumberland style (Smith and Miller 2009, 20–32) though he shares some interesting similarities to several of the Cahokian flint clay statues. He has traces of red ochre in material cavities on his back. This would infer that he was either partially painted with red ochre, as were at least two of the male flint clay statues (Keesee, Arkansas and Resting Warrior, Spiro Site, Oklahoma) and the Bear-Cape sandstone figure, or placed on his back on bed of red ochre, similar to the Exchange Avenue statue from the East St Louis Mound complex (Emerson and Boles 2010, 481). Both arms were broken off with only one recovered. This breakage may have occurred during its discovery or perhaps more likely when it was buried. Similar damage has been noted for many of the flint clay statues and appears to be associated with the decommissioning of sacred or ritual objects (Prentice 1986, 247–8; Emerson *et al.* 2002, 325; Emerson and Boles 2011, 170).

As mentioned earlier, the Tolu statue and some of the Cahokian flint clay statues share a number of similarities. These include how the ears are carved, hairstyles including back hair buns, and the depiction of male genitalia (see Boles 2011 for additional details and figures). The last feature has been noted on a few flint clay male statues but the Tolu statue is the only fluorite statue with this feature. In fact, the Tolu statue differs dramatically from the other fluorite statues in all aspects including hairstyle and seating position. Moreover, the Tolu statue and Cahokia-carved Resting Warrior statue are the only figures in either medium seated in cross-legged or Lotus fashion and are also within about a 15 mm of being the same height. Given the numerous similarities, it appears that one statue was at the very least patterned from the other (Boles 2011).

For the record: Cahokia statue

As mentioned in the introduction, a fluorite statue was attributed to Cahokia although some researchers doubt the accuracy of this reporting (Figs 9.1, 1; 9.8A). Warren K. Moorehead illustrated the fluorite statue in question in his 1923 publication on Cahokia Mounds (pl xvii, no.7). In the section of his report in which this statue is mentioned, Moorehead states that after considerable investigation, they were able to trace the location of a number of Cahokia objects found by previous investigators and collectors. Many of these items resided in a museum at the nearby Monticello Seminary in Godfrey, Illinois. There, Moorehead mentions an interesting collection of local material was on exhibition and made possible by William McAdams some 25–40 years prior (*c.* 1895–1900). He mentions two stone idols curated at Monticello including a large, flint clay male statue and a fluorite one. The flint clay statue was reportedly found in a small mound along Caseyville Road and the fluorite example was reportedly found on the bluffs directly east of Cahokia Mounds (Moorehead 1923, 43-6).

Thomas Emerson, in his study of Mississippian stone images from Illinois, noted that there was discrepancy in the provenance for the flint clay statue provided by McAdams (and subsequently Moorehead) and that listed by the accession records at the Missouri Historical Society that owns the statue (Emerson 1982, 11–13). Smith and Miller also state that the Cahokia fluorite statue illustrated and mentioned by Moorehead was actually the fluorite statue from the Ware Site in Union County, Illinois (Smith and Miller 2009, 150; Fig. 9.1, 3). Although they do not elaborate, it appears that their assertion is based on the close similarity in form between the Cahokia and Ware statues.

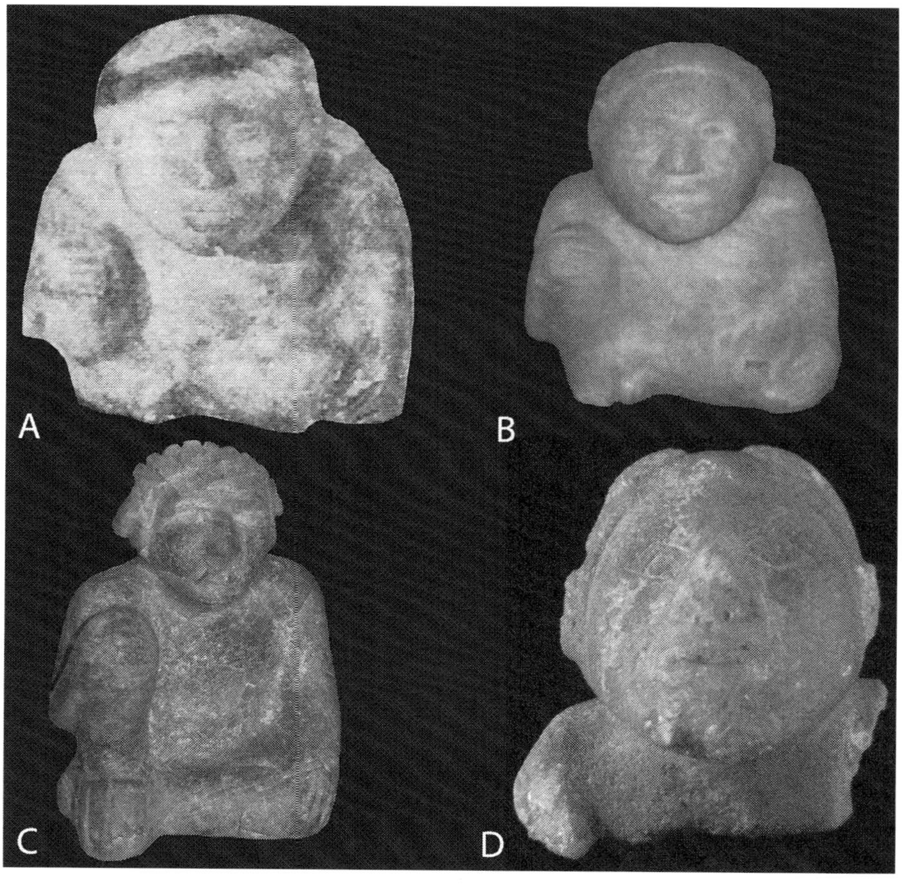

Fig. 9.8 Fluorite Tennessee-Cumberland statues recovered outside core area for style: A. Cahokia; B. Ware; C. Angel; D. unreported site in Edwards County, Illinois.

The Ware statue, often referred to as the Anna statue, was found in a mound at the Ware Site (11U31) by Thomas M. Perrine in 1873 (Fig. 9.8B; Perrine 1873, 410). In 1876, the statue was loaned to the Smithsonian for casting and display at the Centennial Exhibition. It was also exhibited in the 1893 World's Columbian Exposition in Chicago and subsequently acquired by the Field Museum, which opened in 1894. According to research conducted by the late James Marlen, McAdams was involved with providing artifacts for the 1893 exposition (Marlen pers. comm. 2015). McAdams was a prolific collector and excavated a number of mounds in the Cahokia area. He is credited with the discovery of a flint clay frog effigy pipe from the bluffs east of East St Louis in 1883. Unfortunately, for the fluorite statue reported from the same general locale, the Monticello Seminary closed in 1971, becoming part of the Lewis and Clark Community College, leaving the mention and photograph by Moorehead in 1923 as the only known record.

The bulk of the Monticello Seminary museum collections were donated to the Illinois State Historical Society and the Illinois State Museum in the mid-20th century. Contact with both institutions in 2008 revealed neither had an accession record regarding the Cahokia fluorite statue. However, a rumor has persisted for years among the local collecting community that a prominent old-time collector (deceased) had bribed a seminary employee to filter out top-end artifacts from the museum when its collections were being de-accessioned back in the 1950s. This would certainly account for the missing fluorite statue as well as other known missing McAdams artifacts (Emerson 1982, 26).

In returning to Smith and Miller's belief that the Ware and Cahokia statues are one-and-the-same, I agree that both are nearly identical in form, as is a third statue recovered from Angel Mounds (Figs 9.1, 6; 9.8C); Black 1967). Typical of male statuary carved in the Tennessee-Cumberland style, all three are depicted in the same posture with the right hand resting on the right raised knee and the left hand on the knee of the left leg, which is crossed in front of the body. Additionally, all share the same facial characteristics with thick closed lips, large noses, and eyes in relief as well as a rolled hairstyle. None is depicted with additional regalia. My belief that the Cahokia and the Ware statues are not one in the same is based on comparing pictures of both statues and familiarity of fluorite and fluorite artifacts (Boles 2012).

First and foremost, the Cahokia statue has a dark band encircling the upper portion of the head that comes across the hair roll on the left side and dips down below the hair roll on the right side of the forehead before circling back across the right ear and hair roll (Fig. 9.8A). It is at a perpendicular angle to the width of the forehead and looks like a tilted halo. This dark band is pronounced in Moorehead's black and white photo and it most likely represents a dark purple seam in a lighter colored yellow or clear piece of fluorite. In contrast, the statue from Ware is homogenous and light in color and does not have a dark halo about the head (Fig. 9.8B). Although I feel this observation in-and-of-itself is sufficient to validate the existence of the Cahokia statue, there are a few more differences to separate the two statues. The left eye on the Cahokia statue is clearly oval in shape compared to the elliptical shape of the same eye on the Ware statue. The Cahokia statue also appears to have wide indentions or bands below the shoulders on both sides; the Ware statue does not. The left hand of the Ware statue also appears to be holding something relatively flat against the left knee. Whatever this object represents, it appears to corner with right-angles just past the fingertips on the lower leg. Although Moorehead's photo is not of great quality, no such object is discernable on the Cahokia statue. In fact, the left knee looks damaged with part of it missing.

As for the provenance of the Cahokia statue, the bluff line east of Cahokia borders the American Bottom and is basically a large, continuous mortuary area. A search of archaeological and historical literature as well as the Illinois site file reveals that a number of mounds have been reported along the bluffs east of downtown Cahokia. Some of the mounds in this area have the potential to have been the locale for the fluorite statue (assuming it was placed in a mound) due to known disturbances or excavations. Greg Perino noted that a land developer bulldozed three mounds on the bluff edge 2.2 miles due east of Cahokia Mounds in the 1940s. He also reported that the developer recovered the head of a human effigy statue (flint clay) at that time and that a village area was located adjacent to the mounds. (Perino 1971, 120). Two other mounds (11MS2088) are located in an active cemetery 2.5 miles (3.5 km) to the northeast of downtown Cahokia along the bluff edge. The earliest modern interments in the mounds date to the mid-1800s. A cache of large unfinished Mississippian celts was recovered adjacent to the cemetery and infers that a village or at least special use area lies near the mounds (Boles 2022b).

Discussion

The statuary described above, while differing in style and varied raw material use, share a connection to Cahokia in that they were made at Cahokia or by Cahokians, deposited at Cahokia, or likely influenced by Cahokians. They have commonly been interpreted as representations of either important individuals or mythological personas. As such, these statues were likely considered religious sacra and had restricted ownership and use and were likely curated in sacred bundles or baskets within temple or special use structures. When these statues were no longer to be curated most appear to have been ritually decommissioned in a similar fashion via breakage and burning, whether deposited in a special use feature or as mortuary accompaniments (Emerson and Boles 2010; Boles 2020). These shared aspects are discussed below in detail, starting with interpretative possibilities, followed by use and decommissioning, and concluding with an exploration on the movement and deposition of religious sacra outside of the cultural area in which they were produced.

Iconography and ethno-historic correlates

The combined use of iconographic study and ethno-historic and ethnographic correlates has been very useful in providing insights into past American Indian cosmology and possible identifications of ancestral and mythological personas depicted in various media. F. Kent Reilly III of Texas State University and esteemed members of his annual Mississippian Iconography Workshop have advocated this line of study and built upon similar works by Robert Hall (1991; 1997), Guy Prentice (1986), Thomas Emerson (1989, 90–1), Robert Salzer and Grace Rajnovich (2000); Timothy Pauketat (2004, 114–18; 2009, 85–98), Carol Diaz-Granados and James Duncan (Diaz-Granados and Duncan 2000), and many others.

Before delving into discussion, criticisms of this interpretative approach often point to the temporal and sometimes spatial disconnects between the archaeological record and ethnographic correlates, the relevance of an ethnography chosen for comparisons, and the problematic identification of specific Pre-contact mythological personas from much later recorded accounts. While these are legitimate concerns, the use of ethno-historical accounts herein is done so to provide loose correlates to provoke thought and inform speculation (for examples see Diaz-Granados and Duncan 2000, 214; Smith and Miller 2009, 165–6). Admittedly, it is unfortunate that we have so few ethno-historical accounts to use in this interpretative approach. Therefore, in cases where an archaeological figure is identified as a representation of an ethno-historically recorded being, this should be viewed as but one possibility via the account(s) used for the interpretation. Additionally, the intent is not to suggest static religious beliefs between Pre- and Post-contact American Indians. However, not noting similarities between ethno-historic accounts and Pre-contact imagery is to deny the possibility of core cosmological personas and that oral mythologies were maintained with some level of integrity through time.

Interpretation of the statues follows the order of introduction with the Cahokia style Westbrook, Harlan, and Bear-Cape statues to be discussed first. There are a few ethno-historical parallels of interest offered here for consideration that pertain to corn, female supernaturals, snakes, and bears. The Westbrook statue, as described earlier, depicts a kneeling female figure that is emerging from a basket behind her and has sunflower and probable corn plants sprouting from her upturned hands, with the stalks arching over her shoulders. Numerous researchers have written about this statue with most in agreement that she represents a general Earth Mother persona, a mythological being associated with fertility and vegetation and common among groups across much of North America (Hultkrantz 1957, 101–2; Prentice 1986; Emerson 1989; Colvin 2012). The Harlan female is also likely another depiction of the Earth Mother as she carries a small strapped "seed" pouch in her left hand. Several of the other Cahokia female statues are depicted with identical hand-held or similar backpack-like pouches and include the New Madrid (Missouri), McBeth (Ohio), Spiro, and Bostrom (uplands near Cahokia) figures (Boles 2022a). The Caddo, as well as numerous eastern tribes, refer to the Earth Mother persona as Corn Mother (Alexander 1916, 91–2, 107–8; Witthoft 1949) while many Siouan tribes referred to her as Old-Woman-Who-Never-Dies or Grandmother (Bowers 1965).

The Bear-Cape male figure, as described earlier, depicts a male figure kneeling with a compound jar resting between his knees and appearing full of possibly maize ears. His arms extend out to the upper vessel and his oversized hands are grasping the sides of the vessel. He has what I interpret as a bear cape draped over his shoulders and down his back. He is wearing earspools and has an elaborate headdress or hairstyle. I include this statue with the Cahokia style based on the overall level of detail and that the figure is kneeling on a disk. Although most Cahokia style statues were carved from red Missouri flint clay, others have been recorded in both sandstone and limestone (Emerson 1982; Boles and Lewis 2019; 2022a; Lepper 2020). Additionally, and perhaps circumstantially, the Bear-Cape statue was carved from a red piece of sandstone or it was burned thus creating the red color; regardless, it shares the color red with the flint clay suite and the choice of using or creating a red piece of sandstone may have been by design. Also circumstantially, the find location of the Bear-Cape statue was relatively near the Mississippian Schild Site where Perino discovered a female flint clay pipe. Lastly, the compound jar held by the Bear Cape male is not without precedent within the flint clay suite. The Schild female has a vessel behind her and the Keesee statue has a pot before him and like the pot in front of the Bear-Cape figure, the Keesee vessel is also mounded over with substance.

As for ethno-historic correlates, the first comes from the Siouan-speaking Mandan and pertains to the Old-Woman-Who-Never-Dies mythology. In the narrative, two hunters appear at the Old Woman's lodge located on an island. She hands them a pot with corn mush to eat. They do not feel that it will be enough but upon eating their fill, the pot is just as full as it was when they began. Later on, when the hunters wish to return home, the Old Woman's husband, which is a large serpent, gives them a ride on his back to the mainland (Bowers 2004, 198–9). Accounts from southeastern tribes such as the Yuchi and Alabama state that the Old Woman feeds two men food that replenishes itself and helped them find the spirits of their deceased wives, trapping them in gourds. She then instructs them on how to resurrect their wives (Swanton 1929; Grantham 2002).

In a generalization of the Old Woman concept, as discussed in earlier chapters in this book, she is identified as the mother or grandmother of the creative boy or Hero Twins, as they are often referred, (Hultkrantz 1957; Prentice 1986, 249–50). The mounded over pots with both the Bear-Cape and Keesee figures therefore could be functioning as an avatar of the Old Woman. The male or Hero twins are a common myth cycle in both North and South America and it has been suggested that they were part of the oral literature of the founding populations in the New World (Hall 1997, 161). While the narratives and twin's names vary between groups, there is generally a good boy and a mischievous boy, the latter often a personification of the placenta or umbilical cord and characterized as a throw away or wild boy (Hall 1997, 163; Lankford 2011; 160–75). The twins are generally associated with the origin of death and mourning (Hall 1997, 162).

The Bear-Cape figure and his paw-like hands are without a known analog in the Siouan Red Horn mythology. However, there are a number of Siouan mythologies concerning bears for consideration. The Earthmaker is said to have created four bears to act as island weights to help stop the incessant spinning of the primordial Earth. One of the four bears was the Red Bear, a grizzly bear, who was placed in the west. The four Bear Spirits were actually men manifested as bears. The Bear Clan, that functioned as soldiers or police, were descendants of the Bear Spirits.

They were given this role because they suppressed the chaotic nature of the Earth and because of their furious spirit (Funmaker 1974). The Red Bear is also the guardian of the gateway to the great beyond (Funmaker 1986). Some war leaders were blessed from the spirit chief of the race of bears and given the ability to change into a raging grizzly bear during battle (Blackhawk 1926). Bear Spirits were also associated with evil deeds. Grandmother Earth was said to have had such a mischievous Bear Spirit as one of her brothers (Radin 1948). Other Bear Spirits could shape-shift to a human form and would wreak havoc even in their communities (Radin n.d.). While none of the above mythologies mentions a bear cape figure, they do provide a general concept of a bear-like male or bear association with a bold or intimidating male figure who is associated with the Old-Woman-Who-Never-Dies or Grandmother.

Now turning to the fluorite statues, as mentioned in the description, the Cahokia statue is almost identical in form to the fluorite statues from Angel and Ware. A fourth fluorite statue found at the Obion site in Tennessee (Fig. 9.1, 7) was also likely identical but was largely destroyed in a house fire and only the head remains. All the complete statues were carved in the classic Tennessee-Cumberland male pose with the right knee raised and the left flat and in front of the seated figures. Also consistent with the style, all appear to be without clothing or other accoutrements and the facial features are the most detailed on the figures, especially the crenulated hair rolls depicted on the Cahokia, Angel, Ware, and Obion statues. Interpretations are limited without motifs and as Smith and Miller suggest, single Tennessee-Cumberland statues may reference a specific but as-yet unidentifiable supernatural character of significance such as First Man, Venerable Man, First Creator, or Old Man Immortal, all progenitors mentioned in many oral traditions (2009, 173–4).

The Tolu statue, as described earlier, is also carved without clothing but departs considerably from the other fluorite statues. Five of the seven known are complete or were found complete. Four of these are nearly identical and appear to have been carved by the same artisan or artisan group and, as mentioned above, likely portray the same supernatural but unidentified persona. While it is possible that the Tolu statue represents another version of one of these personas, given his similarities with the Cahokian flint clay Resting Warrior statue, it is possible that he represents a supernatural persona associated with a different mythology.

F. Kent Reilly III, building on the works of Robert Hall (1989, 240–3, 1997, 150) made a compelling argument that the Resting Warrior statue was a representation of Red Horn, also known as He-Who-Wears-Human-Heads-As-Earrings, based on the Dhegiha Sioux Red Horn mythology (Duncan and Diaz-Granados 2000, 20–1). Reilly suggested that other flint clay statues might represent other personas in this mythology (2004, 132–3). In line with Reilly, James Brown (2011, 56) has suggested that the WPA Warrior pipe from Spiro represents Turtle, one of Red Horn's companions. In identifying Turtle, Brown noted accoutrements such as the heavy body armor, a claw-like knife, and a turban headdress or helmet. A key element not mentioned by Brown that adds to his interpretation is a turtle depicted on top of the headdress (Boles 2014; 2020, 69). If the shield and a turban headdress are also identifiers of Turtle, then the Guy Smith pipe and the Kingston pipe are also possible representations of Turtle. If posture is any indication, then the Moundville Man and Gahagan Man may also be possible representations of Turtle. Two other flint clay statues have also been linked to Red Horn's companions, the WPA Conquering Warrior as Otter and the WPA Rattler as Wolf (Boles 2020, 69–74).

In following this interpretative vein, it has been proposed that the Tolu figure was possibly portraying Red Horn's main companion and equal, Storms-As-He-Walks, a Thunderbird (Boles 2010; 2011). This interpretation is based primarily upon the numerous similarities between the Tolu and Resting Warrior statues as mentioned above. The weight of this assertion also rests heavily on two assumptions. First, Emerson's (1989, 52) and Smith and Miller's (2009, 21) conjecture about detail, whether present or absent, as intentional rather than an expression or lack of artistic talent. The second assumption is that the Red Horn mythology extended back to the 12th century and was maintained with considerable integrity, at least in regards to key motifs or other identifying characteristics.

Pictographs, some dating to the late 10th or early 11th century from Missouri's Picture Cave and those in the Gottschall rock shelter in Wisconsin (Diaz-Granados *et al.* 2001; 2015; Salzer 1987; Salzer and Rajnovich 2001; Duncan 2015, 227) infer that these same personas mentioned in the Red Horn mythology (Radin 1948) likely existed by the 12th century in the Midwest. Other personas mentioned in the Red Horn mythology are also represented at these rock art sites and include Turtle and an avian "Thunderbird" image.

As for the carving of the Tolu statue, if it can be assumed that every detail is intentional, then the color and composition of the raw material were likely important factors as well. Though fluorite comes in many colors, blue is the least common and the streaked material is known to have been associated with one small source near Cave-In-Rock, Illinois. Both factors would not only have made the right piece of fluorite hard to locate, but such coloring would have been the natural choice to portray an upper world being such as Storms, a Thunderbird deity, often described without accoutrements.

The physical characteristics of fluorite, which is a crystalline mineral, may also have played into the choice of using this raw material. Fluorite is relatively soft, at 4 on the Mohs scale of mineral hardness, and thus easily carvable with a sharp chert flake. It is translucent, thermo-luminescent when heated, and smokes when carved. Among many Historic tribes, crystals were associated with powerful forces and general uses included charming or dazzling the viewer and as aides in prophetic visions (Wolforth and Wolforth 2000, 458). According to a Cherokee legend, the scales of the Uktena, a creature resembling the Chief-of-the-Water-Spirits, were crystals and a large crystal was also in the center of the Uktena's forehead. This large crystal was used by the Uktena to daze victims with piercing rays of light (Hudson 1976, 147).

If the blue color of fluorite and possibly other notable attributes of this crystalline mineral were chosen specifically to portray Storms, then it is suggested that the artist who crafted the Tolu statue intentionally carved the figure so that the yellow and white streak ran through the right eye and down his cheek (Fig. 9.7).

Also of importance, not only is his head disproportionately bigger than his body, but his right eye is also 18% bigger top to bottom than his left. Both exaggerations and the alignment of color would have drawn the viewer to his face and right eye. Such artistic conventions would aide in portraying a deity that could shoot lightning bolts from his eyes to slay enemies (Boles 2011).

Incidentally, none of the other fluorite statues is made from blue material. It is also noteworthy that the Resting Warrior also has an exaggerated right eye. This might be coincidental but could be viewed as a means of showing connectedness between the two statues, especially when taken in conjunction with all the other shared traits (identical back hair buns, hair rolls with lock in front of the ears, depiction of genitals, Lotus seating position). The exaggerated eyes could also be viewed as an artist's signature thus inferring the possibility that the same artisan carved both statues. The likelihood of that is of course debatable but what does seem rather apparent, is that one statue was patterned from the other, not just in seating style and other noted attributes but in size, as the statues are within 15 mm of being the same height. This equality of size may be symbolic of the relationship between Red Horn and Storms (Boles 2011). In the narratives, both are main characters and seem to be of equal importance throughout their exploits.

As mentioned earlier, the proposed identification of Post-contact ethno-historically recorded mythological personas with Pre-contact statuary is but one possibility via the Winnebago (Ho-Chunk) mythologies recorded by Paul Radin (1948).

Contexts: ritual deposition, shrines, funerary objects

Although most of the statuary in either style was unfortunately discovered by chance and typically by farmers or early antiquarians digging for artifacts, general patterns have been parsed from their discoveries and provide comparisons with the five presented here.

Smith and Miller's (2009) extensive study of the Tennessee-Cumberland style statuary documents 86 statues and provides an exemplary analysis and discussion of depositional contexts. They incorporated four sources of data in their depositional analysis starting with direct evidence (archaeological excavation), anecdotal records (general or site-specific geographic location and/or limited intra-site information), indirect associations (artifacts, excavation data, and radiocarbon dates from sites where statues were reportedly found), and ending with the features of the statues themselves. They also utilize ethno-historic accounts to provide background information on ancestor shrines and human figural sculptures (Smith and Miller 2009, 158–65).

Their analysis revealed that Tennessee-Cumberland statues entered the archaeological record in a variety of locales and contexts over a probable span of 200 years from AD 1200 to 1400. To summarize their findings, Tennessee-Cumberland statues were placed with human interments as funerary belongings in stone box burials, seemingly treated as humans and buried in a stone box crypt by themselves, placed with human interments in burial mounds but also placed in mounds without human burials, deposited in non-mortuary features some distance from mounds, and deposited at sites without evidence of mounds. Several statues not associated with mortuary contexts or mounds appear to have been deposited in elite residential areas perhaps in or near ceremonial structures, or at special geographic locations.

Smith and Miller offer that the statues were important objects that end up in sacred places and contexts at each site and suggest that trajectories ending in deposition were different in each case (2009, 160). More specifically, they note that the creation and distribution of male/female paired statues, possibly physical representations of ancestral chiefly couples, was restricted to the "Heartland" for the style in Middle Tennessee and northern Georgia from AD 1250 to 1350 and associated with ancestral mortuary shrines (Smith and Miller 2009, 179). On occasion, a third statue representing a female and possibly a version of the mythological Old Woman accompanied the ancestral pair. Lone female statues were also found at smaller settlements and isolated contexts such as springs and caves.

Lone male statues represent a third subset and are also found outside the heartland for the style. Several males, especially those made from fluorite, were included in their discussion of statues that were widely scattered from the heartland. Smith and Miller note that the statues were made from a variety of lithic material and typically deposited not far from the site of manufacture (2009, 144). As such, those made from fluorite were found not far from a major fluorite source in Hardin and Pope Counties in Illinois and across the Ohio River in Crittenden County, Kentucky. Of the fluorite statues mentioned in their study, the Tolu statue was recovered in the heart of the fluorite district while the others varied in distances. The Angel statue in southern Indiana was the next closest to the fluorite source at approximately 56 miles (90 km); the statue from the Ware site in Union County, Illinois at 60 miles (96.5 km); the statue from Edwards County, Illinois at 75 miles (121 km) (Figs 9.1, 4; 9.8D); the statue from the Obion site in western Tennessee at 105 miles (169 km); and the statue from Cahokia the farthest from the fluorite source at 130 miles (209 km).

As for known contexts, the Angel statue was recovered from a non-mortuary mound, both the Ware and Tolu statues were reported from mortuary mounds, the Obion statue possibly from a borrow pit, and the Edwards County statue was recovered near a shallow ford in the Little Wabash River. The statue from Cahokia is likely from a mortuary context given the ubiquity of mounds and cemeteries located along the bluff line as well as the foreign nature of Tennessee-Cumberland sacra to the region. Although speculative, the fluorite statue could have arrived with a religious leader who either immigrated to Cahokia post-AD 1200 or who visited Cahokia for other reasons. Personal adornments made from fluorite along with raw and worked fluorite and bead production failures have been recovered from a few scattered locales at Cahokia and all come from post-AD 1200 contexts. While some researchers attribute the fluorite to trade, it is also possible that these fluorite locales represent Lower Ohio River Valley immigrants to Cahokia. Long-handled spuds made from greenstone are also distinctive of the Tennessee-Cumberland region and have been found at Cahokia as well. These have however been recovered from early and late contexts at Cahokia and from both domestic and mortuary features (Pauketat 1983; Boles *et al.* 2018). In summation, the fluorite statue from Cahokia is possibly related to immigration and deposition with the last bundle keeper (see below) while the Tolu statue fits a noted pattern of deposition in a relatively unassuming locale.

Now turning to the Cahokia style statuary as defined by Emerson and extensively researched by Emerson and colleagues, as well as others. The Cahokia statues, as mentioned earlier, are predominately made from Missouri flint clay although sandstone and limestone were used on occasion. The Cahokia style statues originate perhaps a century or more before the Tennessee-Cumberland statues during the Stirling phase, AD 1100–1200 (Emerson and Hughes 2000), if not a little earlier (Boles *et al.* 2018). In contrast to the Tennessee-Cumberland statues, the Cahokia statues are largely carved in great detail and anatomically correct.

At present, roughly 100 flint clay Cahokia style figures have been documented, including both complete and fragmented pieces (Boles 2020). Of those that can be assigned to a distinct category, 14 are zoomorphic, 18 are male, 12 are indeterminate sex, and nine are female; of note, no two are alike although various themes are represented. Biological sex is not always depicted and thus some statues are separated into the male and female groups based on motifs or other signifiers of gender. All the female statues have associated items that they interact with in some way. Associated items include baskets, vessels, pouches, bags, serpents, and garden vegetation such as corn, sunflowers, and gourds. As mentioned with the Westbrook statue, these female figures have been interpreted as representations of the Earthmother persona. Early archaeological evidence suggested that the female statues were kept at small rural civic-ceremonial settlements and were retained by Cahokia's religious leaders whereas the male and animal statues were allowed to leave. Recent research has however revealed that a greater number of Cahokia female statues have been recovered outside of Cahokia (most well outside) than have been recovered at Cahokia (Emerson 1982, fig. 10; Lepper 2020, fig. 3; Boles 2022a). Those recovered at Cahokia have almost all been broken and/or burned and deposited in numerous ceremonial deposits. Similarly, those recovered outside Cahokia have also been decommissioned via breakage and/or burning but in contrast, those with known context were associated with human burials or human remains (Boles 2022a).

Cahokia statues representing human males depict some adorned with regalia while some are depicted nude but in different stances. A few males are depicted interacting with other characters or objects such as a ceramic vessel, discoidal, and possibly a bundle. Distribution of male statues does appear to differ dramatically from that of females, not only in terms of recovery in or outside Cahokia, but also in terms of contexts. This is not unexpected when we consider the likelihood that these statues were created, curated, and utilized for various purposes by different cultural institutions.

The female statues have been associated with a fertility cult and were likely curated by female religious leaders. Conversely, some male statues are depicted in warrior regalia or combat related interactions with subordinate figures. As for distribution, only three male figures have been recovered at Cahokia and the rest (n = 18) outside the Greater Cahokia area (Boles 2020, table 3.1a). Contexts are known for two of the three from Cahokia with one reportedly recovered from a mound and the other recently recovered in the wall trench of a Stirling structure at the East St Louis site (Boles *et al.* 2018). Of the 16 with known contexts from outside Cahokia, 13 came from burials, ten of which were in mounds, one was cached in a mound, one from a mound with unknown context, and one from a house basin at a non-mound site. The discrepancy of males recovered within or outside Cahokia could, however, be associated with sampling bias, especially if the males were deposited in mound top shrines or elite mortuary contexts. Although a number of Stirling phase burial mounds have been "excavated", they were done so in an unscientific manner during the process of removing the mounds for construction purposes, mainly in the mid- to late 1800s or early 1900s. Very few Stirling phase mound top shrines and burials have since been professionally excavated at Cahokia.

Cahokia style animal effigy statues made from flint clay were typically created as figure pipes. This is an important observation as it shows that Cahokians were creating these effigies to be used for smoking and not merely as statues. The suite of animals includes mainly frogs, followed by avian figures, with single examples of a squirrel and a crayfish. The animal figure pipes are important to the discussion here, as they were occasionally placed with human interments along with other Cahokian statues, or with separate interments within the same burial mound. To date, the only known animal type associated with other Cahokian statues, directly or with nearby burials, is the frog. Associated frog effigy statues are almost exclusively made from flint clay.

The frogs carved from flint clay at Cahokia are sometimes depicted with the frog holding an object that appears to represent a rattle and equated as shaman helpers or shaman shape-shifting forms, while the majority are depicted in a natural stance without accoutrements (Emerson 2003). As just mentioned, frog effigy statues were also carved from other lithic materials such as sandstone or limestone and were also sometimes sculpted from clay. The realistic depiction of frogs varies, even among those carved from flint clay. The frog effigy pipe also has a broad distribution and was crafted by various groups. Researchers have noted that frogs were the most common animal depicted by Illinois Mississippians (Perino 1971, 117; Brown 1976, 248; Emerson 1982, 33; Aftandilian 2007, 65). Frog effigy pipes were first made during the TLW Merrell phase, as were bird effigy pipes (Koldehoff 1996, 48; 2016, 302). These large figure pipes are likely the predecessors of the later Mississippian Cahokia style statues/figurines and figure pipes. Aftandilian argues that frog symbolism was imported along with maize from the southwest during the TLW period. He provides a number of ethnohistoric analogies from southwestern tribes that associate the frog with fertility and rain (Aftandilian 2007). It stands to reason that the refinement of the images and change in raw material during the later Mississippian phases are a continuation and elaboration of effigy pipe smoking rituals and traditions that were rooted in the TLW period and likely associated with the introduction of maize agriculture.

Now we turn our attention to the depositional contexts for the statues highlighted in this chapter. While little is known about the discovery of the Bear-

Cape statue, inferences can be drawn from the limited details and what is known about the area from previous archaeological investigations. The dark red color of the statue suggests possible exposure to heat and thus it is possible that the statue was located within a burned special use structure similar to the Exchange figurine from the East St Louis Site (Emerson and Boles 2010; Boles *et al.* 2018). As mentioned earlier, Perino noted the existence of a Mississippian village in the adjacent valley that contained a temple mound with a burned structure. This observation also provides for the possibility of the Bear-Cape statue being deposited in a special-use feature. If this was the case, it follows the use pattern for both female and animal effigy statues and figure pipes at Cahokia but not the burial deposition for Cahokian statues outside Cahokia. The Westbrook and Harlan female statues however, do follow the noted mortuary deposition for Cahokian statues recovered from outside Cahokia although each differs in mortuary rituals.

The Westbrook statue was buried in a Caddo style shaft tomb that was intrusive into an earlier, low relief, Coles Creek conical burial mound. The statue was buried with one individual thought to be a female whose skull was removed and a conch shell cup put in its place. Other items accompanied the remains in addition to the flint clay statue. According to a relative of one of the collectors, there was at least one other Caddo burial in the mound. Recovered from the second burial was a frog effigy pipe and a pair of copper covered, wooden, bear canine effigy ear adornments, identical to the ones discovered with the Westbrook burial. The late James Marlen, who acquired the Westbrook statue, had the wooden adornments from the second burial dated at the University of Illinois. The one-sigma date range is cal AD 1019–1118. While this does not provide a date for the Westbrook burial, it seems likely that both burials are relatively close in time as they are intrusive into an earlier mound. The date range includes the early Stirling phase at Cahokia. This is noteworthy as this is when the flint clay statues were produced.

The Harlan statue was placed in a Caddo burial mound with numerous contemporaneous interments dating to the late Harlan phase (AD 1100s to mid-1200s). The Harlan statue was buried with a group of at least eight cremated individuals. Other items accompanied the remains including three conch shells. Of interest, other Cahokia related artifacts were also recovered with cremated remains in the central mound and includes a ground-stone spud and two bi-pointed Ramey-type knives. A third (non-cremated) central mound burial contained two copper, long-nosed god maskettes.

A third Cahokia style statue-pipe was recovered from Caddo contexts at the Spiro Mound site in Le Flore County, Oklahoma. This statue was carved from sandstone and was part of an elaborate mortuary event in the hollow chamber of the Craig Mound. She was placed in the center of the chamber and next to curated human remains that likely represented a sacred bundle (Hamilton 1952; Brown *et al.* 2020; Boles 2022a).

While the particular context differs for each of the above examples, all were placed with or near human remains within mounds. This differs from ritual use and decommissioning in special use structures and/or nearby pit features as seen at Cahokia where they were crafted.

Foreign material culture: trade vs. immigration

Paramount to understanding how non-local objects end up where they are discovered lies in understanding how these items were used within the society that produced them. In the past, researchers offered the default explanation of trade or some type of exchange to account for non-local pieces. If the non-local item in question were elaborate or refined, then it is assumed that these objects would have been highly sought by non-local, high-status leaders and therefore part of an elite exchange network. This model largely reflects western notions of consumerism whereby refined items were viewed as art and the accumulation of such objects displayed wealth and status. It also does not take into consideration the spiritual aspects and taboos that were likely associated with certain objects.

Other types of exchange have been linked to fictive adoption rituals similar to the Calumet ceremony practiced by Plains tribes to form trade relationships. Robert Hall suggested that a similar ceremony was practiced in Early Mississippian times and that long-nose maskettes were distributed from Cahokia to non-local elites in such a ritual manner (1991). Others have argued that the wide distribution of flint clay statues from Cahokia might also have been the result of similar alliance building ceremonies.

There is quite a difference however between personal items meant to be worn and displayed versus a statue or statue-pipe that represented a supernatural and was likely incorporated in a sacred bundle and served as temple statuary. Views differ of course on whether bundles containing religious sacra could or would be transferred to outsiders and whether outsiders would seek to acquire such objects through trade or exchange. And, while there are examples of bundle transfers between disparate groups, it bears keeping in mind that life was much different for Post-contact native groups than it was for Pre-contact groups. Native populations were decimated by the time Euro-American researchers recorded bundle transfers. It seems reasonable to assume that regulations for bundle transfers loosened during this time when native groups were forming alliances in an effort to mitigate decreased populations, resource shortages, and combat Euro-American expansion into their homelands.

Even so, there are still a number of recorded examples of tight restrictions on bundles regarding use and transfers (Boles 2020, 80–2). The objects within bundles were considered sacred and powerful; only priests had the ritual knowledge to control and use the power. Ritual knowledge was guarded and only given to worthy initiates (Bailey 1995, 18, 62; Hall 1997, 69). For instance, the ownership of the Morning and Evening Star bundles of the Skidi Pawnee (Caddoan language) were hereditary and had to be purchased by the apprentice (Dorsey 1904, xx–xxii). The war bundle of the Winnebago (Siouan speaking) was passed from father to son within a clan and although they were primarily a family possession, they were also a clan possession to some extent (Radin 1990, 394). War bundles were viewed as sacred and dangerous by many southeastern tribes, and no one, including the enemy would dare touch these bundles on any account (Dye 2007, 160; Adair 2009). For the Hidatsa (Siouan language), a man's personal sacred or medicine bundles were buried with him while any tribal bundles were passed on to the next of kin (Bowers 1965, 171). The Mandan (Siouan language) had two types of sacred bundles, one associated with a culture hero and the other with the Old-Woman-Who-Never-Dies. These were passed on through clan inheritance (Bowers 1965, 201). In instances when there were no worthy apprentices, the bundle would be buried with the last bundle keeper or properly disposed of through burning or immersion in water (Bailey 1995, 23; Hall 1997, 69).

From the discussion above and with even the brief review of bundle restrictions just noted, it is reasonable to suggest that the Cahokia style statues recovered from afar arrived there in sacred bundles with Cahokian immigrants. These statues were religious sacra of the highest order and as such would not be given to, exchanged with, or traded to outsiders. Research has shown that Cahokia was built with the aid of people migrating there from various directions at the onset *c.* AD 1050. Research has also shown that people began departing Cahokia by the early to mid-1100s and in droves during the late 1100s (Benson *et al.* 2009). Of interest, Cahokia style statues have not been found in the Greater Cahokia area post-AD 1200. A few of the Cahokia statues with datable contexts recovered outside Cahokia were deposited within the time of production or shortly thereafter. Other statues recovered from afar were curated and passed down to descendants for generations before decommissioning and deposition.

Many of the Cahokian statues are relatively large and may have been transported in a sacred basket on a litter, perhaps along with other baskets carrying venerated human remains. This notion is validated or at least reasonable based on the emergence of several female statues from baskets. The weight of the larger statues would have been burdensome to carry via a pack and the fragility of the statues, especially those made from fluorite, would create additional stress if carried in this manner. Additionally, while one individual may have been entrusted with curating a statue (bundle keeper), some statues were likely associated with clans or even larger groups and thus not viewed as personal possessions. It follows then that numerous people rather than an individual would be tasked with the movement or relocation of these statues. The final deposition of these statues varies with some buried with an individual (last bundle keeper) or more than one individual (clan burial), some placed in temples that are decommissioned with fire, and some seemingly placed or hidden in isolated pits in unassuming locales. Prior to deposition these statues were almost always broken and/or burned. The consistent ritual decommissioning of these statues, whether at Cahokia or afar, and whether made from flint clay or some sedimentary rock, attests to the sacred nature of the Cahokian statues and that Cahokians or their descendants were present when they no longer retained purpose.

In returning to earlier distribution theories it seems unlikely that such objects would enter an elite trade network or be exchanged in a Calumet-like ceremony. As Hall noted, the Calumet Ceremony was about adoption and rebirth and typically involved children as the recipients of the gesture. Typical exchanges involved food staples or other easily obtained items (Hall 1991). If Cahokians practiced a similar alliance forming ceremony, it seems doubtful that exchange items would include their religious statues or even god maskettes, the latter, which were likely imbued with power by association with the mythological Red Horn

(Hall 1983; 1991). Even taking the religious nature of the statues and maskettes aside, the exchange of such refined and unequaled objects would have created a trade imbalance and potentially awkward reciprocity events with other leaders. These factors diminish the likelihood of both elite trade and alliance forming exchanges. In many locales where Cahokia statues or god maskettes have been recovered, there are other Cahokia related items such as discoidals, Ramey knives, spuds, and arrow points. Harlan is a prime example as is Spiro, Gahagan, Schild, Yokem, Twin Mounds, as well as regions such as southern Wisconsin, northwest Iowa, southwest Ohio, southeast Missouri, and eastern Arkansas.

Common, everyday Cahokia arrow points were recovered at many of the locales mentioned above. Conversely, non-local arrow points are the most common type of exotic material recovered at Cahokia's East St Louis Precinct and predominately from domestic contexts (Boles *et al.* 2018). These non-local points are not gem quality points and show resharpening from use, indications that these were likely brought with people that migrated to a given site and were not part of a trade network. Additionally, some non-local points are made from local cherts, again suggesting that migrants continued to make their own styles but out of necessity had to use local, expedient cherts (Boles 2020). Research has shown that, at Cahokia for instance, at any given time from its inception until abandonment, approximately one-third of the population was non-local (Slater *et al.* 2014).

While migration could easily account for a certain percentage of non-local material at any given site, other factors such as trade and exchange assuredly occurred but likely involved non-religious items and basic necessity staples. For instance, digging and woodworking implements made from Mill Creek and Kaolin cherts are ubiquitous at Cahokia (and other Midcontinent Mississippian sites) but were produced by local knappers near the source area for these cherts, some 90 km south of Cahokia. What was exchanged for these implements is not readily discerned from the archaeological record, as Cahokia material culture is all but absent at the large workshop villages. Cahokians may have traded perishables such as grain, other foodstuffs, or clothing/animal hides but, of course, such staples would be archaeologically invisible.

Conclusion

In closing, the main goal of this chapter is to present new or corrected data on five statues with ties to Cahokia. These examples were also used as a means of discussing the religious aspects of these statues, the likely Terminal Late Woodland origin of the Cahokia style statuary, and the manner in which they were transported and ritually deposited in distant lands. Ethno-historic accounts were utilized to discuss sacred bundles and restrictions on bundle transfers as a means of providing insight for similar Pre-contact items. Ethno-historic accounts also provided insights into what or who the various statues may have represented from general Earth Mother personas, specific individuals associated with the Siouan

Red Horn mythology, or portraits of individuals. Of course, the identification of specific representations via ethno-historic accounts is limited by the available data and/or the data used for comparisons. That stated, other interpretations than the ones proposed here are certainly possible. However, proposed identities for the statues aside, the ritual decommissioning and deposition of these statues, suggests that these objects were religious sacra and as such likely retained by the groups that crafted and utilized them, whether deposited within or outside the homeland where they were created.

Bibliography

Adair, J. (2009) *The History of the American Indians*. University of Alabama Press, Tuscaloosa AL.

Aftandilian, D. (2007) Animals, Agriculture, and Religion Among Native Americans in Precontact Illinois: An Interdisciplinary Analysis of Perception and Representation. Unpublished Ph.D. thesis, University of Chicago.

Alexander, H.B. (1916) *North American Mythology*. Cambridge University Press, Cambridge MA.

Bailey, G.A. (1995) *The Osage and the Invisible World: From the Works of Francis La Flesche*. University of Oklahoma Press, Norman OK.

Bell, R.E. (1972) *The Harlan Site, CK-6, A Prehistoric Mound Center in Cherokee County, Oklahoma*. Memoir No. 2, Oklahoma Anthropological Society, Norman OH.

Benson, L.V., Pauketat, T.R. and Cook, E.R. (2009) Cahokia's boom or bust in the context of climate change. *American Antiquity* 74(3), 467–83.

Black, G. (1967) *Angel Site: An Archaeological, Historical, and Ethnological Study*. Indiana Historical Society, Indianapolis IN.

Blackhawk, J. (1926) Wazunka. *The Wisconsin Archaeologist* 7(4), 223–6.

Boles, S.L. (2010) Thunder on the Ohio: Connections to Cahokia. Unpublished paper presented at the Cahokia/Mississippian Archaeological Conference at the Cahokia Mounds State Historic Site, Collinsville, Illinois, 31 July 2010.

Boles, S.L (2011) Thunder on the Ohio: introducing Storms-as-he-walks, Red Horn's Companion. *Central States Archaeological Journal* 58, 237–44.

Boles, S.L (2012) Fluorite: A Mineral of Importance in Midcontinental Prehistory. Unpublished M.A. thesis on file in Southern Illinois University, Carbondale IL.

Boles, S.L (2014) Supernaturals in the Confluence Region. Unpublished paper presented at the 71st Annual Meeting of the Southeastern Archaeological Conference. Greenville SC.

Boles, S.L (2020) Tracking Cahokians through material culture. In *Cahokia in Context: Hegemony and Diaspora*, C.H. McNutt and R.M. Parish (eds), 49–86. University of Florida Press, Gainesville FL.

Boles, S.L (2022a) Cahokia's wandering supernaturals: what does it mean when the Earth Mother leaves town? In *Archaeologies of the Cosmoscapes in the Americas*, J.G. Stauffer, B.T. Giles, and S.P. Lambert (eds), 47–66. American Landscapes 5, Oxford.

Boles, S.L (2022b) Cary Celt Cache site (11S2234). Illinois Archaeological Survey site form (electronic document available at https://maps.dnr.illinois.gov/ias/sitedoc.ashx?id=S02234.pdf).

Boles, S.L., Ensor, H.B., Poling, A.I., Kitchen, C.A. and Holschen, M.S.(2018) *East St Louis Precinct (11S706) Terminal Late Woodland and Mississippian Lithics: Data Summary and Interpretation*, S.L. Boles (ed.) Illinois State Archaeological Survey 41, Prairie Research Institute, University of Illinois at Urbana-Champaign IL.

Boles, S.L. and Lewis, M. (2019) Solving the McBeth Figurine mystery: professional and avocational collaboration. *Prehistoric Archaeology* 53(4).

Bowers, A.W. (1965) *Hidatsa Social and Ceremonial Organization.* U.S. Government Printing Office, Washington D.C.

Bowers, A.W. (2004) *Mandan Social and Ceremonial Organization.* University of Nebraska Press, Lincoln NE.

Brown, J.A. (1976) *Spiro Studies, Volume 4: The Artifacts.* Second part of the Third Annual Report of Caddoan Archaeology, Spiro Focus Research, University of Oklahoma, Norman OK.

Brown, J.A. (1996) *The Spiro Ceremonial Center: The Archaeology of Arkansas Valley Caddoan Culture in Eastern Oklahoma.* Museum of Anthropology, Ann Arbor MI.

Brown, J.A. (2011) The regional culture signature of the Braden art style. In *Visualizing the Sacred: Cosmic Visions, Regionalism, and the Art of the Mississippian World.* G.E. Lankford, F.K. Reilly III, and J.F. Garber (eds), 37–53. University of Texas Press, Austin

Brown, J.A., Barker, A.W. and Sabo, G. III (2020) The Spirit Lodge, Spiro ritual, and cosmic renewal. In *Recovering Ancient Spiro: Native American Art, Ritual, and Cosmic Renewal,* E.D. Singleton and F.K. Reilly III (eds), 92–113. National Cowboy and Western Heritage Museum, Oklahoma City OK.

Colvin, M.H. (2012) Old-Woman-Who-Never Dies: A Mississippian Survival in the Hidatsa World. Unpublished manuscript on file, Department of Anthropology, Texas State University-San Marcos TX.

Corbin, J.E. and Hart, J.P. (1998) The Washington Square Mound Site: A Middle Caddo Mound Complex in South Central Texas. *Bulletin of the Texas Archaeological Society* 69, 47–78.

Diaz-Granados, C. and Duncan, J.R. (2000) *The Petroglyphs and Pictographs of Missouri.* University of Alabama Press, Tuscaloosa AL.

Diaz-Granados, C., Duncan, J.R. and Reilly, F.K. III (eds) (2015) *Picture Cave: Unraveling the Mysteries of the Mississippian Cosmos.* University of Texas Press, Austin TX.

Diaz-Granados, C., Rowe, M.W., Hymann, M., Duncan, J.R. and Southon, J.R. (2001) AMS radiocarbon dates from three Missouri pictographs and their associated iconography. *American Antiquity* 66, 481–92.

Dorsey, G.A. (1904) *Traditions of the Skidi Pawnee.* Memoirs of the American Folklore Society 8, New York.

Duncan, J.R. (2015) Identifying the characters on the walls of Picture Cave. In Diaz-Granados *et al.* (eds) 2015, 209–37.

Duncan, J.R. and Diaz-Granados, C. (2000) Of Masks and myths, pp. in *Midcontinental Journal of Archaeology* 25, 1-26.

Dye, D.H. (2007) Ritual, medicine, and the war trophy iconographic theme in the Mississippian Southeast. In *Ancient Objects and Sacred Realms: Interpretations of Mississippian Iconography,* F.K. Reilly III and J.F. Garber (eds), 152–73. University of Texas Press, Austin TX.

Early, A.M. (1988) *Caddoan Settlement in a Mountain Environment.* Arkansas Archaeological Survey Research Series 2, Lincoln NE.

Emerson, T.E. (1982) *Mississippian Stone Images in Illinois.* Illinois Archaeological Survey, University of Illinois Urbana-Champaign IL.

Emerson, T.E. (1983) The Bostrom figure pipe and the Cahokian effigy style in the American Bottom. *Midcontinental Journal of Archaeology* 8, 257–67.

Emerson, T.E. (1989) Water, serpents, and the Underworld: an exploration into Cahokian symbolism. In *The Southeastern Ceremonial Complex: Artifacts and Analysis,* P.G. Galloway (ed.), 45–92. University of Nebraska Press, Lincoln NE.

Emerson, T.E. (2003) Materializing Cahokia shamans. *Southeastern Archaeology* 22(2), 135–54.

Emerson, T.E. and Boles, S.L. (2010) Contextualizing flint clay Cahokia figures at the East St. Louis Mound Center. *Illinois Archaeology* 22, 473–90.

Emerson, T.E. and Boles, S.L. (2011) Sourcing and interpreting the St. Francois Raptor Figurine. *Illinois Archaeology* 23, 158–72.

Emerson, T.E. and Girard, J.S. (2004) Dating Gahagan and its implications for understanding Cahokia-Caddo interactions. *Southeastern Archaeology* 23, 57–64.

Emerson, T.E. and Hughes, R.E. (2000) Figurines, flint clay sourcing, the Ozark Highlands, and Cahokian acquisition. *American Antiquity* 65, 79–101.

Emerson, T.E., Koldehoff, B.H. and Brennan, T.K. (eds) (2018) *Revealing Greater Cahokia, North America's First Native City: Rediscovery and Large-Scale Excavations of the East St. Louis Precinct.* Studies in Archaeology 12, Illinois State Archaeological Survey, Prairie Research Institute, University of Illinois at Urbana-Champaign IL.

Emerson, T.E., Hughes, R.E., Hynes, M.R. and Wisseman S.U. (2002) Implications of sourcing Cahokia-style flint clay figures in the American Bottom and the Upper Mississippi River Valley. *Midcontinental Journal of Archaeology* 27, 309–38.

Emerson, T.E., Hughes, R.E., Hynes, M.R. and Wisseman S.U. (2003) The sourcing and interpretations of Cahokia-style figurines in the trans-Mississippi South and Southeast. *American Antiquity* 68, 287–313.

Engle, N.L. (1957) Prehistoric Human Figurines of the Eastern United States and Their Significance. Unpublished M.A. thesis, University of Illinois at Urbana-Champaign IL.

Fundaburk, E.L. and Fundaburk Foreman, M.D. (eds) (1957) *Sun Circles and Human Hands: The Southeastern Indians Art and Industries.* E.L. Fundaburk, Luverne AL.

Funmaker, W.W. (1974) The Bear in Winnebago Culture: A Study in Cosmology and Society. Unpublished manuscript on file, Department of Anthropology, University of Minnesota, Minneapolis MN.

Funmaker, W.W. (1986) The Winnebago Black Bear Subclan: A Defended Culture. Unpublished manuscript on file, Department of Anthropology, University of Minnesota, Minneapolis MN.

Girard, J.S., Perttula, T.K. and Trubitt, M.B. (2014) *Caddo Connections Within and Beyond the Caddo World.* Issues in Eastern Woodlands Archaeology Series, Lanham MD.

Goldstein, L.G. (1980) *Mississippian Mortuary Practices: A Case Study of Two Cemeteries in the Lower Illinois Valley.* Scientific Paper 4, Northwestern University Archaeological Program, Evanston IL.

Grantham, B. (2002) *Creation Myths and Legends of the Creek Indians.* University of Florida Press, Gainesville FL.

Hall, R.L. (1983) Long Distance Connections of Some Long-nosed Gods. Unpublished paper presented at the annual meeting of the American Anthropological Association, Chicago, 17–20 November.

Hall, R.L. (1989) The cultural background of Mississippian symbolism. In *The Southeastern Ceremonial Complex: Artifacts and Analysis*, P. Galloway (ed.), 239–78. University of Nebraska Press, Lincoln NE.

Hall, R.L. (1991) Cahokia Identity and Interaction Models of Cahokia Mississippian. In *Cahokia and the Hinterlands: Middle Mississippian Cultures of the Midwest*, T.E. Emerson and R.B. Lewis (eds), 3–34. University of Illinois Press, Urbana IL.

Hall, R.L. (1997) *An Archaeology of the Soul: North American Indian Belief and Ritual.* University of Illinois Press, Urbana IL.

Hamilton, H. (1952) *The Spiro Mound. The Missouri Archaeologist* 14.

Hudson, C. (1976) *The Southeastern Indians.* University of Tennessee Press, Knoxville TN.

Hultkrantz, A. (1957) *The North American Indian Orpheus Tradition.* The Ethnological Museum of Sweden Monograph Series 2. Stockholm.

Jeter, M.D., Scott, R.J. Jr and House, J.H. (2020) Possible Cahokia contacts in eastern and southeastern Arkansas. In *Cahokia in Context: Hegemony and Diaspora*, C.H. McNutt and R.M. Parish (eds), 185–204. University of Florida Press, Gainesville FL.

Koldehoff, B.H. (1996) Pits and grooves, feathers, and fertility: interpreting the AG Church bird pipe. *Illinois Antiquity* 31, 6–10.

Koldehoff, B.H. (2016) Appendix E: lithic artifacts from the 1963 Illinois State Museum excavations. In *The Kane Village Site: A Terminal Late Woodland Habitation in Madison County, Illinois*, B.H. Koldehoff and C.R. Moffat (eds), 299–312. Technical Report 109,

Illinois State Archaeological Survey, Prairie Research Institute, University of Illinois Urbana-Champaign IL.

Lankford, G.E. (2011) *Native American Legends of the Southeast*. University of Alabama Press, Tuscaloosa AL.

Lepper, B.T. (2020) The Mississippian iconography of Serpent Mound. *Journal of Ohio Archaeology* 7, 38–55.

Moorehead, W.K. and Leighton, M.M. (1923)*The Cahokia Mounds*. University of Illinois Bulletin 21(6), University of Illinois, Urbana IL.

Parks, C. and Thompson, B.W. (1972) *Who's Who in Indian Relics* 3. Messenger, Kirkwood IL.

Pauketat, T.R. (1983) A long-stemmed spud from the American Bottom. *Midcontinental Journal of Archaeology* 8, 1–15.

Pauketat, T.R. (2004) *Ancient Cahokians and the Mississippians*. Cambridge University Press, Cambridge.

Pauketat, T.R. (2009) *Cahokia: Ancient America's Great City on the Mississippi*. Penguin Press, New York.

Pauketat, T.R. (2013) *An Archaeology of the Cosmos: Rethinking Agency and Religion in Ancient America*. Routledge, London.

Pauketat, T.R. and Alt, S.M. (eds) (2015) *Medieval Mississippians: The Cahokian World*. School for Advanced Research Press, Santa Fe NM.

Perino, G.H. (1963) Tentative classification of two projectile points and a knife from west central Illinois. *Central States Archaeological Journal* 10(3), 95–100.

Perino, G.H. (1971) The Mississippian component at the Schild Site (No. 4), Greene County, Illinois. In *Mississippian Site Archaeology in Illinois*, J.A. Brown (ed.), 90–140. Archaeological Survey, Urbana IL.

Perrine, T.M. (1873) Mounds near Anna, Union County, Illinois. *Smithsonian Institution Annual Report for 1872*,418–20.

Prentice, G. (1986) An analysis of the symbolism expressed by the Birger Figurine. *American Antiquity* 51, 239–66.

Radin, P. (n.d.) The Squirrel. *Winnebago Notebooks* 22, 1–85. American Philosophical Society, Philadelphia PA.

Radin, P. (1948) Winnebago Hero cycles: a study in Aboriginal literature. *International Journal of American Linguistics* 14(3)

Radin, P. (1990) *The Winnebago Tribe*. University of Nebraska Press, Lincoln NE.

Reilly, F.K. III (2004) People of the earth, people of the sky: visualizing the sacred in Native American art of the Mississippian Period. In *Hero, Hawk, and Open Hand: American Indian Art of the Ancient Midwest and South*, R.F. Townsend and R.V. Sharp (eds), 125–37. Yale University Press/Art Institute of Chicago, New Have CO and London.

Salzer, R.J. (1987) Preliminary report on the Gottschall Site (47Ia80). *Wisconsin Archaeologist* 68, 419–72.

Salzer, R.J. and Rajnovich, G. (2000) *The Gottschall Rockshelter: An Archaeological Mystery*. Prairie Smoke Press, St Paul MN.

Sharp, R.V. (2011) What New Additions to the Flint Clay Corpus Can Tell Us About Mississippian Sculpture. Unpublished paper presented at the 68th annual Southeastern Archaeological Conference, Jacksonville FL.

Sharp, R.V. (2012) Mythic Figures or Shamanic Practitioners: What New Additions to the Flint-Clay Corpus Suggest. Unpublished paper presented at the 77th annual meeting of the Society for American Archaeology, Memphis, TN.

Sharp, R.V. (2013) Sacred Narratives of Cosmic Significance: The Place of the Keesee Figurine in the Mississippian Mythos. Unpublished paper presented as part of the symposium "Visions of Other Worlds: Ideological and Ritual Functions of Mississippian Symbols" at the 79th annual meeting of the Society of American Archaeology, Austin TX.

Slater, P.A., Hedman, K.M. and Emerson, T.E. (2014) Immigrants at the Mississippian polity of Cahokia: strontium isotope evidence for population movement. *Journal of Archaeological Science* 44, 117–27.

Smith, K.E. and Miller, J.V. (2009) *Speaking with the Ancestors: Mississippian Stone Statuary of the Tennessee-Cumberland Region*. University of Alabama Press, Tuscaloosa AL.

Swanton, J.R. (1929) Myths and tales of the Southeastern Indians. *Bureau of American Ethnology Bulletin* 88.

Thomas, C. (1985) *Reports on the Mound Explorations of the Bureau of Ethnology*. Smithsonian Institution Press, Washington DC.

Webb, W.S. and Funkhouser, W.D. (1931) The Tolu Site in Crittenden County, Kentucky. *University of Kentucky Reports in Archaeology and Anthropology* 1(5), 307–410.

West, G.A. (1934) *Tobacco, Pipes, and Smoking Customs of the American Indians. Bulletin of the Public Museum of the City of Milwaukee* 17.

Witthoft, J. (1949) *Green Corn Ceremonialism in the Eastern Woodlands*. University of Michigan Museum Occasional Publication 13. Ann Arbor MI.

Wolforth, T.R. and Wolforth, L.M. (2000) Fluorite figurines from the Midcontinent. In *Mounds, Modoc, and Mesoamerica*, S.R. Ahler (ed.), 455–68. Illinois State Museum Scientific Papers 28, Springfield IL.

10

The great importance of the Great Serpent

James R. Duncan

When we began mapping and recording the petroglyphs and pictographs (Fig. 10.1C) of Missouri in the 1980s we encountered many petroglyph sites with large numbers of serpentine images, clustered in the southeastern quadrant of the Missouri Ozarks, adjacent to major sites of Mississippian occupation. In addition to the southeastern petroglyphs we rediscovered a trove of unique pictographs in a cave on the lower Missouri River near its confluence with the Mississippi River. After taking a cue from Robert Hall, we began to link the serpent motifs to oral traditions. This spirit's motif has possibly achieved a universal presence within the North American Indian oral traditions. This is, at least in part, because of his eternal presence in the night sky. This spirit being, the Great Serpent, is associated with the Milky Way. We are not the first to discuss the Great Serpent (Emerson 1989; Knight 1989; Lankford 2004; 2007; Reilly 2011; 2015; Lepper 2018). We find this spirit to be a paradox. Early European explorers and French missionaries were shocked to see his images in temples. Because one of this spirit's salient features is a pair of white-tailed deer antlers, his gender is believed to be male. His presence is widespread and his image exists as everything from a tiny copper serpent (?Fig. 10.1B) to the largest effigy mound in North America (Fig. 10.1A). In delving into his importance, it becomes apparent that he is not a member of the commonly understood celestial family, nor is he always adversarial. Finally, we will focus on his presence in the corpus of imagery originating in the area around the confluence of the Missouri and Mississippi Rivers, especially the Cahokia region and the central Mississippi valley.

Just after the formation of the new republic, the United States, the fertile lands west of the Appalachian Mountains, especially the Ohio River valley, were coveted by numerous land speculators eager to replace and disinherit the rightful American Indian inhabitants. At the heart was the Missouri/Mississippi River confluence where, just to the east, Cahokia, the largest of the many mound groups, stood abandoned and silent. As was the nature of many at the time, public opinion cast the Indian Nations as incapable of creating such works, and the myth of the

"Moundbuilders" was born – a "Lost Race" of creators of the great mound groups which had been destroyed by contemporary Indians (Bailey 2004, 86). Academic research beginning in the period just before1900 and particularly after World War II unraveled some of the stifling mythology, created largely by greed and ignorance, that has long obscured the purpose and origins of the largest mound groups. The Cahokia group, the largest, was considered to be an outlier with its environs shrouded by urban and industrial development, and was not appreciated for its eminency and influence. Work by James B. Griffin (1952a; 1952b), Philip Phillips and James Ford (1951), James Howard (1968), Fred Eggan (1970), Robert Hall (1991; 1997), Alice Kehoe (2007), James Brown (2007; 2011) and others began a gradual weaving together of ethnographic collections, archaeological finds, and archival descriptions of North American Indian rituals. Gradually, archaeological investigations increased at Cahokia, especially during federally financed highway construction which employed newly legislated funding for archaeological salvage and preservation. Sadly, a few members of the craft of North American archaeology retain vestiges of colonial bias and a refusal to believe in the longevity of the cultural memory of American Indians.

Using ethnographic data along with archaeological findings, we will describe and define this principal spirit personage and his attributes and add to our previous work concerning the Cahokia area's seminal role. We have found that this spirit being often changes its shape over time while still retaining his puissance and purpose. We will also discuss the age and cultural associations of this spirit's imagery and attempt to describe and define its complex nature. Recent interpretation of early Spanish and French documents name the Dhegiha as prominent in the mid-Mississippi valley (Hall 2004, 102; Kehoe 2007, 246–7). Using this as our starting point, we will travel back in time to their earliest ancestors looking for evidence of the Great Serpent.

The antiquity of the Great Serpent

The earliest evidence we have for a spirit associated with water, especially springs, although indirect, is during the Paleo-Indian (13,400–12,300 BP) and the (Paleo-Archaic) Dalton periods (12,000–9800 BP). Both single examples or group caches of large, skillfully made Clovis or Dalton points have been found closely adjacent to, or directly in, springs in the mid-Mississippi and lower Missouri River valleys (McMillan 2019; 393; Kolderhoff 2020, 8–9, Loebel and Koldehoff 2020, 138–9). Ritual behavior, such as leaving a "valuable" gift, a reciprocal gift in exchange for a gift from a spirit being, has been a commonly practiced human characteristic worldwide for a long time. Springs, some quite large and spectacular, are sources of water and, in pre-Columbian times, clean water, especially those along the Ozark marginal karst and on the Ozark plateau. These springs provided water for foraging and hunting camp sites. This ancient gift is still acknowledged during Osage (Dhegiha) funeral ceremonies. The rite begins with a holy man, called the Roadman washing the grave walls with spring water. At the commencement of the post-funerary meal, after all of the participants have been ritually cleansed, the Roadman presides over the water ceremony. A cup of spring water has been placed at each place setting and the Roadman reminds all, Osages and other attendees, that water is The Great Mystery's (*Wa-kon'-da*) greatest gift, the gift of life itself ... there can be no life without water and all drink the spring water, the water of life. Ritual caches associated with springs continued to occur during the Early (9800–6000 BP) and Middle Archaic (6400–3400 BP) periods (Ray *et al.* 2020, 39–62).

It is during the Late Archaic period (*c.* 3700–2700 BP) that caches associated with springs and sinkholes become more elaborate. The Late Archaic sites along the lower Missouri River can be quite large, and evidence of long-range exchange of exotic materials, including eastern banded slate, southern rhyolite, and other exotic materials, such as copper from the Great Lakes and marine shells from the Gulf of Mexico, becomes evident. Several spectacular caches have been found by collectors. The DeWille or Cole Junction Bottom cache of hypertrophic, bifacially worked blades, housed in the Missouri History Museum collections in Forest Park (St Louis, Missouri) is truly exceptional. Hypertrophic Etley points, Wadlow preforms, three-quarter grooved axes manufactured from exotic hardstone, and even atlatl weights made from heat treated quartzite occur in caches near springs and sinkholes. An example of the size of several central Missouri Late Archaic sites located on elevations near the Missouri River was neatly recorded by Judge S.P. Dalton. In the early 1950s he and Hadley Irwin found, in one afternoon, more than 1000 bifacially worked Late Archaic tools, blades, and points at the Edward O. Buel farm on a ridge top near the confluence of the Moreau and Missouri rivers. Included in this collection were several Etley points and Wadlow preforms measuring more than 16.0 cm in length. Judge Dalton's extensive collections also included several of the ground and polished chert "lizard effigies" associated with the Late Archaic (Fig. 10.1F). We believe that these ground and polished chert objects are Water Spirit representations and were probably kept in small portable shrines or bundles (Duncan 2021, 29). These large Late Archaic sites were sites of early plant domestication. Not only were springs viewed as the realm of Water Spirits, regular rains brought by these spirit beings were a much needed stimulus for early agriculture.

The Late Archaic period (3700–3100 BP) earthworks at Poverty Point, interpreted as expressing a layered cosmos, certainly provides a home for an early version of the chief of the Water Spirits, the Great Serpent (Townsend 2004; 17; Hargrave *et al.* 2021, 192–3). Evidence for the widespread influence of Poverty Point is found as far up the Mississippi valley as the Missouri River confluence. Symbolism involving the Beneath World is found on drilled cylindrical hard stone beads (Fig 10.1E?), elaborately decorated hard stone bolas weights, and cross hatched reptilian patterns found on atlatl weights. The antiquity and importance of the Great Serpent as an essential part of principal rituals cannot be overstated. The earliest serpent imagery, adorning hunting devices and processing tools, along with small three-dimensional objects, small personal hunting talismans is often associated with a feminine image of baked clay. Both are found at Poverty Point (Fig. 10.1D) and in Late Archaic rock art (McNutt 1996, 201–4; Ward *et al.* 2022, 770–5). Surprisingly, hunting, fishing, and especially foraging seem to have sustained the immense Poverty Point site.

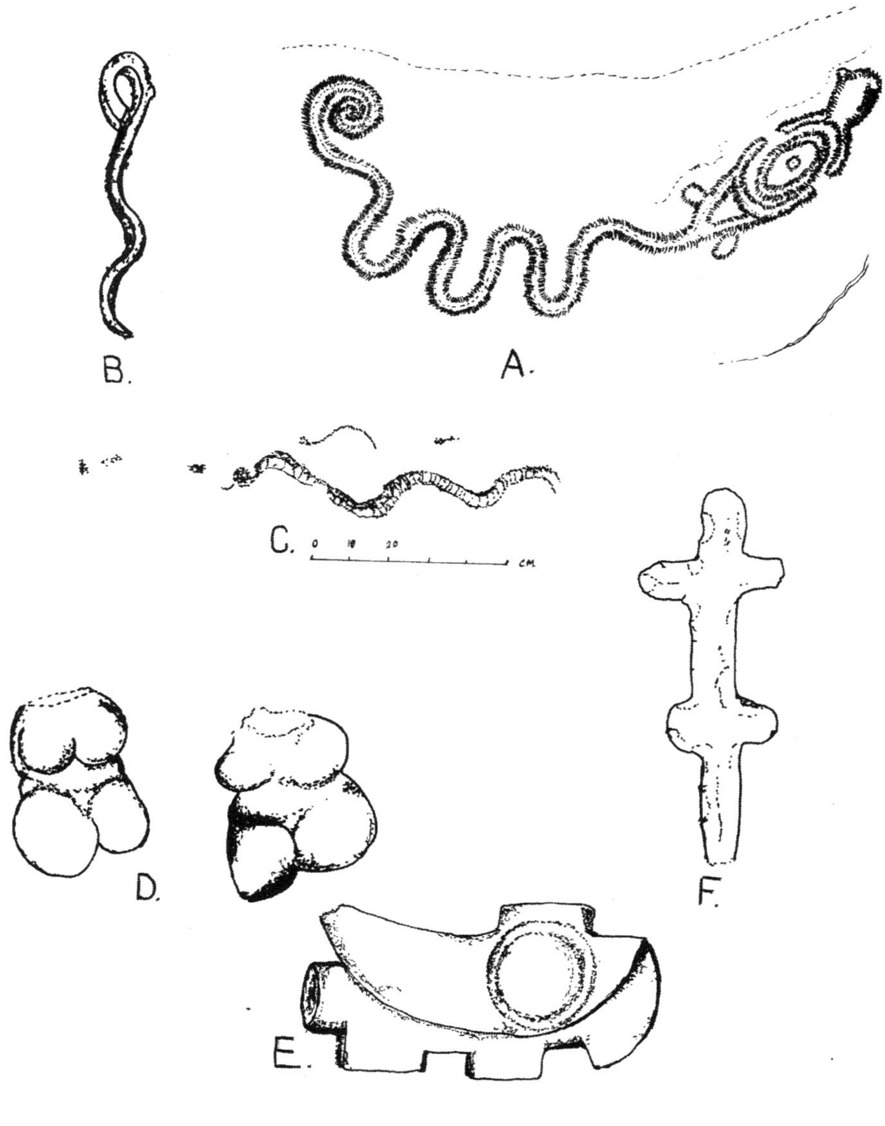

Fig. 10.1 A. Drawn from MacLean's (1885) map, the Great Serpent Mound, Adams County, Ohio (after Lepper 2018); B. copper serpent, Cahokia Mounds, St Clair County, Illinois; C. serpent pictograph, Rattlesnake Bluff, Franklin County, Missouri; D. ceramic female figures, Poverty Point, Louisiana; E. jasper bead, Water Spirit(?) Poverty Point; F. Burlington chert "lizard effigy", S.P. Dalton Collection, Moniteau County, Missouri.

Beginning at least by the Late Archaic, the Great Serpent begins moving away from the watery Beneath World and his probable title as lord of all the animals, especially those that are hunted for food. He adds another dimension to his kingdom, he becomes attracted to places where feminine activities such as food processing take place, especially vegetable foods. Rock art images of vulvas, serpentine cross-hatching and an occasional serpent have been found associated with bedrock mortars in the upper Cumberland plateau. Dates associated with charred nut shells and acorns fall into the Late Archaic period at Cloudsplitter and Cold Oak shelters (Claassen 2016, 26). The western segment of the prairie peninsula adjacent to the lower Missouri River and its confluence with the Mississippi was home to large Late Archaic populations. These people used a different set of tools than their eastern neighbors to process starchy seeds, roots, nuts, and acorns. Rather than manufacturing bedrock mortars, portable tabular sandstone metates, some with almost bowl like cavities surrounded by shallow "nutting" depressions were used to grind the seeds and nuts. Occasional petroglyphic footprints on the east side of the central Mississippi River valley are attributed to these Late Archaic peoples (Wagner *et al.* 2018, 108–9). These Late Archaic groups constructed low mounds on bluff tops overlooking river valleys. The scattered or bundled bones were covered with limestone flags and accompanied by large, phallus-like Burlington chert blades along with copious amounts of red ochre, three-quarter grooved axes, bolas weights, occasional atlatl weights, and stone pendants. The presence of human and dog internments on Late Archaic village sites indicates that the bundled and scattered bones in the mounds belonged to a minority group who were being subjected to special treatment, likely indicating social stratigraphy.

Late Archaic people, often referred to as foragers, were excellent hunters and fisherfolk, their physical remains reflect their efficiency. Some, but not all, were also engaging in early agriculture (Johannessen 1984, 198–9b; Claassen 2016, 5; Ward *et al.* 2022, 770–3). Spreading quickly throughout the Mississippi Valley and its adjacent watersheds, the conjoined botanical foraging and early agriculture were primarily the realm of the Great Serpent and his partner, First Woman or Grandmother Earth. The shift away from gathering to the domestication of botanical resources was solely the work of women (Colvin 2012; Mueller and Fritz 2016).

It is during the Middle Woodland period (2250–1750 BP) that we see a definitive, three-dimensional, therianthropic representation of the Chief of the Water Spirits expertly carved from a piece of mineralized wood or red slate. This effigy (Fig. 10.2A) was found, broken into many pieces, associated with altar 1 in Mound 1 at the famous Turner Site in Hamilton County, Ohio (Willoughby 1922, 70–1; Townsend 2004, 20–1). It is important to examine and describe this image carefully as there are multiple features that will consistently survive through the centuries into the post-Columbian era. The Turner figurine is a quadruped, with short clawed legs and a muscular body with what appears to be a rattlesnake's three button tail and a cervid head. The dorsal part of the body has six longitudinal bands of cross hatching arranged in two symmetrically engraved parallel stripes. Cross hatching is a representational signature trait of this character in the North American Indian Art tradition. The cervid head and the figure's belly are carved with reptilian scaled plates or scutes, two pairs of bilaterally symmetrical bovid horns and what look to be round dot-in-pupil eyes. The spirit being depicted is a theriomorphic combination of a felid, the puma (*Felis concolor*); a reptile, the timber rattlesnake (*Crotalus horridus*); the eastern white-tail deer (*Odocoileus virginianus*), and possible parts of several additional animals such as the beaver and the bison (Fig. 10.2A). It is our belief that the presence of horns is another important signature, perhaps even as much as the cross hatching, the serpent's skin. In the same altar, a beautiful mica serpent with an inlaid freshwater pearl eye was also found (Fig. 10.2B).

Perhaps the most important link to the Chief of the Water Spirits and his consort, First or Old Woman is the recent analysis of the immense Hopewellian earthworks at Newark, in Licking County, Ohio. Lepper and his associates Hively, Horn, and Walker, have determined that the Moon, the traditional home of First or Old Woman, and the Moon's maximum and minimum rises and settings are principal alignments of this site. The location of these earthworks is closely associated with water, in the form of large glacial ponds (Lepper 2004, 73–81). The association of this habitat of the Water Spirits linked to lunar observations reinforces the antiquity of these associated spirit beings and their governing of the cycle of death and rebirth. We can also connect a feminine presence as First Woman and the exchange of seeds and agricultural lore are essential during the annual gatherings at these impressive geometric earthworks.

The domestication and improvement of cultigens by selection and seed exchange rituals has a long history in North America. This gender specific technology, beginning during Archaic times, becomes more evident in the archaeological record by Middle Woodland times, especially in the Eastern Woodlands (Johannessen 1984a, 201–2; Mueller and Fritz 2016, 111). The rapid expansion of agriculture and its rites gives rise to the canonical depictions of many spirit beings. The images of these spirit beings, especially the Great Serpent and First Woman, are found on village sites and in burial mounds. The image of the Great Serpent found at the Turner Mounds is actually an atlatl weight. Because of its relatively fragile nature, the Turner figurine was probably not actually used on a hunting atlatl. It may have been part of a sacred bundle used in communal hunting rites since the Great Serpent is the "Lord of the animals" (Hall 1997, 84: Lankford 2004, 214–5). Middle Woodland people were fine hunters and keen observers of all the animals that they saw and hunted. We can only guess as to why generous amounts of material wealth was deposited in their burial mounds with the honored dead, as sacrificial economics never to be seen or used. The wealth placed in the mound was a gift, a reciprocity gift in many cases for either the Great Serpent or First Woman, the Spirit of the Earth, or both (Hall 1997, 156). This deposition of valuable objects, artisan products, and sacred icons was gifted not only for animals and plants consumed by the populace but also for the continuing gifts of life, the ability to enter the great cycle of rebirth or reincarnation experienced by all living things.

Further examination of Middle Woodland traditions, especially Havana from Illinois, Iowa, and Missouri, reveals skillfully rendered, ceramic human figures in the form of females in elaborate regalia dominate (Fig. 10.2C).

While the figurines can be associated with living areas, indicating clan or family shrines, the superbly carved stone platform pipes, 22% (66 of 305) of which realistically depict animals and birds, which are usually found in mortuary deposits (Farnsworth *et al.* 2021, 703) and suggest personal, ancestral sacra: bundles. Other accompanying mortuary objects are cut, perforated, and polished human and wolf mandibles, along with bear canine teeth. Reptilian depictions are rare, Beneath World beings depicted on platform pipes are usually frogs, along with bears, beavers, and otters, possibly fulfilling the role of the Great Serpent's avatars (Fig. 10.3A, B).

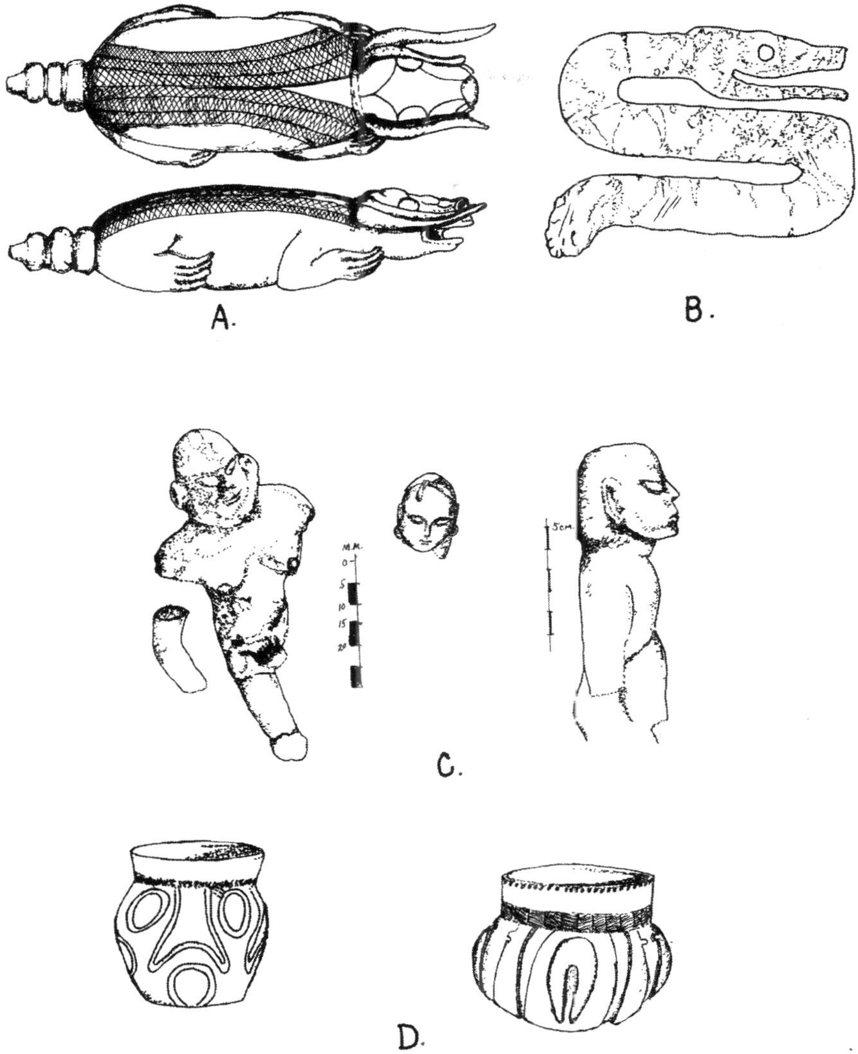

Fig. 10.2 A. theriomorphic Water Spirit, Turner Mound 1, Hamilton County, Ohio; B. mica serpent, Turner Mound 1; C. left to right: female figurine, white painted skirt, female figurine head, male figurine, Grafton, Illinois; D. mortuary pottery vessels, Mound 6, Havana Mounds, Mason County, Illinois.

With female figurines present in the collections we can surmise that the Old Woman or First Woman was definitely present in Middle Woodland oral traditions (Fig. 10.2C). Old Woman or First Woman symbolism is also present on ceramic vessels from the Havana type site in Illinois. Vessel "A" from Havana Mound 6 has an anthropomorphic face with large round eyes; can this be the face of the Chief of the Water Spirits? Vessel "C", also from Havana Mound 6 has alternating vulvar and phallic designs. This unique collection of pottery was excavated as a unit by Moorehead in 1928 (McGregor 1952, 75–8; Fig. 10.2D).

Engraved bone, along with marine shell gorgets with a central perforation, are not uncommon in Middle Woodland, especially Hopewellian, mortuary art. While most occur as badly preserved or burnt fragments, avian and felid designs are discernable (Phillips and Brown 1978, 157–90). It is the engraved felid or Underwater Panther motifs, along with carved stone pipes depicting the same character, the lord of the lower watery world, whose rites and bundles would be addressed as an aid, especially by Middle Woodland female agriculturists.

With the fading matrix of communication between various Middle Woodland clans and villages, regionalism became more pronounced. Happily, a Late Middle Woodland population prospered in western Illinois along the lower Illinois river and adjacent Clear Lake area, manufacturing red-slipped ceramics, especially T-rimmed bowls, Brandenburg ware, and other exotic, well-made, thin ware pottery along with at least one outstanding abstract platform pipe (Griffin 1952, 118). It is possible that a wonderfully talented artist among this small group created a monumental work, using marine shell, the famous Jaguar Gorget found in the Fairfield Mound 23BE6/2 in the western Ozarks of Missouri (Fig. 10.3C). The gorget was with a burial in a small earth and rock mound, along with a mammiform object and three large triangular knife preforms (Chapman 1980. 94–8). The Fairfield Jaguar Gorget may even represent the curation of heirloom sacra by elite clans or families. The Chief of the Water Spirits has at least two principal shapes. Lankford assigns the guise of both the Great Serpent and the Great Puma, or Underwater Panther, or Jaguar in this case, as being one and the same spirit being (2004, 214).

As the Middle Woodland interaction sphere gradually disintegrated, regionally isolated groups continued to develop their agricultural technologies. We believe that post-Middle Woodland societies continued to exchange seeds and gardening techniques with neighboring groups. However, two factors came into play by AD 600: First: growing populations caused friction among these groups as competition for territory increased with the growing populations and, secondly, the introduction of the bow and arrow added to cultural stress and casualties (Nassaney and Pyle 1999, 259–60). Late Woodland people made great strides with hunting equipment, the bow and arrow became the hunter's chief means of harvesting game. However, this technology was also used in warfare, resulting in much increased tension and cultural stress in Late Woodland societies.

Late Woodland populations in the lower Missouri River valley and at the confluence region were likely dichotomous, there being gender specific industries. The farming activities

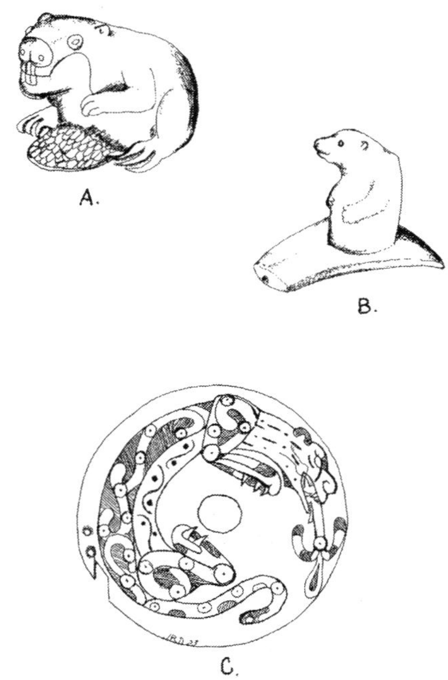

Fig. 10.3 A. carved and inlaid pipestone beaver, platform pipe, the bowl, Bedford Mound Group, Pike County, Illinois; B. river otter platform pipe, Wilson Mound Group, White County, Illinois; C. jaguar, engraved whelk shell gorget, Fairfield Mound 2, Benton County, Missouri.

were feminine as were the manufacture of ceramic containers, for example. As Late Woodland agricultural technology and production progressed, around AD 550, villages along the Lower Missouri Valley began to increase in size and complexity. Villages with accompanying burial mounds occupied hilltops adjacent to bottomlands where smaller streams joined the Missouri River and its larger tributaries. Expanding agricultural production, growing populations, and increasing conflict over territory for both hunting and farming placed growing stress on the competing communities. Feminine agricultural societies grew in importance. Their efforts to avoid conflict expanded the use of the ancient rituals of adoption establishing a synthetic kinship, the *Wa'-wa-thon* or pipe ceremony and Walking with the buffalo also referred to as the "Uniting of the blood" by early Europeans. Evidence for this increased aggression has been archaeologically recovered, especially in the central Mississippi River valley and its tributaries (Perino 1973, 66–106). The increased aggressive interaction, warfare involving the seizure of territory and captives (especially women, the clan centered corporate farmers and a source for the production of foodstuffs and its ancillary industries) made amelioration rites more common. These rites usually involve both successful warriors and prominent women, the women engaging in exchanging both foodstuffs and manufactured goods during seasonal gatherings (Duncan and Diaz-Granados 2000, 20–1; Bowers 2004, 324–5).

Benn suggests that Great Serpent and Underwater Panther effigy mounds were being used as focal points for seed exchange and agricultural rites by Late Woodland and later Oneota female age-graded societies (1995, 91–140). During the Late Woodland Period the small, portable images of the Chief of the Water Spirits almost disappear. They have been replaced by effigy mounds in the upper Midwest (Lepper *et al.* 2018, 433–50). During the last 20 years or so, these groups of effigy mounds, as well as singular examples, have been subjected to re-analysis and surprising links have been made, especially to the oral traditions of the Nations that occupied the areas of concern at the time of first European contact. Several of these mound groups have been interpreted to form vignettes of the paramount "Great Medicine Rites", oral traditions collected in the 18th, 19th, and early 20th centuries. It is not surprising that as sacred imagery, the effigy mounds should be made of earth, earth taken from the body of an almost universally revered spirit being, the spirit of the Earth, the mother of all things visible and invisible. Vignettes, groups of characters found in ontological oral traditions can be recognized as being portrayed in several effigy mound groups (Lepper *et al.* 2018).

It is during the terminus of the Late Woodland period where we see an increase in the performance of the ancient adoption rituals between adversarial groups, to avoid revenge raids and killings (Hall 1997, 42–7; Duncan and Diaz-Granados 2000, 8–12; Bowers 2004, 63–6). This renewed interest in adoption formed the basis for the principal amelioration rite, present in the Eastern Woodlands for millennia and was especially strong in the Missouri/Mississippi River confluence and its hinterlands, as demonstrated by the widespread distribution of an iconographic symbol, the Long-nosed ear ornaments. It is the accompanying oral traditions of the adoption rites that involve the Great Serpent, Chief of the Water Spirits, and his progeny.

Outside the Missouri/Mississippi River confluence, especially the northern region between the Great Lakes and the lower Missouri River valley, terminal Late Woodland groups and emergent Oneota groups increasingly engage in agricultural seed exchange rites. Berres describes this increase in the important reciprocal exchange systems: salient features of the adoption rites (2001, 37–8).

We have, in the past, assigned the Hidatsa/Mandan name to the spirit of the Earth, The-Old-Woman-Who-Never-Dies or simply "Old Woman". The first time the author was able to speak to Gerard Baker (Mandan-Hidatsa; see Baker 2004), I asked him to describe her, to hear if she was one and the same as First Woman among the Dhegiha. I was not disappointed, because she appeared to be the same spirit. Sharing the findings with two Osage elders and friends, William Samuel Fletcher and John W. Williams, it became apparent that Fletcher had visited the Hidatsa and he remarked that it was not difficult for an Osage to understand the Hidatsa (Baker 2004; Fletcher pers. comm. 2005; Williams pers. comm. 2021). It is absolute that many of the oral traditions collected under the heading of "The Great Medicine Rite" are rooted in an ancient, pre-Columbian legacy centered around a group of powerful spirit beings having been created by a universal, mysterious, animistic power variously known as "Earth Maker", "The Great Mystery" or even "*Wa-kon-da*". The increased importance of the rites of adoption and the accompanying reciprocal exchanges begin to forge new connections between prominent band leaders, elite holy men and women, and admired warriors. This in turn results in an increase in the exchange of culturally valuable information, particularly religious information. Dated genesis images from sources such as Picture Cave and contextually dated imagery on shell cups, copper plates, and as stone sculptures anchor the key narration in pre-Columbian times. This widespread and important narration is called the Great Medicine Rite (Hall 1997, 70–6; Weeks 2009). All of the extant versions of the Great Medicine Rite involve the Great Serpent, Old Woman or First Woman, First Man, and the Celestial Twins (Duncan 2015).

We will begin our description of the ancestral spirits by referring to a well-preserved collection of images made during the Late Woodland and Early Western Mississippian Periods, found in a sandstone cave, called Picture Cave, near the confluence of the Missouri and Mississippi Rivers. As discussed in earlier chapters, we have long believed the images that cover the sandstone walls of this dark zone cave were the work of ancestors of today's Dhegiha. When descending into Picture Cave, into the dark zone in which the walls are filled with an amazing array of kinetic figures, the first image that greets you is the looming visage of the Chief of the Water Spirits, the Great Serpent, *We'-ts'a Ton-ga* (La Flesche 1975, 215). Drawn in black, with great antlers and wide dot-in-pupil eyes, the Great Serpent bares his mouth full of sharp teeth as if to caution visitors to feel the aura of this sacred place (Fig. 10.4C). This great Chief of the Water Spirits, with his dark mask, antlers, and sharp teeth is accompanied by an eye-less figure, drooling blood ... death! These powerful images remind the visitor of the immense power and importance of this sacred place, The First Woman's womb,

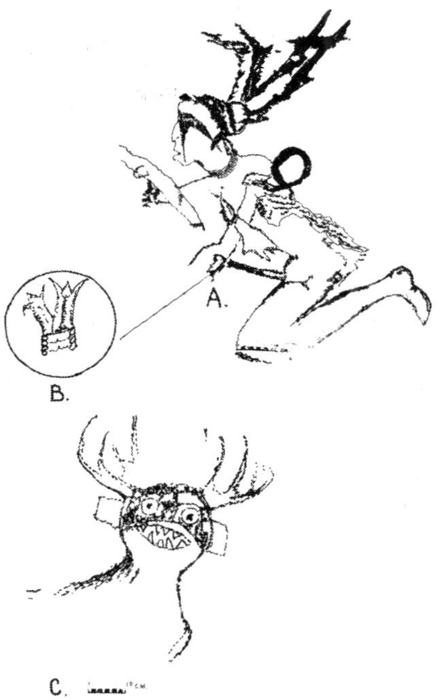

Fig. 10.4 A. "Snake Hide" Formative Braden style figure of the Great Serpent, a shape-shifter with an unusual penile terminus, Picture Cave, Warren County, Missouri; B. drawing of a male rattlesnake's bi-lobed penis; C. the antlered theriomorphic Great Serpent, Picture Cavei.

the "Womb of the Universe" (Pratt in Duncan 2015, 210).

The many images of the Great Serpent and his offspring dominate the vignettes on the sandstone walls asserting the importance of him and his clan. He is depicted not only in his many theriomorphic states, but also in his human form, the spiritual founder of the Omaha "Shell Society" and a related unnamed Osage society (Fletcher and La Flesche 1992, 509). This proto-Braden image has a penile terminus that closely resembles a rattlesnake's penis (Fig.10.4A, B). This image is the largest human figural rendering in the cave. Of the three prominent styles, only the latest style which involved the largest images yielded enough carbon from pigment samples to obtain AMS dates. These dates clustered tightly for a weighted average of AD 1025 (Diaz-Granados *et al.* 2001, 481–93).

His gigantic, full faced image probably represents him as the Milky Way with his serpentine body which seems to loom up from a dark cleft in the sandstone wall. It is in this form that we encounter him most often in the iconography of the Western Mississippian world. In this form he is the "Grandfather" of all the snakes, who transports the celestial twins, Stone and Black or Dark Wolf, the sons of Evening Star, to and from the lodge of their grandmother, Old-Woman-Who-Never-Dies (Bowers 2004, 263–5). Several of the oral traditions that Alfred Bowers collected recount how the Great Serpent, the Milky Way, transports the spirits. Among the Osage, when an older relative is getting near death, they often tell family members and close friends that they are "getting ready to walk the Milky Way". It is on this journey that spirits approach the bright star Deneb where the Milky Way divides (Lankford 2007, 185). The Dhegiha say that here the judge sits. He is red on his "heart" or left side and white on his right side. The judge is another powerful spirit being, the eldest of the celestial twins, the Thunderers, *In-gthon'* (Stone). What his younger brother, the Man of Mystery, *Shon'-ge Ca-be* (Dark Wolf) does in the daytime, Stone does at night when their roles are reversed (Fletcher and La Flesche 1992, 590; Charles Pratt pers. comm. 2009). The Dhegiha do not believe that human beings have a multiplicity of souls, they believe a person has only one, *Wa-non'-xe*, and that soul travels the Way of Souls aided by the Great Serpent and the spirits of deceased relatives to the spirit place, a key feature of the Genesis narration (La Flesche 1975, 197; Fletcher and La Flesche 1992, 589–91).

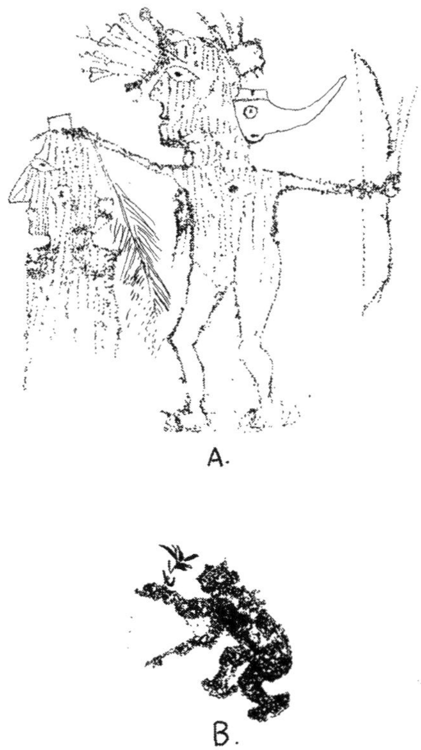

Fig. 10.5 A. "Morning Star" raising his father, the Sun, on the first day after First Woman created the Middle World. This early image, engraved, abraded, and painted is possibly Terminal Late Woodland in age. Picture Cave, Warren County, Missouri; B. A *He'Dewachi* dancer performing a unity dance that involves the First Man Pole or Staff and the vulvar Earth Altar (Fletcher and La Flesche 1992, 251). Picture Cave, Formative Braden Silhouette Style, not dated, Warren County, Missouri.

Two of these rites directly involved segments of the Genesis or Great Medicine Rite's oral traditions relating to the Chief of the Water Spirits, the Great Serpent. It is here that we find the mechanisms and traditions of unification and rebirth among the sedentary farming societies of the lower Missouri River, the southern Siouan "Five Cognate Tribes", the Dhegiha, as well as their northern Siouan speaking neighbors the Mandan and the Hidatsa. It is these rites that allow warring communities to peaceably resolve their differences as well as aiding in the unification of communities, especially if they are linguistically compatible. As their shared agricultural technology increased in effectiveness, stable food supplies invited more cooperation and additional unification. We believe the importance of the early stone sculptures of the First or Old Woman from the Cahokia area are displayed for discerning ritual participants in rites of seed exchange indicated by the strap handled bags, containers of seeds carried by several of these figures (see Fig. 9.5 for instance).

The earliest seminal Braden style image at Picture Cave, where the Great Serpent is well represented, likely belongs to this spectacular period of rapid growth focusing on adoption or synthesizing kinship, as demonstrated by the brilliant white depiction of a Long-nosed ear ornament worn by Morning Star (Fig. 10.5A). These definitive ear ornaments are the adopted nephews/sons who give Thunder power to the wearer. Their round dot-in-pupil eyes are identical to the eyes of the Chief of the Water Spirits, the source of the power to renew and become reborn, the original adopter (Hall 1997, 147–53; Duncan and Diaz-Granados 2000, 1–26; Duncan 2022). Although the proto-Braden pictographs of Picture Cave were rendered as consecratory iconography, these symbols recorded the children of First Woman. The cave being considered the "Womb of the Universe". A short distance away, in the confluence area, a geophysical center, Cahokia was on its way to becoming a major religious center (Kelly *et al* 1984, 154–7, Duncan 2015, 102–5).

During the Terminal Late Woodland, archaeological evidence appears of synthetic kinships, interrelated with gifting, supported by an increase in exotic artifacts (Kelly 1991, 63–70). Most importantly, unification rites appear on the lower Missouri River and confluence region. One of the figures at Picture Cave, a dancer holding a willow branch, appears to be performing the *He'dewachi* rite, a celebration where enfeebled separated bands unite, discouraging enemy attacks (Fig. 10.5B). More significantly, this rite involves the sacred, Striped Pole or Staff and the most important vulva (*Uzhin' eti, Ushje'*) shaped alter or portal as a small mound (Fletcher and La Flesche 1992, 252–5; Duncan 2015, 225). This Grand Portal, First Woman's vulva is a cave, bursting with colorful flowers that opens to a kaleidoscopic night sky with moving stars (Ponziglione 1897, 9–12).

Excavations of intermediate Late Woodland sites in the Cahokia area (Patrick phase) have revealed a new settlement pattern: structures clustered around an open space with a single pole in the center (Kelly *et al.* 1984, 124). These poles are a common feature found throughout the southeast and are still in use by the Chickasaw nation. They are also important in Sedentary Siouan speaking communities and recorded by early visitors in the 18th and 19th centuries (Duncan 2021, 32–7). Expanding the context of the lone Sacred Poles, they represent a powerful spirit, sent by a supreme creative entity, who "saves" humanity and who promotes unity, as in the case of the Mandan Lone Man Pole and the Dhegiha First Man Pole. These poles or staffs are found in Indigenous communities today, especially among the Native American Peyote Church followers, and become the focus or center of the Universe, when they are "dressed" in their regalia and blessed. They then become embodied with a powerful spirit that animates the 15-hour Dhegiha rite. It was this spirit and his two adopted sons that subdued the Chief of the Water Spirits and his children at the creation of the Earth, as narrated in the Genesis traditions (Duncan 2015, 209–40). Visiting members of other Native American Churches travel long distances to participate in these meetings, not only in a spirit of unity and peace but also because the service is essential to the healing and wellbeing of the Universe.

For many archaeologists the complex of three large mound groups at the confluence of the Missouri River with the Mississippi, especially the easternmost, Cahokia, presents an enigma, a persistent riddle. Some insist that this outlier, by far the largest center containing the greatest mound, is the earliest expression of "Mississippian". The origins of these monuments have continued to be the focus of intense study and they have been attributed principally to the Dhegiha Siouan linguistic group (Eggan 1952, 40–2; Howard 1968, 4; Diaz-Granados 1993, 334–42; Knight 1997, 232; Diaz-Granados and Duncan 2000, 244–5; Hall 2004, 100–3; Brown 2007, 56; 2011, 39–62; Kehoe 2007, 246–61). We will link our iconographical explanations, in conjunction with oral traditions concerning the Great Serpent, to the Dhegiha and their close kin, plains/prairie folk rather than the more distant southeastern cultures. We find some basic differences, as well as similarities when comparing the oral traditions and for that reason we will refer to the populations along the central Mississippi Valley as Western Mississippians. These population centers, especially Cahokia, have long been classified as either urbanized foci of mercantile activity, defined using Mesoamerican economic paradigms or as large "Southeastern, tiered settlements supported by a developing Maize centered agricultural economy" (Pauketat and Emerson 1997, 3–7). Recent research has provided data that create a new and somewhat different image.

The social structure at the greater Cahokia area was a variation of the Plains/ Prairie type, similar to the Hidatsa (Bowers 1992) and Mandan (Bowers 2004), possessing a complex agricultural system that was gender specific (Duncan and Diaz-Granados 2016, 88–9; 2018, 74; Mueller and Fritz 2016, 109–43; Fritz 2019, 58–73). The patrilineal, matrilocal society of the Dhegiha places women in an advantaged position as production specialists with major economic domination. It is this dominant factor that allows the women to foster and control ideal Plains/Prairie male behaviors which are: piety, bravery, generosity, and the eloquence of communication, especially oral traditions. While we accept Cahokia and the East St Louis Mound groups as well as the St Louis or Mound City group as being co-functional and linguistically compatible, we do believe that they were different. We simply refer to the three centers, together, as the Greater Cahokia area. The cosmological importance of the builders' designs is monumental. The easternmost and largest site, Cahokia, is an earthen replica of the "center" of the universe, the westernmost site, the St Louis or Mound City group, now largely destroyed, seems to have been replicating, in part, the Beneath Worlds. These mound groups, especially Cahokia, make up the most sacred place in the universe, the naval or the "center of all that matters", for their creators! Not only is this primal ontological site echoing the unique ritual iconography's style, Braden, also found in Picture Cave, Cahokia's Mound 72 presents the entire genesis story as a tableau (Fowler 1974, 18–23; Brown 2011, 37–63). While the three large mound groups had been the location of substantial residential villages, with many surrounding hamlets and farmsteads beginning at least by AD 900 with the Fairmount phase, after AD 1050, a rapid and dramatic change occurred, especially at Cahokia (Pauketat and Emerson 1997, 5).

A rapid population increase and massive construction projects quickly changed the Cahokia landscape. Immense plaza areas were filled, raised, and leveled on the four cardinal sides of the largest mound, Monks Mound. To the south of Monks Mound, south of the grand plaza, a causeway leads south through a wetland to the southernmost mound, Rattlesnake Mound, the home of the Great Serpent. Not only were the remnants of the previous residential areas covered by the newly constructed plazas, new mounds were constructed on platforms of clean soils and, by about AD 1060, the major structure on top of Monks Mound was dismantled, terminal offerings were buried, and the foundations were buried or capped with a layer of clean soils (Reed 2009). There seems to have been a significant removal of residents from the central area to accommodate the building of new ecclesiastical structures including the plaza areas (Pauketat and Emerson 1997, 8). This sort of exclusion, restricting populace from sacred areas, was also present in fortified Mandan towns (Bowers 2004, 111–13).

After this restrictive move and the removal of residential populations to surrounding areas, populations began a migration outward, away from the core ritual areas at the centers at Cahokia, East St Louis and St Louis Mound City. It is with the initial dispersal of residents, around AD 1200, that important sacra also began to leave the Cahokia area. Included in the inventory of sacra are Classic Braden style repoussé copper plaques, stone and flint clay sculptures of ancestral spirits,

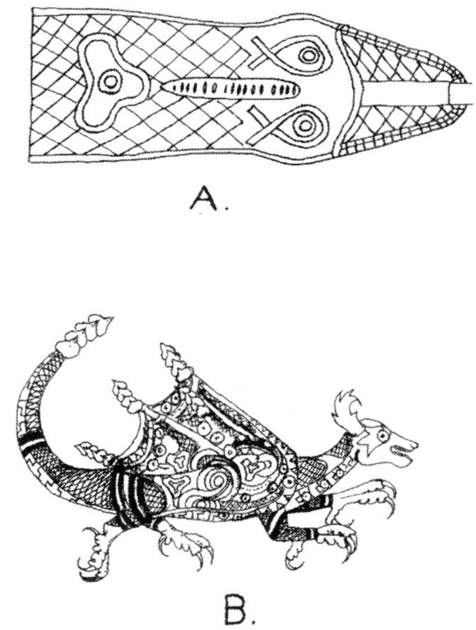

Fig. 10.6 A. The engraved head of the Water Spirit diorite bowl from Moundville, Alabama. The "mobius" eye surround occurs only at one other site, as a petroglyph, at Maddin Creek in Washington County, Missouri (see Chapter 2); B. a Classic Braden style Water Spirit reconstructed from shell cup fragments found in the Craig Mound, Spiro, Oklahoma (after Reilly 2011).

and engraved shell cups and gorgets that moved along with specific clan members. Several heirloom engraved shell cups were found at Spiro in the Great Mortuary and the Spirit Lodge, both in the Craig Mound. A Classic Braden image of a rare "winged" Water Spirit has been reconstructed from several fragmentary engraved shell cups found at Spiro (Phillips and Brown 1978, pls 8, 20, 32 and 33; Reilly 2011, 132; Fig. 10.6B). Another possible example of migrating sacra is a carved diorite bowl adorned with a classic Braden style amphisbaena head with the mobius strip eye surround found at Moundville, Alabama (Fig. 10.6A). This unusual eye surround also exists at the Maddin Creek petroglyph site southwest of Cahokia in the Big River valley of Missouri (Diaz-Granados and Duncan 2000, 135).

The Great Serpent survives migration and post-Cahokia. resettlement, quite a feat!

As Cahokia was evolving into a large complex society during the Terminal Late Woodland and Emerging Mississippian Periods, the same cultural movement was occurring in the Mississippi Valley to the south of Cahokia, especially adjacent to and south of the Ohio/Mississippi River confluence, the Cairo Lowlands, and Cumberland and northeastern Arkansas (Morse and Morse 1983, 233–46; 2000, 351–7). Findings by Ray Williams, Stephen Williams, Richard Marshall, and Dan and Phyllis Morse describe the simultaneous appearance of mound groups along with fortified towns and accompanying earthworks. Closely related ceramic forms, especially decorative techniques, ritual lithic artifacts, imagery on engraved shell, copper repoussé plates, and stone sculptures are common to both areas (Morse and Morse 1983; 241–3, 2000, 351–3; D. Morse 1990, 94–7). Shared symbolism is also common, especially the Great Serpent's image and his consort, Old Woman or First Woman.

Not surprisingly, spurred by a probable onset of a lengthy, severe drought, the Mississippian populations in the American Bottom began to decrease by dispersion after AD 1050. Erroneous conclusions have been drawn concerning the decreasing population of Cahokia; at least one writer believed that the population simply "disappeared" (Emerson 1989, 45) We definitely do not agree with this premise. We believe the best answer can be based on the archaeological record and Dhegiha oral traditions as well as archaeological context! A large part of the Cahokia area's populations, the Dhegiha proto-Osage, began migrating to the area around the junction of the Ohio and Mississippi River. Francis La Flesche, while collecting oral traditions from the Osage found an important key – traditions describing the exodus of large populations: the Cahokia diaspora. Around AD 1200, just after the Omaha and Ponca left, another large number of clans asked permission and were allowed to travel south along the great river to find additional supplies of persimmons, paw paws, plums, and grapes to dry for winter use (La Flesche in Bailey 2010, 75).

The Mississippian populations of the broad alluvial floodplain began to experience rapid growth at the same time as Cahokia area's diaspora. This growth was most evident in the Cairo lowlands of southeast Missouri. As these populations rapidly grew, their construction and residential debris obscured earlier features including modest mound centers. New construction enlarged ritual centers while the associated farming hamlets greatly increased in number and size (Morse and Morse 1983, 237–8; La Flesche in Bailey 2010, 76). One of the largest ritual centers, Lilbourn (23NM38) at the south end of Sikeston Ridge, was so large that it attracted scholarly attention before the Civil War. W.B. Potter excavated a large collection of artifacts including a much misunderstood, engraved shell gorget (see below), along with many ceramic vessels depicting the Great Serpent, mostly from Mound 3 (Potter 1880; Fig. 10.7B). Another unusual shell gorget was found in 1887, probably in the same mound and was discussed at length by Gates P. Thruston (1897, 346–8; Fig. 10.7A). These two human figure gorgets probably depict spirit ancestors and seem to be Braden in style.

With the several-fold population increase, agricultural technology in the Cairo lowlands expanded its inventory, especially after AD 1200 with increasing varieties of maize and the possible addition of beans (D. Morse 1990, 86). Ceramic vessels become quite elaborate and the Great Serpent is modeled as a quadrupedal "bottle", often painted, and his consort the Old-Woman-Who-Never-Dies makes her debut as a favored mortuary ceramic effigy accompanying children (Mueller and Fritz 2016, 138). These pottery vessels are striking in their iconography (Fig. 10.8D, E). Many of the ceramic containers are graphic, accentuated vulvas adorn images of First Woman. The Chief of the Water Spirits, often called a "dog", is often adorned with polysemous portal imagery (Fig. 10.8A–C). These engaging ceramic containers were usually manufactured as burial furniture and were often looted from indigenous cemeteries.

The large populations resided in extensive farmsteads, hamlets, and small villages surrounding the major mound centers, occupying elevations made up of the lighter silty loam soils ideal for farming. Cemeteries are interspersed among the habitation areas and are also concentrated in low mounds integral with the mound centers. About AD 1350 the Cairo lowland villages were quickly abandoned, some burned by the inhabitants as these populations begin to push southward, along the east side of Crowley's ridge following the Mississippi River (O'Brien 1994, 17). As the Great Serpent and his followers moved south, previous inhabitants were pushed southward or adopted. Few investigators are happy to agree with using a general catch-all called the Pemiscot phase (O'Brien 1994, 50–3). Whatever happened,

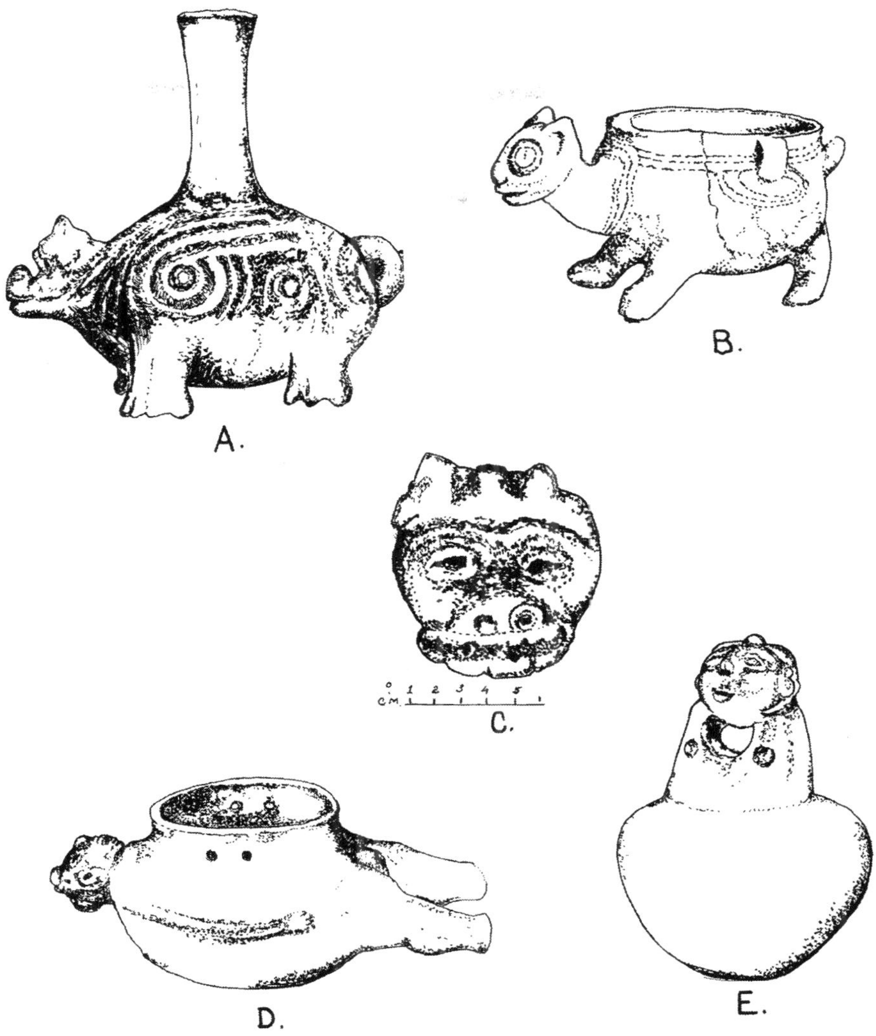

Fig. 10.7 Early Middle Mississippian negative painted Water Spirit pottery carafe, AD 1200–1250, LaFerth Site, Cape Girardeau County, Missouri; B. young puma or mountain lion tetrapodal jar with handles and "Mound Place" incising representing the Milky Way and portals in the night sky. LaPlant site, New Madrid County, Missouri; C. Water Spirit head from Lilbourn Mound group, W.E. Potter collection, drawn from a Leonard Blake photograph; D. jar depicting Old Woman with her graphic vulvar portal, the Drinkwater Site, Mississippi County, Missouri; E. a unique way of expressing the portal through First Woman's body. A fine ware "stirrup bottle", New Madrid County, Missouri.

after AD 1350, a cluster of towns with many artistically talented potters appeared along the Mississippi River and these talented potters manufactured images of the principal characters of their Genesis traditions, including the Great Serpent in his most fearsome visage, to be placed in the graves of specific individuals according to clan, age, and gender. This phase has been labelled Armorel by Stephen Williams (1980), and they are closely linked ritually to Moundville. Leo Anderson's collection from the Pemiscot County sites contained three fragmentary Moundville style stone pallets including one with a felid headed, serpentine Water Spirit. Additionally, at least two complete pallets have been found, one in the shaft grave excavated by the Main brothers at the Campbell site 23PM5. At the base of the shaft was a terminal deposit, a rectangular stone pallet, and placed on top of it was a large catlinite disc pipe (Aid 2016, 114, 116). Although the Water Spirit

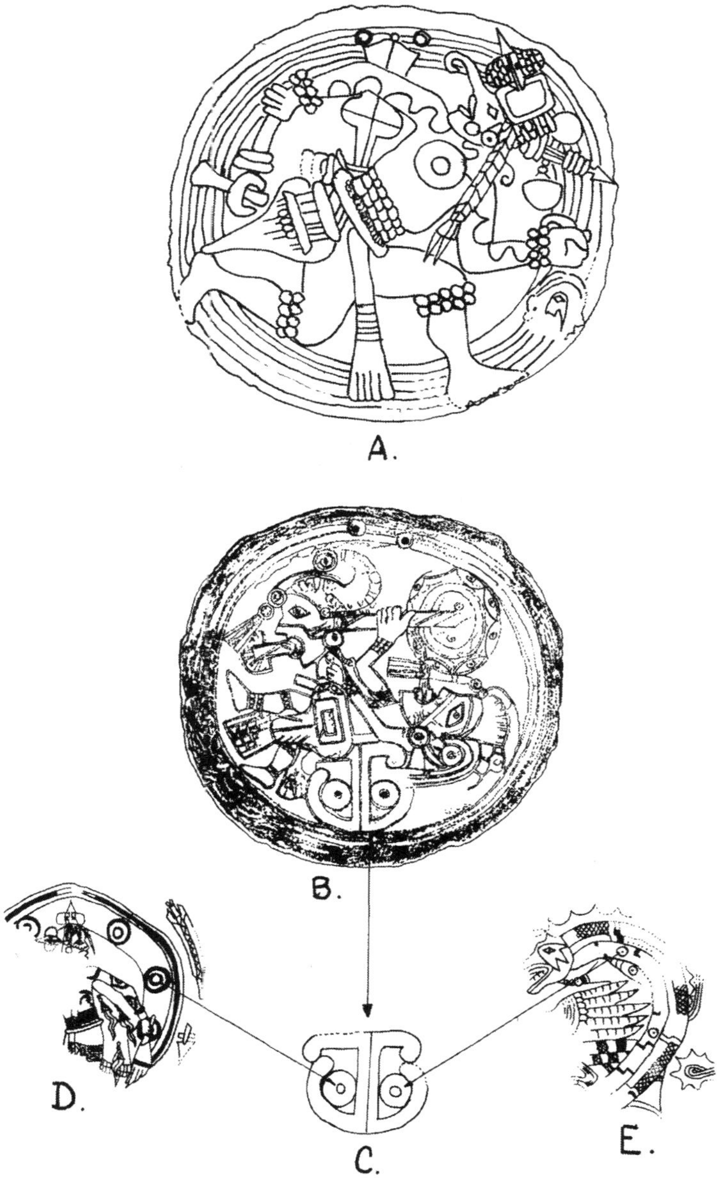

Fig. 10.8 A. The Douglass Gorget, Mound 3, Lilbourn Site, New Madrid County, Missouri. The figure is probably the younger of the Celestial Twins with his serpentine arm tattoos and his long proboscis; B. The W.E. Potter Gorget, Mound 3, Lilbourn Site; C. the Earth pot with its two fire altars, portals that are opened by the eldest Celestial Twin as a priest or doctor; D. and E. are these same portals on engraved shell, both patterns represent the Milky Way.

motifs are similar to the Moundville examples, they differ stylistically. Looters did not find them to be prolific, but neither were they rare. Local variations of the Chief of the Water Spirits are exceptional and they are artistically rendered; however, they are rarely winged, the eye markings are usually the only indication that they are in the sky (Reilly 2011, 126–7; Fig. 10.9A).

Most archaeological maps of the Mississippi corridor below the confluence of the Ohio and Mississippi Rivers show only a single large Late Mississippian phase, the Nodena phase, and is identified as Quapaw (Dhegiha; P. Morse 1990, 132–4).

Morse discusses the association of the Nodena phase sites and the exceptional quality of silty loam soils so necessary for the complex agricultural needs of these hyper-productive farmers. More importantly, these similar soils are associated with the closely related, northern Armorel phase described by Stephen Williams (1980, 105–10). Both phases are composed of towns usually containing at least one mound and a plaza, which are compact and often fortified, surrounded by palisades. It is apparent that these cultural centers were made up of closely interrelated populations with a common linguistic heritage and a common ideology. Surveys in the 1950s–1970s also found scattered hamlets and farmsteads along the ridges adjacent to the fortified towns. The surrounding wetlands were ideal habitat for fish, waterfowl, and game animals.

Both James B. Griffin and Dan Morse attribute the large Late Mississippian towns, grouped into the Nodena phase, as possible Siouan speaking people (Morse and Morse 1983, 233). A review of the ceramic material recovered from the Nodena and Armorel phase sites is surprising. This small area is responsible for an astonishing amount of the most exquisite pottery in the Eastern Woodlands, a continuum of the ancient Braden art tradition that began on the lower Missouri River (O'Brien 1984, 1–7; Fig. 10.9D–F). Sadly, the immense collections treasured by museums and collectors were looted from thousands of human burials. Fine ware Bell Plain bowls adorned with engraved designs, effigy adornos, and/or incised designs representing possible copies of wooden feast bowls, dominate these collections, the best quality pieces are truly magnificent (Fig. 10.9B, C). The myriad red slipped, painted and polychrome effigy vessels, some depicting Water Spirits, amaze the eye. The creators of this fabulous ceramic universe seem to have been largely Southern Siouan, Dhegiha (Phillips *et al.* 1951, 418–21; D. Morse 1990, 96–7).

The migrants from the Cairo Lowlands establishing large, fortified towns along the Mississippi River, capitalizing on the richest wetlands and the accompanying silt bearing soils for their dichotomous industries, hunting and agriculture. This southward movement displaced other populations. There are archaeological hints of aggressive confrontations, such as burned living areas and at least one entire burnt village, the Snodgrass Site (Morse 1983, 259–60). Also, human remains have been found dating to the same period showing evidence of a violent death. Early Spanish accounts describe entire towns of farming folk under vassalage to a dominant town (Phillips *et al.* 1951, 352; Moselage 1962; P. Morse 1990, 128–33). The northernmost group of towns along Pemiscot Bayou were likely the *Hon'-ga u-ta non-dsi*, a large divisional group also known as the Keepers of the Rites. This group, we remember, detached from the elite super group by permission (Duncan 2015, 108–10). The fortified Nodena phase towns south of this group belonged to the Quapaw or the Pacaha, closely related Dhegiha speakers (Hudson 1985; Hoffman 1990, 211–25; D. Morse 1990, 73–97). According to Dan Morse, both the Nodena and accompanying Armorel phases lasted until 1650 or later (D. Morse 1990, 69-77). This is corroborated by the amounts of European manufactured artifacts and especially a European skull with an unhealed arrow wound from the Nodena plantation (Powell 1990, 105).

The most plentiful effigy pottery form found with burials on the Armorel and Nodena sites is the bowl form made of plain fine ware (Bell Plain) and many of

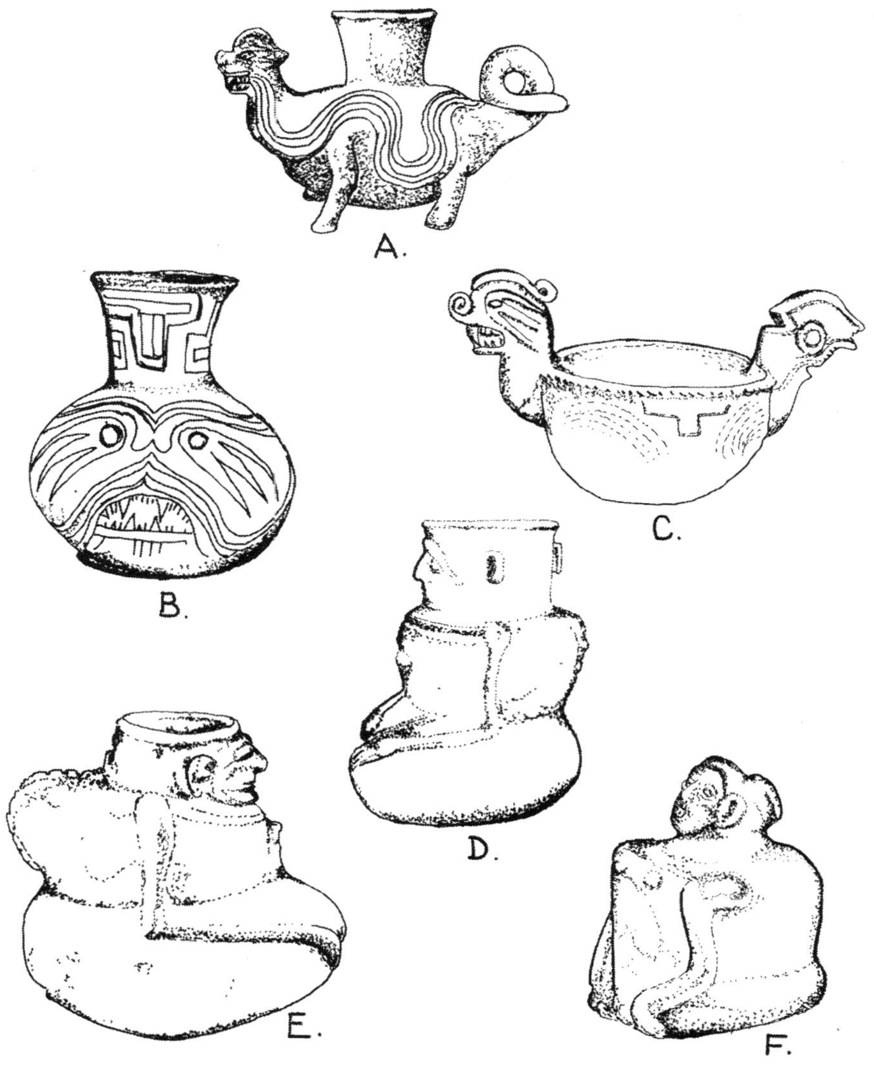

Fig. 10.9 A. Tetrapodal Water Spirit fine ware bottle, with engraved Milky Way; B. Bellaire style Water Spirit fine ware bottle; C. Water Spirit bowl with engraved Milky Way (A–C from the Berry Site, Pemiscot County, Missouri: D–F. The Old Woman who Never Dies, consort of the Chief of the Water Spirits, fine ware pottery. The mortuary context for Old Woman vessels associated with children. All are from the Campbell Site, Pemiscot County, Missouri.

these depict the Great Serpent, Chief of the Water Spirits (D. Morse 1990, 88). Several of the Armorel phase towns are special in that the vessels have specific motifs relating to the Great Serpent and rituals directly involving him. Of these sites, the Murphy Mound (23PM43) is not only a large terraced mound (120 × 75 × 12 m), it also has some of the earliest Armorel phase ceramics. These engraved fine ware bottles have a large corpus of ritual symbolism, much of it a continuum with the earlier Cairo Lowlands. Murphy Mound mortuary pottery seems to have plentiful explicit cosmic symbolism, especially on engraved fine ware bottle forms. One engraved bottle in particular displays four headless, handless figures "leaping" into portal symbols carried by a two-headed serpent reminiscent of the headless, handless burials interred in Episode 4 at Mound 72, Cahokia

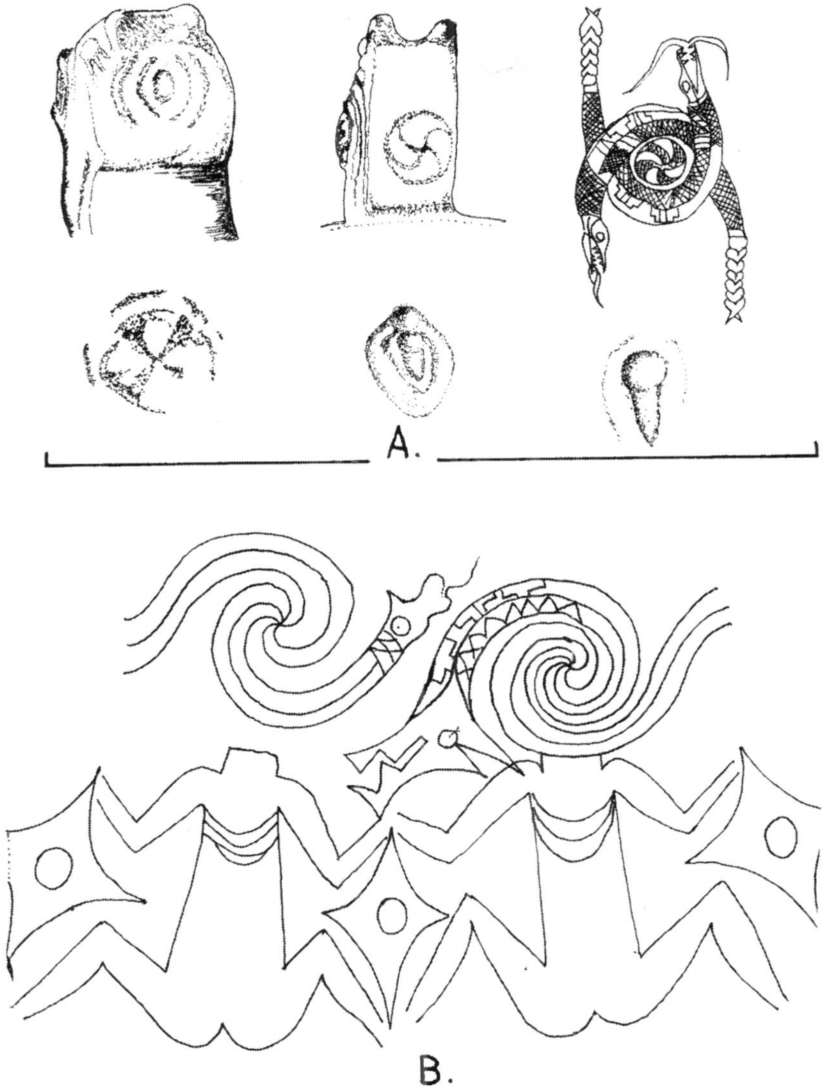

Fig. 10.10 A. six examples of portraying the Great Portal illustrating its polysemic nature. These run from naturalistic vulvar petroglyphs to engraved and modeled examples found on pottery. All are from Missouri; B. a Walls Engraved scene on a short neck bottle. Headless and handless male figures jumping into the vortex of the Great Portal on the two-headed Milky Way Great Serpent with interspersed stars. Notice that one of the Great Serpent's heads is inverted. The Dhegiha Osage believed the earth inverted at sunset and returned at sunrise (Duncan 2011).

(Fowler 1974, 21–2; Fig. 10.10B). This symbolism has clear links to ancient Cahokia and to contemporary Moundville.

An encounter between the Dhegiha Grand Chief "Pacaha", a direct descendant of the First Man and the Chief of the Casqui, was recorded during de Soto's visit. The "Lord" of Pacaha was acknowledged to be superior in his descent by the Tunican Grand Chief of the Casqui, and this concession was heard and recorded by the Spaniards (P. Morse 1990, 131–4). After many years of excavations and survey works, the site of Pacaha was finally identified by the Morses. It is the Bradley Site 3CT7, located on a low ridge near the west bank of the Mississippi River. While most of this large site was destroyed by levee construction, a large flat-topped mound still exists and the associated pottery is spectacular. Late Mississippian ceramic forms and motifs, including the Great Serpent, are present as well as early European artifacts (P. Morse 1990, 131–3).

Along with the brass bells, glass beads, bits of iron, and the herd of European swine, a more profound European contribution appeared among the closely populated towns and ritual centers: pandemic disease introduced to a population isolated genetically from the Euro-Asiatic gene pool for at least 25,000 years (Phillips *et al.* 1951, 351). When the French began to explore the central Mississippi River valley after the 1670s, the great mound centers and populous towns were deserted. The Mississippian farmers and their families were, for the most part, dead. Survivors had fled, uniting with their kinsmen, bison hunters of the tall grass prairie regions to the north and west (Duncan 2015, 108–10; La Flesche in Bailey 1995, 63–4). The descendants of Pacaha were reduced to a few towns near the mouth of the Arkansas River.

Discussion and conclusions

In interpreting the symbolism and meanings attached to the Great Serpent and his Dhegiha followers we must resort to the methodology and tools that we have learned to use in our Iconography Workshops memorializing Linda Schele and two of her best students: F. Kent Reilly III and David Freidel. In linking the symbolism with meaning, attention to the ethnography, the oral traditions are most important because they are the principal source of information. Most congruent symbolism with the 19th and 20th century Dhegiha is found at the Cairo Lowland and Armorel phase sites. This cluster of mound groups and later fortified towns, because of the large corpus of looted grave furnishings, especially pottery, has distinctive motifs that closely relate to modern Osage rituals (Fig. 10.11).

Much of the information we have found concerning the Great Serpent has been taken from the Osage Native American Church rites, including the *In-lon'-shka* ceremonial dances that occur during the summer solstice. We have never met with any resistance in discussing the various facets of these rites. The modern Dhegiha are proud of their ancient heritage, especially the Osage. Since we were shown the James Lacey Red Corn cosmic chart, we have added to the corpus of oral traditions surrounding the cosmology. We found that the Celestial Family, First Man and First Woman, and their six offspring are all travelers of the path of the Sun, the solar ecliptic; the Sun, the Moon, and

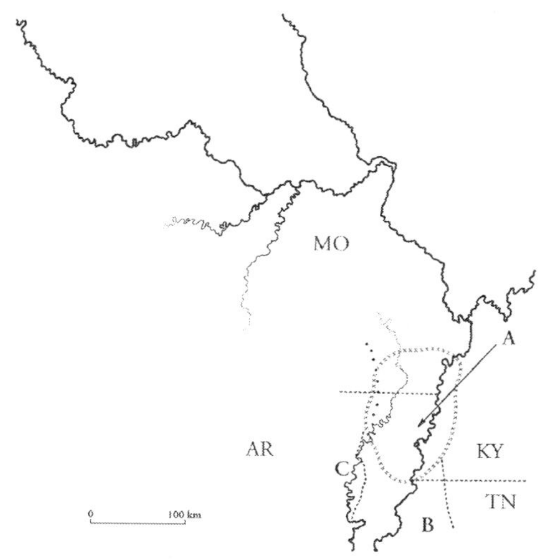

Fig. 10.11 Map: Missouri, Arkansas, Kentucky and Tennessee with Groups named: A. the group that *Pa-nee-wa-with-tah* would not identify for La Flesche. Because of their affinity with their northern Siouan relations, they were designated "Armorel" Phase by Williams. They were the *Hon-ga Uta-non-dsi*, the large Osage group that requested to leave the Cahokia area and later re-united with the Osage after 1670–1700; B. The Quapaw Nodena Phase; C. The Tunica Parkin Phase.

the five visible planets. Venus has two phases, the morning star and the evening star, which account for the two eldest children. Discussions with Osage informants has added to our knowledge of the workings of the night sky. The Pleiades is the great portal, the vulva of the First Woman, whose lodge is the Moon. All of the Osage, the star people, came from this portal (La Flesche in Bailey 1995, 31; Mary Jo Mercer pers. comm. 2006). The Sky clans or Tsi-Zhu people have the Pleiades as one of their symbols. The Isolated Earth clan has the rattlesnake and the spider as their Life Symbol. It is the Great Serpent and First Woman as the rattlesnake and the spider who have coitus in which he transfers to her his power of rebirth, resulting in the making of the *Ho-e-ga*, the web or trap of the breath of life (La Flesche in Bailey 1995, 35–41). The star people, the children of First Woman's children, the Osage, are then born from the great portal, First Woman's vulva, the Pleiades.

Several foundational characteristics of the Great Serpent, Chief of the Water Spirits, come to mind: First, he is associated with and considered to be the source of life-giving water by all Dhegiha. In the Osage Native American Church, he is personified and honored as the *pe'-xe*, the gourd rattle, which is a metaphor; it becomes the head of the Great Puma. Most of this rite takes place when the five great stars at the head of the Way of Souls (Milky Way) are visible (at night). His heart beat and life-giving fluid, water, is the *Tse'-xe-ni*, also a metaphor. It is the water drum used in singing during the church meeting and its use is ancient (Lepper 2018)! Represented by these two instruments, the Great Serpent moves around the vulvar shaped altar, the portal of death (grave) and rebirth with the Symbolic Man, the axis of the universe. The purpose of the spring water during burial rites, is to wash the grave and the coffin. This action is a symbol of rebirth or re-incarnation.

Second, when an Osage man is dressed for the dance honoring the Eldest Son (Morning Star) he is dressed so that he represents a cosmogram, the center or axis of the universe. Starting at his windpipe (in front), the path of the breath of life, and hanging straight down his back to where it almost touches the ground, is the hide of a river otter. This otter hide represents the watery Beneath Worlds from which all living things draw their life. On his head he wears a roach made of turkey beard hackles and red dyed, deer tail hair representing the Earth, the mother of all life. Finally, fastened to his roach and standing straight and tall, is an eagle feather, a metaphor that represents the collective bravery of all Osage warriors and also *Wa-kon'-da*, the Great Mystery who gives all things life and who infuses the cosmos with order and stability. The strict adherence to an orderly cosmology is an indication that other powerful forms of sanctioning exist, especially in Dhegiha and related Plains Indian cultures where a strong centralized authority is absent for the infliction of penalties for disorderly and antisocial behavior.

Although these societies are warlike and often engage in semi-nomadic buffalo hunting, they have extended jurisdiction of their social control and the means to extend that control is strong and effective (Provinse 1970, 341–51). It is important to remember that, among the Dhegiha, the principal clans and divisions responsible for making war rites were well represented by the life symbols related to the Great Serpent or Puma as well as water (La Flesche in Bailey 1995, 69). We believe that these sanctions, in part, evolved from the formation of early agricultural exchange groups that required artificial kinship rites to establish a stable, aggression free environment in order to accomplish tasks that resulted in benefits for all participating societies. To define the opposite role, we will give an inherited example, the Town Makers. The Town Makers among the Osage are members of the Red Eagle clan of the Tsi-Zhu (Sky) division (as stated by Eddy Red Eagle Jr, pers. comm. 2022). The Town Makers are sanctioned by inherited clan membership, the role being passed from Father to son. The Town Maker is in charge of laying out the town according to a complex cosmic diagram that he carries in his head.

The Great Serpent is an integral part of this complex and effective system of sanctions. He is seen in the many vignettes encoding proper behavior at Picture Cave. The principal and most important oral tradition depicted in Picture Cave is the Dhegiha Genesis narrative (Duncan 2015, 209–37). When descending into the main room, the visitor is greeted by the visage of the Great Serpent, an awe-inspiring image. Arranged in vignettes, on the sandstone walls the visitor then sees his children, the snakes, who play a stick-ball game with First Man and friends. The snakes make a clever bet and win First Man's head as well those of as his friends. Taking their prize, the snakes return to their town, the Beneath World under the night sky, and they celebrate by hanging First Man's shining head on a pole in the center of their town.

First Woman, finding her headless husband wandering about in the darkness, takes him to her house. First Woman then summons her grandsons, the Celestial Twins, Stone and the Dark Wolf. She feeds the two young men, paints, and equips them with ancient and powerful weapons including ancient bows with black arrows. The Celestial Twins attack the Great Serpent's town with thunderous war cries, defeating the snakes, and wounding, disarming, and capturing the Great Serpent. Tying a bull-snake skin on the Great Serpent's upper left arm, they lead him to their Grandmother, First Woman, and present him to her as a *da'-gthe*, a captive to be kindly treated (La Flesche 1975, 35; Fig. 10.10). She adopts him, feeds him, and they exchange gifts since they are now synthetically linked as kindred wife and husband. First Woman and the Great Serpent accomplish an even greater gift exchange – she engages in sexual intercourse, or "walks with the buffalo" and he gives her his power, his ability to resurrect himself (Kehoe 1970; Bowers 2004, 284–5). Water Spirits are immortal, like snakes, they never die. All indigenous people know that snakes simply come out of hibernation in the spring, shedding their skins; they are reborn. This is the defining moment of the Dhegiha Genesis traditions, this event warranted the First Woman's ability to infuse the *Ho'-e-ga*, the web or snare of the breath of life, the Middle World between sky and water, with the ability to rebirth any and all of her children, including human beings (La Flesche 1975, 63).

The importance of the Great Serpent cannot be overstated, he is *Ni'-wa-the*, "the giver of life" (La Flesche 1975, 111; John W. Williams, pers. comm. 2022). The gentle treatment of the captive Great Serpent by the Celestial Twins and the Grandmother is a contrast to the treatment of war captives in southeastern North America. The adoption and "coitus" with the Great Serpent by First Woman point out two major sanctions, the social power possessed by women in the matrilocal Dhegiha society and the gentle treatment of war captives. These sanctions seem more at home with a Plains/Prairie culture rather than their neighbors to the east. The Great Serpent's role as a Life Symbol is also a paradox. Among many southeastern groups Water Spirits are feared and they are locked in perpetual combat with the Thunderers; this is not the case with the Dhegiha, even when the Chief of the Water Spirits is in his most warlike form, the Great Puma, he is still a benevolent spirit being. The Great Puma is not only a Life Symbol, he is a source of gifts, important food, and medicinal plants, especially the American Lotus (*Nelumbo lutea*). With an entire clan named after him among the Osage, the Great Puma is considered a progenitor, truly an honor when human beings bestow it. Finally, the Dhegiha ethnogenesis linguistic study by Michael Hoffman firmly anchors the continuity of the Dhegiha, especially the Quapaw, with the central Mississippi River valley Mississippian period cultures, especially the Nodena and Armorel phases (1990, 208–9).

Robert Rankin's linguistic work involved a distant relative of the author, Ardina Revard Moore, a Quapaw/Osage. Rankin found no cross-amalgamation in the Quapaw language. The fidelity with which Quapaw inflection matches that of Dhegiha language is absolute (Hoffman 1990). The linguistic congruency along with the lack of autocratic chiefdoms strongly reflects the presence of Plains style sanctions among the Dhegiha Armorel and Nodena phases. These traits and the archaeological findings support the premise for a late movement of populations from the Cairo Lowlands, the *Hon-ga* Osage population and the lower Ohio Valley population "Paheka" Quapaw to the Pemiscot bayou and northeastern Arkansas (Morse and Morse 1983, 271–320; Hoffman 1990, 221).

As a part of our closing remarks, we would like to address some important concepts that surfaced during our study. Although there is often very little satisfaction with the one-to-one correlation with phases, ceramic collections, and ethnic groupings when attempting to unravel the identity of a cluster of archaeological sites. The archaeological evidence we have used is a large corpus of fine ware, pottery that was placed in Indigenous graves to accompany the dead, largely dug out by pot hunters seeking monetary gain. However, we believe that examining these looted collections has merit. There must be some sort of taxonomic framework to use for an initial attempt at synthesizing a solution. We believe that both the Morses, Dan and Phyllis, and Steve Williams provided evidence to focus attention on the uniqueness of the Armorel cluster. We hope that we have successfully linked a body of oral traditions, ceramic imagery, and archaeological data into what we think is a very plausible argument, especially to keep a sizable Dhegiha population and their altruistic Great Serpent from disappearing almost 800 years ago (Emerson 1989, 45). We also believe that a large part of the "lost texts" can be recovered by carefully examining oral traditions preserved into the present day (Knight *et al.* 2001, 131). The Osage of today still maintain their family or clan *Tsi Wa-kan-da-gi*, "Church Houses", religious structures of great importance to the Osage Native American Church (La Flesche 1975, 164). These structures have a round floor plan and are kept clean and maintained near residences. They house carefully aligned vulvar shaped fire altars, the portals of birth and death. There are two distinct types, one with an eastern portal, the other a western portal, after all, the great portal has two sides. The dual nature of these structures preserves the all-important balance of sacred forces, *wa-kan*.

Most circular Church Houses have a rectangular structure in association, a "Summer House" where church members and visitors have meals before and after services. Adam King has found similar structures at Etowah, stating that they have to be carefully excavated, and since they contain only a minimum of disturbed or residential soils, they are also difficult to detect electronically. We wonder how many of these enigmatic structures exist on major post-AD 1200 Mississippian sites, especially along Sawyer's (2011) Braden corridor? If, indeed these special structures exist in a more widespread pattern, does it then mean that Cahokia's sacred objects were only a small part of an expansive religious movement originating in the all-important central Mississippi Valley between the confluences of the Missouri and Ohio with the Mississippi River? Was it likely a nodal expansion of an ancient ideology embodying the Great Serpent that moved anew throughout the Eastern Woodlands and the prairie/plains? While many regional differences exist, plentiful serpentine images are found on shell gorgets extending up into post-Columbian times. We have to agree with Brain and Phillips with their "Bellaire style overlap" found on engraved ceramic bottles from at least two of the Armorel phase sites in Missouri (1996, 392–3). These bottles, with the full face of the Great Serpent, represent a tight, small interval of time and style. They were found only at the Berry Site (23PM58) and the Campbell Site (23PM5) in the Pemiscot Bayou cluster; these two sites are separated by only 7 km. A single, talented artist was likely the creator of these images.

After examining several large collections of pottery from the Armorel phase archaeological sites in Missouri and Arkansas, we can only say that every possible theriomorphic image of the Great Serpent imaginable is present during a relatively short span of time, AD 1450–1700. These images are widespread and represent a great sharing of similar religious symbolism involving a large area. This sharing resembles the stress induced movement that evolved into the "Ghost Dance" doctrine of the late 19th century (Mooney 1996, 16–17). Two of the most important actors depicted in the iconography are the Great Serpent and his adopter and consort, First Woman. We believe that they are ancient and yes, their presence is still with the Dhegiha Osage. The corridor from the Missouri-Mississippi river confluence to the Armorel phase towns, south of the Ohio-Mississippi River confluence contains a trove of congruent symbols. From the early expressions at Picture Cave in the lower Missouri River valley and Mound 72 at Cahokia, in the American Bottom, the signature ideology migrated southward evolving in a spectacular manner. Many superb artifacts reach across the centuries. However, three significant, immensely powerful examples exist that greatly shorten the distance between the seminal expressions and the Osage Native American Church of today. They are the Potter Gorget from Mound 3 at Lilbourn, the engraved fine ware vessel from Murphy's Mound, and Black Dog's Striped Pole preserved by his great-grandson, William Samuel Fletcher.

These stress induced revivals were pan-Indigenous and crossed many linguistic groups involving large populations spread over sizable regions. Nodal revivals seem to exist within the entire time span of this corpus of evolving and intertwining belief systems belonging to various regional populations but related by a core religious ideology. What we have examined is one such core systemic expression, one principal spirit being, an ancestor as well as a personified bundle of natural forces, the Great Serpent, the chief of the Water Spirits.

Acknowledgements

I am eternally grateful for all the help, time and timely conversations over many years with my late Osage friends and relatives: Cora Jean Big Elk, Uncle Louis F. Burns, Mary Carter, Aunt Francis Holding, Yvonne Lookout, Alma Jean Maker, Leonard Maker, Preston Morrell, Charles Pratt, Andrew "Bud" Red Corn, Charles Red Corn, Frank Red Corn, Uncle Raymond Red Corn, Sr, Edward Red Eagle, Sr, Delmer Rennick, Mary Renn, Ardina Revard Moore, Carter Revard, Romaine Shackleford, Robert Smith, Jake Waller, Dudley Whitehorn, and John Williams.

Bibliography

Aid, C.T. (2016) *The Roy Hathcock Collection*. Privately published.

Bailey, G.A. (ed.) (1995) *The Osage and the Invisible World: From the Works of Francis La Flesche*. University of Oklahoma Press, Norman OK.

Bailey, G.A. (2010) *Traditions of the Osage*. University of New Mexico Press, Albuquerque NM.

Bailey, G.A. (2004) Continuity and change in Mississippian civilization. In R.F. Townsend and R.V. Sharp (eds) 2004, 83–92.

Baker, G. (2004) Foreword. In Bowers 2004, vii–x.

Benn, D.W. (1995) Woodland people and the roots of the Oneota. In *Oneota Archaeology: Past Present and Future*, W. Green (ed.), 91–140. Office of State Archaeologist Report 20, University of Iowa, Iowa City IA.

Berres, T.E. (2001) *Power and Gender in Oneota Culture*. Northern Illinois University Press, Dekalb IL.

Bowers, A.W. (1992) *Hidatsa Social and Ceremonial Organization*. University of Nebraska Press, Lincoln NE.

Bowers, A.W. (2004) *Mandan Social and Ceremonial Organization*. University of Nebraska Press, Lincoln NE.

Brain, J.P. and Phillips, P. (1996) *Shell Gorgets*. Peabody Museum of Archaeology and Ethnology, Harvard University, Cambridge MA.

Brown, J.A. (2007) Sequencing the Braden art style within Mississippian Period art and iconography. In Reilly and Garber (eds) 2007, 213–45.

Brown, J.A. (2011) The regional culture signature of the Braden art style. In Lankford *et al.* (eds) 2011, 37–63.

Chapman, C.H. (1980) *The Archaeology of Missouri*, II. University of Missouri Press, Columbia MO.

Claassen, C. (2016) Rock shelters, boulders, and bleeding rocks of women's ritual landscape in the Midcontinent. In *Native American Landscapes: An Engendered Perspective*, C. Claassen (ed.), 3–34. University of Tennessee, Knoxville TN.

Colvin, M. (2012) Old-Woman-Who-Never-Dies: a Mississippian survival in the Hidatsa world. Unpublished M.A. Thesis, Texas State University, San Marcos TX.

Diaz-Granados, C. (1993) Petroglyphs and pictographs of Missouri: a distributional, stylistic, contextual, functional, and temporal analysis of the state's rock graphics. Unpublished Ph.D. Dissertation, Washington University, St Louis MO.

Diaz-Granados, C. and Duncan, J.R. (2000) *The Petroglyphs and Pictographs of Missouri*. University of Alabama Press, Tuscaloosa AL.

Diaz-Granados, C., Duncan, J.R. and Reilly, F.K. III (eds) (2015) *Picture Cave: Unraveling the Mysteries of the Mississippian Cosmos*. University of Texas Press, Austin TX.

Diaz-Granados, C., Rowe, M.W., Hyman, M., Duncan, J.R. and Southon, J.R. (2001) AMS Radiocarbon dates for charcoal from three pictographs and their associated iconography. *American Antiquity* 66(3), 481–93.

Duncan, J.R. (2011) The cosmology of the Osage, In Lankford *et al.* (eds) 2011, 18–33.

Duncan, J.R. (2015) Identifying the characters on the walls of Picture Cave. In Diaz-Granados *et al.* (eds) 2015, 209–37.

Duncan, J.R. (2021) Dressing and caring for the spirits: the role of sacred bundles in Siouan society. In *Mississippian Culture Heroes, Ritual Regalia, and Sacred Bundles*, D.H. Dye (ed.), 29–56. Lexington Books, New York and London.

Duncan, J.R. and Diaz-Granados, C. (2000) Of masks and myths. 1–26 *Midcontinental Journal of Archaeology* 25(1), 1–26.

Duncan, J.R. and Diaz-Granados, C. (2016) Rock art, gender, and the Dhegihan landscape. In *Native American Landscapes, An Engendered Perspective*, C. Claassen (ed.), 109–50. University of Tennessee Press, Knoxville TN.

Duncan, J.R. and Diaz-Granados, C. (2018) Landscape, cosmology and the Old Woman: a strong feminine presence. In *Transforming the Landscape: Rock Art and the Mississippian Cosmos*, C. Diaz-Granados, J. Simek, G. Sabo III and M. Wagner (eds), 57–74. American Landscapes 4, Oxford.

Duncan, J.R. and Diaz-Granados, C. (2022) Picture Cave and the birth of the Braden art style. In *Archaeologies of Cosmoscapes in the Americas*. J.G. Stauffer, B.T. Giles and S. Lambert (eds), 175–192. American Landscapes 6, Oxford.

Dye, D.H., and Cox, C.A. (eds) (1990) *Towns and Temples along the Mississippi*. University of Alabama Press, Tuscaloosa AL.

Eggan, F. (1952) The ethnological cultures and their archaeological backgrounds. In *Archaeology of the Eastern United States*, J.B. Griffin (ed.), 35–45. University of Chicago Press, Chicago IL.

Eggan, F. (1970) *Social Anthropology of North American Tribes*. University of Chicago Press, Chicago IL.

Emerson, T.E. (1989) Water Serpents, and the Underworld: an exploration into Cahokian symbolism. In Galloway (ed.) 1989, 45–92.

Farnsworth, K.B., Emerson, T.E. and Hughes, R. (2021) Havana tradition platform pipe production and disposition. *American Antiquity* 86(4), 696–714.

Fletcher, A. and La Flesche, F. (1992)[1911] *The Omaha Tribe*. University of Nebraska Press, Lincoln NE.

Fowler, M.L. (1974) Cahokia: ancient capitol of the Midwest. *Addison-Wesley Module in Anthropology* 48, 3–38.

Fritz, G.J. (2019) *Feeding Cahokia*. University of Alabama Press, Tucaloosa AL.

Galloway, P. (ed.) (1989) *The Southeastern Ceremonial Complex: Artifacts and Analysis*. University of Nebraska Press, Lincoln NE.

Griffin, J.B. (ed.) (1952a) *Archaeology of Eastern United States*. University of Chicago Press, Chicago IL.

Griffin, J.B. (1952b) Prehistoric cultures of the Central Mississippi Valley. In Griffin (ed.) 1952a, 226–38.

Hall, R.L. (1991) Cahokia identity and interaction models of Cahokia Mississippian. In *Cahokia and the Hinterlands*, T.E. Emerson and R.B. Lewis (eds), 3–32. University of Illinois Press, Urbana IL.

Hall, R.L. (1997) *An Archaeology of the Soul*. University of Illinois Press, Urbana and Chicago IL.

Hall, R.L. (2004) The Cahokia site and its people. In R.F. Townsend and R.V. Sharp (eds) 2004, 93–104.

Hargrave, M.L., Clay, R.B., Dalan, R.A. and Greenlee, D.M (2021) The complex construction history of Poverty Points timber circles and concentric ridges. *Southeastern Archaeology* 40(3), 192–211

Hoffman, M.P. (1990) The Terminal Mississippian Period in the Arkansas River Valley and Quapaw ethnogenesis. In Dye and Cox (eds) 1990, 208–26.

Howard, J.H. (1968) *The Southeastern Ceremonial Complex and its Interpretation*, Memoir 6, Missouri Archaeological Society, Columbia MO.

Hudson, C. (1985) *DeSoto in Arkansas: a brief synopsis*. Arkansas Archaeological Society Field Notes 205, Fayetteville AR.

Johannessen, S. (1984a) Middle Woodland paleoethnobotany. In *American Bottom Archaeology*, C.J. Bareis and J.W. Porter (eds), 201–2. I.D.O.T., University of Illinois Press, Urbana IL.

Johannessen, S. (1984b) Late Archaic paleoethnobotany. In *American Bottom Archaeology*, C.J. Bareis and J.W. Porter (eds), 197–9. I.D.O.T., University of Illinois Press, Urbana IL.

Kehoe, A.B. (2007) Osage texts and Cahokia data. In Reilly and Garber (eds) 2007, 246–62.

Kehoe, A.B. (2020) The function of ceremonial sexual intercourse among Northern Plains Indians. *Plains Anthropologist* 15(48), 99–103.

Kelly, J.E. (1991) Cahokia and its role as a gateway center in interregional exchange.,In *Cahokia and the Hinterlands*, T.E. Emerson and R.B. Lewis (eds), 61–82. University of Illinois Press, Urbana IL.

Kelly, J.E., Ozuk, S.J., Jackson, D.K., McElrath, D.L., Finney, F.A. and Esarey, D. (1984) Emergent Mississippian Period. In *American Bottom Archaeology*, C.J. Bareis and J.W. Porter (eds), 12–57. I.D.O.T., University of Illinois Press, Urbana IL.

Knight, V.J. Jr (1989) Some speculations on Mississippian monsters. In P. Galloway (ed.) 1989, 205–10.

Knight, V.R. Jr (1997) Some developmental parallels between Cahokia and Moundville. In T.R. Pauketat and T.E. Emerson (eds) *Introduction to Cahokia Domination and Ideology in the Mississippian World*, 229–47. University of Nebraska Press, Lincoln NE.

Knight, V.J. Jr, Brown, J.A. and Lankford, G.E. (2001) On the subject matter of Southwestern Ceremonial Complex art. *Southeastern Archaeology* 20, 129–41.

Koldehoff, B.H.(2020) Lithic caches of Missouri. Resource or ritual? *The Missouri Archaeologist* 81, 1–13.

Lankford, G.E. (2004) World on a string: some cosmological components of the Southeastern Ceremonial Complex. In R.F. Townsend and R.V. Sharp (eds) 2004, 207–18.

Lankford, G.E. (2007) The Path of Souls: some death Imagery in the Southeastern Ceremonial Complex. In Reilly and Garber (eds) 2007, 174–212.

Lankford, G.E., Reilly, F.K. III and Garber, J.F. (eds) (2011) *Visualizing the Sacred: Cosmic Visions, Regionalism, and the Art of the Mississippian World*. University of Texas Press, Austin TX.

La Flesche, F. (1975) *A Dictionary of the Osage Language*. Smithsonian Institution Bulletin 109, Washington DC.

Lepper, B.T. (2004) The Newark Earthworks, monumental geometry and astronomy. In Townsend and Sharp (eds) 2004, 73–82.

Lepper, B.T. (2018). Insights into Hopewell material culture derived from the contemporary ceremonial practices of the Shawnee Tribe: a case study supporting the value of collaborative research with Native American Tribes. *Current Research in Ohio Archaeology* 2018, 1–5. [www.Ohioarchaeology.org]

Lepper, B.T., Duncan, J.R., Diaz-Granados, C. and Frolking, T. (2018) Arguments for the age of Serpent Mound. *Cambridge Archaeological Journal* 28(3), 433–50.

Loebel, T.J. and Koldehoff, B.H. (2020) A Cache of Pitkin Chert Dalton Points from Montgomery County, IL. *Illinois Archaeology* 32, 133–42.

McGregor, J.C. (1952) The Havana Site. In *Hopewellian Communities in Illinois*, T. Duel (ed.), 43–92. Illinois State Museum, Springfield IL.

McMillan, R.B. (2019) Underwater Spirits and sacred places: artesian springs in Southwest Missouri. *Plains Anthropologist* 64, 382–413.

McNutt, C.H. (1996) The Central Mississippi Valley: a summary. In *Prehistory of the Central Mississippi Valley*, C.H. McNutt (ed.), 155–86.

Mooney, J. (1996) *The Ghost Dance*. J.G. Press, North Dighton MA.

Morse, D.F. (1990) The Nodena phase. In Dye and Cox (eds) 1990, 69–97.

Morse, D.F. and Morse, P.A. (1983) *Archaeology of the Central Mississippi Valley*. Academic Press, New York.

Morse, D.F. and Morse, P.A. (2000) Social interaction between the American Bottom of Cahokia and Crowley's Ridge Lowlands Division of the Lower Mississippi River. In *Mounds, Modoc, and Mesoamerica*, S.R. Ahler (ed.), 347–60. Illinois State Museum Papers 28, Springfield IL.

Morse, P.A. (1990) The Parkin Site and the Parkin phase. In Dye and Cox (eds) 1990, 118–34.

Moselage, J. (1962) The Lawhorn Site. 4–82 *The Missouri Archaeologist* 24, 4–82.

Mueller, N.G. and G.J. Fritz (2016) Women as symbols and actors in the Mississippi Valley. In *Native American Landscapes*, C. Claassen (ed.), 108–48. University of Tennessee Press, Knoxville TN.

Nassaney, M.S. and Pyle, K. (1999) The Adoption of the bow and arrow in Eastern North America: a view from central Arkansas. *American Antiquity* 64(2), 243–64.

O'Brien, M.J. (1994) *Cat Monsters and Head Pots: The Archaeology of Missouri's Pemiscot Bayou*. University of Missouri Press, Columbia MO.

Pauketat, T.R. and Emerson, T.E. (1997) Introduction. In *Introduction to Cahokia Domination and Ideology in the Mississippian World* T.R. Pauketat and T.E Emerson (eds), 1–29. University of Nebraska Press, Lincoln NE.

Perino, G. (1973) The Late Woodland Component at the Schild Sites, Greene County, Illinois. In *Late Woodland Site Archaeology in Illinois I: Investigations in South-Central Illinois*, 90–140. Illinois Archaeological Survey, Inc. Bulletin No. 9, University of Illinois, Urbana.

Phillips, P. and Brown, J.A. (1978) *Pre-Columbian shell engravings from the Craig Mound at Spiro, OK*. Part I, Peabody Museum of Archaeology and Ethnology, Harvard University, Cambridge MA.

Phillips, P., Ford, J.A. and Griffin, J.B. (1951) *Archaeological Survey in the Lower Mississippi Alluvial Vlley, 1940-1947*. Papers of the Peabody Museum of American Archaeology and Ethnology 25, Cambridge MA.

Ponziglione, P.M. (1897) The Osages and Father John Schoenmakers, S.J., Interesting Memoirs Collected from Legends, Traditions and Historical Documents. Unpublished handwritten manuscript, file at Midwest Jesuit Archives, St Louis MI.

Potter, W.B. (1880) *Contributions to the Archaeology of Missouri by The Archaeological Section of the St. Louis Academy of Science*. Smithsonian Contributions to Knowledge 259, Washington DC.

Powell, M.L. (1990) Health and disease at Nodena: a Late Mississippian community in northeastern Arkansas. In Dye and Cox (eds) 1990, 98–117.

Provinse, J.H. (1970) The Underlying sanctions of Plains Indian Culture. In *Social Anthropology of North American Tribes*, F. Eggan (ed.), 341–76. University of Chicago Press, Chicago IL.

Ray, J.H., Meade, T.M. and Powell, G.S. (2020) The Kellner Cache: an Early Archaic Searcy deposit in Benton County, MO. *The Missouri Archaeologist* 81, 39–62.

Reed, N.A. (2009) Excavations on the Third Terrace and Front Ramp of Monk's Mound, Cahokia: a personal narrative. *Illinois Archaeology* 21, 1–89.

Reilly, F.K. III (2011) The Great Serpent in the Lower Mississippi Valley. In Lankford *et al.* (eds) 2011, 118–36.

Reilly, F.K. III (2015) The cave and the Beneath World Spirit. In Diaz-Granados *et al.* (eds) 2015, 133–44.

Reilly, F.K. III and Garber, J.F. (eds) (2007) *Ancient Objects and Sacred Realms: Interpretations of Mississippian Iconography*. University of Texas Press, Austin TX.

Sawyer, J. (2011) Introduction, Map 1. In Lankford *et al.* (eds) 2011, xi–xviii.

Thruston, G.P. (1897) *The Antiquities of Tennessee* (2nd edn). The Robert Clark Company, Cincinnati OH.

Townsend, R.F. (2004) American landscapes, seen and unseen. In Townsend and Sharp (eds) 2004, 15–35.

Wagner, J.J., Sharp, K. and Remo, J. (2018) Transformed spaces: a landscape approach to the rock art. In *Transforming the Landscape:Rock Art and the Mississippian Cosmos*, C. Diaz-Granados, J. Simek, G. Sabo III and M. Wagner (eds), 100–55. American Landscapes 4, Oxford.

Ward, G.M.V., Grooms, S.B., Schroll, A.G. and Kidder, T.R. (2022) The view from Jaketown: Considering variation in the Poverty Point Culture of the Lower Mississippi Valley. *American Antiquity* 87(4), 758–75.

Weeks, R.W. Jr (2009) The antiquity of the Midewiwin. Unpublisehd PhD Dissertation. Arizona State University.

Williams, S. (1980) The Armorel Phase, a very late complex in the Lower Mississipipi Valley. *Southeastern Archaeology* 22, 105–10.

Willoughby, C.C. (1922) *The Turner Group of Earthworks*. Papers of the Peabody Museum of American Archaeology and Ethnology 8(3), Harvard University, Cambridge MA.

Index

Numbers in *italics* denote pages with illustrations, numbers followed by t indicate pages with tables. Note that as most of the text in this book is concerned with oral traditions and the Mississippian period/culture, these terms are not indexed